Author's P...

THIS book does not pret... ...te textbook of the conduct of a chess game; neithei ... ...n to present a new approach to chess strategy: my aim ha... ...ely been to produce a practical guide to the study of the middle-game. Everyone who desires to take up chess seriously is interested in the question: How can I recognize the characteristic features of a position and then lay my plans accordingly? To help answer this question is the task of this book.

We begin with an examination of the peculiarities of the individual pieces and pawns. Then the problem of the centre, material and space advantage on a particular section of the board, pawn formations, and some general problems of the chess struggle are discussed.

As a foundation for the book I have used a large number of games spanning many periods of chess, though naturally examples from recent tournaments predominate. It may be noticed that my own games appear with comparative frequency. This is not because I consider them to be the best examples of correct strategical play, but because every chess player understands his own games better than those of others and can therefore best explain the thought processes he experienced during the game.

LUDĔK PACHMAN

Translator's Preface

MR. PACHMAN, the Czechoslovak Grandmaster, has for many years been a leading Chess expert and theorist on the Continent; only recently, however, have any of his works been translated into English.

The present book is an abridgement that attempts to compress into one volume the material contained in the three volumes of *Moderne Schachstrategie*, the German translation of the Czech original, *Strategie Moderního Šachu*. To do this I have omitted a number of games and left out the opening moves of many others. But, on the whole, I have avoided any omission of ideas and theories presented by Mr. Pachman.

ALAN S. RUSSELL

Contents

MODERN CHESS STRATEGY

By

LUDĚK PACHMAN

Translated and Abridged
by
ALAN S. RUSSELL

DOVER PUBLICATIONS, INC.
NEW YORK

Published in Canada by General Publishing Company, Ltd., 30 Lesmill Road, Don Mills, Toronto, Ontario.

This Dover edition, first published in 1971, is an unabridged and unaltered republication of the work originally published in 1963. It is reprinted by special arrangement with Sir Isaac Pitman and Sons, Ltd., Pitman House, Parker Street, Kingsway, London WC 2, publisher of the original edition.

International Standard Book Number: 0-486-20290-9
Library of Congress Catalog Card Number: 73-176353

Manufactured in the United States of America
Dover Publications, Inc.
180 Varick Street
New York, N. Y. 10014

Contents

Contents

Bibliography

THE middle-game in chess has never received the same attention from chess authors as the opening. The following books, however, can be recommended as worthy of study—

> Nimzowitsch, *My System*
> Euwe, *Judgment and Planning in Chess*
> Fine, *The Middle Game in Chess*
> Kmoch, *Pawn Power in Chess*

For those who can read foreign languages there is, of course, the three-volume unabridged version of the present book, *Strategie Moderního Šachu*, written in Czech, or the German translation, *Moderne Schachstrategie*. Dr. Euwe has done good work in his *Het Middenspel*, a series of twelve booklets in Dutch; these have been translated into German under the title *Das Mittelspiel*.

Annotated games also contain much useful information on strategy; numerous examples can be found in chess magazines, tournament books, and collections of games. Two such collections worthy of mention are *Masters of the Chessboard*, by Réti, and *My Best Games of Chess* (in two volumes), by Alekhine. Both these works are illuminating on many aspects of chess strategy.

CHAPTER I

The Basic Concepts of Chess Strategy

A. STRATEGY AND TACTICS

A WIDELY held view is that the difference between the expert chess player and the novice lies in the extent to which the former can calculate in advance; and the question of how many moves in advance a Grandmaster can reckon is often thrown up for argument. The ability to calculate correctly is undoubtedly a necessity for the top-class player; but it is not the only one, and certainly not the most important difference between the master and the average player. There are many players who have a good command of the art of accurate combinations, but who will never reach master strength: for *they* lack the ability to conduct the entire game on the basis of a correct plan laid out in advance. The calculation of particular variations is only possible, and necessary, in certain clearly defined positions; in most cases one's overall plan of play is the correct pointer to finding a given move.

The plan of play at a particular point in the game is called the strategical plan; the way in which it is laid out, the collection of principles we follow in its determination, is known as strategy. These terms, and others like strategical goal and tactics, have the same meaning as in the science of warfare, political science, etc.

It might be thought that the strategical goal in every game was the mating of the opposing King. And, indeed, such a superficial comprehension of strategy prevailed in the early days of the modern form of chess. Nowadays, however, technique has improved and ideas have become more profound. In the games of good players even the winning of a weak pawn no longer appears with frequency as a strategical goal; more often a small positional advantage (such as control of an open file, the weakening of an opposing pawn, or the creation of a passed-pawn) is the object for which a player puts up a bitter fight.

It is hardly necessary to add that the best of plans come to nothing if they are not carried out correctly; this applies in chess as in life. The collection of measures and methods for executing one's strategical plan or thwarting the opponent's is called tactics. To this field belong manoeuvres, combinations and sacrifices, as well as

1

double attack, pinning, discovered check, traps, etc. To deal with these concepts in detail is, however, not the task of this book, though the reader will become familiar with them by studying the games and examples given in the following pages.

B. THE CHARACTER OF THE POSITION AND CHOICE OF PLAN

The choice of plan is in every case dependent on the concrete position on the board; it must therefore correspond to that position. To judge a position correctly and recognize its peculiarities is an essential prerequisite for finding a suitable strategical plan. We may therefore ask what factors determine the character of a position and how the strategical plan can thereby be deduced. Naturally this cannot be answered in one chapter; it is the basic question with which the whole of this book is concerned. But we can briefly say that the character of a position is determined by the following factors—

1. The material relationship; that is, material equality or the material superiority of one side.
2. The power of the individual pieces.
3. The quality of the individual pawns.
4. The position of the pawns; that is, the pawn structure.
5. The position of the Kings.
6. Co-operation amongst the pieces and pawns.

Some of the factors that determine the character of the position are lasting, others temporary. An important lasting factor is the quality and position of the pawns, for these cannot, in contrast to the pieces, be easily taken from one side of the board to the other; the positions of the pawns as a rule only change gradually, whereas the pieces can mostly take up a new post without undue difficulty. As a result we have the apparent contradiction that it is the pawns, despite their relatively small value, which largely determine the character of the position. Other lasting factors are material superiority and, in many cases, the positions of the Kings.

Now let us look at some positions and see how their characters are determined and how the correct strategical plan is chosen.

In Diagram 1 we have a position from a rarely played variation of the Ruy Lopez. In practice this position has not yet been sufficiently tried out, and the theoreticians have differing views on it. We notice that Black has a material advantage of two pawns, not counting that on d6, which cannot be held; he is, however, behind in development and his pieces are passively placed. White, on the other hand, has his Queen, Knight, and Bishop actively placed, and his Rooks are ready to join in the fight along any of the open files. These factors determine the character of the position and point to the plan to be adopted by both players, which is as follows—

1. White must use his better posted pieces to create tactical threats and to launch a direct onslaught on the opposing King; typical threats would be B × QP, Q–KR5, R–K1, N–KN5, etc.

2. Black must attempt to parry the immediate threats, complete his development, and convert his material advantage by simplification.

DIAGRAM 1

DIAGRAM 2

It is only by accurate and deep analysis of the possibilities of both players that we can state whether White or Black has the better prospects with his plan. But we are not interested in that at the moment; we are much more concerned with the fact that a lasting factor (material advantage) was pitted against a temporary one (lead in development and actively placed pieces). The former is a strategical factor, the latter a dynamic factor. In the last example these factors were opposed to one another and demanded a quite different plan from each side.

In Diagram 2 we again have a position from the Ruy Lopez. Here the material is equal and both sides have the same number of pieces developed. What plan should be adopted by each player? The chief factor here is the asymmetrical position of the pawns. If we divide the board in two by a line between the King and Queen files we see that Black has four pawns against White's three on the Queen-side, whereas on the King-side the position is reversed. Another important factor is White's pawn on e5, which, having crossed the "demarcation line," restricts Black's movements on the

King-side: Black cannot occupy f6, and if he tries P–KB3 (or P–KB4) he must reckon with P×P; furthermore, should he play P–KN3, he gives White the opportunity to occupy f6 with a piece. We can now outline the strategical plans that correspond to this position—

1. White will prepare a piece attack on the King-side with such moves as Q–Q3, B–QB2, N–KN5, etc.; he will be helped in this by the cramping effect of the King-pawn on Black. In addition he will, after thorough preparation, advance with his pawns on the King-side (P–KB4–5).

2. Black will counter the threats on the King-side and will then prepare an advance of his own pawns on the Queen-side (N–QR4, P–QB4, etc.).

In Diagram 3 we have a position from the Rauser Variation of the Sicilian Defence. Here the dominant factor is the position of the Kings on opposite flanks. Both sides must endeavour to set their

DIAGRAM 3

DIAGRAM 4

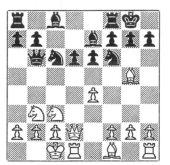
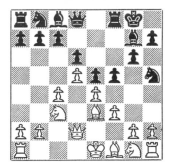

Position after 8 ..., P–KB4

pieces and pawns against the enemy King without loss of time; in such positions the maxim *first come, first served* generally holds true. White will therefore advance his King-side pawns as quickly as possible, and Black his Queen-side pawns. Another, less important, factor is the weakness of Black's pawn on d6; because of this, Black, in carrying out his plan, should try and arrange his pieces so that his pawn can be advantageously covered (e.g. R–Q1 and Q–QB2).

Sometimes positions occur in which a choice of strategical plans is possible. In the Sämisch Variation of the King's Indian, White has (after the moves 1 P–Q4, N–KB3; 2 P–QB4, P–KN3; 3 N–QB3,

B–N2; 4 P–K4, P–Q3; 5 P–B3, O–O; 6 B–K3, P–K4; 7 P–Q5, N–R4; 8 Q–Q2, P–KB4) the choice between two completely different plans (see Diagram 4)—

1. He can play 9 P×P, P×P; 10 O–O–O, and then try to launch a sharp King-side attack with B–Q3, KN–K2, R–KN1, and P–KN4; Black will then go in for an attack on the opposite wing (P–QR3, P–QN4, etc.); the game will have a sharp two-edged character.

2. He can, by 9 O–O–O, P–B5; 10 B–B2, allow Black to obtain a King-side space advantage, which can be increased by P–KN4–5. White, however, will have more space on the Queenside and after the development of his pieces can proceed with the advance P–QN4, P–QB5, etc.

In the transitional period between the opening and the middle-game, the possibility of a choice between two plans often arises. Sometimes it is not possible to decide, after an objective assessment, which is better; then subjective factors (such as one's own style and that of the opponent, as well as the state of the tournament) must be taken into consideration; but that we shall deal with in a later chapter.

When the correct theoretical plan corresponding to the character of the position has been selected, it must be carried out in a consistent manner with all the tactical means available. But a word of warning: the plan should always be kept under control in case a change in the position should occur; even a very slight change may necessitate an immediate alteration to the strategical plan.

C. THE EQUILIBRIUM OF THE POSITION
AND ITS DISTURBANCE

In judging a position we have up to now concerned ourselves with the determination of its strategical character and the choice of the correct strategical plan. A second, and no less important, part of the analysis of a position is the assessment of the prospects of both players for the further course of the game. Such an assessment is especially important if we want to calculate a particular series of moves; it is clear that we should only decide on a manoeuvre or combination when we consider the end position to be more favourable, or at least equal, to the initial one; therefore we must understand how to assess the prospects for both sides in the position before and after every forced manoeuvre or combination. The same type of assessment should also influence the determination of the strategical plan.

If the prospects of both players are equal in a particular position, we speak of the equilibrium of that position. This is often confused with the concept *drawn position*, but to interchange the terms freely is completely wrong, as the following two examples will show.

In Diagram 5 the position of the pawns is symmetrical. Sooner or later an exchange of heavy pieces will take place on the open e-file, leaving, amongst the minor pieces, Bishops of opposite colours,

DIAGRAM 5 DIAGRAM 6

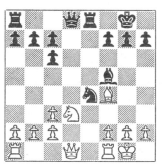 

which act as a strong equalizing factor. Neither side has at the moment a suitable plan that could offer chances of obtaining an advantage. If we ignore the possibility of blunders and assume that the players are of similar strength, then we can say that a draw is the almost certain outcome; the position is an equal one that offers neither side any real prospects.

Somewhat different is the position in Diagram 6. According to the theoreticians this game is also equal, but it is quite clear that it is not equal in the same way as in the preceding example: far from exhibiting drawing characteristics, the position has all the signs of a sharp struggle. White has the advantage on the King-side and is preparing a violent pawn attack there; he intends to castle long after playing Q–Q2. Black, for his part, can operate on the c-file (R–QB1, B–QB5, or N–QB5) and so effect a counter-attack on the side where White will castle. Experience shows that the chances both sides have of realizing their plans are about equal; the outcome of the game will only be decided later, victory going to the player who carries out his action more precisely and consistently and who is able to exploit any possible inaccuracies on the part of his opponent.

Basically, therefore, we have two forms of equilibrium—

1. Drawn positions offering neither side prospects of an active and effective plan.
2. Positions in which the prospects for both sides are equal; here the equilibrium is maintained by individual factors that determine the character of the position.

How is it that equilibrium arises? We know that White has the right to make the first move, and this gives him a certain advantage in development and possibly also in space. Theoreticians once argued about whether the advantage of the first move should suffice, with correct play, to win or whether a faultlessly played game must end in a draw. Recent experience has shown that the advantage of the first move is not so great as was once thought; Black can on the whole neutralize White's initial advantage within the first twelve to twenty moves. However, the first move has some importance: any inaccuracy, no matter how small, on the part of the second player during the opening generally results in disturbance of the equilibrium; White, on the other hand, can generally allow himself more scope and can often choose objectively weaker moves (perhaps for psychological reasons) without risking a seriously unfavourable shift in the equilibrium.

In the first phase of the game Black endeavours to obtain equality, which of course does not mean that he is forced to play for a draw. When he has equalized the position we have an equilibrium. How can this be upset? Basically, only by a mistake on the part of one of the players; but this does not only mean material loss or clear positional disadvantage; a faulty strategical plan or a series of minor inaccuracies that in isolation have little effect can also lead to a disturbance of the equilibrium.

When we maintain that the equilibrium can only be upset by a mistake on the part of one player, we do not imply that one cannot fight to achieve such a change. In order to force an advantage one must create strategical and tactical problems that afford the opponent difficulty. Often in clearly drawn positions it is possible to find a continuation that makes it hard for the opponent to work out the right strategical plan or even one that bamboozles him into making a tactical error.

The equilibrium cannot, however, be advantageously upset by a sudden attack; that would have the reverse effect for its initiator. This is one of Steinitz's principles. A simple example will show it at work.

MEEK–MORPHY

(Mobile 1855)

1	P–K4	P–K4
2	N–KB3	N–QB3
3	P–Q4	P×P
4	B–QB4	B–B4
5	N–N5?	

White's fourth move was, in a way, an attempt to disturb the equilibrium by giving up a pawn for the sake of development. If White had followed up in a consistent manner with 5 P–B3, then there would have been no unfavourable shift in the equilibrium for him. With the text-move, however, he tries to exploit the weakness of f7 by a sudden attack. This is wrong, for Black has obviously not made any error so far; the equilibrium was undisturbed, so White's display of aggression can achieve nothing.

DIAGRAM 7

5	...	N–R3
6	N×BP?!	N×N
7	B×N ch	K×B
8	Q–R5 ch	P–KN3

9	Q×B

DIAGRAM 8

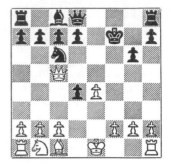

Diagram 7 showed the position before White's combination; diagram 8 gives the picture after it. In the course of the last five moves White has succeeded in recovering the pawn sacrificed on move four and at the same time has exposed Black's King; but he is so much behind in development that the equilibrium has been disturbed in favour of Black!

9	...	P–Q3
10	Q–QN5	R–K1
11	Q–N3 ch?	

A player familiar with the principles of present-day strategy, finding himself in this position, would without hesitation opt for the continuation 11 O–O, R×P; 12 N–Q2, R–K1; 13 N–B3. Although after Black's Q–B3 he would still have insufficient compensation for his pawn, he would at least have completed his development and so be in a position to ward off all immediate threats.

8

11 ...	P–Q4	19 Q–B1
12 P–KB3(?)	N–R4	
13 Q–Q3	P×P	If 19 Q×N, Black answers with
14 P×P	Q–R5 ch	19 ..., R–K7 ch.
15 P–KN3	R×Pch	
16 K–B2	Q–K2	19 ... B–R6!
17 N–Q2	R–K6	20 Q–Q1 R–KB1
18 Q–N5	P–B3!	21 N–B3 K–K1
		22 Resigns

To finish this section we shall examine the concepts *attack* and *initiative* in relation to the equilibrium. By attack we mean a direct threat to the opposing position either by a pawn advance supported by pieces or by a concentration of pieces on a particular section of the board. The well-known principle from the science of warfare that the successful execution of an attack requires a superiority of the attacking forces applies also to chess. Even many beginners know of the slogan, "Do not attack where you are weaker; otherwise you will suffer a disadvantage." In order to carry out an attack we need either a more active placing of the pieces or a space advantage or more mobile pawns or weak points in the enemy position or something similar. We need, in other words, a disturbance of the equilibrium. This rule has only one exception, which occurs in positions of the type shown in Diagram 6. Here the game is equal, but each player has a space advantage on a different section of the board. Either can launch an attack from his region of superiority, but must reckon on a counter-attack on the opposite wing.

We can now consider the consequences of a disturbance of the equilibrium caused by the opponent's inaccurate play. A serious disturbance of the equilibrium can lead to an objectively won game: for example, where material loss without adequate compensation is involved, the question of converting the advantage is generally one of technique; and where the King's position has been seriously weakened, an irresistible attack can often result. But in most cases a disturbance of the equilibrium does not lead at once to an objectively won game; not every advantage can be used to gain victory. A study of the end-game produces positions in which even a large material advantage cannot be converted: for example, a Bishop and a Rook-pawn against a lone King cannot win if the queening square is of a different colour from the Bishop and is controlled by the defending King. The result of a disturbance of the equilibrium is, rather, that one side is enabled to carry out his strategical plan under more favourable conditions and that the execution of the plan will leave its mark on the rest of the game; the opponent is usually

9

forced to ward off tactical and strategical threats so that he has little opportunity to unfold an active plan of his own.

The process of setting the pace with one's plan is called the initiative, which is the natural result of a disturbance of the equilibrium. We should note that it is wrong to equate *initiative* and *attack*; for attack is merely one form of initiative. Initiative can take several forms, e.g. the conversion of material advantage, planned simplification and transposition into an advantageous end-game, forcing the advance of a passed-pawn, etc. It can even happen that one side has the initiative while the other is on the attack; a case of this occurs when one side having lost a pawn makes a desperate, though insufficiently prepared, attack in the hope of saving the game; it is clear that the initiative belongs to the player with the material advantage and not to the one forced to attack. The initiative must necessarily go to the player in whose favour the equilibrium has shifted.

The initiative can not only take different forms but can also be of different degrees. Sometimes it is decisive and leads to a win against even the best counter-play. Sometimes it is not clear whether the advantage obtained is a winning one, although the opponent is forced on to the defensive for a long time and cannot carry out any active plan of his own; in this case we speak of a lasting initiative. Finally we have the case in which one player is forced for a certain time to answer enemy threats, but then, having done so, is able to restore the equilibrium; here it is a question of temporary initiative, an example of which is the initiative that White derives at the beginning of the game through the advantage of making the first move.

CHAPTER II

The Value of the Pieces

ONE of the beginner's first tasks is to become familiar with the working power of the individual pieces, for without a knowledge of this he cannot judge which changes are advantageous for him and which should be avoided. One of the most usual, and simplest, methods of piece evaluation is to take the pawn as a single unit and grade the other pieces accordingly. We then have—

$$\begin{aligned} \text{Bishop or Knight} &= 3 \\ \text{Rook} &= 5 \\ \text{Queen} &= 9 \end{aligned}$$

We can, of course, hardly give a value to the King, for this piece is an absolute factor: when it falls the game is lost.

The relationship of the pieces to one another is more complicated than the above values show; arithmetical values alone cannot express it accurately. A beginner may be able to get along for a while on a system that prescribes exchange on simple arithmetical calculation, but the advanced player knows that this method fails even when comparing a Rook and a minor piece, as the following example shows. A minor piece and two pawns are, on the average, worth a Rook, and here the sum $3 + 2 = 5$ is quite correct; but two Bishops ($2 \times 3 = 6$) are almost always more effective than a Rook and a pawn ($5 + 1 = 6$), while three minor pieces ($3 \times 3 = 9$) are mostly as strong as two Rooks ($2 \times 5 = 10$).

This evaluation is, of course, abstract and cannot be applied to any particular position. It represents the average value of the individual pieces, that is, the mutual relationship in the majority of positions. It should certainly not be taken as valid for all concrete positions. For the value of the pieces is relative; it depends on the character of the position as well as on the actual material on the board at a particular moment.

The minor pieces often show variations in value to one another, and we shall consider this in detail in a later section. Sometimes, however, apparently greater fluctuations occur with other pieces. For example, a Rook is generally much more powerful than a minor piece; but a centrally posted Knight can at times be its equal, as in Diagram 9.

11

Here White would be in advantage if he could get his Rook into action against the Black King; but he cannot do this by way of either a3 or f1; e.g. (*a*) 1 R–R3, P–K5!; 2 R×P, N–B6; 3 R–R3, P–K6! (threatening Q–N8 ch); 4 R–N3, P–K7 winning, or (*b*) 1 R–Q1, N–B6; 2 R–KB1, P–K5; 3 R–Q1, P–K6, etc. In view of this, Black's Knight can be considered as strong as White's Rook, and as Black has an extra pawn as compensation for his loss of the exchange we can say that he has the upper hand.

DIAGRAM 9

Just as variable is the value of the Queen. Normally a Queen is about equal to a Rook, a minor piece, and two pawns; but there are occasions when it can be inferior to a Rook, a minor piece, and one pawn. The following game exemplifies this.

NAJDORF–RAGOSIN

(Interzonal 1948)

DIAGRAM 10

Position after Black's 19th move

Black has sacrificed his Queen for a Rook, a Knight, and a pawn, and obtained a position that most of the competitors at the time considered good for his opponent. White has a material advantage and his position looks quite solid;

only the square b2 is a little weak, but this appears to be of temporary duration. Yet the further course of the game shows that Ragosin had calculated well in giving up his own Queen, for his opponent's remains for more than twenty moves inactive on the one spot.

We may well ask why a Queen should be superior to a Rook and a minor piece; after all its movements are merely the combination of those of a Rook and a Bishop. This is true: but the Queen coordinates these different movements much better than the single pieces; its great mobility makes it an excellent instrument of attack. Therein lies its superiority. Its advantage, however, is diminished when the opponent's pieces are working well in co-operation and cover all weak points. End-game theory produces positions in which a Queen sometimes cannot win against a Rook and a pawn because of the excellent co-ordination of the defending forces; a similar, though more complicated, example of co-operation is the present game, in which the Black pieces make it impossible for the White Queen to find a favourable target for attack.

20	B–Q2	N–K5
21	B–K3	N–Q3!

In the fight against the Queen it is important to prevent the formation of tactical weaknesses that could possibly be attacked by the opponent. The position of the Knights is important in this game, for they possess good operation bases: the Knight on d6, while heading for f5, is threatening to secure the *two Bishops* by N–QB5.

22	R–QB1	N–B4
23	B–KB4	B–Q4
24	B–B4	B × B
25	R × B	P–K4
26	B–N5?	

White's desire to maintain his material superiority (mechanically assessed) is understandable, but it leads to a speedy catastrophe. White's last chance lay in the exchange sacrifice given by

Smyslov: 26 R × N!, P × R; 27 B × P; after that Black, with two Rooks for a Queen, still has the better of it, but his weakened pawns offer White a good target for his Queen and therefore some drawing chances.

26	...	R–Q8 ch
27	K–R2	P–KR3
28	R–B1	R–Q2
29	B–K3	P–K5
30	N–K1	QR–Q1
31	B–B5	B–K4 ch
32	P–KN3	R–Q7
33	R–B2	B × KNP ch
34	K–N2	B–K4

Avoiding 34 ..., B × P?; 35 B × B, P–K6; 36 Q–B3!, P × B; 37 R × R, P × N=Q; 38 R × R ch, and White wins.

35	K–B1	R × R
36	N × R	R–Q8 ch
37	K–K2	R–QN8
38	P–N4	R–N7
39	K–Q1	R–N8 ch
40	K–Q2	B–B3!
41	B × P	N–K4
42	Q–R4	N–B6 ch
43	K–K2	N–N8 ch

White resigned without resuming play; there is nothing to be done after 44 K–Q2, N–B6 ch; 45 K–K2, N–Q3; 46 Q–Q7, N–N8 ch; 47 K–K3, R–Q8.

Now let us look at some other piece groupings. As a general rule three minor pieces have the edge over a Queen. An exception occurs if the Queen can penetrate the enemy position, attacking pawns and pinning the opposing pieces to passive defence; if, however, the side with the minor pieces can consolidate his position, his pieces can usually develop great power and go over to a concentrated attack. Diagram 11 shows a position in which the minor pieces give White the upper hand even though, on a purely mechanical calculation, his opponent has a material advantage (Queen and pawn against two Bishops and a Knight). The reason for White's superiority stems from his opponent's lack of active possibilities; in addition Black's weaknesses caused by the moves P–QN3 and P–KN3 will have their effect. It should be noted that White's isolated pawn on d4 is by no means weak; on the contrary, it plays a useful role by stopping a pawn advance on either the King's or Queen's wing.

DIAGRAM 11

DIAGRAM 12

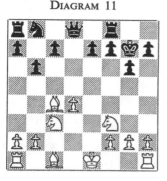

A frequent struggle is that between two Rooks and a Queen. Here the advantage lies almost always with the two Rooks, and the side with the Queen must generally have an extra pawn to have equalizing chances. The strength of the Rooks is best seen when they are united on the seventh or eighth ranks, or operating on open files; then the Queen's limited powers as a defensive piece become apparent. Better for the Queen are those positions in which it can attack weak pawns or an exposed King. The Queen has also improved prospects when its action can be assisted by certain other pieces; for example, a Queen and Bishop against two Rooks and a Knight in an open position offers better chances than a lone Queen against two Rooks; the reason is that the Queen and Bishop can co-ordinate well to attack along a diagonal. Diagram 12 shows this piece grouping at work. Black has the advantage here for several reasons. First, he has the possibility of attacking the weak points b4, f2, and, possibly, e4. Secondly, the White Rooks are not united, and they cannot easily begin to work together on the seventh or eighth ranks because of the need to defend threatened points. Thirdly, the Knight, which is also required for defence, cannot be maintained on its most advantageous operation base, d5; if it goes there, it will soon be driven back to passive defence.

CHAPTER III

The Minor Pieces

As we already know, the Bishop and Knight are about equal in value despite the very great difference in their ways of moving. In the following six sections we shall examine various combinations of these pieces.

A. THE BISHOP AND OPEN DIAGONALS

In order to obtain its full working force, a Bishop must be provided with open diagonals; here its long-range power can be put to good effect. In the opening the moves 1 P–Q4 and 1 P–K4 open up diagonals, but these are generally only ways of getting the Bishops into play; later comes the fight to provide diagonals from where a Bishop can exert a lasting pressure on the enemy position.

The following example shows how the opening of an attacking diagonal can lead to an immediate decision.

ALEKHINE–JOHNER

44 P–K5!!   QP×P

The alternative 44 ..., BP×P is answered by 45 P–B6!, Q×P; 46 Q×P ch followed by 47 B–K4.

45 P–Q6!   P–B4

No better is 45 ..., P×P; 46 P–B5! with the threat of 47 B–N3 ch.

46 B–K4   Q–Q2
47 Q–R6!   Resigns

The position is hopeless; there is no defence after 47 ..., K–B2; 48 B–Q5 ch.

DIAGRAM 13

Position after Black's 43rd move

As may be guessed, a well-posted Bishop is an extremely important strategical factor; on the other hand, a Bishop limited in its movements by its own or enemy pawns can also be an important, even a decisive, factor—for the opposing side. The difficulty is to assess whether a Bishop is good or bad in a particular position, for this cannot be done in any routine fashion. In Diagram 14, for example,

15

the Bishop on g2 can only move to one square, h1; yet this Bishop is by no means weak; in fact it is very strong. On the one hand it protects the White King should Black attack by N–KR4 and P–KB4; on the other it is there to protect the pawn on e4 if White should later decide to play P–KB4.

DIAGRAM 14

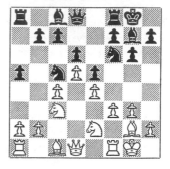

In modern openings the position of a Bishop is often very modest at the beginning; only later in the game does it develop its latent powers. If we compare the Bishop on g2 in the opening system 1 N–KB3, P–Q4; 2 P–KN3, N–KB3; 3 B–N2 with that on c4 in the Giuoco Piano (1 P–K4, P–K4; 2 N–KB3, N–QB3; 3 B–B4) we may at first glance consider it to be much more passive; yet the Bishop on c4 only gets the opportunity to develop a few tactical threats, whereas that on g2 can frequently determine the whole character of the game.

B. THE GOOD AND THE BAD BISHOP

If we look at Diagram 15 we see a position in which the material is exactly equal; nevertheless, White has a considerable advantage, and in fact he managed to win the game in a further ten moves. The explanation of White's advantage is the difference in the Bishops. Whereas the Bishop on d3 is not hemmed in by its own pawns and can attack both on the King's and Queen's wing, its adversary is condemned to inactivity by the Black pawn chain.

The value of a Bishop can usually be assessed by the following rule: the Bishop has good working power if its own pawns are posted on squares of the opposite colour. This of course applies only where the pawn formation cannot easily be altered, as Diagram 16 will make clear. There White has three pawns on squares of the same colour as his Bishop and only two on squares of opposite colour, while the position is reversed with Black. But White's three Queen-side pawns can easily change their positions. What determines whether the Bishops are bad or good are the immobile King-side pawns; so it is White's Bishop which should be considered the good one.

The differing value of Bishops is an important strategical factor. As a rule, each side will endeavour to place his pawns on a colour opposite to that of his Bishop; this makes it easier to block the

16

opponent's pawns on squares accessible to the Bishop. When the position has become simplified and the pawn formation fairly rigid, both sides will try to rid themselves of a bad Bishop and keep a good one. In the middle-game it is sometimes possible to initiate a

DIAGRAM 15

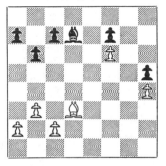

DIAGRAM 16

Black to play

series of exchanges leading to a favourable end-game of good versus bad Bishop. Bronstein employed this idea against Najdorf when he continued 1 ..., B × B; 2 Q × B, Q–K4!; 3 Q × Q, P × Q from the position in Diagram 17. The advantage he obtained from his good Bishop proved sufficient to win the game.

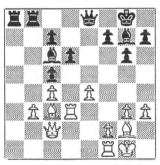

DIAGRAM 17

Black to play

The rule given above for determining whether the Bishop is good or bad must be modified in certain circumstances. So, for example, after the moves 1 P–Q4, P–Q4; 2 P–QB4, P–QB3; 3 P × P, P × P; 4 N–QB3, N–QB3; 5 N–B3, N–B3; 6 B–B4, B–B4; 7 P–K3, P–K3, the Bishops on f4 and f5 can hardly be called bad, although they are the same colour as their own blocked pawns; their position outside the pawn chain makes a difference, and, in fact, they can develop great strength. In a game Botvinnik–Trifunovic (Moscow 1947), which reached this position, Black answered 8 Q–N3 by 8 ..., B–QN5!; after that he exchanged his "good" Bishop on b4 against White's Knight on c3, but nevertheless got a good game on account of the active position of his other minor pieces.

17

We shall follow with a game illustrating how the application of the *good Bishop* rule caused a change in theory on the King's-Indian Defence.

SAKELLAROPOULOS–
BOLESLAVSKI

(Helsinki 1952)

1 P–Q4	N–KB3
2 P–QB4	P–KN3
3 N–QB3	B–N2
4 P–K4	O–O
5 N–B3	P–Q3
6 B–K2	P–K4
7 P–Q5	QN–Q2
8 O–O	N–B4
9 N–Q2	P–QR4
10 Q–B2	

DIAGRAM 18

At one time this position occurred with such frequency that one could almost have called it the normal position. In 1950, however, in the 18th U.S.S.R. Championship, Petrosian employed against Flohr a continuation for Black of such strategic brilliance that the whole variation has now disappeared from master practice. This continuation is repeated here.

10 ...	B–R3!!

Why had this move—which is really a very logical continuation—escaped the attention of both theorists and players? The reason is that, in many variations of the King's Indian, Black's Bishop on g7 plays such an important role that it is White who often attempts to eliminate it by exchange. But that is the case only when White's Queen-pawn is still on d4 or Black has already made the exchange KP×QP; in such cases Black's Bishop on g7 exerts an important positional pressure on the long diagonal. However, once the centre has been blocked, things are different; Black's Bishop on g7 becomes bad while White's on c1 is good. With this in mind, Black makes use of the position of White's Knight on d2 to force the exchange of Bishops; after that his Bishop on c8 will be the good one, and White's on e2 the bad one.

11 N–N3	B × B
12 QR × B	

In his game against Petrosian, Flohr played 12 N × N but, after 12 ..., B–R3, Black was left with the *two Bishops*. At the time, many commentators were still so convinced of the importance to Black of the King's Bishop that they recommended 12 QR × B (as played in this game); they assumed

18

that this continuation would bring White an advantage owing to the supposed weakness of Black's castled position. But this view is wrong; White has no real prospects on the King's wing.

12 ...	KN–Q2
13 N×N	N×N
14 P–B4?	

Correct is the waiting move 14 Q–Q2; the text-move leaves White with a serious weakness on e4.

14 ...	P×P
15 R×P	Q–N4
16 R(4)–B1	B–Q2
17 QR–K1	QR–K1
18 B–Q3	P–B4

19 Q–N1?

After 19 P×P, Black has the strong reply 19 ..., R–K6!; but somewhat better for White is 19 K–R1.

19 ...	P×P
20 N×P	N×N
21 B×N	R×R ch
22 K×R	Q–B5 ch
23 K–N1	Q–K4
24 K–B1	

Otherwise Black plays 24 ..., B–B4.

24 ...	Q×RP
25 B–B3	Q–R8 ch
26 K–B2	Q–R5 ch
27 Resigns	

C. UNLIKE BISHOPS

Almost every novice is familiar with the concept *Bishops of opposite colours.* They are often a means of salvation in positions materially unfavourable, where they present a strong equalizing factor; they place difficulties in the way of converting an extra pawn, or sometimes several. Instructive in this respect is the position worked out by W. Tschechover (Diagram 19); against a superiority of three

DIAGRAM 19

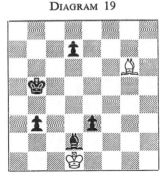

White to play and draw

DIAGRAM 20

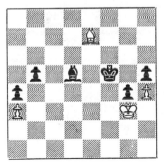

pawns White can draw the game: **1 B–K8!, K–B3** (1 ..., K–N5; 2 B×P, K–R6; 3 B–B5, K–N7; 4 B–K6!, K–R7; 5 B–B7, K–R6;

6 B–N6, draw); **2 K–K2!** (2 B–B7?, P–Q4), **B–B8** (2 ..., K–B2; 3 B–B7, P–N7; 4 B–N6, draw); **3 K–Q1, B–N7; 4 K–K2, B–Q5; 5 K–Q1, K–Q3; 6 B–B7!, P–N7; 7 B–N6, K–B4; 8 K–K2, P–Q4; 9 B–B5, K–N5; 10 B–N6, K–R6; 11 B–N1, K–N6; 12 K–Q1, K–B6; 13 K–K2, B–B4; 14 K–Q1, P–Q5; 15 K–K2, K–N6; 16 K–Q3,** draw. Another drawn position is that in Diagram 20. The reason for the drawing tendency of unlike Bishops should be clear from these examples: the stronger side cannot force pawns over squares controlled by the enemy King and Bishop, for there is no piece apart from the King to give the pawns support; in addition the Bishop cannot attack pawns posted on squares of the opposite colour.

The well-known drawing propensities of unlike Bishops—how often they are blessed by the weaker side!—is lessened or eliminated completely if there are other pieces on the board; in fact they can even work the other way in the middle-game and enable one side to obtain a positional advantage. The reason for this is that the Bishop of the defending side cannot protect a point attacked by the opponent's Bishop. In Diagram 21, Black has a material advantage, but he is powerless against White's attack: 1 ..., K–R1; 2 Q–K5, R–N1; 3 P–N6!, or 1 ..., Q–Q2; 2 Q–K5, P–B3; 3 P×P, B–B2; 4 P×P, KR–K1; 5 Q–N3. The following game shows the Bishops working in a similar way.

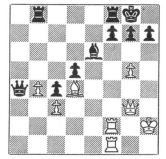

DIAGRAM 21

Black to play; White wins

FILIP–PACHMAN

(Czechoslovak Championship 1953)

At first sight this position looks clearly drawn: the pawns are symmetrically distributed, and at least one pair of Rooks seems bound to be exchanged on the open King's file. In addition, the unlike Bishops appear to make any endgame a certain draw. Yet it is the very presence of these unlike Bishops which gives White winning

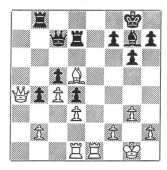

DIAGRAM 22

Position after Black's 28th move

chances: his Bishop on d5 is actively posted, whereas Black's has no great prospects. A further important factor is the open King's file, which White is soon able to use to his advantage.

29	R–K4	R–K2
30	R(Q1)–K1	B–B1

Bad is 30 ..., R(N1)–K1 because of 31 Q×R ch.

| 31 | P–KR4 | K–N2? |

The decisive mistake. Black wants to avoid leaving his pawns on white squares, so he makes preparations for a later advance by P–KR3 and P–KN4. However, it is after these very moves that the weakness of the white squares becomes apparent. Necessary was 31 ..., P–R4, after which Black could have put up a successful defence.

32	P–R5!	R–Q1
33	R×R	B×R
34	Q–Q1	R–Q3
35	Q–K2	B–B3
36	K–N2	R–Q2
37	Q–B3	Q–Q3
38	R–K4	P–N4

White was threatening 39 R–B4.

| 39 | Q–B5 | P–R3 |

White has now obtained a won position. Although the actual game lasted twenty moves longer, there was a quick and elegant win as follows: 40 R–K6!, P×R; 41 Q–N6 ch, K–B1; 42 Q×B ch, etc.

This example shows that Bishops of opposite colours are not always a drawing factor. Perhaps in the end-game their drawing influence is strong; in the middle-game, however, the difference in their respective strengths can often help one side to a decisive advantage.

D. THE KNIGHT AND ITS OPERATION BASE

Because of the special movements of the Knight, an essential requirement for its successful working is an operation base. By this we mean a square on which the Knight is protected from attack by enemy pieces and, more important, pawns. As mentioned in an earlier chapter, a centrally placed and protected Knight often exerts the same power as a Rook. On the other hand, a badly placed Knight is a definite weakness. The old saying, "A Knight on the side brings only trouble," is a clear way of stating that a Knight utilizes only a part of its strength when on the edge of the board. Whereas a Knight in the centre can reach eight squares, one in the corner is limited to two. Because of this, an advantageous posting is extremely important.

AHUES–ALEKHINE

(Bad Nauheim 1936)

1 P–Q4	P–Q4
2 P–QB4	P×P
3 N–KB3	P–QR3
4 P–QR4(?)	N–KB3
5 P–K3	B–N5
6 B×P	P–K3
7 N–B3	N–B3
8 B–K2	B–N5
9 O–O	O–O
10 N–Q2	

Better is B–Q2

10 ...	B×B
11 N×B	P–K4
12 N–KB3	R–K1
13 B–Q2	B–Q3
14 N–N3	P–K5
15 N–K1	

DIAGRAM 23

15 ...	B×N!

At first, this move is surprising, for the Bishop appears to have an important role to play in a future attack on the King's wing. Alekhine, however, has realized that, after this exchange, White's King-side pawns will be immobile, thus

giving him excellent operation bases for his Knights on d5 and g4.

16 RP×B	N–K2!
17 P–QN4	Q–Q2
18 N–B2	N(2)–Q4
19 N–R3	

White also wants an operation base for his Knight—on e5—but his plans for this are quickly frustrated.

19 ...	P–QN4!
20 P×P	P×P
21 Q–K2	P–B3
22 N–B2	Q–B4
23 KR–QB1	P–R3
24 R–R5	QR–B1
25 N–R1?	

White attempts to bring his Knight to the strong operation base c5. For such a manoeuvre, however, it is already too late, for Black's attack meanwhile smashes through. Correct was 25 P–B3 to deprive the Black Knight of the square g4.

25	N–N5

DIAGRAM 24

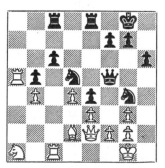

It is clear that Alekhine has carried out his plan successfully. Now he threatens 26 ..., Q–R4.

26 K–B1	R–K3
27 R × NP	R–B3
28 R(1)–B5	N × BP
29 K–K1	N–Q6 ch
30 K–Q1	Q–B8 ch
31 B–K1	R–B7!
32 Resigns	

Noticeable in this game were the differing roles played by the Knights: White's one Knight achieved little, whereas Black's (especially that which remained fully thirteen moves on d5) exerted a crippling influence on the enemy position.

The securing of operation bases for the Knights is certainly one of the most important motifs in chess strategy. What will be interesting to see is whether the unfavourable position of a Knight can be also considered a lasting strategical factor. Undoubtedly such cases will occur less frequently, for the Knight is not bound to squares of a particular colour and its movements are not greatly cramped by pawn chains. Its unfavourable posting is therefore generally a temporary feature only. Nevertheless, there are occasions when the Knight's position cannot be improved without great difficulties; or it can even happen, as in the next game, that the Knight remains completely cut off.

PACHMAN–SZABÓ
(Hilversum 1947)

1 P–Q4	P–K3
2 P–QB4	P–Q4
3 N–QB3	N–KB3
4 B–N5	B–K2
5 N–B3	O–O
6 P–K3	N–K5
7 B × B	Q × B
8 R–B1	P–QB3
9 B–Q3	P–KB4?

Here N × N was necessary. After the text-move the greater activity of the White Knights is apparent. In this case, such a lasting positional factor is more important than Black's purely tactical prospects on the King-side.

10 O–O	N–Q2
11 P–QR3	R–B3
12 N–K5!	N × N

Now Black's Rook is drawn out of play.

13 P × N	R–R3
14 P–KN3!	B–Q2
15 P–B3	

The Black Knight becomes the object of White's attention. An exchange by 15 ..., N × N; 16 R × N is hardly attractive, for then White's attack on the Queen's wing would develop quickly.

| 15 ... | N–N4 |
| 16 P–B4 | N–R6 ch? |

A mistake similar to that on move 9. For the sake of a few tactical threats, Black condemns his Knight to a hopeless post, a

23

fact that will grow in importance when the position becomes simplified. The reason for such an error is probably the lack of attractive alternatives, e.g. 16 ...,
N–K5; 17 P×P, KP×P; 18
Q–N3, N×N; 19 Q×N.

| 17 K–R1 | P–KN4 |
| 18 P×QP | KP×P |

DIAGRAM 25

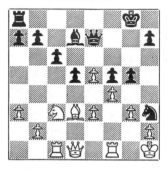

| 19 Q–B2 | P×P |

The first disappointment. Black had probably planned the advance 19 ..., P–Q5?!; 20 P×QP, P×P; 21 P×P?, Q–R5, when, with K–R1, he has a turbulent attack in which his Knight on h3 is admirably placed. However, White has a stronger line in 21 N–K2!, P×P; 22 N×P, P–B5; 23 N–B5, winning the f-pawn. In the game, Black is virtually a piece down, for

his Knight on h3 is eternally locked in.

20 KP×P	Q–B2
21 N–K2!	K–R1
22 N–Q4	

The White Knight, on the other hand, attains a strong position from where it attacks the weak f-pawn. The contrasting powers of the two Knights are quite clear.

22 ...	R–KB1
23 QR–K1	B–K3
24 Q–B5!	

Winning a pawn, for if 24 ...,
P–R3, then 25 Q–Q6 decides the issue.

| 24 ... | R–KN1 |
| 25 N×B | R×N |

25 ..., Q×N fails against 26 Q–Q6, for after the exchange of Queens, the imprisoned Knight on h3 cannot be protected. Now that the threat of R×NP is settled, White has time to take the a-pawn.

26 Q×RP	Q–R4
27 Q–K3	R–R3
28 Q–K2	Q–K1
29 P–K6!	R×NP
30 Q–K5 ch	K–N1
31 B×P	R–N2
32 B×N	R×B
33 R–KN1	Resigns

E. THE STRUGGLE OF BISHOP AGAINST KNIGHT

The struggle of Bishop against Knight is one of the most interesting problems in chess strategy. In the nineteenth century the Bishop was held by some authorities (e.g. Tarrasch) to be superior, on account of its long reach; others, however, preferred the Knight, because of its ability to occupy all squares on the board. Out of these differing views arose the expression *the minor exchange*, which mostly meant the win of a Bishop for a Knight, though sometimes the reverse. However, no such "rule of thumb" method is advisable in considering these pieces: to assess which really is superior we should bear in mind the character, and particularly the pawn formation, of the individual position.

The long-range powers of the Bishop show up best where the position is open, with mobile pawns on both sides of the board; it is also effective when attacking opposing pawns blocked on squares of its own colour. The strength of the Knight, on the other hand, is best felt in blocked positions, where its peculiar movements enable it to find points of attack that are denied to the straight-moving Bishop. Of course, an important requirement for its effective working will be operation bases from which to harass enemy weak points and defend its own.

As a guide we give below positions that show when each of the pieces is working best.

1. THE SUPERIORITY OF THE BISHOP

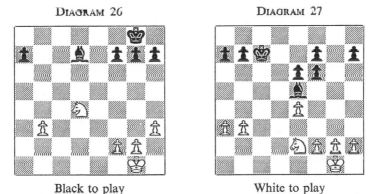

DIAGRAM 26   DIAGRAM 27

Black to play   White to play

From the positions in Diagrams 26, 27, 28 the player with the Bishop managed in each case to win. For example, in Diagram 27 the game went as follows: **1 K–B1, P–N4; 2 K–K1, B–N7; 3 P–QR4, P×P; 4 P×P, K–B3!** (4 K–N3, K–Q2; 5 K–R4?, K–B2); **5 K–Q2, K–B4; 6 N–B3, K–N5; 7 N–N5, P–QR4!; 8 N–Q6, K×P; 9 K–B2, B–B4; 10 N×P, B×P; 11 N–Q8, P–K4;** and Black won.

Generally we can say that in positions similar to those in Diagrams 26 and 27, where the pawns are mobile on both wings, the Bishop is superior. It needs only an additional small advantage, such as a mobile King, to disturb the balance sufficiently for the win. Just as good for the Bishop are positions (like that in Diagram 28) in which the Bishop can subject enemy pawns to attack. The Bishop here attacks the White Kingside (supported by the pawn advance P–KR5) and at the same time defends its own Queen-side. The slower-moving Knight, on the other hand, is only able to operate on one side at a time.

DIAGRAM 28

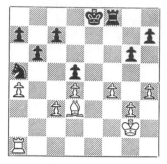

White to play

2. THE SUPERIORITY OF THE KNIGHT

DIAGRAM 29

White to play

DIAGRAM 30

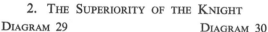

White to play

DIAGRAM 31

Black to play

From the positions in Diagrams 29, 30, 31 the Knight emerged victorious. For example, in Diagram 29 the game continued: **1 N–K1, B–R8; 2 N–B3, B–Q5; 3 N–R4ch, K–B3; 4 K–R5, B–N7; 5 N–B5, B–B8; 6 N–R6, B–N7; 7 N–N4 ch, K–K3; 8 K–N6, B–B8; 9 N–R6, B–Q7; 10 N–B7, B–B5; 11 N–N5 ch!, K–Q3; 12 K–B6** and wins.

All three positions are blocked or semi-blocked, with the Bishop unable to find an object for attack. The

Knight has, in each case, much greater freedom of movement than the bad Bishop and this was sufficient to bring victory.

From the above six examples we can set out an important principle in conducting games where Bishop is opposed by Knight: the side with the Bishop must endeavour to keep the pawns mobile; the opponent, on the other hand, must try to lock the enemy pawns on squares of the same colour as the Bishop and at the same time, by suitable Knight manoeuvres, create points of attack.

We give now two examples in which the Bishop comes off best.

NAJDORF–STÅHLBERG

(Candidates Tournament 1953)

DIAGRAM 32

Position after Black's 25th move

In this position with mobile pawns on both wings, White's Bishop gives him an advantage, which, however, is minimized by the presence of his doubled pawns.

26 R–K4 ch	K–B1
27 R–QR4	P–QR3
28 R–KB4	P–B3?

Generally, the pawns should be placed on squares of opposite colour to the Bishop, but here we have the exception that qualifies many a rule. The move P–B3 actually increases the range and power of the Bishop and allows

White, at a later stage, the possibility of creating a passed-pawn. For this reason 28 ..., N–Q3 was the correct move.

| 29 R–KR4 | P–R3 |
| 30 R–R5! | |

Prevents the mobilization of Black's Queen-side pawns by 30 ..., P–QB4.

30 ...	N–B2
31 P–B4	K–K2
32 R–QB5	R–Q3
33 R–B1?	

It is only on the next move that White finds the right plan. Here he should have played P–B5 forestalling 33 ..., P–KB4, which, if played, would considerably reduce his advantage on the King-side.

| 33 ... | P–QN3? |
| 34 P–B5! | |

This move has a double purpose: it restricts the Knight's movements and at the same time prepares the advance of White's pawns.

34 ...	P–B4
35 P–B4	R–B3
36 P–QR4!	

Makes possible the opening, at a

27

suitable moment, of the a-file, for Black must sooner or later play P–QN4 to set his Queen-side pawns in motion.

36 ...   **P–QN4**
37 B–B2!

A strong move, which aims, by tactical means, at bringing the Bishop to a dominant position on d5. At the moment B–K4 winning a pawn is the threat, which cannot be countered by 37 ..., P–B5 on account of 38 B–K4, R–N3 (or Q3); 39 P–N3, etc.

37 ...   **N–K1**
38 B–K4   **R–B2**
39 B–Q5

DIAGRAM 33

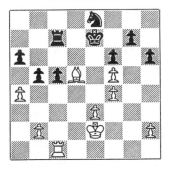

The action of the Bishop has increased considerably. It is now in a strong position to support the break-through P–K4–K5 while at the same time holding the Black Queen-side pawns.

39 ...   **P–B5**

Otherwise White, after the manoeuvre P–K4, P–K5, K–K3, K–K4, B–K6, K–Q5, would penetrate with his King.

40 P–K4   **N–Q3**
41 P × P   **P × P**
42 K–K3   **R–R2**

Black has apparently widened the scope for his pieces. Two moves later, however, he is driven back to passive defence.

43 R–KN1   **K–B1**

Unplayable is N–K1 because of 44 B–B6 winning a pawn.

44 K–Q4   **R–QB2**
45 R–QB1   **N–N2!**

Counters the threat 46 P–QN3, which can now be met by 46 ..., N–B4.

46 R–QR1!   **N–B4**
47 R–R8 ch   **K–K2**
48 P–K5   **N–N6 ch**
49 K–B3   **N–B8**

Other defences are no better; e.g.

(a) 49 ..., R–B4; 50 R–R7 ch, K–Q1 (K–B1; 51 R–Q7 or 50 ..., K–K1; 51 B–B7 ch, K–B1; 52 P–K6); 51 B–K4, P × P; 52 R × P, N–Q5; 53 P–B6!, N–K3; 54 B–B5 winning.

(b) 49 ..., P × P; 50 P × P, R–B4; 51 R–R7 ch, K–K1 (K–B1; 52 R–Q7, K–K1; 53 P–K6); 52 B–B7 ch, K–B1; 53 P–K6, R × P; 54 B–N6, R–R4; 55 R–B7 ch, etc.

50 R–KN8   **N–K7 ch**
51 K–Q2   **N × P**
52 R × P ch   **K–Q1**
53 P × P!   **R–Q2**

Or 53 ..., N × B; 54 R–N8 ch and P–B7.

54 R×R ch   K×R
55 B–B6 ch!   Resigns

White wins both Queen-side pawns because K×B fails against 56 P–B7.

KRYLOW–RUNZA

(Presov 1951)

DIAGRAM 34

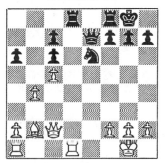

Position after Black's 21st move

Black seems to have a satisfactory position. In fact, a purely mechanical judgement might even say that White, in view of his blocked pawns on the Queen-side, is saddled with a bad Bishop. A deeper probe, however, shows that more important are Black's weak Queen-side pawns, one of which (on c7) is a natural target for the Bishop. Besides, there are pawns on both sides of the board, and this throws the balance in favour of the Bishop.

21 Q–K4   R×R ch
22 R×R   R–Q1
23 R–K1!

White keeps the Rook on the board partly because this piece is admirable for attacking weak pawns in an end-game and partly to facilitate the exchange of Queens, whose disappearance would then leave him with the superior end-game for which he is striving.

23 ...   R–Q4
24 P–B4   Q–R5
25 B–B3   P–R3
26 P–N3   Q–N5
27 Q–K2!   Q×Q
28 R×Q   K–B1
29 K–B2   P–N3
30 K–K3   P–B4
31 R–Q2!

DIAGRAM 35

White has allowed his King-side pawns to be blocked on squares of the same colour as his Bishop. Now he exchanges the Rooks, renouncing any idea of exploiting the Queen-side weaknesses by a manoeuvre such as R–N2–N3–R3. Nevertheless, the lone Bishop is still superior to the Knight, for its action on the long diagonal, together with its threats to the weak pawn on c7, assists the gradual penetration of the White King.

31 ...	R×R
32 B×R	K–K2
33 B–B3	P–KR4
34 B–K5	K–Q2
35 K–Q3	K–B1
36 K–B4	K–Q2
37 P–QR4	K–B1
38 P–N5!	RP×P
39 P×P	K–N2
40 P–KR4!	

Yet another pawn is placed on a square of similar colour to the Bishop. White, however, needs to prevent any possible freeing manoeuvre on Black's part through P–KN4 or P–R5. The point of the advance is that White will not reply to 40 ..., P×P ch with 41 K×P, after which 41 ..., P–B3 ch draws, but with 41 K–Q5!, when the penetration of his King into Black's King-side is decisive.

40 ...	N–Q1
41 B–B6	K–B1?

Even without this mistake the game could not be saved; e.g.

(*a*) 41 ..., N–K3; 42 B–K7, P×P ch (N–N2; 43 K–Q4!, P×P; 44 K–K5); 43 K–Q5, N–N2; 44

P–B6 ch, K–N3; 45 B–B5 ch, K–R4; 46 K–K5, P–N5; 47 K–B6, K–N4; 48 B–Q4, K–B5; 49 B–K5, N–K1 ch; 50 K–K7 and wins.

(*b*) 41 ..., N–B2; 42 B–N7!, P×P ch; 43 K–Q5, P–B3 ch; 44 K–K6, N–Q1 ch; 45 K–K7 winning (Krylow)

42 B×N	P×P ch
43 K×P	K×B
44 K–R6	K–K2!
45 K–R7!	

Not K–N7?, after which Black wins with 45 ..., K–Q2; 45 K–N8, K–B3.

45 ...	K–K3
46 K–N8!	K–Q4

Or 46 ..., K–Q2; 47 K–N7, K–Q1; 48 P–B6, and Black is finished.

| 47 K×P | |

At this point Black resigned in view of the continuation 47 ..., K×P; 48 K–Q7, K–Q4; 49 K–K7, K–K5; 50 K–B6, K–B6; 51 K×NP, K×NP; 52 K–N5!.

Now we follow with two examples where the Knight has the initiative.

LILIENTHAL–BONDAREVSKI

(Moscow 1940)

In this position (Diagram 36) with locked centre pawns, the Bishop has no target for attack; the Knight, for its part, has freedom to manoeuvre. We can therefore judge the position as favourable for White, though it must be admitted that with such a small advantage he could hardly win if he were not able to induce weaknesses on his opponent's Queen-side.

DIAGRAM 36

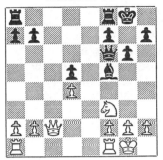

Position after Black's 17th move

18 Q–N3	B–K5
19 N–K5	

Now White has three threats: Q×NP, P–B3, and N–Q7.

19 ...	Q–N3!
20 Q×Q	P×Q
21 KR–QB1	

The attempt to win a pawn by N–Q7 is out of the question: 21 N–Q7, KR–Q1; 22 N×P?, R–R3, and the Knight is trapped.

21 ...	KR–QB1
22 P–QR3	B–B4
23 P–KN4!	B–K3
24 P–R3(?)	

White posts his pawns on squares of the same colour as the Bishop, a course that here is quite correct because the movements of the Bishop are thereby constrained. However, it was better to do this by 24 P–B3, for then, after an exchange of Rooks by 24 ..., R×R ch; 25 R×R, R–QB1; 26 R×R ch, B×R, White could continue immediately with P–KN5,

seriously compromising Black's position.

24 ...	P–B3
25 N–Q3	P–KN4
26 P–B3	K–B2
27 K–B2	K–K2
28 K–K3	K–Q3?

This mistake is decisive. Black ought to have played P–KR4 followed by K–Q3 and P×P; by this means he would have stopped the penetration of White's Rook on the King-side.

29 R×R!	R×R
30 P–KR4!	P–R3

Worse is 30 ..., P×P; 31 R–R1, P–B4; 32 P–N5.

31 P×P	RP×P
32 R–KR1	R–K1
33 K–Q2	B–Q2
34 R–R6	R–KB1

If K–K3, there follows 35 P–B4!, R–KN1; 36 P–B5 ch.

35 N–K1	K–K2
36 N–B2	R–B2
37 N–K3	B–K3
38 K–B3	K–Q3
39 K–N4	B–Q2
40 N–B5 ch !	K–B2

Here exchanging off the Knight leads to a loss: 40 ..., B×N; 41 P×B, K–B3; 42 P–QR4!, R–B1; 43 R–R7, R–Q1; 44 R–KB7, R–Q3; 45 P–N3, P–N4; 46 P–R5, P–N3; 47 P–R6 (Lilienthal).

41 P–QR4	B–K3
42 N–N3	B–Q2

31

43 N–R5!	P–B4
44 N–B6!	

The end of a seven-move manoeuvre in which the Knight has shown great mobility. Now Black loses a pawn and with it the game.

44 ...	P×P
45 N×P ch	K–N1
46 P×P	B×NP
47 N×P	R–B7
48 P–N3	B–Q8
49 P–Q5	K–B2

If R–B6, then 50 P–Q6, R×P ch; 51 K–R5, etc.

50 P–R5	R–Q7
51 R–R7 ch	K–N1
52 P–Q6!	R–Q5 ch

If R×P, then 53 R–R8 ch, K–B2; 54 R–QB8 mate!

53 K–B5	R–KR5
54 P–Q7	K–B2
55 P–Q8=Q ch	K×Q
56 R–Q7 ch	Resigns

SMYSLOV–RUDAKOWSKI

(Moscow 1945)

1 P–K4	P–QB4
2 N–KB3	P–K3
3 P–Q4	P×P
4 N×P	N–KB3
5 N–QB3	P–Q3
6 B–K2	B–K2
7 O–O	O–O
8 B–K3	N–QB3
9 P–B4	Q–B2
10 Q–K1	N×N
11 B×N	P–K4
12 B–K3	B–K3?

Better is B–Q2 followed by B–B3.

13 P–B5	B–B5?

Here it was essential to try 13 ..., B–Q2; 14 P–KN4, B–B3; 15 B–B3, P–Q4!?; 16 P×QP, P–K5; 17 N×P, N×QP, though it must be admitted that in the ensuing sharp play White's prospects are better.

14 B×B	Q×B
15 B–N5!	

Positionally, a decisive move. Black cannot prevent the exchange of his Knight on f6, after which White secures a strong operation base on d5. There now arises a typical and frequently recurring position, where the White Knight is superior to the Bishop, which, in this case, is unable to work up any active counter-play right to the end of the game.

DIAGRAM 37

15 ...	KR–K1
16 B×N	B×B
17 N–Q5!	

White need not worry about losing his QBP, for if 17 ...,

Q×BP; 18 R–B2, Q–B4; 19 R–QB1, Black cannot prevent 20 N–B7 winning the exchange.

17 ...	B–Q1
18 P–B3	P–QN4
19 P–QN3	Q–B4 ch
20 K–R1	R–QB1
21 R–B3	K–R1

Here Black had his last chance to strengthen the defence by P–B3. In this case White would have had the choice between a King-side attack with heavy pieces (22 R–R3, P–QR4; 23 Q–R4, P–R3; 24 Q–N4, K–R1; 25 R–KB1 followed by Q–N6 and QR–B3) and the equally strong manoeuvre of opening the a-file with 22 P–QR4. Now the weakened position of Black's King brings about a quick decision.

22 P–B6	P×P
23 Q–R4	R–KN1
24 N×P	R–N2
25 R–N3!	

Threatening both 26 Q×P ch! and 26 R×R, K×R; 27 Q×RP ch!, K×N; 28 R–KB1 ch.

25 ...	B×N
26 Q×B	QR–KN1
27 R–Q1	P–Q4
28 R×R	Resigns

F. THE TWO BISHOPS

Almost every chess player is familiar with the meaning of this concept. In thousands of annotations to master games the superiority of the *two Bishops* over Knight and Bishop is mentioned; in many games a pawn is given up merely to secure the *two Bishops*; often we encounter the view that, independent of the position, the *two Bishops* can be considered an absolute advantage. Our task here is to explain the reasons for their inherent advantage, in which positions this is valid, and how it can best be exploited.

In a previous section we considered the lone Bishop opposed by a Knight and concluded that in unblocked positions the Bishop was generally the better piece. However, it had one drawback—its confinement to one half of the board. This allowed the opponent to operate freely, even with his King, on squares of opposite colour to that of the Bishop. When, however, there are two Bishops this drawback is greatly diminished: all squares are then controlled and the power of the Bishops in an unblocked position becomes a noticeable factor. A simple example is the following from a game by Botvinnik.

BOTVINNIK–EUWE

(The Hague 1948)

Botvinnik has just played the strong move 17 N–K5 (Diagram 38) offering a pawn to obtain the *two Bishops*, whose activity against the opposing King-side should outweigh the material disadvantage. Black's best course was to decline the offer by 17 ..., B–K3; 18 B–N1, B–Q4, with good defensive possibilities, though even here White would obtain some initiative by 19 P–B3 or P–B4.

DIAGRAM 38

Position after White's 17th move

17 ...	B×N?
18 P×B	Q×KP
19 B–B3	Q–K2
20 P–B3	N–Q4

If P×P, then 21 B–N1, P–R3; 22 R×P, N–Q4; 23 R–N3! winning. Better than the text-move, however, is 20 ..., B–K3, when, after 21 P×P!, B×B; 22 R×N! followed by 23 Q–N5, White has a sharp attack, though the position is unclear.

21 Q×Q	N×Q
22 P×P	

Now we have an interesting endgame (or rather a middle-game without Queens) in which White has broken pawns but strong Bishops. It is important that Black cannot, for tactical reasons, play for the exchange of Bishops: 22 ..., B–K3?; 23 B×B, P×B; 24 R×R ch, K×R; 25 R–KB1 ch,

K–N1; 26 R–Q1, and Black cannot prevent the penetration of the Rook to the seventh rank. The position is already difficult; Euwe's next move makes it quite lost. The best defence lay in active counterplay: 22 ..., B–N5!; 23 R–B4, B–R4; 24 P–KN4, B–N3; 25 R–Q1, QR–Q1; 26 R×R, R×R; 27 B×RP, R–Q8 ch.

DIAGRAM 39

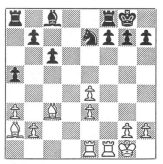

Position after 22 P×P

22 ...	P–QN3?
23 R–Q1	N–N3

It is possible that Black had planned 23 ..., R–R2 and now realizes that this is refuted by 24 R×P.

24 R–Q6	B–R3
25 R–B2	B–N4
26 P–K5	N–K2
27 P–K4!	P–QB4
28 P–K6	

This is much better than 28 R×NP, B–B3.

28 ...	P–B3
29 R×NP	B–B3
30 R×B!	N×R
31 P–K7 dis ch	R–B2
32 B–Q5	Resigns

34

The *two Bishops* in this game worked quite simply on their free diagonals, attacking various points in the enemy position; the Bishop on c3 even managed to direct its attack in two places (a5 and g7) simultaneously. A different use of the *two Bishops* occurs in the next example. There, it is not their intrinsic value which matters; what stands out is the ease with which one of them can exchange itself for an actively placed enemy piece. Generally the possessor of two Bishops is in a much better position to bring about such a favourable exchange than the player with two other minor pieces. And often that is sufficient to win.

BARCZA-PACHMAN

(Prague 1954)

DIAGRAM 40

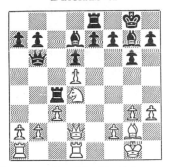

Position after Black's 19th move

White has gained a seemingly strong post for his Knight in return for conceding his opponent the advantage of the *two Bishops*. Black now makes use of these to undermine the Knight's position. The threat is 20 ..., B×N both weakening the White pawns and allowing Black control of the c-file.

20 P-N3

This weakens the QBP, whose advance to QB4 will soon be necessary, depriving the Knight on d4 of support. However, if 20 B-B1, then Black doubles his Rooks while gaining a tempo: 20 ..., R-B4; 21 B-N2, KR-QB1.

20 ...	R-B2
21 QR-B1	P-QR4!

Better than KR QB1. Since White will sooner or later be forced to play P-QB4, Black prepares the opening of a file on the Queen's wing.

22 P-QB4	P-R5
23 R-N1	R-R1!

Black does not fear P×P, for then 23 ..., Q-B4; 24 N-N5, R(2)-B1 leaves the QBP dangerously weak.

24 B-B1	P×P
25 P×P	R(2)-B1
26 Q-K3	

Black was planning to strengthen his position with R-R6 followed by R(B1)-R1. White counters by preparing to exchange Queens; he reckons that the penetration of the Black Rooks will not be dangerous, for his only weakness (the QNP) can easily be protected.

| 26 ... | R-R7! |

27 N–B5	Q×Q
28 N×Q	P–R4
29 R–Q3	P–QN4
30 P×P	B×NP
31 R(3)–Q1	R–N1!

The first offer to exchange. After 32 B×B, R×B Black would have no difficulty in exploiting the weak pawns on b3 and d5, e.g. 33 R–Q3, R(N4)–R4!; 34 N–B4, R–R8; 35 R×R, R×R ch; 36 K–N2, K–B1, and the Black King marches to the Queen-side.

| 32 N–B4 | B–B6! |

The Bishop heads for c5, from where it can attack the weak KBP.

33 R(N1)B1	B–N5
34 R–R1	R(1)–R1
35 R×R	R×R
36 R–N1	B–R3

The other Bishop makes for b7, from where it can put pressure on the QP. White no longer has a satisfactory defence, for, if 37 N–K3, B×B; 38 K×B, K–N2, the entry of the Black King is decisive.

| 37 R–N2 | R–R8 |

| 38 R–B2 | B–N2 |
| 39 N–K3 | B–B4! |

The exchange of the Knight, and with it the loss of at least a pawn, can no longer be avoided. It is interesting to see how the first threat of an exchange (on move 31) confined White's pieces to a passive position and how the second finishes the game. The *two Bishops* have played an important role; their action has facilitated a vital exchange.

| 40 R–Q2 | B×N |
| 41 P×B | B–R3 |

Naturally R–N8 also wins.

| 42 R–KB2 | K–N2 |
| 43 K–N2 | |

Or 43 P–QN4, B–B5; 44 P–K4, B–Q6, etc.

43 ...	R×B
44 R×R	B×R ch
45 K×B	K–B3
46 K–K2	K–K4
47 K–Q3	K×P
48 P–QN4	K–B3
49 K–B4	P–Q4 ch
50 K–Q4	K–Q3
51 Resigns	

In both examples the Bishops triumphed mainly because of their natural co-ordination in an open position. However, it often happens that, even in an open position, such straightforward methods are not sufficient; where the pawns are symmetrically placed and the position simplified we must instead resort to the important strategical plan worked out by Steinitz. This consists of—

(*a*) suitable pawn advances to deprive the enemy Knight (or Knights) of effective operation bases;

(*b*) pressing the Knight back into an unfavourable position;

(*c*) exploitation of the Knight's restricted power by a breakthrough at the right moment.

It was only after Steinitz's methods became known that the concept *advantage of the two Bishops* was formed. Réti in his book *Masters of the Chess Board* gives two games in which Steinitz clearly demonstrates his plan for utilizing the Bishops; we can do no better than repeat these examples.

ROSENTHAL–STEINITZ

(Vienna 1873)

1	P–K4	P–K4
2	N–QB3	N–QB3
3	N–B3	P–KN3?!
4	P–Q4	P×P
5	N×P	B–N2
6	B–K3	KN–K2
7	B–QB4	

Here 7 Q–Q2 followed by O–O–O is strong.

7	...	P–Q3
8	O–O	O–O
9	P–B4?	N–R4!
10	B–Q3	P–Q4
11	P×P	

Not 11 P–K5?, P–QB4!, when a piece is lost.

11	...	N×P
12	N×N	Q×N
13	P–B3	R–Q1

Threatening P–QB4.

| 14 | Q–B2 | |

Intending to answer 14 ..., P–QB4 by B–K4.

14	...	N–B5!
15	B×N	Q×B
16	Q–B2	

Black was threatening 16 ..., B×N; 17 B×B, R×B!.

DIAGRAM 41

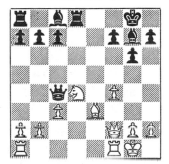

Now we have one of those typical positions in which the *two Bishops* have no direct object of attack; it will therefore be important to restrict the mobility of the White Knight. This game has great historical value, for it is the first example in which Steinitz's method of utilizing the *two Bishops* occurs.

| 16 | ... | P–QB4 |

The first and most important operation base (d4) is taken away from the Knight.

| 17 | N–B3 | P–N3 |

White has already, by his injudicious ninth move (P–KB4), reduced the mobility of his Bishop on the King-side; Black now builds a pawn chain to restrict it on the Queen-side.

18	N–K5	Q–K3	25 Q–N3	R–Q4!
19	Q–B3	B–QR3	26 R×R	Q×R
20	KR–K1	P–B3!	27 R–Q1	Q×BP
21	N–N4	P–R4!	28 Q–B7	B–Q4
22	N–B2	Q–B2	29 P–QN3	R–K1

30 P–B4	B–B2
31 B–B1	R–K7
32 R–KB1	Q–QB7

Takes care of the threat 23 P–B5 and at the same time prepares B–N2 attacking the weak point g2. It is now clear that White is in an inferior position, for both his minor pieces are seriously cramped; his next move, which loses a pawn, makes things even worse and shortens any possible defence.

Threatening R × N

33 Q–N3	Q×RP
34 Q–N8 ch	K–R2
35 Q–N3	B–N3
36 P–R4	P–N5
37 N–Q3	Q×P
38 Q–B7	Q×N
39 Resigns	

23 P–B5	P–KN4
24 QR–Q1	B–N2

It is plain to see how Steinitz's task was made easy by weak moves (9 P–KB4 and 23 P–KB5) on the part of his opponent. For that reason another game by Steinitz, played ten years later, is much more interesting.

ENGLISCH–STEINITZ

(London 1883)

1	P–K4	P–K4
2	N–KB3	N–QB3
3	B–N5	P–KN3
4	P–Q4	P×P
5	N×P	

It was only later that the strong continuation 5 B–KN5! was discovered.

5	...	B–N2
6	B–K3	N–B3
7	QN–B3	O–O
8	O–O	N–K2

Prepares P–Q4 White ought now to have played 9 P–K5, N–K1; 10 B–KB4, securing an advantage in space.

9	Q–Q2	P–Q4
10	P×P	N(2)×P
11	N×N	Q×N
12	B–K2	N–N5
13	B×N	B×B
14	N–N3	Q×Q

More precise was Q–B5! followed by (after 15 P–QB3) QR–Q1. With the text-move Black obtains only a minute advantage; for that very reason, however, its exploitation is extremely instructive.

15 N×Q	QR–Q1!

Not 15 ..., B×P immediately, because of QR–N1. Now, however, the threat is on: 16 ..., B×NP; 17 QR–N1, B–Q5!, and Black must let the pawn go.

16 P–QB3	KR–K1
17 N–N3	

DIAGRAM 42

17 ...	P–N3!

Again Black initiates manoeuvres whose object is to reduce the mobility of the opposing pieces and deprive the Knight of operation bases.

18 P–KR3	B–K3
19 KR–Q1	P–QB4
20 B–N5	P–B3
21 B–B4	K–B2

Here we see another, and frequent, feature of the working of the two Bishops: under their protection the King generally finds it easy to press towards the centre; the enemy King, on the other hand, is kept back by their action (e.g. 22 K–B1, B–B5 ch).

22 P–B3	P–KN4!

In the previous game White's own pawn on f4 limited the range of his Bishop; here it is Black's pawns which press the Bishop back into a passive position. If White now wishes to keep his Bishop in the centre he must con-

cede his opponent control of the Queen's file, for an immediate B–K3 loses a piece: 23 B–K3, R×R ch; 24 R×R, B×N.

23 R×R	R×R
24 B–K3	P–KR3
25 R–K1	P–B4
26 P–B4	

If White were to allow 26 ... P–KB5, he would be completely hemmed in. However, the presence of the pawn on f4 enables Black, at a suitable moment, to open the game (*see* move 30).

26 ...	B–B3
27 P–N3	P–QR4!

Threatens 28 ..., P–R5; 29 N–B1, P–R6, breaking up the White pawn-formation. Now the process of driving back the Knight is complete.

28 N–B1	P–R5
29 P–R3	B–B5
30 K–B2	

DIAGRAM 43

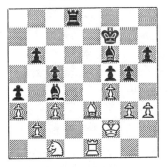

The diagram shows how successful Black has been in his plan to shut out the White Knight; there remains the task of converting

his positional advantage to a win.
White's position still seems quite
solid, for the Bishop on e3 covers
the most important points; Black,
however, can use his Bishops to
get rid of his opponent's only well-
placed piece.

30 ...	P×P
31 B×P(f4)	B–KN4!

Threatening 32 ..., B×B; 33
P×B, R–Q7 ch, which cannot be
forestalled by 32 K–K3, because of
32 ..., R–K1 ch; 33 K–B2, R×R;
34 K×R, B×B; 35 P×B, K–K3
followed by K–Q4.

32 B×B	P×B
33 K–K3	K–B3
34 P–R4	

Or 34 R–R1, K–K4 followed by

P–KB5 ch, and Black's Rook will
gain the seventh rank.

34 ...	P×P
35 P×P	R–K1 ch
36 K–B2	R×R
37 K×R	K–K4
38 N–K2	B×N
39 K×B	K–B5

Even though White has an outside passed-pawn Black wins
because his King is the more active.

40 P–B4	K–N5
41 K–K3	P–B5 ch!

Naturally not K×P??; 42 K–B4
with a win for White!

42 K–K4	P–B6
43 K–K3	K–N6
44 Resigns	

In the examples given so far the *two Bishops* were successful in
positions whose structure would in any case have favoured a single
Bishop against a Knight; the presence of the two merely enhanced
a natural advantage sufficiently to
force a win. Where, however, the
position is such that a Knight is
superior to a single Bishop, the role
of the *two Bishops* is that of mini-
mizing or neutralizing a natural
disadvantage.

DIAGRAM 44

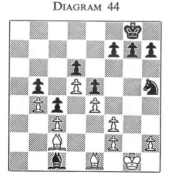

In some cases, of course, the
Knight has so much in its favour that
even two Bishops are quite powerless
to cope with its activities. An extreme
example of this occurs in Diagram 44,
where the imprisoned Bishops soon
succumb: **1 B–Q1, N–B5; 2 B–B2, P–B3; 3 K–B1, K–B2; 4 B–Q1,
K–N3; 5 B–B2, K–N4; 6 B–N1, K–R5; 7 B–B2, K–R6; 8 K–N1,
P–R3; 9 B–N1, P–R4; 10 B–B2, N–Q6; 11 K–B1, K×P; 12 K–K2,
K–N7; 13 B×N, P×B ch** and wins. Such drastic examples of complete powerlessness on the part of the Bishops are not very common;

40

more often we have cases, as in the next example, where the side with the Knight has a positional advantage that two passive Bishops do not quite counterbalance.

SOKOLSKI–KOTOV
(Moscow 1949)

DIAGRAM 45

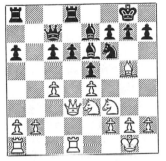

Position after White's 14th move

Black has the *two Bishops*, but at the moment they are inactive. White's plan of campaign is clear: he must prevent the advance P–Q4 in order to keep the Bishop on c7 immobile, thus rendering the *Bishop pair* innocuous. He can also later play P–QB5 to disrupt the enemy pawn position.

14 ...	QR–N1
15 Q–B2	R–N2
16 QR–B1	Q–N1
17 P–QN3	P–R3
18 B–R4	P–N4

A serious weakening of the King's position. However, after other moves such as P–QR4 White would reply 19 P–B5!, P–Q4; 20 P×P, P×P; 21 B–N3.

| 19 B–N3 | N–Q2 |

The obvious-looking N–R4 gives

White the advantage after 20 P–B5!, N×B; 21 P×P!, B×QP; 22 RP×N.

| 20 P–KR4 | P–B3 |
| 21 N–K1 | |

The Knight heads for d3 strengthening the threat P–QB5.

| 21 ... | N–B4 |
| 22 N–Q3! | Q–R2 |

If N×KP then 23 N×P!, QP×N (N×B; 24 N×P, Q–B2; 25 N×R); 24 Q×N, B–B2; 25 Q×BP with advantage to White.

| 23 N×N | Q×N |
| 24 Q–K2! | |

Nothing more can be done on the Queen-side; White, however, has one more trump, the attack on the castled King. His Knight controls the square f5 and his Queen can reach h5 without any trouble.

| 24 ... | B–KB1 |
| 25 Q–R5 | K–R2 |

Weak would be 25 ..., B–B2 because of 26 Q–B3, B–N2; 27 N–N4.

| 26 N–N4 | |

An inaccuracy. White ought to have played Q–B3 followed by N–B5.

| 26 ... | B–N2 |
| 27 N–K3 | |

Only now has White realized that 27 P×P, BP×P; 28 B×KP

41

fails against 28 ..., B×N. Therefore the threat 27 ..., B–B2 had to be taken care of.

27 ...   P–R4
28 Q–B3   P–R5

Helps White's attack, for the tempo lost in regaining the QRP lets him occupy the b-file.

29 P×RP   R–QR1

If R–N7, a possible continuation is 30 R–N1, R(1)–QN1; 31 R×R, R×R; 32 N–B5, B–KB1; 33 N×QP!, B×N; 34 Q×P winning (Sokolski).

30 N–B5   B–KB1
31 R–N1   R–KB2
32 P–QR5!   R×P

Against K–N3 Sokolski gives the following continuation: 33 P–R6, R×P; 34 R–N8, R×P; 35 R×P!, B×R; 36 R–KR8! and wins.

33 R–N8   P–Q4
34 Q–R5   P–Q5

There is no satisfactory alternative as the following variations show—

(*a*) 34 ..., Q×QBP; 35 R×B!;

(*b*) 34 ..., R×P; 35 BP×P, BP×P; 36 KP×P, B×P; 37 R×B(d5)!, Q×R, 38 R×B!;

(*c*) 34 ..., P×KP (or BP); 35 N×P! with a position similar to that in the game.

35 R(1)–N1   R–Q2

Speeds his defeat. However, against White's strong threats no satisfactory defence was left.

36 N×RP!   B×N
37 R–KR8 ch!   K×R
38 Q×B ch   R–KR2
39 Q×BP ch   R–KN2
40 R–N7   Resigns

CHAPTER IV

The Rooks

THIS chapter is one of the most important in the whole book. This is not merely because the Rook, next to the Queen, is the most powerful piece; it is largely because the handling of the Rooks demands a great understanding of the strategy suited to a particular position. When we watch beginners at play, it is clear how often they use only the Queen and minor pieces; the Rooks generally remain throughout on their original squares, making no contribution to the conduct of the game. This is quite understandable, for of all pieces the Rook is the most difficult to bring into play: its development necessitates, amongst other things, carefully planned pawn advances, well chosen exchanges, and correct timing in castling. It is not surprising that such a task is generally beyond the novice.

The material in this chapter has been divided into five parts as follows—

A. The creation and meaning of open files.

B. Open files as a factor in an attack against the King.

C. The use of open files in the centre and on the Queen's wing.

D. The seventh and eighth ranks.

E. Active Rooks in front of the pawn chain.

A. THE CREATION AND MEANING OF OPEN FILES

In contrast to the minor pieces, the Rook can enter into the game only after great preparation. The Knight can be brought into play without any preparatory move; the development of the Bishop requires only one; the Rook, however, has hardly increased its scope after a single move (P–R4), its activity being limited by its own pawn. What the Rook needs to utilize its peculiar powers are files that have been cleared of pawns, especially its own. These open files, as they are called, can arise in a number of ways, illustrated by the following examples.

(a) **Simple pawn exchanges, especially in the centre. 1 P–K4, P–K3; 2 P–Q4, P–Q4; 3 P×P, P×P** (Diagram 46). In this case both White and Black have an open King file. After the moves **1 P–K4, P–QB4; 2 N–KB3, N–QB3; 3 P–Q4, P×P; 4 N×P,**

White has an open Queen file and Black an open Queen-Bishop file (Diagram 47).

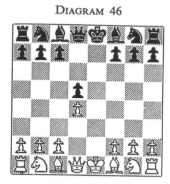

DIAGRAM 46

DIAGRAM 47

(*b*) **Exchange of pieces protected by pawns.** 1 P–K4, P–K4; 2 N–KB3, N–QB3; 3 B–B4, B–B4; 4 N–B3, N–B3; 5 P–Q3, P–Q3; 6 B–K3. Now after 6 ..., B×B; 7 P×B, White would possess the open King-Bishop file. Black, however, has a stronger move in 6 ..., **B–N3**, when an exchange by White would give him an open Queen-Rook file, e.g. **7 B×B, RP×B** (Diagram 48). A further case occurs after the moves 1 P–K4, P–QB3; 2 P–Q4, P–Q4; 3 N–QB3, P×P; 4 N×P, N–B3; 5 N×N ch (Diagram 49), when Black has

DIAGRAM 48

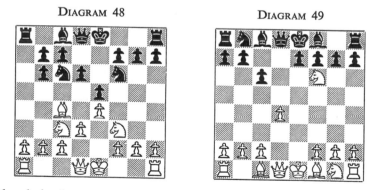

DIAGRAM 49

the choice between opening the King file (KP×N) and the King-Knight file (NP×N). In both cases Black obtains two open files and White one. However, although the possession of open files is essential for bringing Rooks into action, it would be wrong to assess Black's position as superior, merely on account of his two open files. There are other factors to be considered; and some of these may depreciate the value of the open files or prevent their being advantageously used by the Rooks.

(c) **Pawn advance against the enemy pawn chain.** After the moves 1 P–K4, P–K4; 2 N–KB3, N–QB3; 3 B–B4, B–B4; 4 P–Q3, P–Q3; 5 N–B3, N–B3; 6 B–K3, B–N3; 7 Q–Q2, O–O; 8 O–O–O, P–KR3?; 9 P–KR3! (Diagram 50), White can open the g-file by playing P–KN4 and P–KN5.

(d) **Other ways of breaking through the pawn chain.** From the position in Diagram 51 there followed: **22 P–N6, P–N6** (both sides endeavour to open files bearing on the enemy King); **23 BP×P,**

DIAGRAM 50

DIAGRAM 51

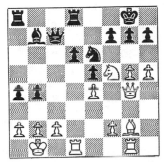

Position after Black's 21st move

QRP×P; **24 R–QB1** (24 RP×P, R–R8 ch!; 25 K×R, Q–B7, and the open Rook file is decisive), **P×P ch; 25 K–R1, Q–Q2;, 26 P×BP ch** (26 P×RP ch, K×P; 27 B–B1, R–KN1; 28 Q–N6 ch K–R1), **K–B1!** (Notice how both the Black and White Kings find protection from the fire of the heavy pieces in front of an enemy pawn); **27 R(N1)–Q1, R(Q1)–B1; 28 R×R ch, Q×R; 29 Q–N3** (29 N×QP, N–B4!; 30 Q–N3, Q–N5! and wins), **Q–B7; 30 R–K1, K×P; 31 N×QP ch, K–N1; 32 P–R6, Q–Q7; 33 P–B4, KP×P; 34 Q–QB3, Q×N; 35 Q–QN3, B B1; 36 R–Q1, R–N1,** and White resigned. This example shows the difficulties involved in opening a file when the opposing pawns remain on their original squares.

B. OPEN FILES AS A FACTOR IN AN ATTACK AGAINST THE KING

The exploitation of open files is strategically one of the simplest methods of attacking the enemy King, and this is where the great power of the Rooks is generally the chief factor in bringing about a successful result. Often, however, the way must be prepared by pawn advances, whose duty it is to open up the vital files. A simple example of such an attack is the following game.

PACHMAN–RUNZA

(Czechoslovak Championship, 1946)

1 P–K4	N–QB3
2 N–KB3	P–K4
3 B–N5	P–QR3
4 B–R4	N–B3
5 O–O	B–K2
6 R–K1	P–QN4
7 B–N3	P–Q3
8 P–B3	N–QR4
9 B–B2	P–B4
10 P–Q4	Q–B2
11 P–KR3	N–B3
12 QN–Q2	B–Q2?

A weak move, which loses time; Black will now have difficulty in developing the strength of his pieces.

13 P×BP	P×P
14 N–B1	R–Q1
15 Q–K2	P–R3

A preventive measure; Black wants to play B–K3 without being molested by (following 16 N–K3) N–N5.

16 N–K3	B–K3
17 P–QR4!	

If N–B5 at once, the reply 17 . . ., B–B5 is troublesome.

17 . . .	P–B5
18 P×P	P×P
19 N–B5	O–O

The retreat B–KB1 followed by P–N3 and B–N2 would have offered more prospects of a successful defence.

DIAGRAM 52

20 P–KN4

The beginning of a characteristic attack. White wants to open the g-file by the manoeuvre K–R2, R–KN1, P–N5; Black tries to prevent this by aiming at control of the square g5. In the end, however, Black's plan allows the opening of the h-file, which proves no less dangerous to him.

20 . . .	N–R2
21 P–R4	R–R1
22 R–N1	

The exchange of Rooks was also good, but White wants to keep his Rook for a possible attack against the enemy King. There is not really a loss of tempo with the text-move, for Black must now waste time vacating the square f8 to give his pieces some freedom.

22 . . .	KR–Q1

23 K–N2

The final preparation for the attack. Black's counter-action is one move too late.

23 ...   P–N5
24 P–N5!

The break-through comes at the right moment, for Black, already burdened with the weak pawn on c4, cannot now afford P–R4, even after P–N6; e.g. 24 ..., P–N6; 25 B–Q1, P–R4; 26 N–Q2, P–N3; 27 N–R6 ch, K–N2; 28 N×QBP, N–Q5; 29 P×N, B×N; 30 Q–B3, R×P; 31 B×P, B×B; 32 Q×B, B–N5; 33 R–Q1, and now 33 ..., R×P fails against Q–Q5. It should be noted that, if Black had not played 23 ..., P–N5, White would have to make further preparations before proceeding with P–N5; otherwise Black could keep the King-side files closed by the reply P–R4.

24 ...   RP×P?

This loses quickly and is certainly worse than the variation in the note to the preceding move.

25 N(3)×NP

This is stronger than re-taking with the pawn, for now the Queen comes quickly into the attack. Black is in any case virtually forced to exchange again because of the threat N(N5)×B, which puts the QBP under fire.

25 ...   N×N
26 P×N   P–N6

DIAGRAM 53

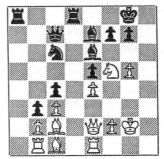

27 Q–R5!

White wastes no time moving his Bishop, but makes immediate use of the open h-file. If now 27 ..., P×B; 28 R–KR1, P–B3; 29 Q–R8 ch, K–B2, then 30 P–N6 ch, etc.

27 ...   P–N3
28 Q–R4   P–B3

The only move. If now 29 R–KR1?, the Black King slips away by K–B2.

29 B–Q1!

Prevents the King's flight, for 29 ..., K–B2 fails against 30 Q–R7 ch, K–K1; 31 N–N7 ch followed by N×B and B–N4 ch. Black is also lost after 29 ..., P×P, 30 Q–R6!, P×N; 31 Q×B ch, K–N2; 32 P×P, B–B3; 33 B×KNP!, etc. Neither does the exchange sacrifice bring relief: 29 ..., R×B; 30 R×R, P×N; 31 R–KR1, K–B2 (K–B1; 32 NP×P); 32 P–N6 ch, etc.

29 ...   P×N?
30 R–KR1   K–B2
31 B–R5 ch   K–B1

47

Only now does Black see that K–N2 leads to mate after 32 B–K8 !!

32 B–N6	B–B4
33 NP × P	Resigns

In this game White's Queen and Rook operated effectively and easily on the open h-file. We notice here that the Queen, as is frequently the case, stood in front of the Rook. In many cases, however, it is better, and sometimes essential, to post the Queen behind the Rook. This allows the Rook to drive the King from the eighth rank while the Queen cuts off his flight squares. An instructive example is that in Diagram 54, where White wins by reversing the positions of his heavy pieces: **1 P–N6!** (weaker is 1 Q–R8 ch, K–K2; 2 Q × P ch, R–KN1; 3 Q–R6, R–KR1), **P × P; 2 Q × P, K–N1; 3 R–R7!, Q–K2; 4 Q–R5,** and mate is unavoidable.

DIAGRAM 54

White to play

In the following game Alekhine uses an open file to break up, in a complicated manner, his opponent's King-side.

STÅHLBERG–ALEKHINE

(Hamburg 1930)

DIAGRAM 55

Position after Black's 17th move

18 P–QR4?

With this move, which aims at opening the a-file, White embarks

on a strategically incorrect plan; this wastes time and leads only to a useless Rook sortie. A much better course was to play on the open Queen file with Q–K5!, threatening Q–B7.

18 ...   **P–B5!**

Black replies energetically, opening the f-file, whose value is strengthened by the action of the Bishop on the white diagonal.

19 P–R5	P × KP
20 Q × KP	N–B4
21 Q–B3	P–Q3
22 P × P	P × P
23 N–K1	P–K4!

By this advance Alekhine creates a strong operation base on d4.

24 R–R7	N–Q5
25 Q–K3	R–Q2!

Not only defends the Bishop but also, because of the threat B–B6, forces back the Rook. At the same time Black prepares the doubling of his Rooks on the f-file.

26 R–R2	R(2)–B2
27 P–B3	

White seems to think that the pawn on f3 prevents any action on the f-file. Alekhine, however, demonstrates ingeniously that even quadruple protection of the square f3 is not enough.

27 ...	R–B5
28 B–Q3	Q–R4

Now he is threatening P–K5!, 30 Q × N, P × P, etc.

| 29 B–B1 | Q–N4! |

Threatening 30 ..., R × P.

| 30 R–KB2 | P–R3! |

An excellent move, which renews the threat 31 ..., R × P (32 Q × Q, R × R). If White tries to forestall this with 31 Q–Q2, then 31 ..., B × P! wins quickly.

31 K–R1	R × P!
32 Resigns	

In the examples so far the attack has been conducted on a single open file. Often, however, an even more dangerous action takes place on two open files simultaneously. An example of this is the following game, in which it is instructive to see how Black overcomes obstructions first on the c-file and finally on the a-file.

BARCZA–FILIP

(Bucharest 1953)

1 P–K4	P–QB4
2 N–KB3	P–Q3
3 P–Q4	P × P
4 N × P	N–KB3
5 N–QB3	P–KN3
6 B–K3	B–N2
7 P–B3	O–O
8 N–N3	

Better is 8 Q–Q2.

8 ...	N–B3
9 Q–Q2	B–K3
10 N–Q5	B × N
11 P × B	N–K4
12 O–O–O?	

Better is 12 B–K2 followed by O–O. To the move 12 P–QB4,

Filip gives the following continuation: 12 ..., R–B1; 13 R–B1, P–QN4; 14 P × P, R × R ch; 15 N × R, Q–R1.

12 ...	Q–B2
13 K–N1	KR–QB1!

One of the most difficult problems in chess is that of deciding which Rook shall occupy a particular open file; its solution demands insight into all possible courses the game may take. In this case it would be wrong to occupy the c-file with the Queen Rook, for this may be needed to open up the b-file in operations against the White King. The threat is now the piece sacrifice 14 ..., N × QP; 15

49

Q×N, Q×P ch; 16 K–R1, N–Q6, and unless White is content with the purely passive 14 R–B1, he must play 14 P–B3; this, however, facilitates the opening of the b-file, after which Black's Queen Rook is ready to join in the attack.

DIAGRAM 56

Position after 13 ..., KR–QB1

14	P–B3	P–QR4
15	N–Q4	N–B5
16	B×N	Q×B
17	N–B2	P–QN4!
18	Q–Q3?	

Loses quickly. A more promising course was 18 N–R3, Q–R5; 19 Q–B2, and after the exchange of Queens, Black, though undoubtedly better placed, has not the same attacking chances.

18	...	Q–B2
19	KR–K1	

After 19 Q×QNP, QR–N1; 20 Q–B6, Q–Q1, Black's attack on the two open files is too strong.

19	...	P–N5!
20	B–Q4	

If 20 P×P, then 20 ..., N×P!

20	...	P×P
21	B×P	QR–N1
22	K–R1	

The Bishop has taken over from the pawn the duty of blocking the open file; but this new obstacle is easily dealt with.

22	...	N×P!
23	B×B	K×B
24	Q×N	Q×N
25	Q–Q2	P–K4!

This prevents a check on d4 by the White Queen; now R×NP becomes a real threat.

DIAGRAM 57

26	P–N3	P–R5!

Undermines the obstacle on the b-file, giving a clearly won game.

27	P×P?	R–N7?

There was an immediate win by 27 ..., R–N8 ch.

28	Q×Q	R(1)×Q
29	R×QP	R×P ch
30	K–N1	R(B7)–N7ch
31	Resigns	

It is noticeable that the outcome of the struggle on the open files was first the penetration of Black's heavy pieces to the seventh rank and then a doubling of his Rooks there. This is generally the important strategical goal to be striven for when manoeuvring on open files.

C. THE CONVERSION OF OPEN FILES IN THE CENTRE AND ON THE QUEEN'S WING

The task of exploiting open files in the centre and on the Queen's wing is beset with many difficult strategical problems. Some things to aim at are the penetration of the Rooks into the enemy position, especially the seventh and eighth ranks; the winning of pawns by pressure on the open files; and the cramping of enemy pieces. However, to formulate general rules for the application of such aims would be complicated, and the result imprecise; so instead we shall content ourselves with a game that illustrates some of the points to be aimed at.

PACHMAN–L. STEINER

(Budapest 1948)

1 P–Q4	P–Q4
2 N–KB3	N–KB3
3 P–QB4	P–K3
4 B–N5	B–K2
5 N–B3	P–KR3
6 B–R4	O–O
7 P–K3	P–QN3
8 P×P	P×P

More usual and better is N×P.

9 N–K5	B–N2

Not 9 ..., B–K3?; 10 B–QN5.

10 R–B1

More precise seems 10 B–K2, KN–Q2; 11 B×B, Q×B; 12 N–Q3!.

10 ...	QN–Q2
11 N×N	

If 11 P–B4?, then 11 ..., N×N; 12 BP×N (12 QP×N, N–K5), N–Q2; 13 B×B, Q×B; 14 N–N5, Q–R5 ch!.

11 ...	Q×N
12 B–Q3	P–QR3?

With this move Black embarks on a faulty plan. Better was 12 ..., N–K5 or even 12 ..., P–B4; 13 Q–B2!, when White's advantage is problematic.

13 O–O	Q–K3
14 Q–N3!	

Black plans to remain passive on the Queen-side and prepare the advance P–KB4; White's chances lie on the open c-file. The text-move prepares the doubling of heavy pieces and also prevents P–QB4 by Black should the latter subsequently renounce his King-side plan.

14 ...	QR–Q1
15 B–N3	B–Q3
16 N–K2	N–K1

Unplayable is 16 ..., N–K5, on account of 17 B×N, P×B; 18 Q×Q, P×Q; 19 B×B, P×B; 20

N–B4, and if 20 ..., KR–K1, then 21 R–B7 followed by N–R5.

| 17 R–B3 | B×B |
| 18 RP×B! | |

After 18 N×B, P–KB4; 19 Q–B2, P–N3, Black would have good attacking prospects with R–Q2–B2.

18 ... P–KN4

Deprives the White Knight of the square f4 and at the same time sets in motion the advance on the King-side. However, the weakness of f5 enables White to break through decisively.

19 Q–B2 P–KB4

DIAGRAM 58

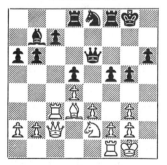

At first sight Black's position seems quite firm, for the only weakness, the pawn on c7, is apparently quite safe. White, however, manages, by a tactical manoeuvre on the King-side, to operate successfully on the open c-file, and eventually wins the QBP.

20 P–KN4!

Black must accept this temporary sacrifice, for if 20 ..., P–B5; 21 P×P, P×P; 22 B–B4, he loses a pawn himself.

| 20 ... | P×P |
| 21 N–N3 | N–N2 |

Now the meaning of White's move 20 becomes clear: Black cannot satisfactorily defend the QBP; e.g. 21 ..., B–B1; 22 B–N6, or 21 ..., P–B3; 22 B–B5 followed by B×P, and Black's King-side is seriously weakened.

| 22 R×P | R–B1 |
| 23 R×R | R×R |

White's action on the c-file has led to the win of the important QBP and with it the weakening of Black's position. Black's control of the c-file is only temporary, for his Rook will soon be needed to defend the weakness in the King's position.

| 24 Q–K2 | P–KR4 |
| 25 B–N1! | |

Naturally not 25 B×P?, B×B; 26 Q×B, R–B7, when the penetration of the Rook to the seventh rank is worth more than the pawn.

25 ... R–KB1!

Virtually forced; for after 25 ..., P–R5; 26 Q–Q3!, Q–R3; 27 N–B5, N×N; 28 Q×N, P–N6; 29 Q–K5, P×P ch; 30 R×P, or 25 ..., Q–R3; 26 N–B5, N×N; 27 B×N, R–KB1; 28 B–Q3, P–QR4; 29 R–QB1, White has a decisive advantage. But now White's Queen can penetrate Black's position by way of the open c-file.

26 Q–B2!	Q–R3
27 Q–B7	B–B1

If 27 ..., P–R5, White should avoid allowing Black a dangerous attack after either 28 Q×B?, P×N; 29 Q×QP ch, K–R1; 30 P×P, R×R ch; 31 K×R, Q–R8 ch or 28 N–B5?, N×N; 29 Q×B, Q–K3. The best answer to 27 ..., P–R5 is 28 N–K2, B–B1; 29 Q–K5.

28 Q–K5	P–R5
29 N–K2	Q–R4?

Black's position is compromised and the eventual loss is unavoidable; the text-move, which brings the Queen out of play, only speeds defeat. Black probably expected 30 Q×QP ch?, after which 30 ..., B–K3 followed by P–N6 would give him a strong attack.

30 N–B3	P–N6!
31 P–B3!	

Simplest and best. After 31 P×P, R×R ch; 32 K×R, P×P; 33 Q×P (g3), Q–R8 ch, the game is drawn, and after 31 N×P, P×P ch; 32 K–R2, Black still has the dangerous exchange sacrifice 32 ..., P–N5!.

31 ...	R–K1

Or 31 ..., B–K3; 32 N×P, Q–B2; 33 B–N6! winning.

32 Q×QP ch	B–K3
33 Q–Q6	B–B5
34 N–Q5	R–K3
35 Q×R ch!	N×Q
36 N–B6 ch	K–B2
37 N×Q	R×R
38 K×B	Resigns

D. THE SEVENTH AND EIGHTH RANKS

It should now be clear that one of the most important strategical aims in exploiting open files is the penetration by the heavy pieces to the seventh and eighth ranks. Heavy pieces on the seventh rank generally cripple the enemy position or force the win of pawns, which on this rank are a rewarding target. On the eighth rank it is the enemy King which comes under fire—and it is not only beginners who have been surprised by many beautiful mating combinations based on the weakness of the back rank.

Of great importance is the use made of the seventh rank in the end-game, and great care is needed in assessing its value before transposing into a Rook end-game. In fact, it is often an important strategical aim to bring about an exchange that leaves a Rook with access to the seventh rank; for even where material is

DIAGRAM 59

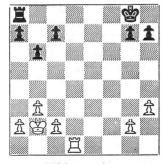

White to play

equal and much reduced, a Rook on the seventh rank can be a decisive factor. So, for example, the position in Diagram 59 is won for White because his King, after **1 R–Q7, R–QB1 (P–B4; 2 K–B3); 2 K–B3,** marches untroubled into play, while Black's pieces are bound to the defence of pawns.

We now give five typical examples in which the Rook on the seventh proves decisive; the way in which victory is secured or a draw snatched in each case aptly illustrates the strategical meaning of the Rook on the seventh. Then we follow with four others showing the two most important aims in controlling the eighth rank: the forcing of mate and the pinning of enemy minor pieces to the back rank.

<table>
<tr><td style="text-align:center">(a)</td><td style="text-align:center">DIAGRAM 61</td></tr>
<tr><td style="text-align:center">DIAGRAM 60</td><td></td></tr>
</table>

White to play and draw

White to play and win

1 Q–KN4, P–KN3; 2 Q–KR4, P–R4; 3 Q × BP and wins. Here White used the position of his Rook to work up a simple mating-attack. It should be noted how important Black's weak pawn formation was; if his KBP had been on f7 instead of f6, White would have had a struggle even to draw.

is not possible owing to 5 R–Q7 mate. The result would have been the same if White's Rook had been on d7 and Black's on b8; for then White's own Rook deprives the Black King of the flight-square d8. This co-operation of Rook on the seventh and Knight to force perpetual check is a frequent strategical goal in positions that are materially or positionally unfavourable.

(b)

1 N × P, P–B7; 2 N–B6 ch, K–B1 (K–R1?; 3 R–R7 mate); 3 N–R7 ch, K–K1; 4 N–B6 ch, and White has saved himself by perpetual check, because 4 ..., K–Q1

(c)

1 P–N6, K–B1; 2 P–N7, R–N1; 3 R–QB7 winning. This is the simplest way of using a Rook on the seventh to assist in the promotion of a passed pawn. It is, however, only available when the enemy King has no nearby pawns (other than Rook pawns) on the second rank to break the power of the Rook; if there are such pawns

DIAGRAM 62

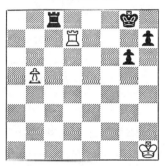

White to play and win

the outcome might well be different. Suppose, for example, that Black's pawns on g6 and h7 were reversed and stood instead on g7 and h6; then White could not win and in fact would have to struggle even to hold the draw: 1 P–N6, R–B8 ch; 2 K–N2, R–QN8; 3 P–N7, K–R2; 4 K–B3, P–R4, etc. The contrasting results in these similar positions underline the care needed in advancing pawns in front of the King when an opposing Rook has access to the seventh rank; a careless placing of pawns (e.g. f5, g6, h7) allows the King to be cut off and may lead to a quick loss. A King so cut off must be considered a serious disadvantage, which even material superiority might not outweigh; the Rook that does the cutting off, on the other hand, has its value enhanced;

in the words of Nimzowitch, it possesses the "absolute seventh."

(*d*)

DIAGRAM 63

White to play and win

1 R–R7 ch, K–N1; 2 R(K7)–N7 ch, K–B1; 3 B×P!, P×B; 4 P–R6 (threatens R–R8 mate), K–K1; 5 R–R8 ch, N–B1; 6 P–R7, P–R8(Q); 7 R×N ch, K×R; 8 P–R8(Q) mate. The result is the same if Black deviates on move three with 3 ..., P–R8=Q (4 B–K7 ch, K–K1; 5 R–N8 ch, N–B1; 6 R×B ch, K–Q2; 7 B–B5 dis ch and mate on the next move) or 3 ..., B–K5 (4 B–K7 ch, K–K1; 5 R–R8 ch, N–B1; 6 B–Q6! followed by 7 R×N mate). This example shows something of the power exerted by two Rooks united on the seventh rank. It is interesting to note the mating threats that arose once the Rook on g7 had been protected by the advance of the Rook pawn; such mating positions are characteristic and are the basis of many a combination.

In this example the united Rooks brought victory. In some cases, however, they act as a saving factor when the material position is unfavourable. If, for example, White were without his Bishop on c1, he could still have drawn by perpetual check: 1 R–R7 ch, K–N1; 2 R(R7)–N7 ch (not R(K7)–N7 ch, K–B1 and the King escapes), K–B1; 3 R(N7)–B7 ch, etc.

(*e*)

DIAGRAM 64

White to play and win

1 R–R7 ch, K–N1; 2 R(K7)–N7 ch, K–B1; 3 R×B! (threatening R–R8 mate), K–N1 (or K–K1; 4 R×BP, K–Q1; 5 R(B7)–KN7, etc.); **4 R(Q7)–N7 ch!, K–B1; 5 R×P, K–N1; 6 R(B7)–N7 ch, K–B1; 7 R×P, K–N1; 8 R(N7)–KN7 ch!** (not R×B?, P–R8(Q)!), K–B1; **9 R×B** and wins. In this case mate cannot be forced, for there is no way of protecting one Rook on g7 while the other gives mate on h8. White, instead, must resort to repeated threats of mate, and by so doing win a decisive advantage in material.

(*f*)

DIAGRAM 65

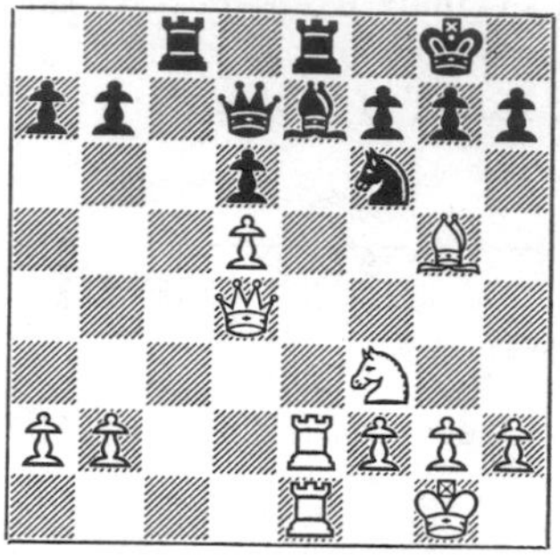

White to play and win

1 B×N!   B×B

After 1 ..., P×B! it would be a mistake to play 2 R×B? on account of 2 ..., Q×R!; 3 R×Q?, R–B8 ch, when White is himself mated. However, re-taking with the pawn does not quite save Black, for, as a result of his weakened King-side and bad Bishop, his position still gives White sufficient opportunity to force a decision, e.g. 2 P–KR3! (now threatening 3 R×B!), R–R1; 3 Q–N4 ch, Q×Q; 4 P×Q, K–B1; 5 N–Q4, etc.

2 Q–KN4!   Q–N4

If 2 ..., Q–Q1, then 3 Q×R.

3 Q–QB4!!   Q–Q2
4 Q–B7!!   Q–N4
5 P–QR4!

Not 5 Q×NP?, Q×R!; 6 R×R, R–B8 ch, when White suffers the same fate as in the note to Black's first move.

5 ...   Q×RP

6 R–K4!   Q–N4
7 Q×NP!   Resigns

Black must give up his Queen to prevent mate on the back rank. This is perhaps the most famous of all combinations directed towards mate on the eighth rank; but the theme is one that occurs again and again under various guises.

(g)

DIAGRAM 66

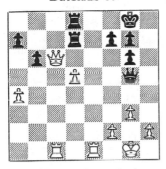

White to play and win

1 Q×R!, R×Q; 2 R–K8 ch, K–R2; 3 R(1)–B8, and Black cannot avoid mate. This combination hinges on the unfortunate placing of Black's Queen, which blocks the freeing move 3 ..., P–KN4.

(h)

1 R–B8 ch, K–R2; 2 N–B8 ch, K–N1; 3 N–N6 dis ch, B–Q1 (holds off mate one move longer); **4 R×B ch, K–B2** (K–R2; 5 R–KR8 mate); **5 R–KB8 mate.** A similar mating combination occurs if

White's Knight on e6 is replaced by a Bishop, e.g. 1 R–B8 ch, K–R2; 2 B–N8 ch, K–R1; 3 B–B7 dis ch,

DIAGRAM 67

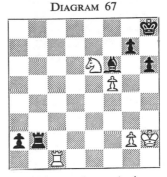

White to play and win

B–Q1;   4 R×B   ch, K–R2;   5 B–N6 mate.

(i)

DIAGRAM 68

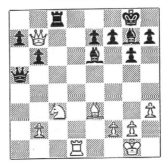

White to play and win

1 Q×R ch!, B×Q; 2 R–Q8 ch, B–B1; 3 B–R6, and Black has no defence against the threat R×B mate. This is a typical example of a piece that is pinned on the back rank leading to an immediate mate.

And now a game showing the Rooks on the seventh.

ALEKHINE–YATES
(London 1922)

1 P–Q4	N–KB3
2 P–QB4	P–K3
3 N–KB3	P–Q4
4 N–B3	B–K2
5 B–N5	O–O
6 P–K3	QN–Q2
7 R–QB1	P–B3
8 Q–B2	R–K1
9 B–Q3	P×P
10 B×BP	N–Q4
11 N–K4	P–KB4?

Positionally a doubtful move because it allows White, at a later stage, to occupy the square e5 with a Knight. Better was P–B3 or B×B.

12 B×B	Q×B
13 QN–Q2	P–QN4?

A similar mistake, which weakens the square c5. Alekhine now uses the two weaknesses to bring about an active posting of his pieces.

14 B×N	BP×B
15 O–O	P–QR4
16 N–N3	P–R5
17 N–B5	N×N
18 Q×N	Q×Q
19 R×Q	

Alekhine assesses the position correctly and does not fear simplification; his positional advantage —control of the c-file and possession of the strong operation-base on e5 for the Knight—will soon begin to tell.

19 ...	P–N5
20 KR–QB1	B–R3

21 N–K5	KR–N1

It is important for White that his opponent dare not exchange Rooks—21 ..., KR–QB1; 22 R×R ch, R×R; 23 R×R ch, B×R; 24 N–B6, P–N6; 25 P×P, P×P; 26 N–R5, and Black loses a pawn—for his domination of the c-file is thus secure. The strategical plan that he must follow consists of doubling Rooks on the seventh, constraining his opponent's Kingside, and eventually using his Knight, and possibly his King, to assist in a mating attack. In the following play, Alekhine pursues this plan with great vigour.

22 P–B3	P–N6
23 P–QR3	P–R3

Again an exchange of Rooks is not possible: 23 ..., R–QB1; 24 R×R ch, R×R; 25 R×R ch, B×R; 26 N–Q3, and after 27 N–B5 White wins either the RP or the KP. Apart from this clear-cut variation, an exchange of Rooks would give White a positionally won game, for his King could then march unhindered to b4.

24 K–B2	K–R2
25 P–R4	R–KB1
26 K–N3	KR–QN1

Black can only mark time and must wait passively while his opponent prepares for action.

27 R–B7	B–N4
28 R(1)–B5	B–R3
29 R(5)–B6	R–K1
30 K–B4	K–N1
31 P–R5!	

DIAGRAM 69

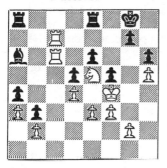

All that now remains is the doubling of Rooks on the seventh. Once this is accomplished, the game will be decided.

31 ...	B–B1
32 P–N3	B–R3
33 R–KB7!	K–R2

| 34 R(6)–B7 | R–KN1 |
| 35 N–Q7! | |

With the killing threat of 36 N–B6 ch. There is now no defence.

35 ...	K–R1
36 N–B6!	KR–KB1
37 R×P!!	R×N
38 K–K5!	Resigns

White wins the Rook, for its retreat to f1 or defence by the other Rook from f1 deprives the Black King of a vital flight square, e.g. 38 ..., R(3)–B1; 39 R–R7 ch, K–N1; 40 R(B7)–KN7 mate. This game shows how control of an open file can first constrict the enemy position and then prepare the final blow by allowing the doubling of Rooks on the seventh.

E. ACTIVE ROOKS IN FRONT OF THE PAWN CHAIN

In the previous sections we were concerned mainly with the basic method of conferring power on the heavy pieces—the creation and use of open files. It does however happen that occupation of an open file is sometimes not sufficient; or the creation of an open file might not be possible when the strategical plan indicates that such a file would be desirable. For example, when both sides have castled on the same side, it assists an attack to open a file against the enemy King; but generally a pawn advance to secure this leads to a weakening of one's own position, while to open a file without advancing a pawn is frequently impossible. In cases like this it is often useful to post the Rook in front of one's own pawn chain. An example is the old variation of the Queen's Gambit in which Pillsbury, after the moves 1 P–Q4, P–Q4; 2 P–QB4, P–K3; 3 N–QB3, N–KB3; 4 B–N5, B–K2; 5 P–K3, O–O; 6 N–B3, QN–Q2; 7 R–B1, P–N3; 8 P×P, P×P; 9 B–Q3, B–N2; 10 O–O, P–B4, used to launch an immediate attack with 11 N–K5 followed by P–B4, R–KB3, and R–KR3.

Similar examples in which the Rook operates in front of its own pawns to attack the enemy King are fairly frequent. In some modern games, however, the Rook is played in front of its own pawns even when there is no question of an attack against the enemy King. The reason for this is that pawn advances are generally necessary to open files, and Steinitz has shown that every advance by a pawn reduces its prospects for the end-game—a principle remembered by Réti in all his systems. In the close positional type of game, the players often endeavour to keep the pawns as long as possible on their original squares; if the Rooks are to operate at all they must then do so from in front of their own pawn chain. To describe a Rook operating in such a way, Tartakover has coined the phrase "the hyper-modern Rook."

We now give two games. In the first the Rooks are used in a direct attack against the enemy King; in the second they exert a positional pressure on the Queen-side. Both are good examples of handling Rooks when the normal methods—open files—are ineffective or not available.

ALEKHINE–KMOCH
(San Remo 1930)

1 P–Q4	N–KB3
2 P–QB4	P–K3
3 N–QB3	B–N5
4 B–Q2	O–O
5 P–K3	P–Q4
6 N–B3	P–B4
7 P–QR3	B×N
8 B×B	N–K5
9 R–B1	N×B
10 R×N	BP×P
11 KP×P	N–B3
12 B–K2	P×P
13 B×BP	Q–B3
14 O–O	R–Q1
15 R–Q3	B–Q2
16 R–K1	

Although Black has emerged from the opening with full equality, White nevertheless plays for a win. He therefore avoids the continuation 16 Q–Q2 and 17 P–Q5, which would eliminate his isolated pawn, and instead prepares an attack on the enemy King-side.

16 ...	B–K1
17 Q–Q2	N–K2
18 N–N5!	

The first attacking move, with which White hopes to induce the weakening advance of the KRP to h6. The threat is 19 N×KP!, P×N; 20 R×P.

18 ...	N–Q4
19 R–KB3	Q–K2
20 R–KN3	

Now the threat is 21 Q–Q3, which, if played, would force the weakening reply 21 ..., P–KN3.

20 ...	P–KR3
21 N–B3	Q–B3
22 R–K4!	

The second Rook now joins in the attack and at the same time prevents Black's Knight from occupying the square f4.

22 ...	N–K2
23 N–K5	N–B4
24 R–Q3	QR–B1
25 P–R3!	

White must first take care of any possible back-rank mate before he can fully develop the powers of his heavy pieces.

| 25 ... | N–Q3? |

Exchanging the Knight for the Bishop is faulty and makes the defence more difficult. After the correct 25 ..., B–B3, Black would have had an equal game.

| 26 R–B4 | N × B |
| 27 N × N | Q–N4 |

Or 27 ..., Q–K2; 28 N–K5, when 28 ..., P–B3 is not good owing to 28 N–N4.

28 R–KN3	Q–Q4
29 N–K3	Q–B3
30 K–R2	

DIAGRAM 70

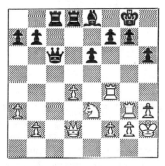

The White Rooks have taken up a menacing position and their action makes an energetic finish possible. Occupation of the eighth rank by Black would serve no purpose, for there is no longer time for doubling Rooks; in any case, White's King is for the moment adequately protected.

| 30 ... | Q–B8 |
| 31 Q–N4 | Q–B2 |

If 31 ..., Q–QN8, then White wins with 32 Q–K7, R–B8; 33 R × P ch, K × R; 34 R–N4 ch, K–R2; 35 Q–B6, R–R8 ch; 36 K–N3.

| 32 P–Q5! | P–QR4 |

Or 32 ..., P × P; 33 Q–Q4 with a decisive attack.

33 Q–K4	R–Q3
34 Q–K5	P–KN3
35 Q–R5!	R × P

Or 35 ..., K–R2; 36 N–N4!, P × Q; 37 N–B6 ch with mate next move.

| 36 N × R | P × N |
| 37 Q × RP | Resigns |

TRIFUNOVIĆ–PACHMAN
(Hilversum 1947)

1 P–K4	P–K4
2 N–KB3	N–QB3
3 N–B3	N–B3
4 B–N5	B–N5
5 O–O	O–O
6 P–Q3	B × N
7 P × B	P–Q3
8 B–N5	Q–K2
9 KB × N	P × B
10 Q–B1	

Better is 10 N–Q2

10 ...	P–KR3
11 B × N	Q × B
12 Q–K3	P–B4!
13 KR–N1?	

Better is 13 QR–N1.

13 ...	B–Q2
14 P–Q4?	

White would have done better to try 14 P–B4, QR–N1; 15 R–N3, R–N3, though Black still has a slight pull owing to the possibility of playing B–QR5. The alternative 14 R–N7, KR–N1!; 15 QR–N1, Q–Q1 also gives Black an advantage.

14 ...	BP×P
15 P×P	P×P
16 N×P	KR–K1!

Should White's Rook now venture on to the seventh rank with 17 R–N7, Black has a strong reply in 17 ..., B–B3! followed by B×KP. Black's last move also threatens P–Q4.

17 R–K1	QR–N1
18 N–N3	

White's plan to control the open b-file has misfired and it is Black's Rooks which threaten to reach the seventh rank. White therefore decides to block the b-file with his Knight, forcing his opponent to find some other means of using the heavy pieces.

18 ...	R–N5
19 P–B3	

Not, of course, 19 Q×QRP, QR×P; 20 R×R, R×R; 21 Q×P?, Q×R ch!; 22 N×Q, R–K8 mate.

19 ...	R–R5

Already one of Black's Rooks has taken up an extremely effective position; from a4 it protects its own QRP while attacking that of White.

20 P–B3	R–K4!

Now the other Rook makes for the Queen-side.

21 R–K2

An attempt to force the pace by 21 P–KB4 fails against 21 ..., R(K4)×P; 22 Q×R, R×Q; 23 R×R, Q×QBP; 24 R–QB1, Q–Q6; 25 R–K7, B–K3; 26 R(7)×QBP, Q–K6 ch, with advantage to Black.

21 ...	B–K3

DIAGRAM 71

Black's pressure on the Queen-side mounts move by move. In attempting to gain counter-play White now loses a pawn and with it virtually the game. Defensive moves, however, would have held out little hope, for Black's Rooks operate too strongly on the Queen-side, e.g. 22 N–Q4, R(K4)–QR4; 23 N×B, Q×N; 24 Q–Q2, Q–B5 followed by R–R6, etc., or 22 R–QB1, R–QN4; 23 N–Q4, R(N4)–QR4; 24 N–B6, R–B4, etc.

22 R–Q1 ?	R×RP!

Wins a pawn, for if 23 R×R, the reply 23 ..., B×N is decisive. The rest is a matter of technique.

23 N–Q4	R(K4)–QR4
24 R×R	R×R
25 R–N1	Q–N3
26 P–N4	Q–B3

Black's Queen, having induced the weakening advance of the KNP to g4, now looks towards h4 with threats against the opponent's King. White cannot bring back his Knight to defence by 27 N–K2 on account of 27 ..., B–B5, winning the QB pawn; so the Rook must give up any ideas of counter-play on the b-file and instead go to the assistance of the King.

27 R–K1	P–B4

28 N×B	Q×N
29 R–K2	R–R6
30 K–N2	Q–B5
31 R–QB2	R–R8
32 R–B1	

If 32 Q–Q2, then 32 ..., Q–B8 ch; 33 K–N3, R–Q8; 34 Q–K2, Q–R8, etc.

32 ...	R–R7 ch
33 K–N3	Q–N6
34 Q–N1	Q–N7
35 P–K5	P×P
36 R–N1	Q×BP
37 R–QB1	Q–Q7
38 R×P	Q–B5 ch
39 K–R3	Q×BP ch
40 Q–N3	Q×Q ch
41 K×Q	R–R6 ch
42 K–N2	P–B3
43 R–B7	K–R2
44 Resigns	

CHAPTER V

The Queen and Play with the Heavy Pieces

As we have mentioned earlier, the main characteristic of the Queen is its great mobility. Both in the end-game and in the middle game its lightning changes of front make it an admirable attacking piece, which operates effectively against direct weaknesses in the enemy position or in an assault on the enemy King. The example below shows how smoothly the Queen can move from one wing to the other even when the position is of a partially blocked character.

BOGULJUBOW–MIESES

(Baden-Baden 1925)

DIAGRAM 72

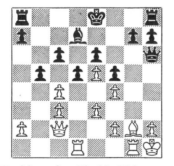

Position after Black's 17th move

In this position neither Queen appears to be actively placed. The succeeding play, however, shows how White is soon able to move his Queen from its present modest position so that it can menace his opponent on both wings; Black's Queen, on the other hand, finds that its premature sortie to h6 has left it quite ineffective.

18 Q–N2!

Not 18 P×NP?, P×P, after which Black has counter-play on the c-file.

18 ...   O–O

Neither 18 ..., QP×P; 19 R–Q6 nor 18 ..., NP×P; 19 Q–N7 is satisfactory for Black.

19 Q–R3!   KR–Q1

If 19 ..., NP×P, then 20 Q–Q6, KR–Q1; 21 R–N1 followed by R–N7.

20 P×NP   P×P
21 Q–R6!

With the threat 22 B×P, P×B; 23 Q×Q. Black ought to counter with 21 ..., Q–R5!, when White could continue with 22 R–Q2, threatening 23 P–QR4!, P×P; 24 P–B4.

21 ...   Q–R4?

Only partially takes care of the above threat; Black now gets the chance of a fine sacrifice, which lets his Queen into Black's lines with a consequent mating net. The combination is merely the logical outcome of White's previous Queen manoeuvres, Q–N2–R3–R6

22	B×P!	P×B
23	R×P ch!	K×R
24	Q–B6 ch	K–N1
25	R–N1 ch	Q–N5
26	R×Q ch	P×R

On a purely mechanical count

Black seems to have sufficient material for his Queen. White's two united passed-pawns, however, now enter the game too strongly and shepherded by the Queen advance with decisive effect.

27	P–B5	KR–QB1
28	P–K6	B–B3
29	Q–B7 ch	K–R1
30	P–B6	R–KN1
31	Q–QB7	QR–QB1
32	Q–K5	P–Q5 dis ch
33	K–N1	Resigns

In modern chess there often occur positions in which neither side allows any weakening of his pawns and in which both Kings are well protected from attack. In such cases it is generally impossible to utilize the Queen's attacking function as in the previous example; so the Queen must for long be content to use only part of its powers. It can then assist the Rooks in the struggle to control an open file; it can also occupy an important diagonal and enhance the power of the Bishop or, where this has been exchanged, even take over the function of the Bishop. Operation by the Queen on diagonals is a common feature of many modern opening systems where Bishops are fianchettoed; for an exchange of Bishops to remove an important defensive piece is often an important aim, and any resultant free diagonal is of use only to the Queen. A simple example is the well-known variation of the Queen's Indian in which Black, after **1 P–Q4, N–KB3; 2 N–KB3, P–K3; 3 P–KN3, P–QN3; 4 B–N2, B–N2; 5 O–O, P–B4; 6 P–B4, P×QP; 7 KN×P, B×B; 8 K×B,** generally continues with 8 ..., Q–B1 followed by Q–N2 ch.

Perhaps the greatest exponent of operating with the Queen on long diagonals was the Czechoslovak Grandmaster R. Réti; his game against the World Champion of that time, Capablanca, has made the rounds of the entire chess world.

RÉTI–CAPABLANCA

(New York 1924)

1	N–KB3	N–KB3
2	P–QB4	P–KN3
3	P–QN4?!	B–N2

Better is 3 ..., P–QR4!, 4 P–N5, P–Q3.

4	B–N2	O–O
5	P–KN3	P–N3
6	B–N2	B–N2
7	O–O	P–Q3
8	P–Q3	QN–Q2
9	QN–Q2	P–K4
10	Q–B2	R–K1
11	KR–Q1!	

The first fine move, which already envisages operations by the Queen on the diagonal a1–h8. Should Black now play 11 ..., P–K5, towards which his previous moves seem aimed, then the continuation 12 P×P, N×P; 13 B×B, K×B; 14 N–Q4, N(2)–B3; 15 Q–N2! gives White the advantage because of the strong position of his Queen.

11 ...	P–QR4
12 P–QR3	P–R3
13 N–B1	P–B4
14 P–N5!	

White could have won a pawn here by 14 P×RP, R×P; 15 N×P, B×B; 16 N×N, B–B3; 17 N×N ch, B×N; 18 B×B, Q×B; but the resulting weakening of his King's position would have given his opponent considerable attacking chances.

14 ...	N–B1
15 P–K3!	

The beginning of a manoeuvre by which White opens both the Queen file and the diagonal a1–h8.

15 ...	Q–B2
16 P–Q4	B–K5
17 Q–B3(?)	

A tactical error that should have cost White a large part of his advantage. More precise was 17 Q–B1, with consequences similar to those in the game.

17 ...	KP×P
18 P×P	N(3)–Q2?

After this mistake, all is again in order for White. Much stronger would have been 18 ..., N–K3; 19 Q–B1, QR–B1, with complicated play.

19 Q–Q2!	P×P

Preferable was the holding of tension in the centre by 19 ..., QR–Q1. The text-move, which wins the QBP in return for the Queen pawn, leaves a serious weakness on b6; it also opens the way for White to the important outpost on c6.

20 B×P	Q×P
21 B×B	K×B
22 Q–N2 ch!	K–N1
23 R×P	

DIAGRAM 73

A glance at the diagram shows just how successful White's strategy has been: his Queen controls the long diagonal and creates hidden threats to the Black King (see note to Black's 27th move). Black's Queen, on the other hand, is only a source of worry: it is subject to the immediate threat 24 N(3)–Q2, and any endeavours to send it on profitable tactical excursions come to nothing. In the end its unfavourable position leads to tactical difficulties contributing to Black's downfall.

23 ...	Q–B4
24 QR–Q1	R–R2
25 N–K3	Q–R4

An apparently logical manoeuvre, the purpose of which is to induce the weakening advance of White's KNP to g4. The text-move also meets the threat 26 N–N4; but a better way of doing this was simply 25 ..., P–R4.

26 N–Q4!

Capablanca probably reckoned only with 26 R(1)–Q5?!, B×R; 27 P–N4, B×N; 28 P×Q, B×P, after which his defensive prospects are quite good.

| 26 ... | B×B |
| 27 K×B | Q–K4 |

Unplayable is 27 ..., R×N; 28 P×R, Q×R; 29 N–B5 (or K6)!, and the long-range power exerted by the Queen against the King is apparent. A better defence, however, lay in 27 ..., N–K4; in this case White could maintain his advantage either with 28 Q–N3 or by transposing into an end-game (28 Q–K2) in which Black's QNP is a serious weakness.

28 N–B4	Q–QB4
29 N–B6	R–B2
30 N–K3	N–K4
31 R(1)–Q5!	Resigns

After 31 ..., N–B5; 32 R×Q, N×Q; 33 R B2, N R5; 34 N–Q5, Black loses a Rook.

It is interesting to observe that the White Queen occupied the long diagonal on move 22 and remained on the same square to the end; yet its latent attacking power was an important factor in the quick victory. Black's Queen, on the other hand, was constantly in action; but its exposed position was more important than the threats it generated, and this finally led to defeat.

We have already mentioned that the Queen is a piece whose action is predominantly of a tactical nature. That is true; but there are also numerous occasions when the many-sided powers of the Queen enable it to assist in the execution of a strategical plan; and there are even some cases where the very presence of the Queen exerts a decisive influence on the strategical character of the position. In this latter category are those positions in which the minor pieces have been eliminated. The game is then in a state of flux between the middle-game and end-game: the Queen supported by a Rook or Rooks can still be a strong weapon in attacking the enemy King; but an exchange of Queens or of all Rooks brings about an end-game. The strategical principles that apply to such a position are therefore a mixture of those applicable to middle-game and end-game separately. A typical example is the following position from a game in a World Championship match.

SCHLECHTER–LASKER

(Match 1910)

Diagram 74

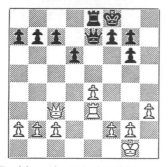

Position after Black's 21st move

At first sight the position seems clearly drawn and one would not be surprised if either player offered a draw. But, in fact, Lasker decides to play for a win—and, as the next few moves underline, with some justification. There are two factors that offer him a winning chance: first, the relative speed and ease with which his King can reach the centre if Queens are exchanged; and second, the unpleasant tactical weakness of White's KP, whose defence by P–B3 would invite the strong advance of Black's QP or KBP. Lasker's plan is twofold: he first moves his King nearer the centre and then, by offers to exchange Queens, brings his pieces to their most effective positions. Schlechter at first chooses the correct counter-plan: by constant Queen manoeuvres he manages to force weaknesses in Black's Queenside pawn position, thus obtaining chances in an end-game in which Black's King would be the first to reach the vital field of play.

22	Q–N4	P–QB3
23	Q–R3	P–R3
24	Q–N3	R–Q1
25	P–QB4	R–Q2
26	Q–Q1	Q–K4
27	Q–N4	K–K1
28	Q–K2	K–Q1
29	Q–Q2	K–B2
30	P–R3	R–K2
31	P–QN4?	

But now he falters. This move shows that he is preparing an advance of his pawns on the Queenside—a course that is tactically unsound. The correct move was 31 P–QR4, though this advance would have been better played on the previous move. Its idea is to hinder Black's action on the Queenside and possibly (after a later P–QN4 with the further threat of a break-through by P–QN5) to obtain counter-play on this wing. After the text-move Black can advantageously change the whole pawn structure.

Diagram 75

31 ... P–QN4!

32 P×P

If 32 Q–Q3, Black replies 32 ..., Q–R8 ch and holds the advantage after 33 K–R2, Q–R7!; 34 P–B5, P×P; 35 P×P, R–Q2; 36 Q–B3, Q–Q7; 37 Q–K5 ch, K–N2 (Romanowski).

32 ...   RP×P

The last two moves have brought such a favourable change in the position for Black that an end-game would be clearly won for him. Besides the weakness of White's Queen-side pawns, Black has always the possibility of advancing either his QBP or his QP, so securing a passed-pawn that the distant enemy King could not halt. Strategically the game is already won for Lasker; his opponent can only hope by tactical threats to make the task of winning as difficult as possible. The fact that the game has a tragic outcome for Lasker is merely proof of the difficulties involved in handling such positions.

33 P–N3

Although this move is necessary to improve the King's position, it creates a new and unpleasant weakness on h3.

33 ...	P–N4!
34 K–N2	R–K1
35 Q–Q1!	P–B3!

The break-through 36 P–QR4, which White prepared with his last move, has been cleverly countered; if now 36 P–QR4, then after 36 ..., P×P; 37 Q×RP, K–N2; 38 R–R3, Q×KP ch; 39 K–N1,

Q–Q5!; 40 Q–R6 ch, K–B2; 41 Q–R7 ch, Q×Q; 42 R×Q ch, K–N3, Black wins because he loses only one pawn on the King-side.

36 Q–N3	Q–K3
37 Q–Q1	R–KR1!
38 P–N4	Q–B5(?)

The first false step. After the correct 38 ..., R–QR1 White has absolutely no counter-play.

39 P–QR4!   Q×NP

A more cautious continuation is 39 ..., R–QR1; 40 P×P, Q×P(b5) with positional advantage to Black. The text-move, which accepts White's pawn offer, is the beginning of a new phase: Black, on account of the now unfavourable position of his King, will soon be forced back on the defensive.

40 P×P	Q×NP
41 R–QN3	Q–R3
42 Q–Q4	

White fights for control of the a-file. He threatens not only Q–N4 followed by R–R3 but also R–N1 followed by R–QR1.

42 ...	R–K1
43 R–N1	R–K4
44 Q–N4	Q–N4

Unplayable is 44 ..., R–N4 on account of 45 Q–B4.

| 45 Q–K1 | Q–Q6 |
| 46 R–N4 | |

Now White has a strong threat in 47 Q–QR1. The safest counter to this would have been 46 ..., R–R4!. Lasker, however, comments that after 46 ..., R–R4; 47

69

R–N3!, Q×R; 48 Q×R ch a
Queen end-game would have arisen
in which his opponent would have
had considerable defensive possibilities, e.g. 48 ..., K–N2; 49
Q–KB5, Q–B2; 50 Q–R5. Nevertheless entry into an end-game was
the right and logical continuation.
In the game Black does indeed gain
a second pawn after two moves,
but White at the same time considerably strengthens the attacking
position of his pieces.

46 ...	P–QB4(?)
47 R–R4	P–B5
48 Q–QR1!	Q×KP ch
49 K–R2	R–N4
50 Q–R2	Q–K4 ch
51 K–N1	Q–K8 ch
52 K–R2	P–Q4
53 R–R8!	Q–N5

Black can obviously draw by
perpetual check; but it is no easy
matter to concede a draw when two
pawns up. The further play,

however, shows the uselessness of
playing for a win.

| 54 K–N2! | Q–B4? |

Black underestimates the threat
55 Q–R6 and loses with surprising
rapidity. He could still have held
the draw by 54 ..., R–N1; 55
Q–R7 ch, R–N2; 56 Q–R6! (56
Q–K3, Q–Q3), Q–N3; 57 Q–R3 or
55 ..., K–B1; 56 Q–R6 ch, K–B2.

| 55 Q–R6! | R–N1? |

Likewise is 55 ..., R–N2; 56
Q–K6 insufficient. Lasker, however, gives 55 ..., P–B6!; 56
R–B8 ch, K–Q2; 57 R×Q, R×R
as a means of still reaching a draw.

56 R–R7 ch	K–Q1
57 R×P	Q–N3
58 Q–R3	K–B1

Or 58 ..., Q–N5; 59 Q–R7.
At this point Lasker resigned,
without waiting for the inevitable
mate in three beginning with 59
Q–B8 ch.

This game is by no means faultless; nevertheless it is extremely
interesting and instructive. In the first phase of the struggle of the
heavy pieces, from moves 22 to 38, Black held a decided initiative.
It soon became clear how strong a centralized King is and how
difficult the game is for the side that must avoid an exchange of
Queens. In the second phase, from move 39 to the end, the picture
changed. White sacrificed first one and then a second pawn to gain
chances in a counter-attack; Black let slip the opportunity to
transpose into a difficult, though won, Queen end-game and finally,
after several mistakes, succumbed to his opponent's assault. It should
be remarked that the errors made by the former World Champion
were not merely chance mistakes; the fight with the heavy pieces
frequently gives rise to serious errors even in Master play. This is
not surprising, for this phase of the game is beset with such difficult
strategical and tactical problems that its correct handling demands

the greatest precision; it is indeed one of the most difficult types of position in chess.

In play with the heavy pieces, weak points in the enemy position have a special importance. Heavy pieces with their long-range powers are ideal for any attacking action, but for defence they are not nearly so effective. When there are weak points in the opposing position alternating attacks soon cause congestion of the defending pieces and are often worth more than an extra pawn. In the next game concentrated action by the heavy pieces brings about a position in which the White pieces are seriously restricted in their movements.

RUBENSTEIN–ALEKHINE
(Dresden 1926)

1 P–Q4	N–KB3
2 N–KB3	P–K3
3 B–B4	P–QN3
4 P–KR3	B–N2
5 QN–Q2	B–Q3!

Strengthens the centre and at the same time opens the c-file.

6 B×B	P×B
7 P–K3	O–O
8 B–K2	

Better is 8 B–Q3

8 ...	P–Q4
9 O–O	N–B3
10 P–B3	N–K5
11 N×N (?)	P×N
12 N–Q2	P–B4
13 P–KB4	P–KN4!
14 N–B4	P–Q4
15 N–K5	N×N
16 QP×N	

If 16 BP×N, then Black can prepare a break-through by P–B5.

16 ...	K–R1
17 P–QR4	R–KN1

Black's heavy pieces offer him great possibilities for action and make up for his bad Bishop.

18 Q–Q2	P×P
19 R×P	

White has no choice, for if 19 P×P, Black replies 19 ..., Q–R5, threatening both Q×RP and R×P ch, and after 20 Q–K3, R–N6 reaches a won position. The text-move, however, leaves White with a tactical weakness on e5, which Black can always attack with his Queen from g7. White must therefore voluntarily restrict the activity of his own Queen in order to stand in readiness to defend his weak KP by Q–Q4.

19 ...	Q–N4
20 B–B1	Q–N6!

A very fine manoeuvre. By the threat of Q×RP Black forces the White King to h1, from where it cannot guard the square f2; Black will soon be able to win an important tempo by a later attack on a Rook standing on this unprotected square.

21 K–R1	Q–N2!

The weakness of the KP makes itself felt. White must withdraw his Queen from the defence of g2, giving Black the opportunity to rid himself of his bad Bishop.

| 22 Q–Q4 | B–R3! |
| 23 R–B2 | Q–N6! |

With his last four moves Black has achieved two things: he is now in a position to exchange his bad Bishop and he has virtually forced the White Rook away from the KB file; for if now 24 K–N1, then 24 ..., B×B; 25 K×B (forced because of the threat 25 ..., Q×RP), Q–R7!; 26 R–Q1, QR–KB1, and Black can break through by P–B5.

| 24 R–QB2 | B×B |
| 25 R×B | |

DIAGRAM 76

Although material is even, the position is quite hopeless for White. His weak pawn and lack of scope for his heavy pieces are in sharp contrast to the activity of Black's pieces on the open g-file; no wonder his position is soon torn asunder.

| 25 ... | QR–QB1 |

Threatening 26 ..., R–B5.

| 26 P–QN3 | R–B2 |

| 27 R–K2 | R(2)–KN2 |
| 28 R–B4 | R–QB2 |

A well-known manoeuvre to gain time to plan the decisive winning action.

29 R–QB2	R(2)–KN2
30 R–K2	R–N3!
31 Q–N4	

If instead 31 Q–Q1, we have after 31 ..., R–R3! a most interesting position, in which not one of White's pieces can move: all Rook moves lose a pawn and a King move is followed by Q×RP; if the Queen leaves the first rank, Black has 32 ..., R×P ch! and if 32 Q–K1 (or KB1), the KP is lost after 32 ..., Q–N2; and if White tries 32 P–B4, he loses to the break-through 32 ..., P–Q5!; 33 Q×P, R×P ch!.

| 31 ... | R–R3 |
| 32 P–R4 | Q–N2! |

This wins much more quickly than 32 ..., R×P ch; 33 R×R, Q×R ch; 34 K–N1. This bears out our earlier statement that a favourable attacking position for the heavy pieces is worth more than an extra pawn. Alekhine carries out the final assault with energy.

| 33 P–B4 | R–N3 |
| 34 Q–Q2 | R–N6! |

Threatening 35 ..., R–R6 ch. If 35 K–N1, then 35 ..., P–Q5; 36 P×P, P–K6!; 37 Q–B2, R–R6 followed by Q–N6.

| 35 Q–K1 | R×NP |
| 36 Resigns | |

CHAPTER VI

The King

OF all pieces the King occupies a special position. On the one hand it is the focal piece of the game; on the other it must for long periods confine itself to a sad and modest role and shelter from attacks by enemy pieces. It is generally pointless to assess the King's value in terms of other pieces, for it cannot be exchanged against any number of pieces. In the end-game, however, the danger of immediate mating attacks is diminished and the King is given the chance to show its working powers; its activity increases sharply and its handling becomes an important strategical element in the game. Experience shows that the power exerted by the King is then greater than that by a minor piece but less than that by a Rook.

The strategical problems associated with the King in the end-game (centralizing, opposition, etc.) are beyond the scope of this book; we shall confine ourselves here to the handling of the King in the middle-game. The treatment has been divided into three sections.

A. THE ACTIVE KING IN THE MIDDLE-GAME

Although the King must generally remain inactive until the end-game there are cases where it enters more quickly into play. Sometimes it joins directly in a mating attack; more frequently it backs up a pawn advance or prepares a break-through. In both cases the King only plays these daring roles with safety when the enemy position is so constricted, or when material is so reduced, that it is not subjected to immediate danger. The most common sortie by the King is in a middle-game without Queens, where one player often renounces castling to bring his King more quickly to bear on the enemy position; the absence of Queens has generally removed mating dangers and the King, after assisting in a break-through, stands actively poised for an ensuing end-game. Although this is the most common, we have chosen more exceptional cases to illustrate the King at work in the middle-game. The fact that the Queens remain on the board highlights the possibilities open to the King and shows that its potential as a working force must not be forgotten.

PACHMAN–UJTELKY

(Czechoslovak Championship 1954)

DIAGRAM 77

Position after Black's 34th move

White has achieved a favourable posting of his pieces; it remains to be seen how best this advantage can be exploited. An attack on the weak c-pawn can hardly be carried out successfully, because the withdrawal of White's Knight from c5 to implement this attack leaves the Queen-pawn under fire; the correct strategical plan must therefore be sought elsewhere. White has a superiority on the King-side and a break-through there by means of a pawn advance is indicated; but first the h-pawn must be protected. To do this by a lengthy Knight tour such as N(N4)–Q3–B4–N2 or to defend it by the Rook (K–N2 followed by R–KR1) would be possible; yet such manoeuvres reduce White's attacking chances. There remains, however, one piece which has not shared in the play and which can easily undertake the protection of

the Rook-pawn; that is the White King. Since Black is in a very constricted position, he will not be able to launch an effective counter-attack against the enemy King should it become exposed; White therefore is well placed to advance his King and shepherd his pawns as they press forward on the King-side.

35	K–R2		Q–N3
36	K–R3!		Q–R2
37	P–B4		P–N3
38	P–N4		N–Q2
39	B–Q3		N × N
40	P × N		Q–Q2

Black endeavours to hold up the attack by exploiting the position of White's King. His efforts, however, are of no avail, for after accomplishing the break-through White will withdraw his King to a safer position; then the attack can be resumed with decisive effect.

41	P–B5!		KP × P
42	P × P		P–N4

Obviously not 42 ..., P × P?; 43 R–N1ch, K–R2; 44 Q–B4, winning for White.

43	K–N2!		P–B3

An attempt to stop at least the advance P–B6, which would lock up Black's second Bishop. A quick loss also results from 43 ..., Q–Q5; 44 Q × Q, R × Q; 45 P–B6, B–Q1; 46 P × P, R–N5 ch (P × P; 47 R–KR1, R–R5; 48 R × R, P × R; 49 K–B3); 47 K–B3, R × P; 48 R–KR1!, etc.

44	P × NP		RP × P

45 P–K6	Q–B2

The final attempt. There is likewise little hope from 45 ..., Q–Q5; 46 Q–R3, Q–R5; 47 Q×Q, P×Q; 48 K–R3.

46 Q–R3	R–Q5
47 R–KR1!	

Wrong would be 47 Q–R5?, R–R5; 48 Q–N6 ch, K–R1; 49 R–KR1, R–KN1!.

47 ...	R–R5
48 Q–B3	R–KB5

Or 48 ..., R×R; 49 K×R, and there is no defence to the threat 50 R–R2.

49 Q–R5	Resigns

In this game the King entered the fight for several moves to prepare a pawn advance, but then withdrew to safety. In a few exceptional cases, however, the King gives up all thoughts of retreat and presses forward to assist in the death blow. Such a case is the following.

TEICHMANN–BERATENDE

(Glasgow 1902)

Black is in the unpleasant position of having no good moves at his disposal. He has just moved his RP to h6 in a rash attempt to avert a smothered mate should his Queen leave the defence of the square e6. The weakness opened up on the King-side gives White the chance to launch a most amazing attack.

DIAGRAM 78

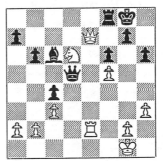

Position after Black's 27th move

28 K–R2	P–QN4
29 K–N3	P–QR4
30 K–R4	P–N3

On this defence Black had obviously pinned his hopes; White cannot take the pawn because of 30 P×P??, Q–N4 mate.

31 R–K3!	Q×NP
32 R–N3!	Q–KB7

If 32 ..., P–N4 ch, White does not allow 33 K–N4??, B–B6 mate, but presses on with his original plan: 33 K–R5, Q×R; 34 K–N6 winning.

33 P×P	Q–B5 ch
34 R–N4	Q–B7 ch
35 K–R5	Resigns

B. CASTLING

In most games both sides protect their Kings by castling, generally in the opening. But castling does not only give protection to the King; it frequently determines the strategical plan for the whole middle-game, especially when one player castles on the Queen-side. This can best be illustrated by a few examples from opening theory.

A. After the moves **1 P–Q4, P–Q4; 2 P–QB4, P–K3; 3 N–QB3, N–KB3; 4 B–N5, B–K2; 5 P–K3, O–O; 6 N–B3, QN–Q2; 7 Q–B2, P–B4** (Diagram 79) White can choose one of two quite different plans—

(*a*) He can isolate Black's Queen pawn and, after castling King-side, concentrate on this weakness: **8 P×QP, N×P; 9 B×B, Q×B; 10 N×N, P×N; 11 B–Q3, P–KN3; 12 P×P, N×P; 13 O–O.**

DIAGRAM 79

Position after 7 ..., P–B4

(*b*) He can produce an entirely different situation by castling Queenside: **8 O–O–O, Q–R4; 9 K–N1.** Then there arises a very sharp position in which White will attack on the King-side aided by a pawn advance (P–KR4, P–KN4), while Black concentrates his counter-action on the Queen-side.

This example shows clearly how the whole course of a game can depend on the decision to castle on a particular side. Generally where players castle on opposite sides a very sharp struggle ensues, for a pawn attack against the enemy King does not then leave one's own King denuded. For this reason it is often wise when behind in development to delay castling until the opponent has committed himself, and then to castle on the same side. The next example illustrates the dangers involved in disregarding this advice.

B. 1 P–K4, P–K4; 2 N–KB3, N–KB3; 3 N×P, P–Q3; 4 N–KB3, N×P; 5 N–B3, N×N; 6 QP×N, B–K2; 7 B–Q3 (Diagram 80). Black is behind in development and would offer White great attacking chances if he castled at once: **7 ..., O–O?; 8 B–K3, N–Q2; 9 P–KR4!.** The correct course for Black is to play **7 ..., N–B3!** and wait until White has castled before likewise committing himself. If White continues with 8 O–O, it is safe for Black to follow suit; if White prepares to

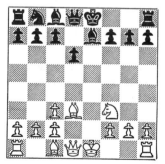

DIAGRAM 80

Position after 7 B–Q3

castle Queen-side, Black must stand in readiness to do the same:
8 B–K3, B–N5; 9 B–K4, Q–Q2, etc.

A similar idea is prominent in the next example—a well-known
line in the Giuoco Pianissimo.

C. After **1 P–K4, P–K4; 2 N–KB3, N–QB3; 3 B–B4, B–B4;
4 P–Q3, P–Q3; 5 N–B3, N–B3** it would not be good for White to
castle at once, for the unpleasant pin arising after 6 O–O?, B–KN5!
cannot be released by 7 P–KR3 because of 7 ..., P–KR4!. White
therefore often plays **6 B–K3,** to which Black must not reply 6 ...,
O–O? giving White the chance, even at the loss of a tempo, to set
up an advantageous pin by **7 B–KN5!.**

It often happens in the opening that a player, for one reason or
another, must renounce castling: then, as in the next example, he
sometimes brings his King to safety in a more roundabout manner.

D. After **1 P–Q4, N–KB3; 2 N–KB3, P–QN3; 3 B–B4, B–N2;
4 P–K3, P–K3; 5 B–Q3, B–K2; 6 QN–Q2, N–R4; 7 B–N3, N×B;
8 RP×N** there are certain difficulties involved for Black in preparing
King-side castling, for his opponent has attacking possibilities on the
open K R file. For this reason it is usual in this position for Black to
play 8 ..., P–KN3 followed by K–B1 and K–N2.

We now give a few games and positions illustrating the difficult
problems associated with the decision to undertake castling.

SZABÓ–BISGUIER

(Buenos Aires 1955)

1	P–Q4	P–Q4
2	P–QB4	P–QB3
3	N–KB3	N–KB3
4	N–B3	P–K3
5	P–K3	QN–Q2
6	B–Q3	B–Q3
7	P–K4	P×KP
8	N×P	N×N
9	B×N	N–B3
10	B–B2	B–N5 ch
11	B–Q2	B×B ch
12	Q×B	O–O

DIAGRAM 81

Position after 12 ..., O–O

This position is very much in
White's favour: he has a superiority in the centre and possesses an
active Bishop, whereas Black's
Bishop has little immediate prospect of joining in the fight. The
problem is to find the right plan to
exploit this advantage. In the same
position Trifunović chose against

Bisguier the faulty 13 O–O and allowed his opponent to equalize. Szabó, however, does better and selects the correct strategical plan: he castles Queen-side and prepares to launch a King-side pawn attack, which puts Black under great pressure.

| 13 N–K5 | Q–B2 |
| 14 O–O–O! | P–B4 |

A logical yet rather routine counter-action. Undoubtedly better was 14 ..., P–QN4! with the idea of securing an operation base for the Knight on d5, though even here White still holds the upper hand after 15 P–B5 because Black's Bishop remains hemmed in.

| 15 Q–K3 | P–QN3 |

Exchanging pawns by 15 ..., P×P; 16 R×P would only assist White's attack. The text move, however, precludes any prospects of a counter-attack on the QB file.

| 16 P×P! | P×P |

The end-game after 16 ..., Q×P; 17 Q×Q, P×Q; 18 P–B3 is very much in White's favour: Black's QBP is weak and the proximity of White's King to the centre is a telling factor.

| 17 P–KN4! | R–N1 |
| 18 KR–N1 | Q–N3 |

Unplayable is 18 ..., N–Q2 on account of 19 N×N, B×N; 20 Q–Q3.

| 19 P–N3 | R–N2 |
| 20 P–N5 | N–K1 |

Just as useless is 20 ..., N–Q2; 21 N–N4, which gives White a decisive attack.

21 B×P ch!	K×B
22 Q–R3 ch	K–N1
23 R–N4	Resigns

The threatened mate on the KR file cannot be averted, e.g. 23 ..., P–B3; 24 R–R4, P×N; 25 P–N6, etc.

This game shows how castling on one side can be a prelude to an attack on the other. Sometimes, however, one player has such a space advantage that castling is possible even on the side where pawn operations are intended. That such a denuding of the King is not without risk can be seen from the following example.

PACHMAN–FICHTL
(Czechoslovak Championship 1954)

(*See* Diagram 81)

In this position it is clear that White's main field of operation will be on the Queen-side, where, besides his space advantage, he has a rewarding target in Black's weak and unprotectable a-pawn. At first sight it might seem that castling King-side is the logical course, but this would be a mistake; Black would reply to 14 O–O by 14 ..., N–K1 followed by P–KB4 and obtain a dangerous counter-attack. The right plan is to castle Queen-side; the only difficulty is the timing. In the game White castled at once and overlooked a strong tactical reply,

DIAGRAM 82

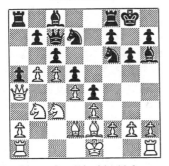

Position after Black's 13th move

which cut across his strategical plan and posed problems for his exposed King. The correct way was first 14 P–N6!, Q–Q1 and only then to castle Queen-side. Black cannot then obtain counter-chances by opening up lines on the Queen-side; he must simply watch while White captures the a-pawn and pushes through his pawn majority.

14 O–O–O?	P–N3!
15 P×BP	N–N1
16 P×P	Q×NP

The last three moves have brought about a great change in the position; the plan to capture the a-pawn must now be abandoned. Playing his Bishop to QN5 offers no great prospects to White because of the reply 16 ..., B–N5 followed by R–QB1 taking advantage of the White King's position. White must search for another plan.

17 Q–N5!

Although White's King appears badly placed at the moment, it will in an end-game be quick to attack Black's weaknesses on a5 and d5. White therefore endeavours to simplify the play as much as possible and exploit his end-game advantage.

17 ...	Q×BP
18 Q×Q	N×Q
19 N–R4	B–N5
20 QR–K1!	

A mistake would be 20 B×B?, N×B; 21 B–K1 (or QR–B1), N–N5. After the text-move White can reply quietly to 20 ..., N–QN5 by 21 K–N1. In the following play Black remains passive and allows a speedy simplification; this policy merely helps White to reach his strategic goal.

20 ...	B×B!
21 R×B	N–Q2?
22 K–N1	KR–QB1
23 R–QB1	B–B1
24 K–N2	N–N5?
25 R×R	R×R
26 B×N	P×B

Or 26 ..., B×B; 27 R–B2, R×R ch; 28 K×R, B–K8; 29 N–B3 (P–B3 followed by N–B3 also wins), B×P; 30 N×QP with a won ending for White.

27 R–B2	R×R ch

Or 27 ..., R–R1; 28 R–B7!, N–B3; 29 N–N6, R–N1 (R–R3; 30 N–Q7); 30 R–B6, etc. In the game the b-pawn is eventually lost, mainly because White's King is much nearer than Black's.

28 K×R	B–Q3
29 P–KR3	K–B1

30	N(3)–B5!	K–K2	36	P–QR4	P–N4
31	K–N3	B–R7	37	P–R5	N–K1
32	K×P	B–N8	38	N–R6 ch	K–N2
33	N–B3	N–B3	39	N–N4	N–B2 ch
34	N–Q1	K–Q3	40	K–B5	P–B4
35	K–N5	K–B2	41	N×P	Resigns

In both examples the active side castled on the Queen's wing. Generally, however, castling King-side occurs much more frequently, for this requires only four moves to accomplish compared with at least five, and mostly six, for castling Queen-side. Besides, the position of the King is much more secure on KN1 than on QB1, from where it is constantly worried by the undefended QRP; often, in fact, the King, after castling Queen-side, must waste a move securing its position by K–QN1. We may say, therefore, that short castling is the general rule; long castling is the exceptional case, undertaken when combined with a predetermined and definite strategical plan.

In certain games it happens that after castling the position of the King becomes unsafe; it is sometimes then thought necessary to bring the King back to the centre or even to the other wing. Such a trek is usually beset with many dangers, for the loss of time involved allows the massing of the enemy pieces for an attack on the wandering King; the whole operation, in fact, is something of an emergency measure, undertaken only when the risks of staying at home are greater than those to be encountered on the journey. Frequently the manoeuvre succumbs to a hostile attack; sometimes it is the means of snatching the game from the fire.

BYRNE–KOTOV
(U.S.S.R.–U.S.A. Match 1954)

(*See* Diagram 83)

In this position Black has good chances on the Queen-side, especially against the pawn on c4. He is, however, faced with a powerful King-side attack, which White will soon reinforce with a pawn advance. There is little time for delay; Black must bring his King to safety immediately.

17 ...   K–B2!

This move is tactically possible

DIAGRAM 83

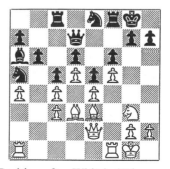

Position after White's 17th move

because Black holds an advantage after 18 Q–R5 ch, K–K2; 19

80

Q × RP, B × P. To his regret White sticks to his original plan of attack on the King-side. This is now pointless and he would have done better to obtain approximate equality by 18 KR–N1! followed by N–B1–Q2–N3. Exchange of Knights would then remove Black's threat to the pawn on c4, freeing the Queen for duty elsewhere and, when the Black King eventually arrived on the Queen's wing, the advance of the Rook pawn to a5 might cause him some trouble.

18 R–B3?	K–K2
19 N–B1	K–Q1
20 R–KR3	R–KR1!

Weaker is 20 ..., P R3 on account of 21 N–Q2 and White's Knight heads for g6.

21 P–N4	K–B2
22 N–N3	K–N1
23 K–B2	N–B2
24 Q–R2	QR–Q1
25 R–KN1	Q–K2
26 B–K2?	

White now indulges in planless waiting moves, after which the initiative passes to Black. 26 N–B1 followed by P–N5 was called for.

26 ...	B–B1
27 N–B1	B–Q2
28 N–Q2	

White misses his last chance to strive for active play by P–N5. On 28 P–N5 Black can reply 28 ..., QR–KN1 followed by P–N3, or even at once 28 ..., P–N3; 29 P × BP, Q–B2!, in both cases obtaining counter-play against White's exposed King.

| 28 ... | P–KN4! |

Having successfully blocked the King-side Black will soon have a free hand for operations on the Queen's wing.

29 N–B1	B–K1
30 N–N3	P–KR3
31 N–R5	B × N
32 P × B	

If 32 R × B, Black plays his Knight to g2, after which he can always threaten to open the KR file by P–KR4.

32 ...	N–K1
33 B–N4	N–N2
34 K–K2	K–B2
35 K–Q3	R–QR1
36 R–QN1	KR–QN1
37 R–N2	P–R3
38 K–B2	

It might be asked why White also brings his King to the Queen-side, especially since it is more exposed to danger there. The answer is that White is thinking of an end-game. He realizes that after P–QN4 the resulting opening of the QN file might lead to an exchange of heavy pieces; if his King were then on the King-side, his weak pawn on c3 would be an easy prize for the Black King.

38 ...	Q–Q2
39 R–KN3	Q–K1
40 B–Q2	R–R2?

With this move, the last before the time-control, Black throws away an almost certain win. After 40 ..., N × RP! 41 R–R3, N–B5; 42 R × RP, Q–K2, Black's heavy pieces break through on the KR file with decisive effect.

41 R–R3	P–N4

This gives White the chance to save himself by a pretty tactical manoeuvre (*see* move 47). The position would certainly offer more for Black if only he could now transfer his King without risk to the King-side; unfortunately this course is too dangerous, for the King-side is not entirely blocked and can always be opened by an advance of White's h-pawn to h4.

42 RP×P	P×P
43 P×P	R×P
44 R×R	Q×R
45 P–B4!	Q×P ch
46 Q×Q	N×Q

47 B×P!

The point of White's defensive plan. If now 47 ..., RP×B; 48 P–R6, R–R1; 49 P×N, R–KN1; 50 B–K2, Black has nothing, and after 47 ..., BP×B?; 48 P–B6, K–Q1; 49 R–QB3, N–QR4; 50 R–KB3, K–K1; 51 P×N, R×P; 52 R–B6, N–B5; 53 K–Q3 he would even lose (Romanovski).

47 ...	N×BP!
48 P×N	BP×B
49 P–B6	P–K5
50 P–B7	R–R1
51 R–QB3	N–K4
52 R–QR3	R–KB1
53 B–K6	K–N3
54 R–N3 ch	K–B2
55 R–QR3	K–N3
56 R–N3 ch	Draw

C. THE EXPOSED KING'S POSITION AS A STRATEGICAL FACTOR

Very frequently an attack on the enemy King is the object of a strategical plan. Often, of course, this is merely part of some other strategical motif, such as exploitation of open files; sometimes, however, it is in itself the dominant part of a plan. In the following example the strategy of the attacking side involves the forcing of the opponent to castle into an exposed position from where his King can be subjected to a direct attack.

ALEKHINE–WINTER

(London 1932)

(*See* Diagram 84)

In this position Black has the better pawn position. If he could only complete his development and castle King-side his prospects would be bright indeed. Alekhine, however, succeeds by his next two moves in preventing Black from castling King-side; his further plan is then to exploit the weakened position of the Black King.

12 P–Q5!	P×P
13 O–O	O–O–O

There is no time for short castling, for if 13 ..., B–K2, then 14 R–K1; the Black King must therefore move to a position in which it receives little pawn protection.

DIAGRAM 84

Position after Black's 11th move

14	B×N	P×B
15	R–N1	Q–B2
16	Q–R4	R–Q2
17	B–Q2!	

Here one could well have expected 17 B–K3, yet this move really threatens nothing. Alekhine's beautiful move, on the other hand, prepares to bring the Bishop to a5.

| 17 | ... | B B4 |
| 18 | P–QB4! | K–Q1 |

The best defence. White was threatening 19 Q R6 ch, K–Q1; 20 B–R5, B–N3; 21 R×B!, which cannot be parried by 18 ..., B–N3, because of 19 P–B5!, B×P; 20 Q–R6 ch, etc.

19	B–R5	B–N3
20	B×B	P×B
21	Q–R8 ch!	

The aim of this move is not simply to win the b-pawn; it is, rather, to free the square a4 for White's Rook. At the same time White prepares to deprive Black's King of the flight-square e7.

21	...	Q–B1
22	Q–R3!	Q–N1
23	P×P	P×P

After 23 ..., R×P; 24 KR–Q1, R–K1; 25 R×R, P×R; 26 R–Q1, R–K4; 27 P–B4 White has likewise a strong attack.

| 24 | R–N4! | Q–Q3 |
| 25 | R–K1 | |

Clearly 25 Q–R8 ch, K–K2; 26 Q×R would be pointless.

| 25 | ... | R–B2 |

If 25 ..., R–K2, Black replies 26 R–Q1! with the threat 27 Q–N3.

26	Q–N3	R–K1
27	R–Q1	R–K4
28	R×NP	R–B3
29	R×R	R–N4 ch

Obviously not 29 ..., Q×R?; 30 Q–N8 ch.

30	K R1	Q×R
31	R–K1!	Q–KB3
32	Q–N8 ch	K–Q2
33	P–B4	R–N3
34	Q–K8 ch	K–B2
35	R–B1 ch	K–N3
36	R–N1 ch	K–B4
37	Q–N5 ch	Resigns

CHAPTER VII
Exchange of Material

In the preceding chapters the reader has been shown the connection between material and the strategical plan and has seen the way in which the quality and number of pieces influence the character of a position. From what was said one obvious conclusion can be drawn: every important exchange of material alters in some way the character of the position and necessitates a change in the strategical and tactical conduct of the game. Not every exchange of a piece, of course, can be considered to be of this importance; on the other hand an exchange of Knight against a Bishop, an exchange of a bad against a good Bishop, an exchange of both Rooks, and naturally an exchange of Queens can all be counted as important exchanges.

The exchange of Queens deserves special attention, for it generally marks the transition from the middle-game to the end-game. Sometimes such an exchange is simply the unavoidable outcome of tactical complications; more often it is the result of a deliberate effort by one of the players. The most common case of a deliberate exchange of Queens occurs where one side has a material advantage. It is clear from a study of end-games that an extra pawn is generally most easily converted in a pawn end-game; end-games with Knights or like-coloured Bishops likewise do not present great obstacles to taking advantage of a pawn superiority; end-games, however, with Queens and Rooks are, together with those in which unlike Bishops participate, much more difficult to win. Consequently the conversion of material advantage often demands simplification involving an exchange of Queens. Generally the side with material advantage will endeavour to transpose into the type of end-game that is most easily won; his opponent, if he cannot prevent an end-game, will strive to bring about one that is impossible, or at least extremely difficult, to win.

Another case in which it is advantageous to bring about a Queen exchange occurs when the opponent is burdened with weak and exposed pawns. Disappearance of the Queens robs him of the opportunity to create counter-chances in an attack and also deprives him of a piece that is perhaps the only one capable of defending his weaknesses; the task of exploiting these strategical pawn weaknesses can then be undertaken without serious hindrance.

We now give an example of a strategically well-conceived exchange action leading to an end-game.

RESHEVSKY–WALISTON

(New York 1940)

DIAGRAM 85

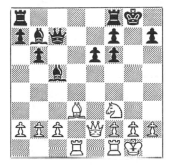

Position after Black's 13th move

At first sight Black's weakened King-side appears to offer his opponent great attacking chances; White's Bishop on d3 seems therefore destined to play an important, aggressive role. A deeper investigation, however, shows that White's scope for attack is limited by the great strength of Black's Bishops; his prospects of a direct mating attack are therefore remote. An immediate sacrifice, for example, is out of the question, for after 14 B×P ch?, K×B; 15 N–N5 ch!, K–N3! (not P×N; 16 Q–R5 ch, K–N2; 17 Q×NP ch, K–R2; 18 R–Q3, etc.) Black wins; there is likewise nothing to be gained by 14 N–R4, Q–B5; 15 Q–R5, P–B4; 16 P–KN3, Q–K4, while after other preparatory moves Black has again an adequate defence in

Q–B5, which gives him good counter-play. Reshevsky assesses the position correctly and in renouncing a frontal attack pins his hopes on simplification. In an end-game Black's doubled pawns will be a decided disadvantage, for they hamper the task of creating a passed pawn; in addition they will present an inviting target for White's pieces, and especially the Knight, which is usually superior to a Bishop when attacking such pawn formations. Consequently White is willing to exchange his active-looking Bishop in order to begin an advantageous simplification.

14	B–K4!	QR–Q1
15	B×B	Q×B
16	N–Q2	R–K2
17	N–K4	R×R?

As already explained exchanges favour White. Black should therefore have refrained from this exchange and played instead P–B4 followed by B–B3. Although White would still retain a definite positional advantage it is doubtful whether this is sufficient to win against an active and precisely played counter-plan.

18	R×R	R–Q1
19	R×R ch	B×R
20	Q–Q3	B–K2
21	P–KR3	Q–B2?

Again P–B4 and B–B3 were

called for. Black, however, makes no attempt to avoid a Queen exchange and allows White to go into a favourable end-game.

22 Q–N3 ch!	Q×Q
23 N×Q	K–B1

The rest of the game revolves round the technical conversion of White's advantage.

24 K–B1	K–K1
25 K–K2	K–Q2
26 K–Q3	K–B3
27 N–K2	B–B4
28 P–KB4	P–N4?

Simplifies White's task of creating a passed-pawn.

29 P–KN4	P–QR3
30 K–K4	B–B1

31 N–Q4 ch	K–Q3
32 N–N3	B–K2
33 N–Q2	B–B1
34 P–B4	K–B4
35 P×P	P×P
36 N–N3 ch	K–Q3
37 N–Q4	K–B4
38 P–B5	P–K4
39 N–B3	

Threatening 40 P–N5.

39 ...	P–R3
40 P–KR4	B–K2
41 P–R5!	B–Q3
42 P–R3	P–N5
43 P–R4	P–N6
44 N–Q2	K–N5
45 P–R5	K×P
46 N–B4 ch	Resigns

Of less frequent occurrence are those positions in which simplification is sought by the side suffering from a positional or material disadvantage. Nevertheless it does sometimes happen that going into a certain type of end-game nullifies an advantage. The most obvious case is that in which the side with a piece up must concede a draw when most of the other pieces and all the pawns have been exchanged. It is well known that one minor piece alone is not sufficient to win; there are also other combinations of pieces that do not suffice to win without support by pawns. Although two minor pieces and a Rook are generally more than a match for a single minor piece and a Rook, any further simplification usually leads to a draw: one minor piece can hold two (except in a few positions where a Knight succumbs to two Bishops) and a lone Rook can obtain, albeit with some difficulty, a draw against Rook and minor piece. These cases are, of course, exceptional, but they do show that automatic simplification does not guarantee the conversion of every material advantage. The same applies to an advantage in position and in fact simplification is sometimes the only way it can be successfully countered. In the following game Black sees an end-game as the one means of preventing a drift into a decidedly inferior position; the pawn sacrifice involved in carrying out the required simplification is a fruitful investment.

H. STEINER–PACHMAN
(Venice 1950)

1 P–Q4	N–KB3
2 P–QB4	P–K3
3 N–QB3	B–N5
4 P–QR3	B × N ch
5 P × B	O–O
6 P–K3	P–Q3
7 B–Q3	P–K4
8 N–K2	P–K5
9 B–N1	P–QN3
10 N–N3	R–K1
11 P–B3	B–N2
12 O–O	QN–Q2
13 R–R2!	

Black's build-up rests on maintenance of control over c4; the text-move endangers the whole system. White will put pressure on the KB-file and force an exchange of pawns on f3 to give himself a strong position in the centre.

13 ...	P–B4
14 R(2)–KB2	

DIAGRAM 86

Black is now confronted with a serious problem, for the loss of his KB pawn is always in the air after 15 P × KP. To meet this threat by

14 ..., P × BP; 15 NP × P is from the strategical point of view quite hopeless: White simply obtains a massive centre after an eventual P–K4 and can then quite easily initiate a King-side attack. Likewise after 14 ..., B–R3; 15 N × P White secures a strong centre and with it a clear positional advantage.

14 ...	P–Q4!

The start of combination that solves the problem. Black sacrifices a pawn in order to achieve an exchange of Queens and minor pieces. To arrive at this move involved the difficult task of correctly assessing the position that would arise after the simplification. In the event Black's decision is vindicated; the resulting Rook end-game brings salvation.

15 P × QP	B × P
16 P × KP	N × P
17 N × N	B × N
18 B × B	R × B
19 R × P	N–B3
20 Q–N3	Q–Q4!
21 Q × Q	N × Q
22 P × P	N × KP!

Better than 22 ..., P × P; 23 R(7)–B5, N × BP; 24 R × P.

23 B × N	R × B
24 P × P	P × P

(*See* Diagram 87)

After ten practically forced moves the position has radically altered and White's chances of deciding the game by direct attack have, as a result of the wholesale exchanges, entirely disappeared. The extra

DIAGRAM 87

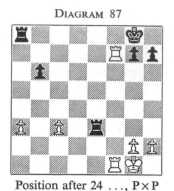

Position after 24 ..., P×P

35	R–QB6	R(2)–K3
36	R×R	R×R
37	K–B4	R–QB3
38	K–K5	R–B4 ch

If 38 ..., R–B5, then 39 R–N3, R×RP; 40 K–Q5 followed by K–B6.

39	K–Q6	R–B5
40	R–N3	K–B2!
41	R–B3 ch	K–K1
42	R–N3	K–B2
43	P–R5!	

pawn cannot be utilized in this position, because White's Queenside pawns are separated and can be subjected to constant attack.

25	R–QB7	R–K3
26	P–QR4	P–R3
27	R–KB4	QR–K1
28	P–R3	R–N3
29	K–B2	R–K4!

Black must play actively and harass the enemy on both wings.

30	P–N4	R(3)–K3
31	P–R4	R–K7 ch
32	K–N3	R(7)–K6 ch
33	R–B3	R(6)–K5
34	P–KR5	R–K2

After 43 K–Q5, R–B4 ch; 44 K–Q4, R–KN4 the game is drawn.

43	...	P×P
44	K–Q5	R–KB5
45	P–B4	K–K1
46	K–B5	K–Q2
47	K–N5	K–B2
48	P–B5	R–B8!
49	P–N5	R–N8 ch
50	K×P	K–B3
51	P×P	P×P
52	R–N6 ch	K×P
53	K–R6	R–KR8
54	R×P	K–Q4
55	R–R8	K–K3
Draw		

So far we have discussed cases in which the Queen has been exchanged. Often, of course, exchanges of other pieces are an equally important part of strategy. Where, for example, one side has a distinct space advantage his opponent can often obtain relief by exchanging several minor pieces. A realization of this has influenced opening theory in the Steinitz defence to the Ruy Lopez. After the moves **1 P–K4, P–K4; 2 N–KB3, N–QB3;**

DIAGRAM 88

Position after 8 ..., O–O

3 B–N5, N–B3; 4 O–O, P–Q3; 5 P–Q4, B–Q2; 6 N–B3, B–K2; 7 R–K1, P×P; 8 N×P, O–O we have the position in Diagram 88. If White now continues with a natural developing move like B–N5 or P–QN3, Black can, by N×N followed by B×B, exchange off two pieces; as practice shows, the relief gained by these exchanges gives him a comfortable game. Theory therefore recommends **9 B×N**, by which only one piece is exchanged; White's pawn on e4 then confers a space advantage that has some importance.

We now list below the main cases where an exchange of pieces is advantageous. These are—

1. When an inactive or badly placed piece is exchanged for a better placed enemy piece.

2. When an exchange prevents the opponent from effectively defending weak points in his position.

3. When an exchange eases the task of converting a material or positional advantage or when simplification makes it harder for the opponent to utilize his advantage.

4. In positions in which exchanges lighten the defence or lessen the effects of an opposing space advantage.

We have up to now looked at exchanges from the point of view of gaining from an exchange. Naturally what is favourable for one side is to be avoided by the other; so the rules given above should also serve as a guide to the avoidance of exchanges. Frequently, indulging in faulty exchanges is the main cause of defeat. Sometimes this arises from an incorrect assessment of a position and the choice of the wrong strategical plan; more often it stems from a reluctance to choose an energetic continuation when this is demanded by strategical considerations. Many players shy away from all complications and by repeated exchanges attempt to deprive the game of its fire; this they hope will ensure a quick and riskless draw. Such a plan is almost always doomed to failure, for every exchange alters the equilibrium of a position. Exchanges should therefore never be undertaken lightly; purely mechanical exchanges bring little reward.

CHAPTER VIII

The Pawns

DESPITE their limited powers, the pawns have special qualities that play a large part in shaping the character of a position and in influencing the strategical plan to be followed. They are, for example, more suitable for covering important points and defending pieces than the pieces themselves; but they also deserve our attention for other reasons. Pawns are best suited for blocking opposing pawns; pawn advances are often the means of opening up important files and diagonals; weaknesses in the enemy position can frequently be created by using pawns; pawns can deprive enemy pieces of important operation bases. Not surprisingly, therefore, the problems associated with the handling of the pawns are many and varied. As a result, this chapter has been divided into seven parts.

A. THE PASSED-PAWN: ITS CREATION AND CONVERSION

For all the modesty of its movements the pawn has in comparison with the other pieces one special advantage: its advance is influenced by the alluring prospect of a huge increase in its value on reaching the eighth rank. A successful pawn advance completely alters the relative material strength on the board and can at a stroke decide the game. The advance, however, is no easy matter; many obstacles must first be overcome.

The greatest impediments to a successful pawn advance are the enemy pawns—those on adjacent files as well as that on the same file. If these cannot all be overcome the pawn advance must eventually come to a standstill. Once, however, these enemy pawns are eliminated or successfully by-passed a new factor enters the game: the passed-pawn has come into existence, a pawn whose way to the eighth rank can no longer be stopped by enemy pawns. This new factor is often of great strategic importance and can be the focal point around which play centres; how it is brought about, therefore, deserves considerable attention.

The passed-pawn can arise in a number of ways, of which the following are the most frequent: utilization of a pawn majority on a particular part of the board; forcing the opponent to exchange a piece, the recapture being made with a pawn; by various tactical devices.

Diagram 89 shows a position that illustrates the first method—

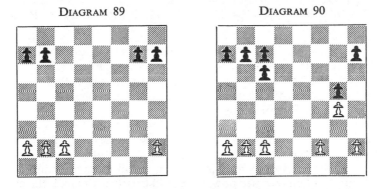

DIAGRAM 89   DIAGRAM 90

both White and Black possess pawn majorities that can be used to produce passed-pawns. Let us see how both sides should proceed. It is clear that P–QN4 for White would be a serious positional error: his opponent has only to counter with P–QN4 and further advance by White is stopped. The same applies to P–KR4 as a first move for Black because White can then reply P–KR4, likewise immobilizing his opponent's majority. Returning to White's majority, we may say that 1 P–QR4 is also generally questionable: it does nothing to further the creation of the passed-pawn, for Black can reply 1 ..., P–QR4, after which White must undertake additional preparations (P–QB3 and P–QN4) before proceeding with his advance. Even more suspect would be 1 P–QR4 followed by P–QB4, allowing P–QR4 by Black to block the pawn majority completely. The logical plan for White is 1 P–QB4 with the idea of creating a passed-pawn after the further moves P–QB5, P–QN4, P–QN5, and P–B6. If Black should try to cut across this plan with 1 ..., P–QR4, then Black should avoid 2 P–QR3, on account of 2 ..., P–QR5!, and first play 2 P–QN3 before proceeding with 3 P–QR3 and 4 P–QN4. Black's best means of creating a passed-pawn from the position in Diagram 89 is similar: P–KN4, P–KR4, P–KN5, P–R5, and P–KN6.

Having examined this simplified position we can now formulate two principles—

1. When one wishes to use a pawn majority to create a passed-pawn, it is generally best to begin by advancing that pawn which is not opposed by an enemy pawn on the same file.

2. The fewer the pawns comprising the majority, the quicker a passed-pawn can be created. In our example Black's majority of 2 against 1 produces a passed-pawn before White's of 3 against 2, even where White has first move; e.g. 1 P–B4, P–QR4!; 2 P–N3, P–KN4; 3 P–QR3, P–N5; 4 P–N4, P×P; 5 P×P, P–R4; 6 P–B5, P–R5; 7 P–N5, P–N6.

These principles have admittedly been drawn from an examination of a schematic pawn structure uninfluenced by pieces. They can however be taken as the general rule; cases in which they do not apply are, rather, the exception, being mostly associated with some special peculiarity in the position.

From the position in Diagram 89 both sides could produce a passed-pawn without much difficulty. In such cases, where the basic pawn structure offers no obstacle to the creation of a passed-pawn, we talk of a mobile pawn majority. In not all cases are majorities so fruitful; often they are powerless by themselves to break through an opposing pawn group and must enlist the services of the pieces. An example is the position in Diagram 90, where both sides have compromised majorities: no matter how he advances Black cannot force the creation of a passed-pawn and White with his majority can only obtain a passed-pawn by conceding one to his opponent. The other pieces must therefore be brought to the aid of the pawns if they are to bear fruit. White will probably prepare the advance P–KB4 with the support of a piece, so that, if Black exchanges pawns, White by recapturing on f4 with the piece leaves himself a mobile pawn majority of 2 to 1. Black in order to use his Queen-side majority must first induce his opponent to play the weakening P–QN3; then he must advance his Queen-Bishop-pawn to c4 and exchange it against White's pawn on b3. In neither case is the task of utilizing such a pawn majority easy: Black can stop White's King-side scheme by keeping control of the square f4 and White likewise can frustrate Black's plans on the Queen-side by exerting pressure on c4. A compromised pawn majority is clearly much more difficult to convert than a mobile one.

Although the utilization of a pawn majority will be examined in detail in a later chapter, we give here a short example showing the successful creation of a passed-pawn.

PACHMAN–FOLTYS

(Prague 1943)

White exerts strong pressure on the diagonal a2–g8 and is ready to improve his position with the manoeuvre B–Q5 followed by N–K4–Q6. Black's best defence would now be 19 ..., B–B3, though it must be admitted that his Bishop

DIAGRAM 91

Position after White's 19th move

might then be embarrassed by a later P-QN5 on White's part.

19 ...   **P-QN3?**

Black believes that after the apparently forced 20 P×P? he can by 20 ..., P×P succeed in hindering his opponent's Queen-side advance, at the same time widening the scope for his own pieces, for White cannot continue 21 P QR4 because of 21 ..., B×N, when the Rook pawn is lost; but Black has overlooked a tactical manoeuvre that gives White a passed-pawn.

20 B-Q5   **QR-B1**
21 P-B6!   **B-K1**

If 21 ..., B×QBP, then 22 B×B, R×B; 23 N Q5 followed by 24 R×R.

22 N-N5

This leads almost by force to the win of a pawn. It may, however, have been better to play for a clear positional advantage by 22 N-K4, K-R1; 23 P-N5.

22 ...   **P-R3!**

Counters the threat 23 P-B7, which would now be answered strongly by 23 ..., R×B!.

23 N×B   **P×N**
24 KR-K1   **Q-Q3**

An immediate loss results from 24 ..., Q-N4; 25 P-KR4!, Q×RP; 26 P-B7, R-Q2; 27 R×B ch, etc. Likewise 24 ..., Q-B2; 25 R-K4, P-Q6; 26 Q×P, B×P?; 27 R-Q4! offers Black little hope.

25 R×B ch!   **R×R**
26 B×P ch   **K-R1**
27 B×R   **R×B**
28 P-R3

Obviously bad is 28 Q-B7?, Q×BP!.

28 ...   **P-Q6**
29 Q-B7   **R-QB1?**

Loses at once as does 29 ..., R-KB1; 30 Q-Q7, P-Q7; 31 R-Q1, R-Q1; 32 Q×Q, R×Q; 33 P-B7, R-QB3; 34 R×P, R×P; 35 R-Q8 ch, K-R2; 36 R-QR8. Much better was 29 ..., R-Q1!; 30 P-B7, R-QB1; 31 R-Q1, R×P; 32 Q-K8 ch, K-R2; 33 Q-K4 ch, and although White will have an extra pawn, the task of winning the ending is difficult in view of the presence of the heavy pieces.

30 Q-Q7!   **Resigns**

Diagram 92

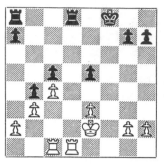

We now come to the second method of obtaining a passed-pawn—recapturing with a pawn after having forced the opponent to exchange pieces. This can best be illustrated by examining the position in Diagram 92. If White plays 1 R–Q5, the threat to the two pawns virtually forces Black to exchange by 1 ..., R×R, whereupon White acquires a passed-pawn after 2 P×R.

The third means of procuring a passed-pawn—tactical devices—comprises many different types of manoeuvre; we shall, however, restrict ourselves to an examination, from schematic diagrams, of three.

In the first, Diagram 93, White can proceed in combinative style with 1 P–N6, and no matter which pawn Black captures with, White ends up with a passed-pawn, e.g. (*a*) 1 ..., RP×P; 2 P–B6!,

Diagram 93   Diagram 94

 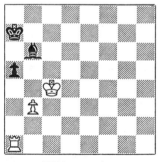

White to play   White to play

P×BP; 3 P–R6 or (*b*) 1 ..., BP×P; 2 P–R6!, P×RP; 3 P–B6. Similar types of break-through can occur in various positions, but since a sacrifice is involved, they can only be carried out successfully when the value of the passed-pawn so created outweighs the material loss.

Diagram 94 shows how an enemy pawn subjected to a pin can be successfully by-passed: 1 P–QN4, K–R3; 2 P–N5 ch.

Discovered check is the theme in Diagram 95: 1 P–B6 dis ch followed by P–B7.

Now we turn to the problem of using the passed-pawn. It might seem obvious, and indeed logical, that queening the passed-pawn is the principal strategic objective; yet the difficulties involved in overcoming all the obstacles that the opponent can place in the way make this an infrequent method of utilizing a passed-pawn in the middle-game. In the end-game, of course, the reduced material offers the passed-pawn great scope for advancing to the queening square, and around this advance the play frequently centres; but in the middle-game the enemy pieces can generally block the pawn some way or other and so make progress to the eighth rank virtually impossible. In view of this we might well ask whether the passed-pawn can, as a general rule, be considered an important factor in the middle-game. The answer is yes, for, although the pawn can usually be stopped, the constant threat of its advance ties up the opponent's pieces on a particular part of the board and allows an attack to be prepared unhindered on another part. A similar possibility of utilizing the passed-pawn is its sacrifice in order to dislocate the enemy pieces. A good example is the following game.

DIAGRAM 95

White to play

SZABÓ–WADE

(Trencianske Teplice 1949)

1	P–Q4	N–KB3
2	P–QB4	P–KN3
3	N–QB3	P–Q4
4	N–B3	B–N2
5	Q–N3	P×P
6	Q×BP	O–O
7	P–K4	N–QR3
8	B–K2	P–B4
9	P–Q5	P–K3
10	O–O	P×P
11	P×P	

Now we have one of those positions in which the passed-pawn has no special dynamic strength, for the White pieces are not well enough posted to support a quick advance; besides, Black has counter-play on the long diagonal a1–h8. According to theory Black should, in this position of the Grünfeld defence, continue with Q–N3, KR–K1, and B–KB4, when he will have the constant threat of counter-action by N–K5.

11 ...   **N–K1(?)**

As we shall see in the next section, such a transfer of the Knight to blockade the enemy passed-pawn from d6 is the correct strategical procedure. Unfortunately in this case it fails on tactical grounds, for White, by his next move, forces his opponent to relinquish his one advantage—the pressure on the long diagonal a1–h8. As a result Black's pieces are given little chance of working together efficiently.

12 B–N5!   **P–B3**

Obviously 12 ..., Q–N3; 13 B–K7 is hopeless.

13 B–B4   **R–B2**

More logical was 13 ..., N–Q3. Then 14 B×N, Q×B; 15 N–QN5 (or K4), Q–N3 gives White nothing. After 14 Q–N3!, however, White's pieces are undoubtedly more active, though it is not easy to exploit this advantage for winning purposes.

14 QR–Q1   **B–B1?**

DIAGRAM 96

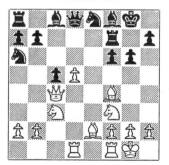

Now N–Q3 was definitely called for. Instead Black plans to bring his Bishop to d6 in order to drive away or exchange White's active Bishop on f4. In the meantime, however, White's passed-pawn

develops a dynamic strength and, at the cost of its life, brings White a decisive positional advantage.

15 P–Q6!   **N–N2!**

The pawn could not be taken at once by either the Bishop or Knight on account of 16 B×B(N) followed by Q–Q5, when White wins a piece. Black therefore prepares to re-group his pieces by B–K3 and R–Q2, after which White can hardly avoid losing the pawn. Black's plan, however, is effectively countered by the following energetic move.

16 P–Q7!

A pawn on d6 under attack would be a distinct weakness in White's position; its immediate sacrifice, on the other hand, disorganizes Black's pieces. Nimzowitsch once wrote that pawns intent on death are the most dangerous.

16 ...	B×P
17 Q–K4	Q–B1

Forced, on account of the threats 18 Q×NP and 18 B–QB4.

18 B–B4	B–K3
19 KR–K1!	B×B
20 Q×B	N–N5
21 N–QN5	N–K1
22 P–QR3	N–R3

The plan to bring the Knight to c6 has proved futile, for if 22 ..., N–B3, then 23 B–Q6, B×B; 24 N×B, N×N; 25 R×N, Q–B4; 26 N–R4, Q–N4; 27 R–Q7, QR–KB1; 28 R–K8!, etc.

23 P–KR4	N(1)–B2

24 B × N	N × B
25 N–Q6	B × N
26 R × B	K–N2

A quick loss results from 26 ..., N–K1; 27 R(6)–K6 followed by 28 R–K7.

27 P–R5!

Threatening 28 P–R6, against which there is no satisfactory defence, for 27 ..., P × P; 28 N–R4! only strengthens White's attack.

27 ...	N–K1
28 P–R6 ch!	K–B1
29 R(6)–K6	Q–B2
30 P–QN4!	N–Q3

Black's Queen-Bishop-pawn can neither take nor be defended. If 30 ..., P × P??, then 31 Q × P ch, and if 30 ..., P–QN3, White replies strongly with 31 Q–K4, Q–Q1 (Q–B1; 32 R–K7); 32 Q–B6, N–B2; 33 R–Q6, etc.

31 Q–B3	N–B4
32 N–N5!	N–Q5
33 N × R	N × R
34 R × N	R–K1

In time trouble Black had hoped to trap the White Knight, which however escapes unharmed along the same route as it had used to collect its prize.

35 N–N5!	Resigns

We now give an example of the less common case that in which the passed-pawn successfully advances to the queening square. It should be noted that White succeeds partly as a result of incorrect defensive measures by Black and partly because he is able to combine the threat to advance the pawn with additional threats on other parts of the board.

FILIP–URBANEC

(Czechoslovak Championship 1954)

DIAGRAM 97

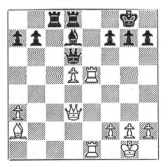

Position after Black's 22nd move

A glance at the diagram gives the impression that the task of queening White's pawn is certainly a difficult one: no fewer than three enemy pieces block the way to the queening square.

23 P–KR4!

This is a dual purpose move. On the one hand White secures himself against tactical threats on the back rank, e.g. 23 ..., Q × R; 24 R × Q, R–B8 ch. On the other he prepares a constricting operation on the King's wing by a pawn advance.

23 ...	R–B8?

A typical example of a faulty exchange action; it simply enables White's Queen-pawn to advance at a future date. After 23 ..., R–K1, Black's position was still tenable.

24 R×R	Q×R
25 Q–B4	

Premature is 25 P–Q6, B–B4!. The text-move is typical of such positions: the advance of the pawn will be preceded, or rather prepared, by favourable piece manoeuvres. In this case White takes control of the c-file and threatens to penetrate to the seventh rank; naturally Black cannot oppose this by 25 ..., R–QB1?? on account of 26 Q×R ch.

25 ...	Q–K1

The only defence. Now 26 Q–B7? fails against 26 ..., R–B1. White therefore re-groups his pieces and prepares to reach the seventh rank by operating on the King-file.

26 Q–QN4	P–QN3

27 R–K1!

Advancing the Queen-pawn is again premature (e.g. 27 P–Q6, B–K3; 28 B×B, Q×B) and playing the Rook directly to the seventh rank is useless: 27 R–B7, R–B1; 28 R×P? R–B8 ch; 29 K–R2, Q–N1 ch.

27 ...	Q–B1
28 R–K7!	P–QR4
29 Q–K4	B–B4
30 Q–K5	B–K3
31 R–B7	B–B1
32 P–Q6!	

At last the struggle is over; the pawn, in view of the threat to f7, cannot be stopped. If 32 ..., B–Q2, then 33 Q–K7!, with the double threat of 34 R×B and 34 B×P ch, is decisive.

32 ...	R–K1
33 Q×R	Resigns

After 33 ..., Q×Q; 34 B×P ch, Q×B; 35 R×B ch, Q–B1; 36 P–Q7 the pawn queens without trouble.

B. THE BLOCKADE

DIAGRAM 98

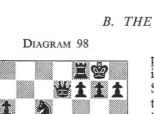

In Diagram 98 White has a passed-pawn whose advance is effectively blocked by the Black Knight. Such an action as that exerted by the Black Knight is termed blockading the passed-pawn; it is the simplest and most effective method of dealing with a passed-pawn and for that reason the most frequent. In this position White has no prospects of forcing his passed-pawn through; so the position is at least equal.

For Black's part, he has a mobile King-side majority, which he can use, after preparing the advance P–B4, P–K5, P–B5, either to attack the opposing King (P–B6) or to create a passed-pawn (P–K6). After the moves 1 ..., P–B4; 2 P–B4, P–K5; 3 N–Q1! followed by 4 N–K3 we have an interesting position: Black now has a passed-pawn, which is, in addition, protected; his position, however, is by no means superior, for White's Knight on e3 will be extremely strong and Black's pawn on e4 can later be undermined by P–R3 and P–KN4.

From this simple example it becomes clear that the blockading piece is important in two ways—

1. As a defensive piece it prevents the gradual advance of the passed-pawn;

2. As an active piece it is protected from frontal attack by the enemy pawn and thereby exerts great pressure, especially when blockading a central pawn.

The following game will throw more light on its important role; we shall see there how a passed-pawn effectively blockaded is worth less than a mobile pawn majority supported by the blockading piece.

VESELY–PACHMAN
(Prague 1951)

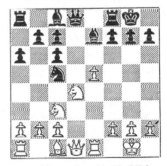

DIAGRAM 99

Position after 11 N–QB3

1 P–K4	P–K4
2 N–KB3	N–QB3
3 B–N5	P–QR3
4 B–R4	N–B3
5 P–Q4	P×P
6 O–O	B–K2
7 P–K5	N–K5
8 N×P	O–O
9 R–K1	N–B4
10 B×N	QP×B
11 N–QB3	

This is a position that had already occurred in my game against Foltys in the 1946 Czechoslovak Championship. At that time, after lengthy deliberation, I reached the conclusion that Black, in view of his two Bishops, would be well placed if only he could deal with White's King-side pawns; this can only be done by a move that at first sight looks unreasonable.

11 ...   P–B4!

Black presents his opponent with a passed-pawn, which, however, he can blockade from the square e6; by this means he obtains play on both wings,

12 QN–K2

The best reply. In his game Foltys played 12 P–B4, N–K3; 13 B–K3, N×N; 14 Q×N, Q×Q; 15 B×Q, B–K3, after which White's position is strategically lost, for he has no effective counter-play against the advance of Black's Queen-side pawns. Another possibility is 12 P×P *e.p.*, B×P, but then Black's pieces come quickly into play.

12 ...	N–K3
13 N×N	Q×Q
14 R×Q	B×N
15 N–B4?	

White endeavours to drive the Bishop from its strong blockading position; but this could be better achieved by 15 N–Q4, for then the reply 15 ..., QR–Q1? fails against 16 B–N5!. After 15 N–Q4 Black can reply 15 ..., K–B2; 16 N×B, K×B, using his King to blockade the pawn; in this position it would fill the role of blockader most effectively, giving White little chance of utilizing his passed-pawn and ensuring a clear draw. But Black has an even stronger continuation after 15 N–Q4; that is 15 ..., B–B1!, after which the White Knight quickly loses its central position; e.g. 16 P–QN3 (16 B–K3, P–B5), P–KN4! followed by P–QB4 and B–K3.

15 ...	QR–Q1!

16 B–K3	B–B1
17 N–Q3	

If 17 N–K2, Black replies P–QB4 followed by P–KN4 and B–K3. The Bishop would then be quite secure on e6 and White would have to defend on both wings.

17 ...	P–QN3
18 P–QN4	

It is understandable that White should avoid mere passive defence and attempt some counter-action. The idea behind the text move is the preparation of the advance P–QR4 and P–QR5; but the plan comes to nothing, for Black immediately begins the decisive action.

18 ...	P–B5!
19 N×P	

Naturally 19 B×BP?, R×N! is hopeless and after 19 B–Q2, P–B6; 20 P–N3, B–KB4 White's position is not very promising.

19 ...	B×P
20 N–K2	

Or 20 N–Q3, B–B6; 21 QR–N1, B–B4; 22 P–B4, P–B4.

20 ...	B–KB4!

A little surprise. The apparently strong reply 21 N–Q4 fails against 21 ..., B–B6; e.g.

(*a*) 22 N×B, B×R; 23 N–K7 ch, K–B2; 24 R×B, K×N; 25 B–N5 ch, K–K3; 26 B×R, R×B; 27 P–KB4, R–Q7, winning for Black.

(*b*) 22 QR–B1, B–N7; 23

R–N1, B×N followed by B×QBP.		25 N–B4	KR–K1
		26 R×R	R×R
		27 P–QR3	R–K1
21 P–QB3	B–R4	28 P–K6	B×KP
22 QR–B1	P–B4	29 N×B	R×N
23 P–B3	B–K3	30 P–QB4	K–B2
		31 B–B4	P–QN4!

Now 24 P–QR3, B–B5 is useless for White; he therefore attempts to create complications.

		32 B–K3	B–N3
		33 P×P	P×P
		34 R–QN1	
24 K–B2	B–B5		

If 34 B×P?, then 34 ..., R–QB3.

In order to deprive White of the counter-chances that arise after 24 ..., R×R; 25 R×R, B×RP; 26 R–Q7 or after 24 ..., B×RP; 25 R×R, R×R; 26 P–QB4.

34 ...		P–B5!	
35 B×B		R×B	
36 K–K3		P–B4	
37 K–K4		K–K3	
38 Resigns			

It might now well be asked which pieces are the most effective in undertaking a blockade. Most frequently it is the Knight which performs this task, but, as we have seen, the Bishop too can fill the role with success; the note to White's move fifteen in the last game showed that even the King is a useful piece for blockading a pawn when the position has an end-game character. The pieces generally least suitable are the Rook and the Queen. This is because they are primarily attacking pieces and their use to blockade a passed-pawn results in a reduction in their striking force; consequently they are mostly given the job of blockader only in cases of emergency.

We have seen how effective a blockade can be in neutralizing a passed-pawn; now we must look at the ways of overcoming a blockade. This can be done in several ways: by direct attack against the blockading piece, thus driving it away; by an attack on another part of the board, drawing the blockading piece to the defence of the newly harassed region; by exchange of the blockading piece. The most common method of eliminating the blockader is the last, and sometimes it is carried out by material sacrifice as in the position in Diagram 100: **1 R–N8 ch, R–B1; 2 R×B, R×R; 3 K–N7,**

DIAGRAM 100

White to play and win

R–KB1; 4 P–R8 (Q), R×Q; 5 K×R, K–B2; 6 K–N7, K–N3; 7 K–B7, K–N4; 8 K–Q7!, K–B4; 9 K–Q6 and wins. White sacrificed the exchange in order to replace an effective blockader, the Bishop, by one less suited to the task; his King was thereby enabled to approach the queening square to assist in the promotion of the pawn.

Sometimes the best way to deal with a blockade is to act before the intended blockader has a chance to take up position; even a sacrifice may be justified to avoid the blockade, as the next example effectively shows.

GRÜNFELD–STEINER

(Ostrava 1933)

DIAGRAM 101

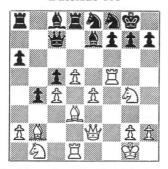

Position after Black's 20th move

In this position it appears that Black, by exchanging off White's Knight after the withdrawal of the Rook from f5, will be well placed to blockade White's central pawns; e.g. 21 R–R5, B×N; 22 Q×B, N–B3; 23 B×N, B×B; or 21 R(5)–B1, B×N; 22 Q×B, B–B3. To avoid having his pawns thus blocked, White sacrifices the exchange; his mobile central pawns, with ample piece support, move forward to unleash a decisive attack.

21	P–K5!	B×R
22	B×B	Q–R4
23	N–Q2	Q×P

After other moves White obtains an irresistible attack by N–K4 or N–B3

24 N–B3

Now besides the threat P–Q6 there is the insecure position of the Queen on a2 to be considered. This Black neglects, but in any case he has no really satisfactory defence, for his minor pieces are completely hemmed in by the forward White pawns.

24	...	P–B3?
25	R–R1!	Q–N6
26	B–B2!	Q×B(N7)
27	B×P ch	N×B
28	Q×Q	P×P
29	Q×KP	B–Q3
30	Q–K6 ch	K–R1
31	N(3)–K5	B×N
32	N×B	N–B1
33	Q–K7	N–Q3
34	R–KB1	K–N1
35	R–B3	Resigns

Now we show an example in which the blockader has already taken up position.

NIMZOWITSCH–
GOTTSCHALL
(Breslau 1925)

DIAGRAM 102

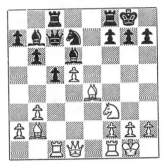

Position after Black's 15th move

Not only is White's passed-pawn blockaded by the Bishop; there is also a Knight on d7 as a second line of defence. Generally a double blockade of this nature is an effective weapon against a passed-pawn, for a withdrawal of the Bishop for some temporary action elsewhere does not release the pawn; its advance is held up one square farther on by the Knight, which acts, in the words of Nimzowitsch, as reserve blockader. In this position, however, the double blockade is not built to endure: White manages to exchange the Bishop and, by attacking threats on the King-side, draws the Knight away from d7. Thereafter the pawn on d5 becomes a very strong weapon.

16 R–K1	Q–Q1
17 B–N1!	KR–K1
18 Q–Q3 (?)	

A slight tactical error, which Black ought to have exploited by 18 ..., R×R ch, improving his defensive possibilities. The correct sequence of moves was 18 R×R ch, Q×R; 19 Q–Q3, N–B1.

18 ...	N–B1 (?)
19 R×R!	Q×R
20 N–R4!	

One of the blockaders is tied to the defence of the Rook-pawn; the other is shortly to be exchanged.

| 20 ... | P–B3 |

After 20 ..., B–K4; 21 B×B, Q×B; 22 P–Q6 (or N–B5) White undoubtedly stands better. The text-move on the other hand is no better, for it allows a tactical thrust that increases White's advantage considerably.

| 21 N–B5 | R–Q1 |
| 22 B×P! | |

Black was probably hoping for 22 N×B?, R×N, when the defence of the Queen-pawn poses some problems. After the text-move the continuation 22 ..., P×B; 23 N×B, R×N; 24 Q–N3 ch is hopeless for Black; his reply is therefore virtually forced.

22 ...	B×P ch
23 K×B	P×B
24 Q–N3 ch	N–N3
25 P–B4!	

The real point of White's twenty-second move: it counters Black's threat to exchange Queens by 25 ..., Q–K4 and safeguards the Queen-pawn for, if 25 ..., R×P (or B×P), then White plays 26

R–K1 followed by 27 N–K7 ch. It is now clear how much Black's position has deteriorated: not only have both blockaders been removed but White can now combine the advance of his passed-pawn with an attack against Black's weakened King-side. By so doing he achieves a decisive material advantage within a few moves.

DIAGRAM 103

Position after 25 P–B4

25 ...	K–R1
26 R–K1	Q–B1
27 P–Q6!	R–Q2

A forced blockading move. Unplayable is 27 ..., B–B1; 28 N–K7,

Q–R3 ch; 29 K–N1, N×P; 30 N×B, R×N; 31 P–Q7.

| 28 Q–QB3! | R×P |

There is no other way to meet the threat 29 R–K8, for 28 ..., R–KB2 fails against 29 P–Q7! R×P; 30 R–K8!, etc.

The rest of the game is now a matter of technique.

29 N×R	Q×N
30 B×N	P×B
31 R–K8 ch	K–N2
32 Q–N3	B–B3
33 R–K3	B–Q2
34 P–B5!	Q×Q ch
35 K×Q	B×P
36 R–K7 ch	K–R3
37 R×P	B–N8
38 R–R6	P–QN4
39 P–R4	P×P
40 P×P	K–N4
41 R–N6	B–K5
42 P–R5	P–KB4
43 P–R6	P–QB5
44 P–R7	P–B6
45 R–N3	P–B5 ch
46 K–B2	P–B7
47 R–QB3	Resigns

To conclude this section on the blockade we give a case in which there is no question of a passed-pawn; the blockade is instead directed at a pair of central pawns.

NIMZOWITSCH–SALVE

(Karlsbad 1911)

1 P–K4	P–K3
2 P–Q4	P–Q4
3 P–K5	P–QB4
4 P–QB3	N–QB3
5 N–B3	Q–N3
6 B–Q3	B–Q2

Better is 6 ..., P×P.

| 7 P×P! | B×P |
| 8 O–O | P–B3 |

(*See* Diagram 104)

The pawn on e5 is an important strategical factor on account of the severe cramping effect it exerts on the opponent's King-side; Black

DIAGRAM 104

Position after 8 ..., P–B3

therefore decides to exchange this dangerous pawn even at the cost of allowing his own King-pawn to become a weakness. It is clear that White cannot avoid the exchange; he can only choose to make it in the most favourable way. An immediate exchange by 9 P×P would only contribute to Black's development, so it would seem that the best course lies in covering the King-pawn and forcing Black to do the exchanging himself. The most obvious line is 9 Q–K2, P×P; 10 N×P, N×N; 11 Q×N, N–B3, when the White Queen acts as a blockader and prevents the formation of a strong Black centre after an eventual P–K4. We have seen, however, that the Queen is generally an unsuitable piece for blockading purposes, and in any case it would be difficult to maintain the Queen on e5, for Black can always threaten B–Q3. Nimzowitsch therefore chooses a different manoeuvre, which shows his deep understanding of the strategical character of the position: he prepares to use his

Bishop to blockade the enemy King-pawn.

9 P–QN4!	B–K2
10 B–KB4	P×P
11 N×P	N×N
12 B×N	N–B3

The attempt to fight at once for control of the square e5 by 12 ..., B–KB3; 13 Q–R5 ch, P–N3; 14 B×P ch!, P×B; 15 Q×NP ch, K–K2; 16 B×B ch, N×B; 17 Q–N7 ch loses for Black.

13 N–Q2!

Here White could have played to win a pawn by Q–B2, but this would have been a false step: after 13 Q–B2, O–O!; 14 B×N, B×B; 15 B×P ch, K–R1 followed by P–K4, Black, in view of his mobile centre and *two Bishops*, has the advantage. The pawn hunt therefore would result in diverting White from the correct strategical plan, which is the blockading of the central squares d4 and e5.

| 13 ... | O–O |
| 14 N–B3 | B–Q3 |

DIAGRAM 105

Black intends to drive off the blockading piece by Q–B2 and possibly N–N5. The correct plan for White now is to replace the blockading Bishop by his Knight and strengthen his position by Q–K2 and R–K1. For tactical reasons the order of moves is important and it would be a mistake to begin with 15 B–Q4?, Q–B2; 16 Q–K2, N–N5!; 17 P–KR3, P–K4!, which gives Black excellent play. White chooses correctly and brings the Knight to e5 without trouble.

15 Q–K2!	QR–B1

Or 15 ..., B×B; 16 N×B, QR–B1; 17 P–QB4!.

16 B–Q4	Q–B2
17 N–K5	

The space advantage enjoyed by White and the weakness of Black's King-pawn decide the game. The further play, in which White utilizes his positional advantage precisely and quickly, is extremely instructive.

17 ...	B–K1
18 QR–K1	B×N

19 B×B	Q–B3
20 B–Q4	B–Q2
21 Q–B2!	

It is worth while to look back at the note to move thirteen. The attack on h7 becomes effective only when Black's centre is blocked.

21 ...	R–KB2
22 R–K3	P–QN3
23 R–N3	K–R1
24 B×RP!	

Now Black cannot reply 24 ..., N×B because of 25 Q–N6.

24 ...	P–K4
25 B–KN6	R–K2
26 R–K1	Q–Q3
27 B–K3	P–Q5
28 B–N5	R×P
29 R×R	P×R
30 Q×P	K–N1
31 P–QR3	K–B1
32 B–R4	B–K1
33 B–B5	Q–Q5
34 Q×Q	P×Q
35 R×R	K×R
36 B–Q3	K–Q3
37 B×N	P×N
38 P–KR4	Resigns

C. SPECIAL TYPES OF PASSED-PAWN

We consider below three special types: the distant passed-pawn, the protected passed-pawn, and united passed-pawns.

The *distant passed-pawn* is principally known as an end-game factor. An example is the position in Diagram 106; in this, White's Rook-pawn is the distant passed-pawn, for it is farther from the blocked pawns on f4 and f5 than is Black's pawn on c4. White wins quite simply by 1 P–R4, K–Q4; 2 P–R5, K–B4; 3 P–R6, K–N3; 4 K×P, etc. The advantage of the distant passed-pawn is here quite clear: by its advance the Black King is drawn from the defence of White's object of attack, in this case the Black pawn on f5.

In the middle-game, of course, the successful utilization of the distant passed-pawn is much more difficult; but even here there are sometimes possibilities to turn it to effect. It may, for example, tie up some of the enemy pieces at the edge of the board and thereby facilitate an attack on another part of the board; or simplification may be possible, with transposition into an end-game. The following example gives some idea of the influence exerted on the play by a distant passed-pawn.

FLOHR–ROMANOWSKI
(Moscow 1935)

DIAGRAM 107

Position after White's 28th move

White has a passed Rook-pawn, which cannot easily be forced through. Its presence, however, obliges Black to keep at least one piece permanently away from the centre in a position from which it exerts little power. White's blockading piece, on the other hand, is well placed on c5.

28 ...	N–B2

DIAGRAM 106
(Distant passed-pawn)

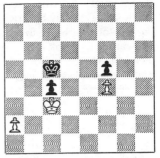

White to play and win

Black wants first of all to drive the Rook from the seventh rank.

29 P–KR3	N–N4
30 R–N7	N–Q3
31 R–N2	N–N4
32 R–Q2	P–B4
33 P–B3	P×P

Helping his opponent, for in the end-game it is White who must strive to open the game on the King's wing. Better was 33 ..., P–B5.

34 P×P	N–N3
35 Q–N4	K–R2

From now on White strives to obtain an end-game with minor pieces.

36 R–KB2	Q–K2
37 R(B1)–KB1	R–KB1
38 Q–K6	Q×Q
39 N×Q	R×R
40 R×R	R–K1
41 N–B5	R–QR1
42 P–R6	K–N1
43 R–R2	N–B1

Even now the pawn cannot be forced through; the remaining Rooks must first be exchanged. White achieves this by driving the Knight on f8 back to g6, thus allowing his Rook to penetrate along the Queen file to the seventh rank; then Black is glad to exchange Rooks.

44 B–B2!	K–B2
45 B–N3	N–N3
46 R–Q2!	R–R2
47 R–Q7 ch	R × R
48 N × R	K–K3
49 N–B5 ch	K–Q3
50 B–B2	N–B2?

This move eases White's task considerably. Stronger was 50 ..., N–B5, after which White must attempt to drive the Knight from its strong position by 51 K–B1 followed by B–K3, K–B2, and K–B3.

51 P–N3	N–QR1

DIAGRAM 108

The conclusion really belongs to a book on the end-game, but it is still a very enlightening example of the theme of converting a distant

passed-pawn: White threatens to advance the pawn and thereby draws Black into an action designed to capture it; the pawn is indeed eventually lost, but Black discovers that its price was too high.

52 K–N2	N–K2
53 K–B3	P–N3
54 N–Q3	N–B1
55 B–B5 ch	

For the time being the Bishop assumes the role of blockader, thus allowing the Knight to prepare an attack on the enemy pawns on e5 and g6.

55 ...	K–K3
56 N–N2	

The duty of constantly guarding the pawn on a6 has confined the Black pieces to inactivity; as a result they are in no position to cope with White's intentions. The immediate threat is 57 N–B4 followed by 58 N–R5 and (after the forced 58 ..., K–Q2) 59 B–B8; then 59 ..., P–R4; 60 P–N4 allows White's King to get among the weak Black pawns.

56 ...	N–Q3

The attempt to foil the above manoeuvre permits decisive simplification.

57 B × N!	K × B
58 N–B4 ch	K–B4

If 58 ..., K–K3, White's King marches to the Queen-side; then after P–R7 it takes up position on b7 to force through the pawn. Black, therefore, prefers to eliminate the arch-enemy, even though he must pay with two of his own pawns.

59 N×P	K–N3
60 N×NP	K×P

Now Black has acquired a distant passed-pawn, on c6, but in view of White's material and positional superiority this is quite unimportant.

61 P–K5	K–N2
62 K–K4	K–B2
63 K–B5	K–Q2
64 P–K6 ch	K–K1
65 N–K5!	P–B4
66 N–Q7!	P–B5
67 N–B6 ch	K–B1
68 N–Q5	K–N2
69 K–K4	Resigns

The second of the three types of passed-pawn to be considered is the *protected passed-pawn*. From the position in Diagram 109 White, who has a protected passed-pawn on g4, wins easily: his King marches to the Queen-side, captures the enemy Queen-Rook-pawn, and returns to the King-side to force through his own passed-pawn. The advantage of the protected passed-pawn is twofold: on the one hand its threat to advance to the queening square at a suitable moment is a decided bind for the enemy King; on the other its immunity to attack by the enemy King leaves its own King free to wander off in search of booty. Even in the middle-game the latent threat of its advance is an important factor, especially as its protected status generally leaves it unworried by attacks from enemy pieces. The following game shows something of its value.

DIAGRAM 109
(Protected passed-pawn)

White wins

GLIGORIĆ–SÁNCHEZ

(Interzonal Tournament 1952)

1 P–Q4	N–KB3
2 P–QB4	P–K3
3 N–QB3	P–Q4
4 P×P	N×P
5 N–B3	B–K2

Better is 5 ..., P–QB4!

6 P–K4	N×N
7 P×N	P–QB4
8 B–QB4	O–O
9 O–O	N–Q2
10 Q–K2	Q–B2

More promising is 10 ..., P×P; 11 P×P, N–B3 followed by P–QN3 and B–N2.

11 R–Q1	P–QR3
12 P–QR4	P–QN3
13 P–Q5	P–K4

Or 13 ..., P×P; 14 B×QP, B–N2; 15 P–B4. After the text-move there arises one of those typical positions that illustrate the advantage of the protected passed-pawn.

DIAGRAM 110

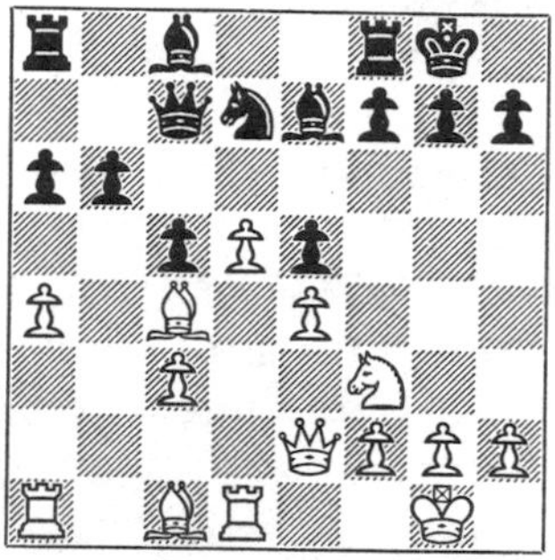

Position after 13 ..., P–K4

14 N–K1!

A very important move, which prevents the Black Knight from blockading the passed-pawn. If now 14 ..., N–B3 (intending N–K1–Q3), then White replies 15 P–B4, with the following pos-sibilities—

(*a*) 15 ..., P×P?; 16 P–K5 winning;

(*b*) 15 ..., N–K1; 16 P×P, Q×P; 17 N–B3, Q×BP; 18 B–N2, etc.

(*c*) 15 ..., B–Q3; 16 N–B3, B–N5; 17 P–B5 with advantage to White.

14 ...	B–Q3
15 N–B2	R–K1
16 B–Q3	N–B1
17 N–K3	N–N3
18 P–N3	

This move not only keeps Black's

Knight from f4; it also prepares the strategically important advance P–KB4. The unfavourable forma-tion of Black's pieces is now apparent; even the natural develo-ping move B–Q2 is unplayable on account of the under-protected pawn on a6, which cannot be advanced to safety without depriv-ing Black of all counter-chances on the Queen-side.

| 18 ... | B–N2 |
| 19 N–B4! | |

A well-known strategical motif. White prepares to exchange the blockading piece and, by threaten-ing to win a pawn with 20 R–N1, gains a tempo.

| 19 ... | KR–N1 |
| 20 B–K3? | |

An inaccuracy, which Black could have exploited by 20 ..., B–KB1!, threatening P–QN4. Cor-rect was the immediate exchange of the blockading Bishop. Fortunately for White, his opponent is blind to the importance of this piece and lets slip the chance of retaining it.

20 ...	B–QB1?
21 N×B	Q×N
22 P–B3	P–KR4
23 Q–KB2!	

A very important move, which on the one hand prepares the advance P–KB4 and on the other forces the blocking of the Queen-side. The immediate threat is 24 P–R5!, winning the pawn on c5.

| 23 ... | P–R4 |
| 24 P–KB4! | |

110

With this move White launches the next stage of his plan—an action on the King's wing. He now threatens 25 P–B5, N–B1; 26 B–K2, P–N3; 27 P×P, P×P; 28 R–KB1, R–R2; 29 Q–B6. In view of this, Black is virtually forced to exchange on f4 in order, after P–B5 by White, to have the square e5 for his Knight. By so exchanging, however, he contributes to a strengthening of White's centre and must, on that account, constantly reckon with the advance P–K5 by White.

24 ...	P×P
25 P×P	B–N5
26 R–Q2	Q–Q2
27 B–KB1	

Also good was 27 P–K5, but White is unwilling to allow his opponent the slightest counterchance, which he might possibly then get by the manoeuvre N–K2–B4.

27 ...	B–R6
28 B×B	Q×B
29 Q–N3!	Q–R5

If 29 ..., Q×Q ch; 30 P×Q, White, by P–B4 and R–QN1, can use his superior position without much trouble. Even after the text-move he could still have played for an exchange of Queens, so obtaining an end-game advantage: 30 Q×Q, N×Q; 31 K–B2, R–K1; 32 P–K5.

| 30 B–B2 | Q–B3 |

Bad would be 30 ..., Q×BP; 31 Q×Q, N×Q; 32 B–N3, P–KN4;

33 B×N, P×B; 34 P–B4, with a won ending for White.

| 31 P–B5 |

White renounces the advance P–K5 and instead selects a rather long-drawn-out plan, which nevertheless is quite safe: he will exchange Black's Knight and in the ensuing end-game with heavy pieces make use of his protected passed-pawn in the attack on Black's b-pawn.

31 ...	N–K4
32 K–R1	R–K1
33 R–K2	N–N5
34 B–N1	Q–K4
35 Q–B3	Q–B3
36 R–KB1	QR–Q1
37 P–R3	Q–R5
38 B–R2	N×B

Weaker is 38 ..., N–B3; 39 R(1)–K1, when White has the threats B–B7 and Q–N3.

| 39 K×N | R–K4 |
| 40 R–KN1 | R–Q2 |

Somewhat better was 40 ..., K–B1; 41 P–B4, when White's task is probably more difficult than in the actual game.

| 41 R(2)–KN2! | P–B3 |
| 42 R–K2 | |

By this Rook manoeuvre, White has completely closed in the Black Queen, which can now be exchanged without trouble.

42 ...	K–R1
43 P–B4	K–N1
44 R(1)–K1	K–B1
45 Q–N3	Q×Q ch

46 K×Q	K–K1
47 R–QN1	R–N2
48 K–B4	K–Q1

DIAGRAM 111

White ends the game with a

characteristic manoeuvre: he sacrifices the protected passed-pawn, winning in exchange the pawn on b6; his Rooks then pierce the enemy position.

49 P–Q6!	K–Q2
50 R(2)–QN2	K–B3
51 P–Q7	K×P
52 R×P	R–B2
53 R–Q1 ch	K–K1
54 R–Q5	Resigns

After 54 ..., R(4)–K2; 55 R–N8 ch, K–B2; 56 R(5)–Q8 there is no way of avoiding loss of material.

The protected passed-pawn is by no means an advantage under all conditions. Its value is much diminished if the opponent can blockade it, preferably with a Knight, and then begin an action designed to undermine it, similar to that arising from the position in Diagram 112. Here Black will endeavour to put pressure on both the supporting pawns, especially that on e4, which is not protected by a neighbouring pawn; his plan will be an attack against c4 by P–QR3 and P–QN4 and against e4 by P–KN3 and P–KB4.

DIAGRAM 112

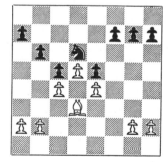

Our next example throws some light on the problems associated with creating and using a protected passed-pawn. The course of the game shows how White's protected passed-pawn is gradually reduced to a mere blocked, and very weak, passed-pawn, whereas Black's is able to advance at a suitable moment and bring him victory.

CHRISTOFFEL–
BOLESLAVSKI

(Groningen 1946)

(*See* Diagram 113)

White has managed to obtain a protected passed-pawn, but in this position it brings him no advantage, for Black has already blockaded the pawn and can soon prepare an action on the King-side by the advance P–KB4.

DIAGRAM 113

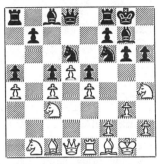

Position after Black's 17th move

18 B–QR3?

A developing move of doubtful value. White allows himself to be misled by the prospects of aggressive tactical threats on the b-file; these, however, in no way make up for the faulty posting of the Bishop. The correct move was 18 P–B3, after which the game is about equal.

| 18 ... | P–QN3 |
| 19 Q–N3 | R–R3 |

Virtually forced, for 19 ..., R–N1? is answered by 20 B×P. The passive position of Black's Rook after the text-move led White to assess the position as in his favour. In the tournament-book, however, Euwe put forward the correct view that Black's Rook on a6 is no worse placed than White's Queen on b3.

| 20 Q–B2 | N–R2 |
| 21 N–N5! | |

A motif that has already appeared in the section dealing with the blockade of a passed-pawn; White intends to exchange off the blockading piece. Tactically the move is based on the following interesting variation: 21 ..., N×N; 22 BP×N (not 22 R×N?, B–Q2; 23 QR–N1, Q–K1, after which White's pawn on a4 is lost), R–R2; 23 N–B3 and it is now White who can blockade a protected passed-pawn with a Knight; his position would certainly be favourable, for the Knight from c4 controls the opponent's blockading square (d6) and at the same time attacks the pawns on e5 and b6.

| 21 ... | N–KN4! |
| 22 K–R1? | |

Now the position has altered and an exchange on b5 brings Black an advantage. White ought therefore to have made the exchange himself with 22 N×N.

| 22 ... | N×N! |
| 23 BP×N | |

Not 23 R×N?, which fails for the same reasons as given in the note to White's twenty-first move.

| 23 ... | R–R2 |

Now White cannot easily bring his Knight to c4: the square f3 is no longer available and 24 N–N2, N–B6 gives Black an overpowering positional advantage after N–Q5 and P–KB4.

| 24 B–QN2 | Q–Q3 |

Generally, as we have said before,

113

the Queen is not a suitable piece for blockading a pawn; in this case, however, it is well placed on d6, for besides acting as blockader it protects the pawns on e5 and g6, thereby preparing the important advance P–KB4.

25	Q–Q2	R–K2
26	B–N2	B–R6!

The exchange of Bishops is in Black's favour because the control that White thereby loses over e4 and d5 adds strength to Black's advance P–KB4.

27	B × B	N × B
28	N–N2	N–N4

White was threatening 29 P–KB4 as well as 29 N–K3 followed by N–B4. Black counters with a threat to win the exchange by N–B6.

29 Q–Q1

Takes care of Black's threat and at the same time prepares the transfer of White's Knight to the blockading square c4. Black cannot indeed counter 30 N–K3 by 31 ..., N × P on account of 32 N–B4; he has, however, already completed his preparations for the decisive action.

29	...	P–KB4!
30	P × P	P × P

(*See* Diagram 114)

The diagram shows just how much the position has changed from that shown in the previous diagram: both supports for White's pawn on d5 have disappeared, leaving this pawn as a weakness in

DIAGRAM 114

Position after 30 ..., P × P

White's position; Black's pawn on c5, on the other hand, has now become very strong and its advance will eventually decide the game. It is important to note that Black's pawn on c5 cannot easily be blockaded by the opposing Knight, for after 31 N–K3, P–KB5!; 32 N–B4, Q–Q2 Black obtains a decisive attack—

(*a*) 33 B × P, Q–R6; 34 B × P, R × R ch; 35 Q × R, R × B!; 36 P × R, Q–KB6 ch; 37 K–N1, N–R6 ch; 38 K–B1, Q–Q6 ch, etc., or 34 B × B, P–B6; 35 R–KN1, R–K7!; 36 R–QN2 (or Q–KB1), N–K5!, etc.

(*b*) 33 N × KP, Q–Q3! (not Q–R6?; 34 N–B6); 34 N–B3, R × R ch; 35 N × R, B–Q5!; 36 B × B, Q × P ch, etc.

(*c*) 33 N × NP, Q–R6; 34 P–Q6, P × P; 35 Q–Q5 ch. R–K3!, etc.

(*d*) 33 P–Q6, Q–QN2 ch, etc.

31 P–B4

This stops the advance P–KB5 by Black, but it leaves the excellent square e4 open for the Black Knight.

31 ...	N–K5
32 K–N1 ?	

Hastens defeat. A longer defence was possible after 32 R–KB1.

32 ...	P–B5 !

The advance at the right moment brings with it two threats: the further advance of the pawn to c3 and the check by the Queen from c5.

33 P×P	B×P

34 B×B	R×B

Now the threats are N–B6 and R×P. The game is as good as over.

35 N–K3	N–B6
36 Q–Q4	N×R
37 R×N	R–K5
38 N×KBP	R×Q
39 N×Q	P–B6
40 R–QB1	R×P
41 N–K4	R–Q5
42 N×P	R–QB1
43 Resigns	

United passed-pawns, the third special type of passed-pawn, are the most valuable of all. Their mutual protection and united advance are severe obstacles to any blockade, so it is not surprising that their formation, even at the cost of material, is often sufficient to decide the game. It is interesting to note the position in which three united passed-pawns are pitted against a minor piece—a struggle which occurs with comparative frequency. In the end-game three united passed-pawns are generally superior to either a Knight or a Bishop, but in the middle-game the position is much more complicated, for the extra piece can be used effectively in an attack before the advance of the pawns gets under way. Of course once the Queens have been exchanged the value of the pawns increases, as the following game shows.

BRONSTEIN–NAJDORF

(Match U.S.S.R.–Argentina 1954)

1 P–K4	P–QB4
2 N–KB3	P–Q3
3 P–Q4	P×P
4 N×P	N–KB3
5 N–QB3	P–QR3
6 B–KN5	P–K3
7 Q–B3	QN–Q2
8 O–O–O	Q–B2

9 Q–N3	P–N4
10 B×P !?	P×B
11 N(4)×NP	Q–N1 ?

Also weak is 11 ..., Q–B4?; 12 B–K3, but there was a better move in 11 ..., Q–R4!. After the text-move the Queens are exchanged and White's task is lightened.

12 N×P ch	B×N
13 Q×B	Q×Q
14 R×Q	

DIAGRAM 115

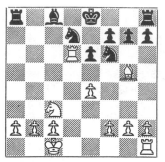

In assessing this position it is worth while repeating Bronstein's remarks on it: "As a result of the piece sacrifice White has won three pawns for the piece, leaving approximate material equality. It would be wrong, however, to judge the position only from the point of view of material advantages. Whereas the activity of the Black Knight can easily be neutralized, the struggle against the White passed-pawns is much more difficult. In this game Black did not fully use the possibilities open to him."

14 ...   P–KR3!
15 B–Q2(?)

Neither 15 B–K3, N–N5 nor 15 B–R4, P–N4 was much good for White. About the possibility of exchanging by 15 B×N Bronstein writes: "In this position White's black-squared Bishop is extremely strong, and it would be a pity to exchange it for a Rook and far more so for a Knight." Probably Bronstein over-estimated the importance of the Bishop, for in a

game from the 1954 Czechoslovak Championship between Fichtl and Dolezal, White played 15 B×N!, N×B; 16 KR–Q1, B–N2; 17 P–B3, K–K2; 18 R–N6!, KR–QN1; 19 P–QN3 and soon used his united pawns to good effect. In the present game Black could still have equalized with correct play.

15 ...   B–N2
16 P–B3   O–O?

The decisive mistake. Correct was 16 ..., O–O–O, after which the King plays an important role in the fight against the White pawns while an attack is launched on the King-side by P–N4–N5. The position would offer several possibilities, with about equal chances for both sides. One thing it does show is the loss of tempo involved in White's fifteenth move, which should have enabled Black to complete his development and castle long.

17 P–QN3	KR–QB1
18 K–N2	N–B4
19 B–K3	P–K4
20 KR–Q1	N–K3
21 R–N6	B–B3
22 N–Q5	B×N
23 P×B	

The number of united passed-pawns has increased to four and the game is virtually decided.

23 ...	N–B4
24 R–N5	N(3)–Q2
25 P–QB4	P–K5
26 B×N	

116

Black's two Knights were becoming an obstacle to the advance of the passed-pawns, so White exchanges his Bishop for one of them. White has also in mind a plan to sacrifice one of his pawns to enable the others to force a decision.

26 ...	N × B
27 P × P	N × KP
28 P–Q6!	R × RP ch
29 K × R	N–B6 ch
30 K–R3	N × R(Q8)
31 P–B5	N–B6
32 R–R5	N–Q4
33 P–B6	N–B3
34 R–R6	K–B1
35 P–QN4	K–K1

| 36 P–N5 | N–Q2 |

The final moves of the game were played under extreme time-trouble, and for that reason Black made an attempt to create complications.

37 R–R7	R–N1
38 R × N	R × P
39 R–R7	R–N1
40 P–Q7 ch	K–K2
41 P–Q8(Q) dbl ch	K × Q
42 P–B7 ch	K–B1
43 P × R(Q) ch	K × Q

At this stage Black at last resigned.

More common than cases of three united passed-pawns are those in which only two are formed. It is important in such cases to ensure that the pawns cannot be blockaded by enemy pieces; so, as a rule, the pawns should advance together. For example, if the pawns stand on QN4 and QB4, the advance P–QB5 or P–QN5 should only be made when the way for the advance of the second pawn has been prepared. The following game illustrates clearly the tremendous effect of a blockade on two united passed-pawns.

GLIGORIĆ–SZABÓ
(Helsinki 1952)

1 P–Q4	N–KB3
2 P–QB4	P–K3
3 N–QB3	B–N5
4 P–K3	P–B4
5 KN–K2	P–Q4
6 P–QR3	P × QP
7 KP × P	B–K2
8 P–B5	O–O
9 P–QN4	P–QN3!
10 P–N3	P × P
11 QP × P	

Weaker is 11 NP × P, for after N–B3 and B–R3 by Black, the White passed-pawn is well blockaded and Black obtains play with his pieces.

| 11 ... | P–QR4! |

On the surface an illogical move, for it gives White two united, and advanced, passed-pawns. These pawns, however, are not nearly so dangerous as they seem, for their advanced position allows them to be easily blockaded.

12 R–QN1

Not 12 B–QN2?, N–B3; 13 P–N5, N–K4.

12 ...	P × P
13 P × P	

DIAGRAM 116

At first sight Black's position looks far from promising: he has only one passed-pawn whereas White has two, and these are already on the fourth and fifth ranks; besides, it is clear that the advance of Black's centre pawns will consume a lot of time. We have already remarked, however, that the advanced position of the White pawns actually renders them less dangerous; their advance has preceded the development of the White pieces, whose position is now so unfavourable that the advance of the pawns cannot be continued. Black now exploits this situation to prepare a blockade on the pawns. His strategical plan will consist of two parts—

(i) Blockading the White pawns, especially that on b4; to achieve this a Knight must be brought to b5 (moves 13 to 27).

(ii) Forcing the advance of his centre pawns (moves 18 to 36).

It is worth noting that in blockading united passed-pawns it is generally most important to blockade the backward standing pawn; that way the pawns are deprived of their greatest strength —their ability to advance together.

13 ...	N–B3!

This first blockading move, which runs counter to the above principle, is playable for tactical reasons: 14 P–N5?, N–K4; 15 P–B4, N–B6 ch!; 16 K–B2, B × P ch; 17 K × N, P–Q5! wins for Black.

14 B–KN2	R–N1!
15 B–QR3	

Again P–N5 fails: 15 P–N5, B × P; 16 P × N, R × R; 17 N × R, Q–N3 and Black obtains a strong attack. If White tries 15 Q–R4 Black can answer 15 ..., B–Q2; 16 P–N5, N–K4; 17 P–B6, N–Q6 ch; 18 K–B1 (18 K–Q2, N × P), B × P!; 19 P × B, R × R; 20 N × R, Q–N3, etc.

15 ...	B–Q2!
16 O–O	

For the third time White must renounce P–N5, for after 16 P–N5, N–R4; 17 O–O, N–B5 Black wins a pawn.

16 ...	N–R2!
17 R–K1	N–K1!

Now the second Knight hastens to join in the struggle for the square b5. Much weaker would be 17 ..., N–N4?, 18 N × N, B × N; 19 N–Q4, when White has the move B–KB1 to assist in overcoming the blockade.

18 B–QB1	B–KB3

The first move in the attacking phase of Black's plan. White ought now to play 19 P–B4, N–B2; 20 B–K3 (N–Q4?, B×N ch; 21 Q×B, N–B3), N(B)–N4, though even here Black stands better. Instead, White embarks on a faulty plan: he attempts to draw Black's centre pawns forward, partly in order to attack them and partly to increase the scope for his Bishop on g2.

19 B–B4?	P–K4
20 B–Q2	P–Q5
21 N–Q5	B–B3
22 N×B ch	

White cannot maintain the Knight on d5, for Black can reply to 22 Q–N3 with N–B2. Nevertheless Q–N3 is superior to the text-move because, as we already know, a Knight is a better blockading piece than a Bishop; consequently it was preferable to allow an exchange of the Knight against Black's Knight, now on e8, rather than purposely to exchange the Knight for the Bishop on f6.

22 ...	Q×N
23 B×B	Q×B
24 P–B4	P–B3

Naturally not 17 ..., P×P, which would break up Black's united pawns.

25 Q–N3 ch	K–R1
26 R–KB1	N–B2

27 Q–B4	N(R2)–N4
28 QR–K1	

The end to all dreams of advancing the Queen-side pawns; the pieces are to be re-grouped to help defend against Black's advancing centre pawns. But already it is too late.

28 ...	P–KR3
29 P–N4	

With the intention of blocking the opposing pawns by N–N3–K4.

29 ...	QR–K1?

A tactical error, which should have made Black's task much more difficult. Correct was 29 ..., KR–K1; 30 N–N3, P–K5, with the end in sight. After Black's mistake White ought to have continued 30 P×P, P×P; 31 N–N3, after which 31 ..., R×R ch; 32 Q×R, P–K5? fails against 33 N×P, R×N; 34 Q–B8 ch, K–R2; 35 Q–B5 ch.

30 P–B5?	

White misses his chance and goes in for a desperate attack on the King-side.

30 ...	Q–Q4
31 Q–B1	

Or 31 Q×Q, N×Q; 32 N–N3, R–R1, and Black, in view of the superior position of his pieces, has a won end-game.

31 ...	K–R2
32 N–N3	P–K5
33 B–B4	P–K6
34 Q–Q1	Q–B5!

Prevents a possible blockade of the pawn on d4 by 35 Q–Q3.

35 P–R4	N–Q4
36 P–N5	P–Q6
37 Q–N4	R–KN1!
38 N–R5	R–K5

(*See* Diagram 117)

It is instructive to compare this diagram with the previous one. The White Queen-side pawns have not progressed a single step, whereas Black's central pawns now decide the game.

| 39 P–N6 ch | K–R1 |

40 Q–N3

White resigned.

DIAGRAM 117

Position after 38 ..., R–K5

D. THE ISOLATED PAWN

Every chess player is aware of the trouble brought by a pawn that has become separated from its fellow-pawns and that cannot be supported by one of them. Such a pawn is called an isolated pawn. Since an isolated pawn cannot be protected by the simplest and most economical means, a neighbouring pawn, it can, under certain circumstances, be captured by the opponent; under others the opponent can, by an attack on the pawn, force the defending pieces into a passive position and use his own relatively more active pieces to obtain an advantage elsewhere.

In many chess books the concept "isolated pawn" is applied only to an isolated pawn that stands on an open file and is subject to frontal attack; this interpretation I believe to be wrong, for in many cases an isolated pawn shielded from frontal attack nevertheless proves to be a strategic weakness. It must be admitted, of course, that, where the pawn is on an open file, the additional pressure from the heavy pieces generally makes the attack on the pawn harder to withstand. An example is the following game.

SOKOLSKI–SIMAGIN

(1st U.S.S.R. Correspondence Chess Championship)

1 P–Q4	N–KB3
2 P–QB4	P–KN3
3 N–QB3	P–Q4
4 P×P	N×P
5 P–KN3	B–N2
6 B–N2	N–N3
7 N–B3	O–O
8 O–O	N–B3
9 P–Q5	N–N5
10 P–K4	P–QB3
11 P–QR3	N–R3

12 P×P   **P×P**

DIAGRAM 118

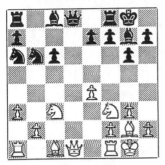

Black is saddled with an unpleasant isolated pawn on c6, but, as some compensation, has an open b-file, which he could use to work up counter-play should White proceed inaccurately. White's task will therefore be to attack the pawn on c6 while at the same time frustrating Black's attempts to exert pressure on b2.

13 Q–B2   **Q–B2**
14 P–QN3!   **P–K4?**

A doubtful move, by which Black voluntarily shuts in his Bishop on g7. Better was 14 ..., B–K3; 15 B–K3, KR–Q1.

15 B–K3   **P–B3**
16 KR–QB1   **B–K3**
17 B–KB1   **Q–N2**
18 N–QR4!

The decisive manoeuvre, after which Black has no reasonable means of protecting the c-pawn.

18 ...   **N×N**

Now White can choose to exploit Black's weak pawn by either direct or indirect methods. If he opts for the former and plays 19 Q×P, Q×Q; 20 R×Q, B×P; 21 R×N, N–N3; 22 B×N, he wins a pawn; but Black has then the advantage of the two Bishops and can put up a stout resistance. White therefore adopts the indirect method of exploiting the weak pawn: he does not take it at once, but instead, by threatening to capture it under more propitious conditions, forces his opponent's pieces into an unfavourable position; he then uses the superior working power of his own pieces to build up a quick attack.

19 P×N   **N–N1**

There is also an easy win after 19 ..., P–QB4; 20 QR–N1, Q–QB3; 21 Q–D3!, B–QB1 (P–B5; 22 R×P!); 22 Q–N3 ch, K–R1; 23 B–QN5, Q–D2; 24 Q–D4, etc.

20 QR–N1   **Q–B2**
21 N–Q2   **R–QB1**
22 P–R5!   **N–Q2**

The threat was 23 P–R6 followed by R–N7. If Black had countered with 22 ..., Q×P; 23 B–QB4, B×B; 24 Q×B ch, K–R1; 25 R–N7, Q–Q1; 26 N–N3, R–B2; 27 R×R, Q×R; 28 R–Q1, he would have been at a loss for a reasonable continuation; e.g. 28 ..., N–Q2; 29 Q–KB7.

23 B–QR6   **Q×P**

This exchange sacrifice does not give Black any great prospects of making a long stand, but the withdrawal of the Rook by 23 ...

KR–N1 is no better, on account of 24 Q×P.

24 B×R	R×B
25 R–N7	P–QB4
26 Q–Q3	Q–R5
27 Q–Q6	R–B3
28 Q–K7	B–B1

As a reply to 28 ..., R–R3, Sokolski gives the continuation 29 Q–K8 ch, N–B1 (B–B1; 30 B–R6); 30 R×B ch!, K×R; 31 Q–K7 ch, B–B2; 32 B–R6 ch!, winning.

29 Q–K8	Resigns

If 29 ..., R–Q3, then 30 B–R6 followed by R×N, and if 29 ..., R–N3, then 30 R×R, B–B2; 31 R–R6!, etc.

Although we have just explained its drawbacks, the isolated pawn should not be considered as a weakness in all circumstances. True, in the end-game it is basically almost always a serious disadvantage; but in the middle-game there are occasions when it can become an important attacking factor. For the sake of simplicity we shall, from now on, deal only with the isolated Queen-pawn, which shows most clearly the conflict between static weakness and dynamic strength. The isolated Queen-pawn occurs in numerous games, especially those opening with the Queen's Gambit; the different positions in which it occurs can be classified according to whether the opponent's Queen-Bishop-pawn or King-pawn has disappeared from the board. The first case can arise after the moves **1 P–Q4, P–Q4; 2 P–QB4, P×P; 3 N–KB3, N–KB3; 4 P–K3, P–K3; 5 B×P, P–B4; 6 O–O, P×P; 7 P×P!** and the second after **1 P–Q4, P–Q4; 2 P–QB4, P–K3; 3 N–QB3, N–KB3; 4 B–N5, B–K2; 5 P–K3, O–O; 6 N–B3, QN–Q2; 7 R–B1, P–B3; 8 B–Q3, P×P; 9 B×BP, N–Q4; 10 B×B, Q×B; 11 O–O, N×N; 12 R×N, P–K4; 13 Q–B2, P×P; 14 P×P.**

DIAGRAM 119

We shall first examine the case in which the isolated Queen-pawn is opposed by a King-pawn on K3; a typical pawn structure is that in Diagram 119. The study of the end-game shows that such a pawn structure is unfavourable to the side with the isolated pawn, the weakness of which in simplified positions can often be exploited for winning purposes by the opponent. In the middle-game the position is much more complicated. There the isolated pawn can, in certain circumstances, attain a dynamic strength when favourable piece development creates the threat of P–Q5; sometimes, even, the pawn may be usefully sacrificed to achieve this advance. Further, the pawn supplies two good operation bases for a Knight: on c5, especially when Black, as he often does, has played P–QR3 and P–QN4 in order to develop his Bishop at b7, and on e5; from this latter square White's Knight can often help to work up an attack against the enemy King, and if Black tries to dislodge it with P–KB3 his King-pawn becomes weak.

We now give some rules as a guide to the correct handling of positions whose pawn structure resembles that schematically presented in Diagram 119.

For White

1. Avoidance of any great simplification.

2. The pieces must be so posted as to allow the advance P–Q5 at a suitable moment or to force Black to tie up his pieces in stopping this advance.

3. He must occupy the square e5 with a Knight and attack on the King-side or occupy the square c5 and operate on the Queen Bishop file.

For Black

1. The advance of the isolated pawn must be prevented; this can best be done by posting a Knight, or failing that a Bishop, on d5 (blockading the isolated pawn).

2. The pieces should be so placed (e.g. Nc6, Bf6) as to tie the opposing pieces to the defence of the pawn.

3. He must seek simplification and endeavour to reach an endgame.

We now follow with a few examples that exemplify the above principles.

	SZABÓ–VAN SETERS	
	(Hilversum 1947)	
1	P–Q4	N–KB3
2	P–QB4	P–K3
3	N–QB3	B–N5
4	P–K3	P–B4
5	B–Q3	P–Q4
6	N–B3	O–O
7	O–O	N–B3

8	P–QR3	P×QP
9	KP×P	P×P
10	B×BP	B–K2

(*See* Diagram 120)

Now we have one of those positions in which there is an isolated pawn on Q4. It is worth noting in this case the importance of White's pawn on QR3. On the one hand it

DIAGRAM 120

Position after 10 ..., B–K2

prevents the blockading of the Queen-pawn by N–QN5–Q4 on the part of Black; on the other it prepares for White the developing move Q–Q3, which, in conjunction with the further moves B–KN5, QR–Q1, and B–QR2–N1, can be used to launch an attack on the King's wing. Another possible set-up of the White pieces, and one recommended by Nimzowitsch, is Q–K2, B–K3, KR–Q1, and QR–B1; in this, White first develops all his pieces and waits for a suitable moment before beginning the attack. However, experience over a number of years, particularly exemplified in some of Alekhine's games, shows that the system adopted here by Szabó is preferable; the speedy action it permits against the opposing King is most effective.

11 R–K1   P–QN3

More solid than 11 .... P–QR3; 12 B–KN5, P–QN4; 13 B–R2, B–N2, after which the weakness of the square c5 makes itself felt; e.g. 14 Q–Q3, N–Q4; 15 N–K4!.

12 Q–Q3   B–N2
13 B–KN5   R–B1(?)

Black underestimates the danger that the aggressive posting of White's pieces presents; he believes he has sufficient time to complete his development undisturbed. After 13 ..., N–Q4 White has the choice between two good continuations—

(*a*) 14 B×N, P×B (B×B; 15 B–K4 with advantage); 15 B×B, N×B; 16 N–KN5, N–N3; 17 P–KR4!, P–KR3; 18 N–K6!, P×N; 19 Q×N, Q×P; 20 Q×KP ch, K–R1; 21 Q–K3, QR–K1!; 22 Q–Q2!, and White has a positional superiority: the Knight is, in this position, better than the Bishop, and White has also the square e5 for his pieces.

(*b*) 14 N–K4, R–B1; 15 B–R2 followed by QR–Q1 and B–N1, giving White good attacking chances.

14 QR–Q1   Q–B2?

A continuation of the faulty plan begun with the previous move. Instead, Black ought to work towards simplification; therefore, 14 ..., N–Q4 was better, though even here White has the upper hand.

15 B–R2   KR–Q1
16 P–R3

Forestalls the tactical complications that would arise after 16 ..., N–KN5.

16 ...   R–Q2

Black continues to play in much

too routine a fashion. He now prepares to double Rooks with 17 ..., QR–Q1 and put pressure on White's Queen-pawn; but meanwhile White achieves the decisive break-through.

DIAGRAM 121

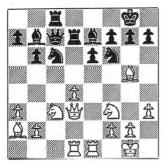

Position after 16 ..., R–Q2

17 P–Q5! N×P

If 17 ..., P×P, White replies decisively with 18 B–N1!, P–N3; 19 R×B and 20 B×N.

18 B×N Q–Q1

Black resorts to this move

because of lack of alternatives: 18 ..., P×B; 19 N×P gives White the exchange and 18 ..., QR–Q1 is answered by 19 R×P!. After the text-move Black can reply to 18 R×P with 19 ..., B×B.

19 Q–K4

The decisive manoeuvre. If Black now goes in for 19 ..., B×B; 20 B×P!, he loses at least the exchange.

19 ...	P×B
20 N×P	B×B
21 N×B	P–N3

Obviously not 21 ..., Q×N; 22 Q–K8 ch and mate next move. The position, however, can no longer be held.

22 Q–KR4	P–KR4
23 N–B6 ch	Q×N
24 R×R	N–Q1
25 R–K8 ch	K–N2
26 R×P ch!	Resigns

After 26 ..., N×R, Black loses his Queen to 27 N–K6 ch.

In this game White decided the issue in his favour by succeeding in playing P–Q5; in the next example White manages to build up a strong attack without advancing the Queen-pawn.

BOTVINNIK–VIDMAR

(Nottingham 1936)

1 P–QB4	P–K3
2 N–KB3	P–Q4
3 P–Q4	N–KB3
4 N–QB3	B–K2
5 B–N5	O–O
6 P–K3	QN–Q2
7 B–Q3	P–B4
8 O–O	P×QP
9 KP×P	

Not 9 KN×P?, N–K4.

9 ...	P×P
10 B×BP	N–N3

According to Botvinnik 10 ... P–QR3 was better; the idea would then be to develop by P–QN4 and B–N2. It should be noted that the weakness of the square c5 is in this case not so important, as it is kept under observation by the Knight, which has been played to d7

125

instead of c6. If in reply to 10
..., P–QR3 White tries 11 P–QR4,
then the weakness of the square
b4 gives Black the opportunity to
establish his pieces advantageously
after the manoeuvre N–N3–Q4.

| 11 B–N3 | B–Q2 |
| 12 Q–Q3 | QN–Q4? |

Here Black neglects an important
principle in the struggle against the
isolated Queen-pawn—simplification. He should have played 12
..., N(B3)–Q4 with the threat of
N–N5. White then achieves
nothing with 13 B–B2, P–N3, and
if instead 13 B–K3, N×N; 14
P×N, B–QR5, or 13 N–K4, B–
QR5!, Black can always obtain a
valuable reduction in material.

| 13 N–K5 | B–B3 |
| 14 QR–Q1 | |

DIAGRAM 122

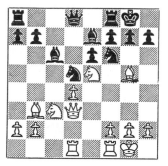

A typical grouping of pieces for
both sides. White's pieces are so
posted that they can be quickly
mobilized for an attack on the
enemy King; they are also well
placed to support the advance
P–Q5, should a suitable opportunity arise. Black for his part has
managed to fortify the important
square d5, so blockading the
isolated pawn. There is however
one disagreeable feature in Black's
set-up, the unfavourable position
of his Bishop on c6, which would
be much better placed on b7. At
present the Bishop hinders the use
of the open c-file, which ought to
be a means for Black of gaining
counter-play; in addition White is
given the opportunity of removing
the Bishop whenever this is favourable. It should be noted, however,
that an immediate exchange of the
Bishop, far from bringing White
an advantage, would merely
strengthen the blockade on d5; the
weakness to Black's c-pawn would
then prove extremely difficult to
exploit.

| 14 ... | N–QN5? |

Black underestimates the dynamic potentialities of his opponent's position and thereby loses.
He embarks on a time-wasting
manoeuvre, allowing White to
initiate a direct King-side attack.
Better was 14 ..., Q–R4 or 14
..., R–B1.

| 15 Q–R3! | B–Q4 |
| 16 N×B | N(5)×N? |

The final mistake, which is
similar to the first (*see* move 12).
It was essential to play 16 ...,
N(3)×N; 17 B–B1, R–B1, a
typical continuation, in which the
offer to exchange gains time for
Black and forces the opposing
pieces to withdraw from their
aggressive positions.

126

17 P–B4!

This move deserves special attention. In many positions with an isolated Queen-pawn it is a weakening move; in this position it is very strong, for it is combined with the irresistible threat P–KB5.

17 ...　　　　**R–B1**

If 17 ..., P–KN3, Black loses the exchange after 18 B–R6, R–K1; 19 B–R4. Should Black try 17 ..., N–K5, the elegant sacrifice 18 N×P!, R×N (K×N; 19 QR–K1!); 19 Q×KP brings White a clearly won position.

18 P–B5　　　　**P×P**

After 18 ..., Q–Q3; 19 P×P, P×P (Q×P, 20 Q–KB3), 20 KR–K1 Black's King-pawn becomes very weak.

19 R×P　　　　**Q–Q3**

Better, though still not sufficient, is 19 ..., R–B2; 20 (R1)–KB1; e.g.—

    (*a*) 20 ..., P–QR3; 21 N×P, R×N; 22 B(3)×N, N×B; 23 R×R, B×B; 24 Q–K6!.

    (*b*) 20 ..., N–N3; 21 Q–R4 (threatening R×N), N(N3)–Q4; 22 N×P, R×N; 23 B(3)×N, N×B; 24 R×R, B×B; 25 Q×B (analysis by Panov).

DIAGRAM 123

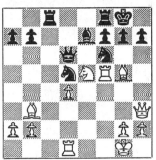

Position after 19 ..., Q–Q3

20 N×P!　　　　**R×N**

Or 20 ..., K×N; 21 B×N ch.

21 B(N5)×N　　　　**B×B**

Here 21 ..., N×B fails against 22 R×N! followed by Q×R ch.

22 R×N　　　　**Q–B3**

A final trap. If now 23 R–QB5?, then Black has the reply 23 ..., B×P ch.

23 R–Q6　　　　**Q–K1**

24 R–Q7　　　　**Resigns**

In these two games the possessor of the isolated pawn was victorious; in each case he managed to secure the better positioning of his pieces and was able either to exploit the dynamic force of the pawn or else to use the operation bases created by the pawn in a decisive attack. It is interesting to note that in many variations of the Queen's Gambit and Nimzo-Indian, the possessor of the isolated Queen-pawn is in practice more likely to succeed in his task than his opponent. This is not to say that possession of the isolated Queen-pawn is an advantage in itself; it merely indicates the difficulties involved in the struggle to exploit the weakness of the isolated Queen-pawn.

In our previous two games, the isolated Queen-pawn was on the winning side mainly owing to faulty defence by the opponent. This is a frequent occurrence; yet it should not be forgotten that the possessor of the isolated Queen-pawn, too, may easily be enticed into faulty play, generally an over-hasty attempt to attack on the King-side. In such cases the weakness of the isolated pawn makes itself felt, especially when most of the minor pieces have been exchanged. Our next example is one in which White, with an isolated Queen-pawn, embarks on an attack, while his opponent defends with skill.

BOTVINNIK–FLOHR

(Groningen 1946)

1 P–Q4	P–Q4
2 N–KB3	N–KB3
3 P–B4	P–K3
4 N–B3	P–B4
5 BP×P	N×P
6 P–K3	QN–B3
7 B–Q3	P×P
8 P×P	B–K2
9 O–O	O–O
10 R–K1	N(3)–N5
11 B–K4	

Better is the immediate B–N1.

11 ...	N–KB3
12 B–N1	P–QN3
13 N–K5	B–N2

DIAGRAM 124

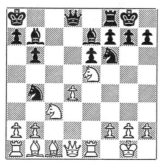

14 R–K3!?

In this position, with the Bishop

already on b1 instead of d3 or b3, Botvinnik decides on a direct attack even though his development is not complete. However, if he were first to proceed with the usual B–N5, P–QR3, and Q–Q3, he would be two tempi behind compared with the normal development in such positions.

14 ...	QN–Q4
15 R–R3	P–N3

A move that sooner or later is necessary, since the continual pressure on h7 is unbearable.

16 B–R6	R–K1
17 Q–Q2	R–QB1
18 B–Q3	P–QR3!
19 R–K1	P–QN4

In this position a good move, for White is not prepared to exploit the weakness on c5. Black's counter-play on the Queen-side just about balances White's King-side attack.

20 R–N3

White now threatens to decide the game by the double sacrifice 21 N×KNP!, RP×N; 22 B×KNP!.

20 ...	N–R4

21 R–R3	KN–B3
22 B–N1	

Since Black has adequate counter-play, a draw by repetition would be a logical conclusion to the game.

22 ...	R–B2
23 R–N3	N–R4
24 R–R3	KN–B3
25 Q–K2	

Now the threat is 26 N×BP, which Black parries by active play.

25 ...	N×N

For a moment Black transforms his opponent's isolated pawn into hanging pawns; with his next move, however, he will deprive the Queen-pawn of its newly acquired protector.

26 P×N	P–N5!

Now 27 N×BP fails against 27 ..., Q–Q4 followed by K×N.

DIAGRAM 125

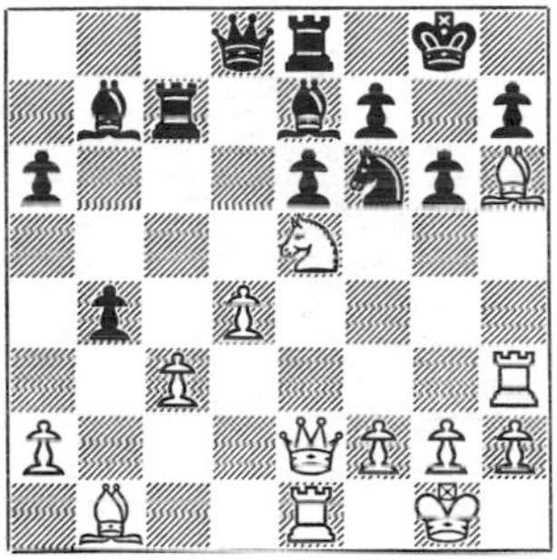

Position after 26 ..., P–N5

27 R–N3	R×P!
28 N×BP!	Q–Q4!
29 N–K5?	

Correct was 29 R–N5!, Q–B5; 30 B×P!, P×B; 31 R×P ch, K×N; 32 R–N7 ch, K–B1; 33 R–N6 dis ch with a draw by perpetual check. Botvinnik either overlooked this fine tactical manoeuvre or else attempted to avoid the draw. Now, however, he suddenly finds himself in an extremely difficult position.

29 ...	R×R
30 BP×R	Q×QP ch
31 K–R1	B–Q3

A quicker way of realizing his advantage was 31 ..., B–Q4.

32 B–B4	N–R4?

A blunder which loses a piece, though, astonishingly, not the game. Correct was 32 ..., N–Q4. After this oversight, the game is deprived of its logical continuity.

33 R–Q1	N×B
34 P×N	Q×P

After 34 ..., Q–B4 or 34 ..., Q–N3, White plays 35 N–Q7! winning.

35 R×B	B–Q4
36 B–B2!	R–KB1

Here and on the next move Black could still have played for a win with B×RP.

37 P–KR3	Q–KB8 ch?
38 Q×Q	R×Q ch
39 K–R2	R–B7
40 R×B!	P×R
41 B–N3	K–N2

Draw agreed, for after 42 N–Q3, R–Q7; 43 N×P, P–QR4; 44 N×P, P–R5; 45 B–B4, R–Q5; 46 N–N6, K–B3 White's advantage is not sufficient to win.

Now let us turn to positions in which the isolated Queen-pawn is not faced by an enemy King-pawn; the pawn structure is that shown in Diagram 126. There are several differences between this and the positions considered earlier. In the first place the open King file is not blocked by minor pieces as in the case of the open Queen-Bishop file, where there were generally

DIAGRAM 126

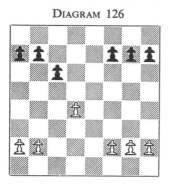

Knights on c3 and c6; consequently there is more scope for the Rooks on the open King file. Sometimes the possessor of the isolated pawn can use the King file to mobilize his pieces for a strong attack; on other occasions the opponent can turn the open King file to his advantage and by exchanging pieces reach a won end-game. A second difference is one associated with the important strategical point c5, which corresponds to e5 in positions of the earlier type; from this square a White Knight is generally less effective than the corresponding Knight on e5, for the Knight on c5 only attacks the point b7 whereas that on e5 is a danger to the opposing King.

We first give an example illustrating the successful fight against the isolated pawn.

BOTVINNIK–BRONSTEIN

(World Championship Match 1951)

1	P–Q4	P–K3
2	P–K4	P–Q4
3	N–Q2	P–QB4
4	KP × P	KP × P
5	KN–B3	N–KB3
6	B–N5 ch	B–Q2
7	B × B ch	QN × B
8	O–O	B–K2
9	P × P	N × P

(*See* Diagram 127)

A position that often results from this variation of the French defence. Although the exchange of white-squared Bishops on move 7

DIAGRAM 127

Position after 9 ..., N × P

was in itself advantageous for Black, it had several favourable features for White too. On the one hand it speeded up White's development; on the other it forced Black's pieces into an unfavourable position, leaving the Bishop on e7 instead of c5 and the Knight on c5 instead of the much more useful square c6.

10 N–Q4!

This well-known blockading of the passed-pawn is combined with the threat N–B5.

10 ...	Q–Q2
11 N(2)–B3	O–O
12 N–K5	Q–B1
13 B–N5	R–K1
14 N–Q3	

This manoeuvre aimed at simplification is correct. Another good idea is 14 P–QB3, strengthening the blockade.

14 ...	N×N
15 Q×N	Q–N5
16 B–K3	B–B4
17 P–KR3	Q–N3?

A frequent mistake in such positions. After the exchange of Queens Black loses all the tactical possibilities that are usual in the middle-game (e.g. attack against the King) and concedes White a lasting positional advantage. For this reason the correct move was 17 ..., Q–R4, after which White can only force the exchange of Queens at the cost of giving Black adequate counter-play; e.g. 18 Q–B5, B×N; 19 Q×Q, N×Q; 20 B×B, R–K7; 21 KR–B1, R–QB1.

18 Q×Q	RP×Q
19 QR–Q1	R–K5
20 P–QB3	P–QN3

21 N–B2	R–Q1
22 R–Q3	K–B1

In positions like this the exchange of the black-squared Bishops frequently hampers the attack against the isolated pawn, for White's Bishop can, if allowed to remain, be used to eliminate the best protection for the pawn—the Knight on f6. Black, however, dare not exchange Bishops at once, owing to the pawn loss which results: 22 ..., B×B; 23 N×B, P–Q5; 24 KR–Q1 or 23 ..., R–Q2; 24 KR–Q1, R–K4; 25 P–QB4, etc.

23 KR–Q1	K–K2
24 K–B1	

Even stronger appears to be 24 P–KN4 followed by K–N2.

24 ...	K–Q2
25 B–N5	K–B3

Black has succeeded in bringing his King, for the time being, to the assistance of the beleaguered pawn. The following forced defence, however, draws Black's pieces into an extremely poor position.

26 P–QN4!	B–B1

After 26 ..., B–K2 White can choose between 27 N–K3 and 27 N–Q4 ch, K–N2; 28 P–N5 followed by 29 N–B6, in both cases with advantage.

27 N–K3	R–K4

(*See* Diagram 128)

All the White pieces are now directed towards the attack on the isolated pawn. The correct and logical continuation is 28 B×N!,

DIAGRAM 128

Position after 27 ..., R-K4

P × B, after which there are three ways of winning the pawn—

(a) 29 P–QB4, P–Q5 (B×P; 30 N×P); 30 N–B2.

(b) 29 P–QR3, and there is no adequate counter to the threat 30 P–QB4.

(c) 29 P–KB4!, R–R4; 30 P–B4, B×P; 31 N×P, B–Q3; 32 N×BP, R(4)–R1; 33 N–K4, B–K2; 34 R×R, R×R; 35 R×R, B×R; 36 K–K2, P–B4; 37 N–N5 and the Knight heads for e5, securing the win.

White misses the correct line and makes a mistake that throws away the win.

28 P–KB4?	R–K5
29 P–B5	

Now 29 B×N fails against 29 ..., R×BP ch; 30 K–N1, R×B.

29 ...	R–K4!
30 B–B4	

Once again exchanging off the Knight leads to failure: 30 B×N, P×B; 31 P–B4, B×P; 32 N×P, R×P ch; 33 K–K2 (K–N1, B–B4 ch), R–K1 ch.

30 ...	R–K5
31 B–N5	R–K4
32 B–B4	R–K5
33 B–N5	
Draw	

Our next example shows the isolated Queen-pawn as a mighty attacking instrument. One feature of interest in this game is the presence of the pawn on the fifth rank instead of the fourth. The pawn so far advanced generally has a cramping effect on the opponent's position, though its defence can often cause considerable difficulty. In the following game the cramping effect predominates.

SMYSLOV–LILIENTHAL

(Moscow 1942)

1 P–Q4	N–KB3
2 P–QB4	P–KN3
3 P–KN3	P–Q4
4 P×QP	N×P
5 B–N2	B–N2
6 N–KB3	O–O
7 O–O	N–N3
8 N–B3	N–B3
9 P–Q5	N–N1
10 N–Q4	

Better is 10 P–K4, P–QB3; 11 Q–N3.

10 ...	P–K3
11 P–K4	P×P?

A serious mistake. Correct was

11 ..., P–QB3!, liquidating the square d5.

12 P × P

DIAGRAM 129

Black's mistake on the previous move was an attempt to benefit by isolating White's Queen-pawn. This pawn, however, backed up by the Bishop on g2, is by no means weak; on the contrary, it restricts the mobility of Black's pieces and blocks his Queen-Bishop-pawn, thereby offering White a ready target on the c-file. Besides, White has the possibility of opening up the long diagonal for the Bishop on g2 by a later advance P–Q6.

12 ...	QN–Q2
13 B–B4	N–K4
14 P–KR3	N(3)–B5
15 P–N3	

Poor would be 15 Q–B2, P–QB4!; e.g. 16 P × P *e.p.*, Q × N; 17 P × P, B × NP; 18 B × B, QR–N1, with good play for Black.

15 ...	N–Q3
16 R–K1	R–K1
17 QR–B1	

The threat is 18 N(3)–N5.

| 17 ... | P–QR3 |

18 N–R4   N–N4

DIAGRAM 130

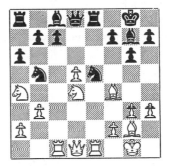

19 N–K6!

A pretty piece of tactical play, made possible by the strong position of the pawn on d5. Black cannot reply 19 ..., P × N, on account of 20 B × N, P × P; 21 Q × P ch, K–R1; 22 B × B ch, K × B; 23 Q × Q, R × Q; 24 R–K7 ch, K–R3; 25 N–B5.

19 ...	B × N
20 P × B	R × P
21 N–B5	Q × Q

White wins after 21 ..., R–Q3; 22 Q–K2, N–Q5; 23 Q–K4, P–B4; 24 Q–K3.

22 KR × Q	R–Q3
23 N × NP	R × R ch
24 R × R	R–N1
25 P–QR4	N–B6
26 R–Q2	R–K1
27 N–B5	P–QR4
28 R–B2!	N–Q8
29 B–Q2	B–B1!

Now if White plays 30 B × P, his opponent obtains counter-play by 30 ..., N × P, since 31 K × N, B × N; 32 R × B, N–Q6 ch is useless for White.

30	N–K4	R–N1	34 P–R5	P–B4
31	B × P	R × P	35 N–Q2	R–R6
32	B × P		36 N–B4!	N × N

Now White has won a pawn, which, with exact play, is sufficient to win.

37	R × N	R–R8
38	B–N6	N–K4
39	R–B3	B–N5
40	R–B8 ch	K–B2
41	K–N2!	Resigns

32 ...   N–Q6
33 B–B1!

Meeting Black's threat of 33 ..., R–N8.

33 ...   N(8)–N7

The passed-pawn will quickly decide the issue and if Black tries 41 ..., B × P; 42 B–Q4, R–K8; 43 R–B5 he loses a piece.

E. THE BACKWARD PAWN

A backward pawn is one which stands behind the pawns on adjacent files and cannot be defended by them. Diagram 131 shows two examples—

DIAGRAM 131

The backward pawns are those on b6 and g4. It is clear that the principles of play to be followed with backward pawns are similar to those adopted with isolated pawns: the backward pawn is also an end-game disadvantage; its advance must be prevented by a blockade; only in exceptional cases can it be won by direct attack. In the next example White is able to exploit the passive position into which Black is forced on account of his backward pawn.

DIAGRAM 132

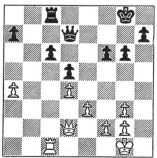

Position after Black's 28th move

The position is very much simplified and it is clear that a direct attack against the weak pawn on c6 brings White nothing; yet it is the weakness of this pawn which can be considered the decisive strategical factor. Black is forced to protect it with his heavy pieces, which are thereby forced into an extremely passive position; White's pieces on the other hand have complete freedom of movement. White too has an advantage in that he can choose his moments to attack the pawn: Black has no such choice as regards its defence; he must defend it when it is attacked. Besides this advantage of setting the pace White also has a big advantage in space: he has the first five ranks in which to manoeuvre for his attack, whereas Black is confined to three for the defence. White's plan should be as follows. He should secure control of the b-file, at the same time exerting pressure on the backward c-pawn; he should post his pieces as actively as possible and then either advance in the centre or launch an attack on the King-side.

| 29 | Q–N4 | K–B2 |
| 30 | P–R5! | |

The further advance to a6 will provide White with a useful operation base on b7. After a possible exchange of pieces there, White would have a passed-pawn on the seventh rank.

| 30 | ... | Q–K2 |
| 31 | Q–N3 | Q–Q3 |

Bad would be 31 ..., Q–B2 on account of 32 P–K4!, Q×RP; 33 P×P.

In the game White now played the faulty 32 Q–N7 ch and won only after several mistakes on Black's part. The proper continuation was 32 P–R6, and after 32 ..., R–QN1; 33 R×P, Q×R; 34 Q×R, Q×P; 35 Q–B7 ch, White wins a pawn; the better position of his King—an important factor in all Queen endings—would soon have produced a decision.

We now follow with an example in which the backward pawn is blockaded.

BERATENDE–NIMZOWITSCH
(1921)

1	P–K4	N–QB3
2	P–Q4	P–Q4
3	P–K5	P–B3
4	B–QN5	

Better is 4 P–KB4, B–B4; 5 N–K2.

4	...	B–B4
5	N–KB3	Q–Q2
6	P–B4	B×N
7	R×B	O–O–O
8	BP×P	

If 8 P–B5, then 8 ..., P–KN4!;

9 Q–K2, Q–K3 followed by N–R3–B2.

8	...	Q×P
9	B×N	Q×B
10	O–O	P–K3

As a result of his bad opening play, White is saddled with a weak pawn on d4 as well as a bad Bishop on c1. If he now decides on the exchange P×P the resulting opening of the g-file will give Black good attacking chances; yet the alternatives are worse, and this exchange would at least have allowed White some counter-chances in the form of an attack on e6.

135

11 B–K3	N–K2
12 Q–K2	N–Q4
13 KR–QB1	Q–Q2
14 R–B4	K–N1
15 Q–Q2	R–B1

In his commentary on the game Nimzowitsch draws attention to the clever rearrangement of the Rooks on c8 and d8. In my opinion the whole manoeuvre is too artificial. I should have given preference to the simple P–KB4 followed by B–K2.

16 N–K1	B–K2
17 N–Q3	KR–Q1
18 Q–B2	P–KB4

DIAGRAM 133

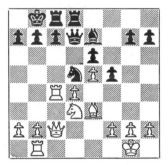

Black has now a marked advantage and can begin the advance of his King-side pawns. White ought now to look for counter-chances on the Queen's wing with 19 P–QN4!, though even then Black has a good game.

19 R–QB1 ?	P–KN4
20 N–B5	B × N
21 R × B	R–N1
22 Q–K2	P–KR4!
23 B–Q2	

The faulty 23 Q × RP would open

attacking lines for Black and leave the White Queen shut in after 23 ..., P–N5.

23 ...	P–R5
24 P–QR4	P–N5
25 P–R5	P–R3

Black's attack comes almost automatically, whereas White's counter-play is non-existent. The Knight on d5 supports the King-side pawn advance and protects the Queen's wing at the same time.

26 P–N4	P–B3
27 R–N1	Q–KB2
28 R–N3	P–B5
29 Q–K4	P–B6!
30 R–B1	P × P
31 K × P	QR–KB1
32 R–KB1	P–N6!
33 RP × P	P × P
34 P–B4	

Bad is 34 R × P, R × R ch, for the White King is then in a mating net.

34 ...	N–K2!

DIAGRAM 134

Another backward pawn has arisen in White's position and the Knight quickly moves to blockade it, at the same time reinforcing the attack on the King. Now 35 R×P, N–B4!; 36 R–N5, R×R ch; 37 P×R, N–R5 ch wins for Black.

35 B–K1	N–B4
36 R–R1	R–N5
37 B×P	Q–N3
38 Q–K1	N×B!

Black succeeds in exploiting the weakness of the two backward pawns and decides the game by their capture.

39 R×N	R(1)×P
40 R(1)–R3	R×P
41 Q–B2	R×R ch
42 R×R	Q–K5 ch
43 K–R2	Q×P

Now the King-pawn falls too; it had been protected first by one and then by two backward pawns.

44 K–N2	Q–Q4 ch
45 Resigns	

An important factor in play with a backward pawn is the advantage in space that the opponent is given; generally this is greater the nearer the pawn is to its original square. Often this space advantage allows a favourable concentration of forces on the backward pawn, which can at the right moment be exchanged to allow the attacking forces access to the enemy position; sometimes too the pawn formerly protected by the backward pawn becomes easy prey when left without support. An example of play involving the exchange of the backward pawn arises from Diagram 135.

DIAGRAM 135

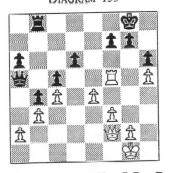

After **1 R–Q5, Q–B2; 2 Q–Q2, R–N3** (if 2 ..., R–Q1, White wins by 3 P–K5, making use of the pin on the backward pawn—a common tactical motif); **3 P–K5!, P×P; 4 R–Q8 ch, K R2; 5 R–Q7, Q–B3; 6 Q–Q3 ch**, White wins; e.g. 6 ..., P–K5; 7 P×P, Q–K3; 8 P–K5 dis ch, P–N3; 9 P×P ch, Q×NP; 10 R×P ch, or 6 ..., P–N3: 7 R×P ch, K–N1; 8 P×P, Q×NP; 9 Q×Q ch, R×Q; 10 R–QB7, etc.

In the section dealing with the isolated pawn it was pointed out that there are occasions when this need not be a disadvantage; so too it is with the backward pawn. Sometimes the backward pawn is purposely created in the hope of bringing an advantage to its possessor. Under certain conditions the pawn can block an open file, so preventing the exchange of heavy pieces or the penetration of the enemy pieces; it can also protect important squares in the centre; and its tendency to advance, after preparation, forces the enemy pieces into a position that prevents the advance. If the backward pawn is not to be a disadvantage, two conditions must as a rule be fulfilled—

1. The backward pawn must be protected in the simplest and most economical way.

2. One's own pieces must exert effective control over the squares in front of the backward pawn.

With a pawn formation d3, e4 against e5 it would be, for example, best to protect the pawn by a Bishop on e2; then the other Bishop could be posted on e3 or b2 and a Knight on f3 or possibly b3. Such a formation hinders the occupation of d4 by an enemy piece and also threatens the advance P–Q4: if Black does play his Knight to d4, then White can reply B×N, forcing P×N, after which White's pawn is no longer backward; in fact the exchange gives mobility to the White King-side pawns.

In the Sicilian defence two systems are often played in which Black as early as the sixth move quite voluntarily allows a backward pawn with all its attendant risks. Numerous games, however, have proved the vitality of both the Opocensky system (1 P–K4, P–QB4; 2 N–KB3, P–Q3; 3 P–Q4, P×P; 4 N×P, N–KB3; 5 QN–B3, P–QR3; 6 B–K2, P–K4!) and the Boleslavski set-up (2 ..., N–QB3; 3 P–Q4, P×P; 4 N×P, N–B3; 5 QN–B3, P–Q3; 6 B–K2, P–K4!). In both cases Black's formation became so feared that the move 6 B–K2 almost ceased to be played; it was replaced by 6 B–KN5, the main purpose of which was to prevent the advance 6 ..., P–K4.

We might well ask: What idea lies at the back of the advance of Black's King-pawn? First of all, and most important, Black wants to obtain superiority in the centre (by controlling d4 and f4) and stop White occupying d4 (on which square a White piece is often an important strategical factor, e.g. in the Dragon and Scheveninger variations). Secondly, Black builds a solid centre and prevents the advance by White of P–K5, which in the usual variations is a thrust to be feared. Thirdly, Black prepares a speedy development (B–K2, B–K3), and one, moreover, in which he has control over the square d5. Often he succeeds in playing P–Q4, thereby obtaining a clear superiority in the centre. If White seeks to prevent this advance, he must generally occupy the square d5 with a Knight and, after Black exchanges the piece, retake with his King-pawn; the result is then a superiority on the King's wing for Black. Finally, Black can, by the move P–K4, considerably reduce White's attacking prospects on the King-side and so give himself a better chance to carry out his own plans on the Queen-side, in which the exploitation of the

The Pawns

c-file is of importance; it is interesting to note that Black's operations on the c-file are mostly more effective than White's on the d-file, for the pawn on d6 protected by the Bishop on e7 is a great barrier for White. As the next two games show, the systems in which Black plays an early P–K4 in the Sicilian defence contain a variety of extremely interesting strategical and tactical problems.

UNZICKER–BRONSTEIN

(Interzonal Tournament 1955)

1 P–K4	P–QB4
2 N–KB3	P–Q3
3 P–Q4	P × P
4 N × P	N–KB3
5 N–QB3	P–QR3
6 B–K2	P–K4
7 N–N3	

A move that is almost exclusively played today. After the alternative 7 N–B3, Black replies with 7 ..., P–KR3!, so preventing White from exerting pressure on d5 by means of 8 B–KN5; with this ruled out White has less prospects of active play, for 8 B–QB4 is countered by 8 ..., B–K3 (maintaining control over d5) and after a possible exchange Black has, in view of his strong position in the centre, a good game, e.g. 9 B × B, P × B; 10 N–KR4, K–B2! followed by B–K2 and R–B1.

7 ...	B–K2

Less precise is 7 ..., B–K3; 8 O–O, QN–Q2; 9 P–KB4!, P × P; 10 B × P, after which White has more freedom of movement; should Black try 9 ..., Q–B2, White continues with 10 P–B5, B–B5; 11 P–QR4!, R–B1; 12 B–K3, B–K2; 13 P–R5, P–KR4 (if 13 ..., O–O, then 14 P–KN4);

14 B × B, Q × B; 15 R–R4, Q–B2; 16 P–R3, and has much the better of it, as can be seen from the game Geller–Najdorf in the 1953 Candidates Tournament. The exchange of the white-squared Bishops is always favourable for White here, because it weakens Black's control over d5.

With the text-move Black retains the possibility of developing his Queen Bishop at b7, should White play P–KB4. From b7 the Bishop would not only keep the square d5 under control but would also put pressure on White's King-pawn; therefore the advance P–KB4 by White is unfavourable; e.g. 8 O–O, O–O; 9 P–KB4, QN–Q2; 10 B–K3, P–QN4; 11 P–QR3, B–N2, and Black stands well.

8 O–O	O–O
9 B–K3	

(*See* Diagram 136)

Now Black is faced with the question of how to complete his development. The move 9 ..., B–K3, which from the point of view of the struggle in the centre appears logical, is here unfavourable, as White again plays P–KB4, and after 10 ..., P × P (otherwise 11 P–B5); 11 B × BP, N–B3; 12 K–R1, Q–N3 (better is 12 ..., P–Q4, after which White has only

139

a minimal advantage); 13 Q–Q2, QR–B1; 14 B–K3, Q–B2; 15 N–Q4, White has a slight advantage (Smyslov–Panno, Candidates Tournament 1956).

DIAGRAM 136

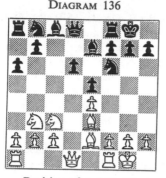

Position after 9 B–K3

9 ...   Q–B2!

The most precise move, giving Black the chance to develop his Bishop on either e6 or b7 as the occasion suits. Less precise would have been 9 ..., P–QN4; 10 P–QR4!, P–N5; 11 N–Q5.

10 P–QR4   P–QN3
11 Q–Q2

White is striving for the set-up that proved good in the game Stcherbakov–Simagin from the 22nd U.S.S.R. Championship: 11 ..., B–N2; 12 P–B3, QN–Q2(?); 13 KR–Q1, KR–Q1; 14 B–KB1!, and after 15 Q–B2 White had the better game. In the same tournament Simagin, defending against Averbach, improved Black's play by refraining from developing the Knight on d2; instead he played B–N2 and R–Q1, and then started

a successful campaign to force the advance P–Q4; with such a set-up of pieces, this would normally lead to exchanges and equality. In the present game Bronstein with his next few moves carries out an original manoeuvre, which likewise brings him control of the square d5, but also gives him simultaneous pressure on the c-file.

11 ...   B–K3
12 KR–Q1   R–B1!
13 Q–K1   Q–N2!

Now Black's plan becomes clear: he will secure control of d5 with the help of his Queen as well as his Bishop. White can only prevent the advance P–Q4 by placing his Bishop on f3, but this would mean renouncing his present plan (P–KB3 and Q–KB2) and giving up hopes of any active operations; Black could meet 14 B–B3 by 14 ..., QN–Q2 followed by R–B2 and QR–QB1.

14 R–Q2   QN–Q2

Obviously not 14 ..., N×P?; 15 N×N, Q×N; 16 B–B3. Also bad is 14 ..., P–Q4?; 15 P×P, N×P; 16 B–B3.

15 P–B3

If White instead tries to prevent the advance P–Q4 by 15 QR–Q1 the importance of White's Rook on c8 becomes clear: Black can, by the exchange sacrifice 15 ..., R×N; 16 P×R, N×P; 17 B–B3, P–Q4; 18 B×N, P×B followed by P–B4, obtain excellent attacking chances. After the text-move Black can, under favourable conditions, effect

140

the advance P–Q4, one of the strategical goals of this opening.

DIAGRAM 137

Position after 15 P–B3

15 ...	P–Q4
16 P×P	N×P
17 N×N	B×N
18 QR–Q1	N–B3

Threatening to win a pawn by 19 ..., R×P!; 20 R×R, B×N.

19 N–B1	P–K5
20 Q–B2	B–B4
21 B×B	P×B

Now Black has two spheres of attack: the King's wing, where he has a pawn majority, and the open b-file.

| 22 Q–K3 | R–K1 |
| 23 P–KB4 | |

The passed-pawn on e4 is now blockaded in the most uneconomical way—by the White Queen.

| 23 ... | P–B5 |
| 24 P–QN3 | |

The threat was 24 ..., P–B6; 25 P×P, QR–B1. If White attempts to forestall this by 24 P–B3, he weakens his pawn on a4 and at the same time presents his opponent with the strong square d3, which the Black Knight can soon occupy.

24 ...	QR–B1
25 P–R3	B–K3
26 K–R2	Q–B2
27 R–Q6	

White's last two moves were not good, as both the Rook on d6 and the pawn on f4 are under pressure from the Black Queen. However, it is well known that in bad positions good moves are difficult to find, and here White had no possibility of an active continuation.

27 ...	P–QR4
28 P×P	B×BP
29 N–N3	B×B
30 Q×B	P–K6!

Now Black is already threatening 31 ..., N–K5, winning the pawn on f4.

31 R–Q4	N–K5!
32 Q–B3	N–N4
33 Q–N4	N–K3
34 R–K4	P–R4!
35 Q–B3	N–N4

The simple 35 ..., N×P; 36 Q×N (36 R×N, P–N4), R×R also leads to a win.

36 R×R ch	R×R
37 Q–N3	Q×QBP
38 R–Q5	P–K7!
39 R×N	P–K8=Q
40 R×NP ch	K–R1
41 Q–N5	Q×P ch!
42 Q×Q	R–K7
43 Resigns	

The execution of the advance P–Q4 is always a characteristic sign of the success of Black's strategy. Sometimes it is only accomplished late in the game, at the end of Black's operations; so the backward pawn remains on d6 for a long time without White being able to take advantage of it.

UNZICKER–TAIMANOV
(Interzonal 1952)

1 P–K4	P–QB4
2 N–KB3	N–QB3
3 P–Q4	P×P
4 N×P	N–B3
5 N–B3	P–Q3
6 B–K2	P–K4
7 N–B3	P–KR3!
8 O–O	B–K2
9 R–K1	

If White continues his development by 9 B–K3, the answer is 9 ..., B–K3, after which Black's advance P–Q4 cannot be stopped; with the text-move White prevents this advance by the threat to the pawn on e5 (9 ..., B–K3; 10 B–B1!). The same idea lies behind the continuation 9 P–QN3 followed by B–N2; indeed with this White can succeed in holding up Black's advance: but the Bishop on b2 is biting on granite, and the disadvantage of the backward pawn is more than counterbalanced by the passive position of White's pieces.

9 ...	O–O
10 P–KR3	P–R3!

White's whole set up was made with the continuation 10 ..., B–K3; 11 B–B1, R–K1 (in order to play P–Q4 after B–B1); 12 N–Q5, B×N; 13 P×B, N–N1; 14 P–QB4 in mind; White would

then have had better prospects than in other similar positions, as he would have been in a position to use his two bishops and his pawn majority on the Queen-side. In this game Taimanov succeeds in refuting White's plan: he gives up the attempt to play an early P–Q4 and instead concentrates first on ending his development so that he can begin operations on the Queen's wing; he develops his Bishop to b7 partly in order to be able to exchange off White's Knight, should it venture to d5, and partly to combine his action on the c-file with pressure on White's King-pawn.

11 B–B1	P–QN4
12 P–R3	B–N2

DIAGRAM 138

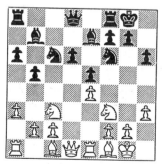

Again one of those positions in which the backward pawn is by no means a disadvantage. Black is ready to carry out his plan to attack along the c-file: White, on the other hand, is not only at a loss for a good plan, but is also in difficulties with the completion of his development; for example, after 13 B–K3, R–B1, he must reckon with N–QR4–B5.

13 P–QN3	R–B1
14 B–N2	R–B2
15 N–N1	

After 15 N–Q5, N×N; 16 P×N, N–N1; 17 P–B4, P×P; 18 P×P, N–Q2, it is White who gets a backward pawn; this can be blockaded by a Black Knight on c5, after which White's Queen-side majority is worthless; Black can then proceed in peace to prepare for his advance on the King-side. It should be pointed out, however, that this continuation, although unattractive, holds more prospects than the cul-de-sac that White enters with his next few moves.

| 15 ... | Q–R1! |
| 16 QN–Q2 | N–Q1! |

The beginning of a manoeuvre that leads to the complete containment of the White position.

| 17 B–Q3 | N–K3 |

Here the Knight has a splendid field of action and can be played, as desired, to c5, d4, or f4.

18 QR–B1	KR–QB1
19 N–R2	N–Q2!
20 N(R2)–B1	N(2)–B4
21 N–N3	P–N3!

The White Knights have no operation bases from where they can work effectively.

22 N–K2

Enticing Black to play for the win of a pawn by 22 ..., N×KP; 23 N×N, B×N; 24 B×B, Q×B, whereupon White can continue with N–B3–Q5, taking up a strong blockading position with his Knight.

22 ...	B–N4!
23 N–QB3	N–Q5
24 N(3)–N	P–Q4!

DIAGRAM 139

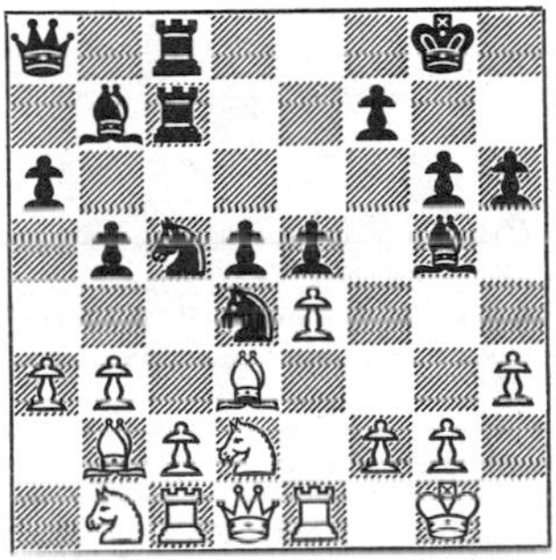

In the end, the advance of the pawn decides the game. Now 25 B×N fails against 25 ..., N×B.

25 P×P	N×B
26 P×N	R×R
27 B×R	B×P
28 P–B3	R–B7!

Now none of White's pieces has a reasonable move. The continuation 29 R×P, Q–B3; 30 R–K1, R×B!; 31 Q×R, Q×Q; 32 R×Q, N–K7 ch is hopeless for White.

29 P–QR4	P–N5
30 K–R1	Q–B3
31 Resigns	

In the last two games Black's plans differed fundamentally. In the first game he achieved an early P–Q4 and with it the opening of lines of attack, which enabled him to obtain superiority on the King-side. In the second game, White was allowed to prevent the advance P–Q4; but, as this was his only goal, and carried out with detrimental effect to the functioning of his pieces, it gave Black the chance to manoeuvre freely and prepare an action on the open c-file.

F. THE ISOLATED PAWN-PAIR

Diagram 140 shows a typical pawn formation. Generally such positions arise when a Knight blockading an isolated Queen-pawn is

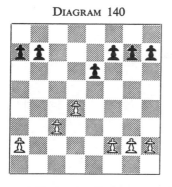

DIAGRAM 140

exchanged against a Knight on c3 or c6. Often the pawns on QB3 and Q4 are a serious weakness if the opponent can blockade the c-pawn and subject it to attack (for example, by P–QN3, B–N2–Q4, N–QB3–R4, R–QB1, Q–B2, etc); in this case the c-pawn can be considered as a backward pawn. The opponent then generally gets a space advantage on the Queen's wing on account of the blocked position and his control of the c-file; the isolated a-pawn also contributes to the opponent's advantage, especially if it has been advanced to QR3, where it can be attacked by B–K2, N–B5, or R–QB1–B5–R5.

Just how important the weakness of the isolated pawn-pair can be is clearly seen in the following game between Flohr and Vidmar.

Black's position shows two weaknesses, the pawns on a6 and c6; but a direct attack against them brings nothing on account of the reduced material. The right plan is the following: White pins the opposing pieces to the weaknesses and then, to give himself more freedom to manoeuvre, exchanges off the opposing Queen-pawn by P–K4; he follows this by forcing a weakening of the enemy King-side, which he can then attack

DIAGRAM 141

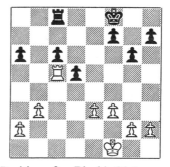

Position after Black's 31st move

successfully, as the defending pieces are on the other side of the board.

32 K–K2	K–K2
33 K–Q3	K–Q3
34 R–R5	R–QR1
35 K–Q4	P–KB4

Black has perceived White's plan and wants to simplify the position on the King-side by a double exchange on e4; but a passive formation, with a pawn on f6, would have afforded stiffer resistance.

36 P–QN4	R–QN1
37 P–QR3	R–QR1

Bad is 37 ..., R–N3, since, with the Rook closed in, Black would soon be in *zugzwang*.

38 P–K4!

The importance of this move has already been explained. It should, however, be further mentioned that such a pawn exchange in play against an isolated pawn-pair is a common strategical motif.

38 ...	BP × P
39 P × P	P × P
40 K × P	R–R2
41 K–B4	P–R3

The threat was 42 K–N5 followed by 43 K–R6.

42 P–KR4!	K–K3
43 K–N4	R–R1
44 P–R5	P–N4
45 P–N3	R–R2
46 K–B3	R–R1
47 K–K4	R–R2
48 K–Q4	K–Q3
49 K–K4	K–K3
50 R–K5 ch!	

The deciding manoeuvre. If the King goes back to the second rank, then 51 K–B5 wins; if it does not, White's Rook penetrates Black's position.

50 ...	K–Q3
51 R–K8	P–B4

After 51 ..., R–K2 ch; 52 R × R, K × R; 53 K–K5, the game is over.

52 R–Q8 ch	K–B3

Or 52 ..., K–B2; 53 R–KR8, winning.

53 R–QB 8ch	K–N3
54 R × P	R–KR2
55 R–K5	K–B3
56 R–K6 ch	K–N4
57 K–B5	R–B2 ch
58 R–KB6	Resigns

Our next example comes from a game by Alekhine; this has become a classic and has already appeared in many textbooks.

(*See* Diagram 142)

Black plans to bind the White pieces to the defence of the Queen's wing and then to launch an attack on the King's wing. An exchange of Queens is favourable for Black, as it reduces the opponent's tactical possibilities and promotes the active working of his own King on the King-side; with his big advantage in space it should not be too difficult to achieve this exchange under favourable conditions.

29 Q–N3!	R–Q3!

DIAGRAM 142

Position after Black's 28th move

The start of an excellent man-oeuvre. Black intends a re-group-ing of his pieces with the Queen on c4 and the Rooks on a4 and a6; then by pressure on a2 he will force the exchange of Queens.

30 K–R2	R–R3
31 KR–B1	B–K2
32 K–R1	R(5)–B3
33 KR–K1	

A little trap. If now 33 ..., B–K3?, there follows 34 R×P!, P×R; 35 Q×KP ch with per-petual check, for 35 ..., K–N2 fails against 36 P–Q5! followed by P–B4 dis ch.

| 33 ... | B–R5! |

An excellent counter. Now 34 R–K5?, Q×Q; 35 P×Q, R×R; 36 B×R, R–R3; 37 B–N2, R–R7; 38 R–K2, B–N6 wins for Black; and no better for White is 34 R–K2, Q×Q; 35 P×Q, R×R ch; 36 B×R, B–N6, etc.

| 34 R–KB1 | Q–B4 |

DIAGRAM 143

35 Q×Q

Otherwise the above-mentioned manoeuvre of placing the Rooks on a4 and a6 would follow. Such play with the Rooks is common in exploiting pawn weaknesses like those on a2 and c3.

35 ...	R×Q
36 P–R3	B–K2
37 KR–QN1	B–Q3
38 P–N3	K–B1

Black cannot yet win the pawn on a3 by playing R(5)–R5, as his own pawn on b5 is indirectly attacked. He therefore first brings his King to c6, making the threat to the pawn on a3 a reality; as a result he will force the Black Rooks into a passive position on a1 and a2.

39 K–N2	K–K2
40 K–B2	K–Q2
41 K–K2	K–B3
42 R–R2	R(5)–R5
43 R(1)–QR1	K–Q4
44 K–Q3	R(3)–R4
45 B–B1	P–QR3
46 B–N2	P–KR4!

Black now threatens P–KR5, which White can prevent only by leaving the square g4 accessible to the Black Rook; next Black will open the way to the King-side by P–KB3 and P–K4.

47 P–R4	P–B3!
48 B–B1	P–K4
49 BP×P	P×P

50 B–N2

Or 50 P×P, B×KP; 51 R–KN2, R–KN5, with a win for Black.

50 ...	P×P
51 P×P	P–N5
52 P×P	R×R
53 P×R	R×B
54 Resigns	

We have now examined those positions in which the opponent succeeded in preventing the advance P–QB4; we convinced ourselves that the isolated pawn-pair was a serious strategical disadvantage if the opponent could keep the c-pawn blockaded and use his superiority on the Queen-side. Frequently, however, the player with the isolated pawn-pair manages to make the advance P–QB4, giving a pawn structure like that in Diagram 144. In this case the position is more complicated. Obviously the pawns on QB4 and Q4 can be made an object of attack: the opponent can put the Queen-pawn under fire by N–QB3, B–KB3, and R (or Q) –Q1, and the Queen-Bishop-pawn by B–QR3, N–QR4, and R–QB1. On the other hand, both pawns—mostly we designate them *hanging pawns*—have important dynamic power. We noticed that the isolated Queen-pawn had a tendency to advance to Q5; with hanging pawns this is much stronger. From Diagram 144 it can be seen at a glance that there is a possibility of creating a passed-pawn by P–Q5 or P–QB5 (in practice the latter move is less common); the obligation to meet this threat prevents, or at least hinders, the attack on the hanging pawns. Further, the pawns control several centre squares (QB5, Q5, and K5) and therefore can be looked upon as a definite pawn centre. The possibilities and plans open to both players are given below, White having the hanging pawns.

DIAGRAM 144

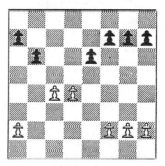

White

1. He can so post his pieces that he threatens to create a strong passed-pawn by advancing one of his pawns.

2. He can occupy e5 with a Knight and prepare an attack on the King-side with the aid of the advance P–KB4–KB5. If Black should then exchange (KP × BP), he opens the f-file for White's attack and also gives White a passed-pawn on d4; if, instead, he allows White to exchange (BP × KP), then his pawn on e6 becomes weak.

3. He can possibly carry out the advance P–QR4–5. Then, if Black exchanges, White is presented with a passed-pawn on c4 and also has prospects of attacking the pawn on a7; if he does not exchange, White can do so, leaving Black with a weak pawn on b6.

Black

1. He can, by the suitable placing of his pieces (e.g. B–N2, B–K2, N–KB3), stop the hanging pawns from advancing, or, should they succeed in advancing, he can prepare to blockade the resulting passed-pawn (e.g. after 1 P–Q5, P × P; 2 P × P, he can play N–K1–Q3).

2. He can at a suitable moment launch an attack on the hanging pawns, so that the opponent is forced to tie his pieces to their defence.

3. Sometimes Black can undertake the advance P–K4 or P–QN4. Then, if White exchanges, he is given an isolated pawn; if he pushes on (P–Q5 or P–QB5), Black can blockade the resulting passed-pawn and attack the adjacent pawn, which will have become backward.

BARCZA–GOLOMBEK

(Interzonal Tournament 1952)

1 P–QB4	N–KB3
2 P–Q4	P–K3
3 N–KB3	P–QN3
4 P–K3	B–N2
5 B–Q3	B–K2
6 O–O	O–O
7 N–B3	P–Q4
8 P–QN3	P–B4
9 Q–K2	P × QP
10 KP × P	N–B3
11 R–Q1	

White places his pieces in readiness to support the break-through P–Q5 after the exchange on c4. Black ought to play now, or next

move, N–QN5 in order to force White's Bishop to retreat to b1; this would lock up the White Queen Rook for the time being.

11 ...	R–QB1
12 B–N2	R–K1(?)
13 QR–B1	P × P(?)

Black is already the worse off. The manoeuvre N–QN5 no longer serves any purpose, as, after 14 B–N1, P × P; 15 P × P, B–QR3, White can obtain an advantage by 16 N–K5 or 16 N–QN5, B × N; 17 P × N; in the latter case the operation base on c6 is more important than the opponent's on d5. The text-move, followed by another incautious move, gives White the possibility of launching a direct attack by means of a breakthrough in the centre.

14 P×P   Q–B2

DIAGRAM 145

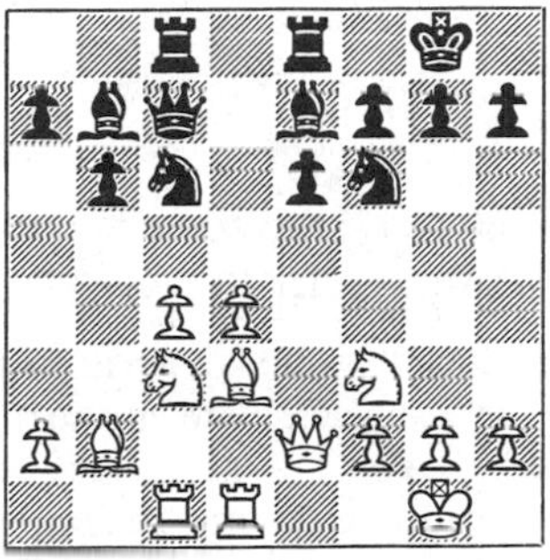

15 P–Q5!   P×P
16 N×P!

A motif that occurs frequently in such positions: Black is forced, either at once or in the near future, to exchange on d5, thereby depriving himself of an important defensive piece; in addition White opens the diagonal for his Bishop on b2.

16 ...   Q–N1
17 Q–Q2

Even stronger is 17 B–N1!, after which 18 B×N followed by Q–Q3 is threatened. If Black replies 17 ..., N×N; 18 P×N, B–B3, then White wins by 19 Q–B2, B×B; 20 P×N!, B×R; 21 Q×P ch, K–B1; 22 Q–R8 ch, K–K2; 23 R–Q7 ch, with mate in three moves.

17 ...   N×N
18 P×N   N–N5
19 B–K4   R×R
20 R×R   R–Q1?

Black could have put up a better fight with 20 ..., B–KB1, though this would have involved giving up the exchange: 21 N–N5, R×B (not 21 ..., P–KR3; 22 B–R7 ch, K–R1; 23 B–B5! P×N; 24 Q×P); 22 N×R.

21 Q–Q4   P–B3

Or 21 ..., B–KB1; 22 B×RP ch! K×B; 23 Q–R4 ch, K–N1; 24 N–N5, etc.

22 B×RP ch!   K×B
23 Q–K4 ch   K–N1

Or 23 ..., K–R1; 24 N–N5!, P×N; 25 Q×B.

24 Q×B   N×QP
25 Q–K6 ch   K–R1
26 Q–R3 ch   K–N1

DIAGRAM 146

27 N–N5!   P×N
28 Q–K6 ch   Resigns

If 28 ..., K–R2, then 29 Q–B7, R–N1; 30 Q–R5 mate, and if 28 ..., K–R1, then 29 Q–R6 ch, etc.

BOTVINNIK–SZABÓ
(Groningen 1946)

1 P–Q4   P–Q4
2 N–KB3   N–KB3

3 P–QB4	P–K3
4 N–B3	P–B4
5 BP × P	N × P
6 P–K3	N–QB3
7 B–B4	

When seen against White's 11th move (B–Q3), this seems to be a loss of tempo: but if White plays 7 B–Q3, his opponent need not exchange on c3; he can, instead, answer with 7 ..., P × P; 8 P × P, B–K2; 9 O–O, O–O; 10 R–K1, B–Q2 followed by R–B1. White therefore plans to put pressure on d5, thereby forcing Black to exchange on c3.

7 ...	N × N(?)

This is not an accurate move; Black should have delayed the exchange as long as possible, in order to make White adapt his development to a position with an isolated pawn and not hanging pawns; therefore, the correct continuation was 7 ..., P × P; 8 P × P, B–K2; 9 O–O, O–O; 10 R–K1, N × N; 11 P × N, P–QN3, with the exchange kept back until White had played 10 R–K1.

8 P × N	P × P
9 KP × P	

After 9 BP × P, B–N5 ch; 10 B–Q2, B × B ch; 11 Q × B, O–O; 12 O–O, P–QN3, Black has a comfortable game.

9 ...	B–K2
10 O–O	O–O

(*See* Diagram 147)

11 B–Q3	

DIAGRAM 147

Position after 10 ..., O–O

White intends to launch an attack on the King-side with all possible speed. This attack, however, never gains sufficient strength, and only causes White to neglect his isolated pawn-pair. A better move was 11 Q–K2, as played by Ståhlberg against Szabó in Helsinki, 1952; on that occasion White managed to break through in the centre (P–Q5) with decisive effect.

11 ...	P–QN3
12 Q–B2	P–N3

The continuation 12 ..., P–KR3?; 13 Q–K2, B–N2; 14 Q–K4 loses a pawn for Black.

13 B–KR6	R–K1
14 B–QN5	

With this move White achieves the advance P–QB4, thus preventing the blockade of his hanging pawns; but the price is very high: the exchange of his active white-squared Bishop.

14 ...	B–N2
15 P–B4	P–R3
16 B × N	B × B

17 N–K5	R–QB1
18 Q–N2	B–R1
19 QR–B1	

DIAGRAM 148

Black has undoubtedly reached his strategical goal, for White has now only slight prospects of an attack against Black's King and must keep his hanging pawns covered. White, however, does still have one tactical trump left: he can at a suitable moment threaten P–Q5 and then by N–N4 begin an attack along the diagonal a1–h8.

19 ...	P–QN4!

This decides the game strategically. White cannot exchange (20 P×P, Q–Q4!), and after 20 P–Q5?, P–B3; 21 N–N4, P–K4, the hanging pawns soon fall to pieces.

20 P–B5	Q–Q4

A better continuation is 20 ..., B–Q4, after which Black can move his Queen to b7 and use his majority on the Queen-side.

21 P–B3	P–B3?

Black wants to cut off the Bishop on h6; but there is little logic in such a plan. His two Bishops and the blockade of the Queen-pawn give him a clear positional advantage; therefore it was unjustifiable to allow tactical complications that give the opponent opportunities for active play.

22 N–N4	KR–Q1
23 KR–Q1	P–N4
24 N–K3	Q–B3
25 P–KR4!	

Black's faulty play on the 21st move already makes itself felt, although he still has the better position. Now after 25 ..., P×P?; 26 P–Q5, P×P; 27 Q–Q4!, White gets a strong attack, e.g. 27 ..., B×P; 28 Q–N4 ch, K–B2; 29 Q–N7 ch, K–K3; 30 Q×RP, or 27 ..., Q–K3; 28 Q×RP, B×P?; 29 R×B!, R×R; 30 Q–N3 ch, K–B2; 31 Q–N7 ch, K–K1; 32 Q–B8 ch.

25 ...	Q–K1
26 P×P	P×P
27 N–N4	Q–N3
28 R–K1	B–KB3
29 QR–Q1	R–Q4??

A blunder that leads to a quick loss. After 29 ..., B–KR1, or even 29 ..., B–Q4, the position remains complicated but, in my opinion, Black has the better prospects.

30 R×KP!	B×P ch
31 Q×B!	

Black had overlooked this move. After 31 ..., R×Q; 32 R×Q ch, he loses a piece, and after 31 ..., Q×R, he is mated; he therefore resigned.

SZABÓ–PACHMAN

(Interzonal 1952)

DIAGRAM 149

Position after Black's 19th move

In this position the hanging pawns are no disadvantage, although their dynamic strength cannot be utilized. The disappearance of two minor pieces has reduced the possibility of a successful attack against the pawns; on the other hand, Black has neither attacking prospects on the King-side nor the chance of carrying out the effective advance of his Queen-pawn. For that reason I offered my opponent a draw. After brief consideration, Szabó decided on active measures against the hanging pawns; this course, however, appears to have little justification.

| 20 P–K4? | P–Q5 |
| 21 QN–K2 | |

After 21 N–R4, N×N; 22 Q×N, P–KR4!, Black has also a good game.

21 ...	P–KR4!
22 P–B3	KR–Q1
23 P–N3	KN–Q2!

White probably assumes that he will be able to blockade the pawns with his Knights from c4 and d3; but the road to those squares is a long one, and the time lost getting there can be used by Black, who will post his pieces so actively that White will have to reckon with the advance of the passed-pawn.

| 24 Q–Q2 | N–K4 |
| 25 Q–R6 | |

With the intention of 26 N–B4, threatening both N×RP and N–Q3.

| 25 ... | R–B3 |
| 26 N–B1 | R(1)–Q3! |

Threatening to shut in the White Queen by P–KN4!; White is therefore forced to withdraw.

| 27 Q–Q2 | R–Q2 |
| 28 P–B4 | |

If 28 N–B4, Black answers strongly with P–B5; in any case White cannot allow the Knight to stay permanently on e5.

28 ...	N–N5
29 P–KR3	N–R3
30 Q–Q3	

White hopes to consolidate his position by N–Q2; however, he is in for an unpleasant surprise.

| 30 ... | R–K3! |
| 31 N–Q2 | N–B4! |

The decisive manoeuvre with the Knight. Now 32 P×N is answered by R–K6!, followed by R×N.

| 32 R–K1 | N–K6 |
| 33 P–K5 | QN–Q4 |

34 N–K4	R–B2

Black now threatens 35 ...,
N×BP; 36 N×N, R×P followed
by Q–N4. White therefore decides
on a doubtful piece sacrifice, which
is surprisingly successful.

35 N×QP?!	P×N
36 Q×P	R×R??

After 36 ..., Q–R5! the game is
clearly won for Black, e.g. 37
N–B6 ch, N×N; 38 Q×N, N–Q4.

37 R×R	N×BP

White's threats N–B6 ch and
R–B8 ch are so strong that Black
must force a draw.

38 Q×N	R×P
39 R–B8 ch	

Or 39 R–K1, K–N2!; 40 Q×N,
P–B4, draw.

39 ...	K–N2
40 Q×N	R×N
Drawn	

Although there was nothing to indicate the fact in the tournament
table, White suffered a strategical defeat as a consequence of his
faulty advance P–K4. We might well ask the reason for this. First
of all White did not succeed in blockading the hanging pawns;
secondly, Black quickly managed to post his pieces in such a way that
the threat to advance his pawns to d3 or c4 was constantly in the air;
finally, Black was able to occupy strong operation bases in the centre
with his Knights. This game once more underlines the importance of
weighing carefully the advantages and disadvantages that would
result from provoking the advance of one of the hanging pawns.

G. DOUBLED PAWNS

In the course of play it often happens that a piece protected by a
pawn is exchanged with the result that two pawns find themselves on
the same file. These doubled pawns, as they are called, form a
concept well known even to weak players, who mostly believe that
they automatically mean a serious
weakness and must therefore be
avoided at all costs. Just when
doubled pawns are a weakness, how
this can be exploited, and when they
can be an advantage, are important
strategical problems.

DIAGRAM 150

Every player knows that the advance of doubled pawns with the
intention of creating a passed-pawn
is beset with greater difficulties than
the advance of other pawns. So in
Diagram 150 the game is quite

hopeless for White, for his doubled pawns on the Queen-side cannot force their way through, whereas Black's King-side pawns will soon create a passed-pawn; the reader can easily verify this. The forced win for Black is entirely due to the doubled pawns, which virtually make the position an ending where White is one pawn down; if the pawn on b3 were moved to c3 the game would be equal.

Additional pawns on f2 (White) and c7 (Black) change the position in Diagram 150 completely and make it quite drawn. The doubled pawns are then no disadvantage, as they block the advance of the opponent's pawns just as effectively as undoubled pawns. From this we can draw the conclusion that the disadvantage of double pawns shows up most strongly in the offensive, when their advance affords difficulties; in defence, on the other hand, they are the equal of two normal pawns in stopping the advance of enemy pawns.

The most unfavourable case of doubled pawns arises with isolated doubled pawns on an open file. A single isolated pawn is itself a disadvantage, but doubled isolated pawns are even worse, for they cannot be protected and supported in their advance by a Rook from behind. Only the superior mobility and striking power of one's own pieces can counterbalance this strategic weakness.

In this chapter we shall deal mainly with doubled pawns that have some contact with their neighbours and therefore do not appear such an obvious weakness.

PODGORNY–PACHMAN
(Czechoslovak Championship 1954)

DIAGRAM 151

Position after Black's 14th move

Both sides have doubled pawns

but there is a big difference. The pressure on a7 will soon force White to play P–QR3, whereupon Black can set his Queen-side pawns in motion, eventually eliminating his doubled pawns by P–QN5. White, on the other hand, has little prospect of mobilizing his King-side majority and creating a passed-pawn. It should be noted that White cannot foil Black's plans by 15 N–Q5, for after 15 ..., P–QB3!; 16 N×P, R×P; 17 P–B4?, B–R3!; 18 P×N, B×R ch; 19 K×B, R×P ch, Black has a won position.

| 15 O–O | P–QB3 |
| 16 KR–Q1 | |

The immediate P–B4 was not possible on account of the reply 16 ..., B–R3; but now it becomes a real threat.

16 ...   **P–KN4!**

16 ..., B–R3 to blockade the doubled pawns would have been premature: Black needs his Bishop on the diagonal a3–f8 in order to support his own doubled pawns in their advance.

17 P–QR3   **P–QN4**
18 N–R2

The Knight heads for the strong operation base f5. In making his 16th move Black had to consider carefully whether the weakness created by that move would be greater than the advantage it brought. The further course of the game shows that the blockade of the doubled pawns was, as Black had assessed, the more important consideration.

18 ...   **KR–K1**
19 N–N4   **B–B1**
20 N–B2   **B–B4**
21 N–K3   **K–B1 !**
22 N–B5   **P–QN5**

The first stage in the conversion of Black's positional advantage is over; now the main task is to improve the position of his pieces and set the Queen-side pawns in motion.

23 P×P   **B×NP**
24 R–Q4   **B–B4**
25 R(4)–Q2   **R–R7!**

Now the importance of Black's 21st move becomes clear; Black's

Queen Rook is not bound to the task of defending the back rank.

26 P–KR4!

White adopts the correct strategical plan—raising the blockade on his King-side pawns. This plan fails against the tactics of his opponent, but only by a hair's breadth.

26 ...   **B–N5**

Obviously not 26 ..., P×P, which would allow the opponent's pawns to begin a dangerous march: 27 P–B4!, N–N3; 28 B–B4, R–R5; 29 P–N3, QR–R1; 30 R–Q7.

27 R–B2   **P–B3**
28 P×P   **P×P**
29 N–N3   **KR–R1**
30 N–R5   **R–R8!**
31 QR–B1

White could indeed have exchanged off one of his doubled pawns by 31 R×R, R×R ch; 32 K–N2, but then he is drawn into the variation 32 ..., R–R7; 33 P–B4, P×P; 34 N×P, B–R6; 35 N–K6 ch, K–K2; 36 N–B5, B×N; 37 R×B, R×P!; 38 R×N ch, K–Q3; 39 R–KR5, R×B; 40 R×P, P–N4, after which Black has a won game in view of the superior position of his pieces. With this variation White just narrowly fails to save the day, but can nevertheless feel justified in having chosen with his last few moves a plan that came near to success. As, however, the variation proved unplayable, White is left with a strategically lost position.

| 31 ... | R × R |
| 32 R × R | K–K2! |

Otherwise there follows 33 P–B4, P × P; 34 N × P, B–Q7; 35 N–K6 ch, K–K2; 36 R–Q1.

| 33 R–Q1 | R–R7 |
| 34 R–N1 | B–Q7! |

The pawn on f3 is again effectively blocked, so that Black has virtually an extra pawn. There is no need to fear the exchange of Knights, as the two passed-pawns that Black will have are on different sides of the board; therefore the ending is won despite the unlike Bishops.

35 K–N2	P–QN4
36 N–N3	K–B3
37 N–B1	B–B6!

With this move an advantageous simplification on the Queen's wing is obtained.

| 38 B × P! | B × P |
| 39 B–K2 | B–Q5 |

Now after 40 N–N3, K–K3!, followed by P–R4, Black wins easily.

| 40 R–Q1! | N–N3! |

After 40 ..., P–B4; 41 R–Q2, Black would also win, but only after a long and tedious struggle. The text-move, which offers a pawn, wins much more quickly.

| 41 R × B | N–B5 ch |
| 42 K–R1 | |

After 42 K–R2, R × B; 43 R–Q6 ch, K–K4; 44 R × P, R × P ch; 45 K–N1, N–R6 ch; 46 K–R1, R × P,

Black has an extra pawn, and, despite the reduced material, has a won position in view of the bad position of White's King; for example—

(*a*) 47 K–N2, P–N5; 48 N–R2, N–B5 ch; 49 K–N1, R–N6 ch followed by P–R4.

(*b*) 47 R–KR6, R × N ch; 48 K–N2, R–QR8!; 49 R × N, R–R7 ch; 50 K–N1, R–R2.

(*c*) 47 N–R2, R–KN6; 48 N–B1, R–N8 ch; 49 K–R2, R × N; 50 K × N, P–R4.

(*d*) 47 N–Q2, R–Q6; 48 R–B5 ch, K–Q3; 49 R–B2, P–R4.

After the text-move the point of Black's combination becomes clear.

| 42 ... | N × B! |
| 43 R–Q1 | |

After 43 R–Q6 ch, K–K2; 44 R × P, R–R8; 45 K–N2, N–B5 ch; 46 K–N1, P–R4, White, despite his extra pawn, is helpless, as his blocked doubled pawns are an obstacle that severely restricts the movement of his King; Black would eventually win the Knight by combining the advance of his Rook-pawn with N–K7 ch.

43 ...	R–B7!
44 K–R2	N–B5
45 K–N3	P–R4!
46 N–K3	R–B8!
47 R–Q6 ch?	

Overlooking the mating threat. But, in any case, the ending is lost after 47 R × R, N–K7 ch; 48 K–N2, N × R.

47 ...	K–K4
48 R–Q8 ?	R–KR8 !
49 N–B4 ch	K–K3
50 Resigns	

This is one of my best positional

games; it is interesting in that it shows the correct handling of the strategical plan to blockade the White doubled pawns.

Very frequently doubled pawns arise after a Knight has been exchanged on QB3 or KB3. We shall deal first with positions in which the doubled pawns are on the Queen-side and in which the foremost doubled pawn is on the third rank; this type of formation occurs in the Steinitz defence, and is shown schematically in Diagram 152.

DIAGRAM 152

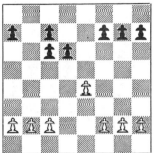

In this example Black's pawn on c6 controls d5, so preventing White from operating effectively on the Queen file. Black, for his part, can often post his Knight on e5, and if White drives it off with P–KB4, the pawn on e4 can be subjected to pressure. A further advantage for Black is the open b file, which can offer him prospects of an action on the Queen-side: he can, for example, move his Rook to the open file and, after provoking the advance P–QN3, proceed against the b-pawn by P–QR4–5; he can then follow this, after preparation, by P–QB4. This last advance requires a lot of caution, for control of d5 is thereby lost; this means relinquishing one of the advantages of the formation and presenting White with a good outpost: therefore Black should play P–QB4 only when he has secured control over d5 with his pieces or when his action on the Queen-side has already developed sufficient momentum to prevent White from exploiting the weakness of d5.

We have seen that the doubled pawns on c6 and c7 are by no means a disadvantage for Black. Now we must ask whether White has any good means of proceeding against them. One way is to attack the pawns by P–K5 or P–QB4–5; then if Black should exchange he is left with doubled isolated pawns. The possibilities open to both sides can best be seen from a study of the following games.

BOLESLAVSKI–FINE

(Radio Match U.S.S.R. *v.* U.S.A. 1945)

1 P–K4	P–K4
2 N–KB3	N–QB3
3 B–N5	P–QR3
4 B–R4	P–Q3
5 P–B4	B–Q2
6 N–B3	P–KN3

7 P–Q4	P×P

Safer is 7 ..., B–N2, although after 8 B–KN5 White has a positional advantage.

8 N×P	B–N2
9 N×N	P×N

Better in this position is 9 ..., B×N, after which White has only a slight advantage.

10 O–O	N–K2

DIAGRAM 153

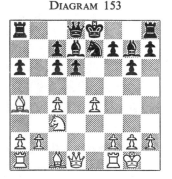

11 P–B5!

A typical attack against Black's type of Queen-side pawn formation. Its execution at this early stage of the game is possible because White had already with this fifth move played P–QB4; in addition his pieces are well developed. Tactically the advance is based on the fact that Black is badly placed after 11 ..., P×P; 12 B–K3 followed by QB×P, and quite lost after 11 ..., P–Q4; 12 P×P, P×P; 13 N×P, N×N; 14 Q×N, B×B; 15 Q–K4 ch. Black must now passively protect his Queen-pawn, after which White can

quietly prepare an action on the King-side.

11 ...	N–B1
12 B–K3	O–O
13 Q–Q2	Q–K2
14 QR–Q1	B–K1

Somewhat better is 14 ..., R–Q1, but even then Black's position is poor, as the pawn on c5 has a horrible cramping effect.

15 P–B4!	P–B4

It is unthinkable to win a pawn here: after 15 ..., B×N; 16 Q×B, Q×P; 17 B–B2 followed by P–B5, White's attack comes of its own accord.

16 KP×P	NP×P
17 KR–K1	P×P

Black has no alternative if he wants to bring the Knight into play; but now he has doubled pawns on an open file, and that constitutes a serious weakness.

18 Q–KB2	N–Q3
19 QB×P	Q–Q1
20 B–Q4!	

White could indeed have won a pawn by 20 Q–B3, but then Black would have been given counter-chances in the form of pressure on the b-file. With the text-move White converts his advantage much more safely: he exchanges off his opponent's single active piece, the Bishop on g7, and creates a weakness in the position of his King; then he forces a transposition into an end-game in which Black's doubled pawns are a fatal burden.

20 ...	B × B
21 Q × B	Q–B3
22 B–N3 ch	K–R1
23 Q × Q ch	R × Q
24 R–K7	R–QB1
25 QR–K1	

A quicker win is possible by 25 N–R4, N–K5; 26 B–K6, R–N1; 27 B × P, though even after the text-move Black cannot resist for long.

25 ...	B–N3
26 R(1)–K6	R × R
27 B × R	R–K1
28 R × R ch	B × R
29 N–R4	K–N2
30 N–B5	P–QR4
31 K–B2	B–B2
32 B × B	K × B
33 P–QN3	P–R4
34 P–N3	K–K2
35 K–K3	N–N4

Or 35 ..., K–B3; 36 P–QR4, K–K2; 37 K–Q4, and Black is in *zugzwang*.

36 N–N7	P–B4
37 N × RP	K–Q3
38 N–B4 ch	K–Q4
39 K–Q3	N–Q3
40 N × N	P × N
41 P–QR3	Resigns

ZVETKOV–PACHMAN

(Hilversum 1947)

(*See* Diagram 154)

Black has just moved his Queen to the b-file in order to begin an action on the Queen-side; he is following the usual plan of forcing his opponent to play P–QN3, after which he will prepare the advances P–QR4–5 and P–QB4–5. White's counter-chances are mainly in the centre.

DIAGRAM 154

Position after Black's 11th move

12 P–QN3	P–QR4
13 N(4)–K2	Q–N5!

Black's Queen is actively placed on b4, especially as its presence there would lead to an exchange of Queens if White should play N–Q5 in reply to P–QB4. White's best plan is now 14 P–KN4 followed by N–N3; he gives this up, however, in an attempt to demonstrate that Black's last move was a loss of tempo.

14 N–B4

This seems to be very strong in view of the threat 15 N–Q3 followed by P–K5; but after the immediate retreat of Black's Queen it proves innocuous.

14 ...	Q–N2!
15 QR–Q1	

After 15 N–Q3, B–K3; 16 P–K5,

N–Q2, Black has a good game, e.g. 17 B–B4, P–Q4, or 17 P×P, P×P.

15 ...	KR–Q1
16 Q–B2	KB–B1
17 R–Q3	P–B4

This move comes at the right moment: with the White Rook on d3 Black threatens to win a tempo by P–QB5. White ought now to simplify the position by 18 N(4)–Q5.

18 KR–Q1	R–K1

Three moves previously Black had moved his Rook to the d-file as a counter to a possible P–K5 by White: now that the White Queen has quitted the d-file leaving doubled Rooks there Black's Rook no longer serves any purpose on d8; he therefore moves it to a more promising post. White should now take the chance to obtain equality by 19 N(4)–Q5, N×N; 20 N×N, P–R5, but, instead, he goes in for a King-side attack that is completely unjustified from a strategical point of view: as Black's King-side has not been weakened, the creation of serious threats against it will take such time that White will meanwhile be overcome by the attack on the Queen-side.

19 P–KN4?	B–B3
20 P–N5	N–Q2
21 Q–N3	P–R5
22 R(3)–Q2	P×P
23 RP×P	R–R6!

Now Black threatens 24 ..., P–B5.

DIAGRAM 155

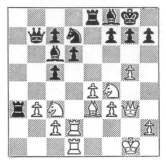

Position after 23 ..., R–R6

24 N(4)–Q5	R–K3

Prevents 25 N–B6 ch with all its accompanying complications.

25 P–R4	B×N
26 N×B	P–B5!

Now Black wins a pawn, which ought to bring victory. White is quite lost after 27 P×P, P–B3; 28 N–B4, R×B; 29 N×R, P×N; 30 Q–N4, N–B4.

27 B–Q4	P×P
28 P×P	R×NP
29 P–R5	N–K4??

With this move I lost first place in the tournament (the game was played in the last round). There was an immediate win by 29 ..., R×KP, e.g. 30 N–B6 ch, N×N; 31 P×N, R×B; 32 R×R, R×P; 33 Q–N2, Q–N6. I saw this variation quite clearly, but at the last moment I hesitated on account of the continuation 29 ..., R×KP; 30 B×P?, B×B??; 31 N–B6 ch winning for White; I had, however, completely overlooked the fact that Black can take the Bishop on g7 with his King, after which White is lost.

30 B×N	R×B
31 P–R6	R–N8

After 31 ..., R–K3; 32 P×P, B×P; 33 N–B6 ch, K–R1; 34 R–KR2!, B×N; 35 P×B, R×P (f6); 36 Q–R4, or 32 ..., K×P!;

33 N–B6, White has a decisive attack.

32 P×P	B×P

Black still does not see the threat. However, after 32 ..., K×P, White replies strongly with 33 Q–R4.

33 N–B6 ch	K–R1
34 Q×R!	Resigns

With doubled pawns on the King-side the strategical problems are similar, especially where both sides castle on the Queen-side; where the Kings remain on the King-side there are, however, some additional factors that affect the situation. On the one hand doubled pawns mean a weakening of the King's position; on the other, they open up a line of attack against the enemy King. Our next example shows Black using for attacking purposes the open file that arose with his doubled pawns; he is helped in this game, it is true, by the fact that he has not castled, but it often is possible even after castling to conduct such an attack by playing K–R1 or K–R2.

SZABÓ–EUWE

(Groningen 1946)

DIAGRAM 156

Position after Black's 15th move

The doubled pawns have arisen in favourable circumstances for Black: he has two Bishops, of which the one on b7, aimed at g2, is extremely dangerous, and his King can remain in the centre, allowing him to occupy the open g-file without loss of time. White should now meet the threatening attack by 16 Q×BP, R–KN1; 17 B–B4, Q–Q4; 18 B–N3; after this, although his position is not particularly good, he would have better defensive possibilities than he had in the game.

16 Q–R4 ch	Q–Q2
17 Q×BP	

Strategically hopeless is 17 Q×Q ch, K×Q; 18 P×P, R–KN1; 19 K–B1, B–Q3, or 19 N–K1, B–Q4, for White has then no counter-play at all.

17 ...	R–B1
18 Q–K2	R–KN1
19 N–K1	Q–Q4

161

20 P–B3	B–Q3
21 K–R1	Q–KR4

More energetic is 21 ..., P–B7!;
22 R–Q3, Q–KR4; 23 P–KR3,
R–N6, with a very strong attack, in
which White is troubled by the
pawn on c7. The variation 21 ...,
P–B7!; 22 N×P?, R×N!; 23
Q×R, Q×BP; 24 R–KN1,
Q–KR6; 25 Q–B8 ch, B×Q; 26
P×Q, B–N2 ch is hopeless for
White.

22 P–KR3	R–N6

It was still possible to continue
with the strong move P–B7.

23 B–K3	K–K2
24 Q–B1	QR–KN1!

As the pressure on the g-file is
irresistible, Black has no need to
worry about his pawn.

DIAGRAM 157

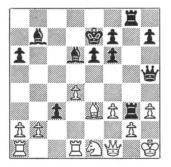

25 P×P	R×NP!

The simplest conclusion of
Black's attack: he gives up two
Rooks for the Queen, but White's
King is thereby so exposed that
Black is left in complete control.
Obviously 26 N×R, Q×RP ch;
27 K–N1, B×P; 28 R–Q2, B–R7
ch is hopeless.

26 Q×R	R×Q
27 K×R	Q–N3 ch
28 K–B2	B–N6 ch
29 K–K2	B×N
30 R×B	Q–N7 ch
31 K–Q3	B×P
32 P–QR4	B–K5 ch
33 K–B4	Q–QB7
34 P–Q5	B×P ch
35 K–N4	K–Q2
36 P–B4	

A despairing attempt to win
space for his pieces in the hope of
warding off the mating threats.

36 ...	Q×BP ch
37 K–R5	Q–B6 ch
38 K×P	B–B5 ch
39 K–N7	Q–N6 ch
40 B–N6	Q–KB6 ch
41 K–N8	B–R3
42 KR–Q1 ch	K–K1
43 Resigns	

Our next example shows the weakness of doubled pawns on the
King-side.

JANOWSKI–LASKER

(World Championship match
1909)

(*See* Diagram 158)

In this interesting position White,
with two sets of doubled pawns,
has a proud-looking centre; he
also controls the open g-file and
has a Bishop that is more active
than his opponent's Knight: nevertheless it is Black who has a clear
positional advantage. This assertion may sound astonishing, for

DIAGRAM 158

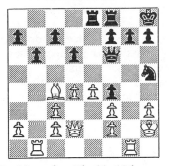

Position after Black's 19th move

even Janowski considered the set-up so much in his favour that, despite a bad experience in this game, he chose it again; but the result was the same. White's advantages are imaginary, for his centre, strong at first sight, lacks mobility and is thus deprived of its main value. It should be noted that after the advance P–QB4 White lacks a pawn on b4 to support the further advance P–QB5; likewise P–K5, which in normal pawn formations constitutes a threat, is here out of the question, as White then remains with two sets of isolated doubled pawns. Black, on the other hand, has a clear plan: he can prepare an action against White's weakened King-side.

20 R–QN5   Q–R3

A bad positional mistake would be 20 ..., P–B4?, after which White gets a target on the b-file; he could then continue with P–QR4–5, which would give him the advantage.

21	QR–KN5	P–B3
22	QR–N4	P–N3!
23	B–Q3	R–K2
24	P–B4?	

In bad positions it is often difficult to wait and see which action the opponent will choose to convert to his advantage. The text-move gives Black the opportunity of bringing his Knight to an attacking position without loss of time.

24 ...   N–N2!

Now the continuation 25 Q×P, Q×Q; 26 R×Q, N–K3; 27 R(4)–N4, N×P leads to an ending that is easily won for Black on account of White's pawn weaknesses.

25 P–B3   N–K3

Threatens N–N4 attacking f3 and h3 simultaneously.

26	B–B1	P–KB4
27	R(4)–N2	R–B3
28	B–Q3	P–KN4!

Threatening Q×RP ch followed by R–R3 mate.

29 R–KR1   P–N5!

Again threatening N–N4, against which there is no defence. If Black had played 29 ..., Q×P ch instead, White could have held out longer by 30 K–N1, Q×P; 31 P×P.

30	B–K2	N–N4!
31	BP×P	P–B6
32	R–N3	P×B
33	Resigns	

As a general rule we might say that pawn formations that include doubled pawns are better not set in motion, as advances mostly leave weaknesses behind; there are of course exceptions, but these arise mainly when the side undertaking the advance of doubled-pawn formations has superior piece mobility. On examination of the pawn skeleton in Diagram 159, we see that the advance P–QB4 is out of the question, for it leaves White with doubled isolated pawns. The advance P–Q5 is more difficult to assess. Generally, however, with pawns on e4 and d5 opposed by pawns on e5 and d6, it is essential for White to prepare the break-through P–QB5; but without the assistance of a pawn on b4, White can be frustrated quite simply by P–QN3 on the part of Black. Besides this, the advance P–Q5 presents Black with a fine square on c5 for his Knight, which cannot be driven off by P–QN4. Furthermore Black has the possibility of placing his Rook on c8 and, after opening the c-file by P–QB3, putting pressure on the doubled pawns; often it does not matter if White plays P–QB4 to rid himself of his doubled pawn by recapturing with his Bishop-pawn after Black plays BP×QP, for the pawn on c2 is then subjected to most unpleasant pressure. The situation is different, of course, if Black plays P–QB4 in order to force White to P–Q5; then Black has not the same possibilities of exploiting the doubled pawns, and the struggle will probably shift to the King-side. If, however, Black does not play P–QB4, White should endeavour to maintain his central pawns on c3, d4, and e4; his active position in the centre should then counterbalance the weakness of his doubled pawns.

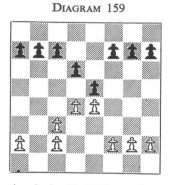

DIAGRAM 159

DIAGRAM 160

We now turn to a pawn formation that arises in several variations of the Nimzo-Indian Defence; it is schematically shown in Diagram 160. In such positions White should aim to play P–K4 and P–KB4–5, and then attack on the King-side; Black, for his part, must try to exploit the weakness of the doubled pawns. It would be good for Black if without P–QB4 he could induce White to play P–Q5; for example, after 1 ..., P–Q3; 2 P–K4, P–K4; 3 P–Q5? we have a position where Black can occupy c5 with his Knight and also operate on the c-file after P–QB3. Generally, however, P–K4 by Black rarely succeeds in getting White to advance his Queen-pawn: White simply maintains his pawn formation and seeks attacking chances on the King-side. If Black then plays P–QB4, White usually finds it quite safe to reply P–Q5, for the completely blocked position virtually neutralizes the disadvantage of the doubled pawns. In view of this, a quite different plan has been developed for Black in recent years; this can be summarized as follows—

1. Black renounces the advance P–K4.

2. He blocks the doubled pawns by P–QB4.

3. He attacks the pawns by P–QN3, B–QR3, and N–QR4; he also has the threat to increase the pressure at a suitable moment by R–QB1 and P×QP.

4. He meets White's King-side attack in one of two ways: after castling short he replies to P–K4 and P–KB4 by P–KB4, thus stopping any further advance; or, a less frequent case, he castles long.

The pawn formation in Diagram 160 is therefore unfavourable for White, who must seek counter-play with pieces; he will of course have two Bishops to help him, as the doubled pawns are the result of an exchange of a Bishop on b4 against a Knight on c3. Very often he sacrifices the pawn on c4, thereby gaining time for his attack, which Black's pieces, largely directed against c4, are not well placed to meet.

The next game shows us some of the problems associated with the doubled pawns in the Nimzo-Indian Defence.

BOTVINNIK–RESHEVSKY

(World Championship 1948)

1	P–Q4	N–KB3
2	P–QB4	P–K3
3	N–QB3	B–N5
4	P–K3	P–B4
5	P–QR3	B×N ch
6	P×B	N–B3

Experience of late has shown that 6 ..., P–QN3!; 7 B–Q3,

B–N2 is much stronger, because it forces 8 P–KB3, a move that has disadvantages for White. The annotation to White's tenth move shows further why the tempo move B–N2 is important for Black.

7	B–Q3	O–O
8	N–K2	P–QN3
9	P–K4	N–K1!

A very important tactical

manoeuvre: Black prevents the pin 10 B–KN5 and leaves the way open to reply to P–KB4 by P–KB4.

10 B–K3?

This is a serious mistake. In the present position White must seek compensation for the weakness of his doubled pawns in active play with his pieces; therefore, a quiet move is wrong; it was essential to prepare a King-side attack as quickly as possible. In a game from the 1948 Interzonal between Lilienthal and Najdorf, White continued: 10 O–O, P–Q3; 11 P–K5! (taking advantage of the exposed position of Black's Queen, a manoeuvre that would not be possible if Black's Bishop were already on b7), QP×P; 12 P×P, B–N2 (12 ..., N×P??; 13 B×RP ch); 13 B–B4, P–B4; 14 P×P *e.p.*, P–K4? (14 ..., Q×P; 15 Q–B2, P–N3; 16 QR–K1 is better, but White still has an advantage); 15 B×RP ch!, and White won quickly. Even better for White is the immediate advance of the King-pawn, as occurred in a game from the 16th Russian Championship between Averbach and Taimanov: 10 P–K5!, P–B4; 11 P×P *e.p.*, Q×P; 12 B–K3, P×P (12 ..., P–Q3; 13 Q–B2, P–N3; 14 P–KR4); 13 P×P, B–R3; 14 Q–B2, with clear advantage.

| 10 ... | P–Q3 |
| 11 O–O | N–R4 |

(*See* Diagram 161)

In this position, White's prospects of active play are not suffi-

DIAGRAM 161

Position after 11 ..., N–R4

cient compensation for the weakness of his doubled pawns. His main disadvantage is the difficulty of supporting his attack with a pawn advance; for example, after 12 P–KB4, Black refrains from 12 ..., B–R3; 13 P–B5!, B×P; 14 P–B6!, N×P; 15 B–N5, which after 16 N–N3 gives White a tremendous attack for his two sacrificed pawns; instead, he simply plays 12 ..., P–KB4, stopping White's advance and restricting the mobility of both his Bishops.

| 12 N–N3 | B–R3 |
| 13 Q–K2 | Q–Q2! |

A good move, threatening to win the pawn on c4 by Q–R5. If White answers by 14 P–QR4, he still loses the pawn after 14 ..., P×P; 15 P×P, R–B1. Therefore, 14 P–K5! was essential in order to give White tactical chances on the King-side.

| 14 P–KB4? | P–KB4! |

White's attack is thus stopped;

his positional disadvantage meanwhile has become greater owing to the immobility of the Bishop on e3. The best chance for White now is to force open a file by P–K5 or P–Q5; unfortunately the immediate P–Q5 is useless, for after 15 P–Q5, P–KN3!; 16 P×KP, Q×P; 17 P×BP, P×P, White loses his pawn on c4 before he has a chance to exploit the weakened position of Black's King.

15 QR–K1

Better was 15 KR–K1 followed by QR–Q1, after which Black must reckon with both P–Q5 and P–K5.

| 15 ... | P–N3 |
| 16 R–Q1 | |

Now the advance 16 P–Q5 can be answered by 16 ..., N–N2; therefore White decides to prepare the break-through P–K5. Black still cannot afford the Queen sortie Q–R5, as the absence of his Queen would give White a very strong attack: 16 ..., Q–R5; 17 P–Q5, B×P; 18 P×KP, B×P; 19 P×P. However, Black has no need to hurry over capturing the pawn on c4.

16 ...	Q–KB2
17 P–K5	R–B1
18 KR–K1	

After 18 P×QP, N×P, White can no longer hold his pawn on c4. The text-move sets a trap, for if now 18 ..., BP×P?, 19 B×QP!, B×P?, there follows 20 P×P, N×P; 21 Q–K5.

| 18 ... | QP×P! |

As White must recapture with his Queen-pawn (19 BP×P?, P×P), Black succeeds in blocking the centre, thereby freeing his pieces. The game is already strategically won for him.

19 QP×KP	N–N2
20 N–B1	KR–Q1
21 B–KB2	N–R4!
22 B–N3	

An unpleasant, but necessary, move. The square e3 must be kept open, and 22 P–N3? leads to a decisive weakening of the diagonal a8–h1 after 22 ..., B–N2! followed by B–R1 and Q–QN2.

22 ...	Q–K1
23 N–K3	Q–R5
24 Q–R2	N×B

There was a quicker win by 24 ..., P–KN4, but Black apparently feared the consequences of White's attack after 25 P×P, P–B5; this attack, however, would never have gained sufficient strength.

25 P×N

DIAGRAM 162

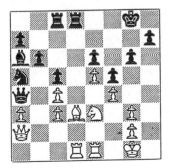

It is clear that Black has achieved his strategic goal in the attack against the isolated pawns. He ought now to seek an exchange of Queens with 25 ..., Q–N6, e.g. 26 Q×Q, N×Q; 27 P–KN4, P×P; 28 N×P, N–R4; 29 N–K3, K–B2 followed by R–Q2 and QR–Q1.

| 25 ... | P–R4? |

In an endeavour to make the square g4 inaccessible to White, Black presents his opponent with an interesting tactical possibility.

26 B–K2?

White misses his opportunity. After 26 B–B2!, Black cannot well continue 26 ..., B×P; 27 B×Q, B×Q; 28 B–Q7, R–N1; 29 P–B4. He has indeed the better position after 26 B–B2!, Q–B3; 27 P–R4, but his immediate attack on the Queen's wing has been repulsed.

26 ...	K–B2
27 K–B2	Q–N6!
28 Q×Q	N×Q
29 B–Q3	

Otherwise Black wins by playing N–R4, and then, after exchanging Rooks with the aid of K–K2, marching with his King to h6 in order to support the advance P–KN4 and P–KR5.

| 29 ... | K–K2(?) |

| 30 K–K2 | N–R4 |
| 31 R–Q2 | R–B2? |

A serious mistake, after which White obtains counter-play. Correct was 31 ..., K–B2!, which shows that Black's twenty-ninth move was not good. The end phase of the game is marked by errors on the part of both players as a result of time-trouble.

| 32 P–N4! | R(2)–Q2 |

After 32 ..., RP×P; 33 R–KR1!, White has good counter-play on the h-file.

| 33 P×BP | NP×P |
| 34 R(1)–Q1?? | |

A bad mistake, which leaves White almost without a single reasonable move. Correct was 34 R(2)–Q1! followed by R–R1, giving him counter-play and depriving Black of any clear-cut way to a win.

34 ...	P–R5!
35 K–K1	N–N6
36 N–Q5 ch	P×N
37 B×P	N×R
38 R×N	P×P
39 B×R	R×B
40 R–KB2	K–K3
41 R–B3	R–Q6
42 K–K2	

And White resigned.

CHAPTER IX

The Centre

BY the centre of the chessboard, we mean the four squares d4, d5, e4, e5 (*see* Diagram 163): sometimes we also use the concept *large centre*, which includes all the adjacent squares; it is the area enclosed by the broken line in Diagram 163. We might well ask why this central region is so favoured; why the struggle for the centre is such an important element in chess strategy.

First of all, as we noted in an earlier chapter, the working power of a piece is influenced greatly by the space it commands, and a piece in the centre generally controls the greatest space. Secondly, the attainment of stable pawns in the centre usually prevents the opponent from manoeuvring freely with his pieces, which are denied access to the central squares; further, the pawns threaten to advance and drive the enemy pieces from neighbouring files; for example, P–K5 by White can drive back an enemy Knight on f6 or a Bishop on d6. Thus control of the centre brings with it a space

DIAGRAM 163

advantage that allows the relatively easy manoeuvring of one's own pieces and restricts the functioning of the opponent's.

The best known and most common type of central control takes the form of pawns in the centre, and indeed many players understand by the concept *struggle for the centre* only the attempt to set up a pawn centre; Tarrasch, for example, presented the problem in such terms. Nimzowitsch, however, in a long dispute with Tarrasch, showed that the centre can be controlled by other means—by centralization of pieces or by pressure on the centre from the flanks; for example, a Knight on f3 and Bishop on b2 can control the squares d4 and e5. The centre is therefore an area, a group of squares; it does not consist of pawns.

Generally, control of the centre by pawns is more lasting than control by pieces; so we shall begin by examining the different types of pawn centre.

A. THE CLASSICAL CENTRE
(Pawns on Q4 and K4)

The majority of openings that were used during the classical period aimed at setting up pawns on Q4 and K4. One example of this is the Giuoco Piano, in which White, after 1 P–K4, P–K4; 2 N–KB3, N–QB3; 3 B–B4, B–B4, continues with 4 P–B3 in an attempt to achieve the desired central pawn formation. As, however, the loss of time involved enables Black to launch a counter-attack that liquidates the centre (4 ..., N–B3! 5 P–Q4, P×P; 6 P×P, B–N5 ch; 7 B–Q2, B×B ch; 8 QN×B, P–Q4!), an improvement in White's plan was eventually sought; this was the Evans Gambit (4 P–QN4?!, B×NP; 5 P–B3), which gave White, for the price of a pawn, the necessary time to control the centre with pawns on Q4 and K4. Another opening of this period, the King's Gambit, is similarly based; in this, White again offers a pawn (1 P–K4, P–K4; 2 P–KB4, P×P) to remove the obstacle to P–Q4; he receives in addition the possibility of drawing advantage from the later opening of the f-file. The idea behind this opening comes most clearly to the fore in the incorrect Steinitz Gambit (1 P–K4, P–K4; 2 N–QB3, N–QB3; 3 P–KB4, P×P; 4 P–Q4?!); here White not only offers a pawn, but also jeopardizes the safety of his King, in his fight to attain the desired pawn centre.

The position of the pawns on Q4 and K4 corresponds best with the way known to the Italian School of using the centre: use of the dynamic power of the central pawns and their advance to force back the enemy pieces, with the resultant creation of possibilities for an attack with pieces. A drastic example of such a use of the pawn centre is the following well-known variation of the Giuoco Piano.

White	Black
1 P–K4	P–K4
2 N–KB3	N–QB3
3 B–B4	B–B4
4 P–B3	N–B3
5 P–Q4	P×P
6 P×P	B–N3?

(*See* Diagram 164)

7 P–Q5!	N–K2
8 P–K5	N–K5

Or 8 ..., N–N5; 9 P–Q6, P×P; 10 P×P, N–QB3; 11 O–O.

DIAGRAM 164

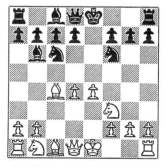

Position after 6 ..., B–N3

170

9 P–Q6	P×P
10 P×P	N×BP

Or 10 ..., N–QB3; 11 Q–Q5.

| 11 Q–N3 | N×R |

12 B×P ch	K–B1
13 B–N5	

And White wins.

A more complicated use of a mobile pawn centre occurs in the following game.

PACHMAN–VESELY
(Prague 1953)

1 P–Q4	P–Q4
2 P–QB4	P–QB3
3 N–QB3	N–KB3
4 P–K3	P–K3
5 N–B3	QN–Q2
6 Q–B2	B–Q3
7 P–QN3	O–O
8 B–K2	Q–K2?

Better is 8 ..., P×P; 9 P×P, P–K4; 10 O–O, R–K1; 11 B–N2, P×P; 12 P×P, N–B1. After the text-move, the exchange on d4 is hardly possible, as the Black Queen would have to lose time withdrawing from the open e-file.

9 O–O	P×P
10 P×P	P–K4
11 R–K1!	

As White, after Black's advance P–K5, will aim at opening the f-file by means of N–Q2 and P–B3, it would have been better strategically to play the other Rook to e1; however, this has a tactical drawback: 11 B–N2, R–K1; 12 QR–K1, P–K5; 13 N–Q2, N–B1; 14 P–B3, P×P; 15 B×P, N–N5!, and White is forced to play 16 B×N, leaving Black the Bishop-pair as a counterbalance to his strong centre.

11 ...	R–K1
12 B–N2	P–K5
13 N–Q2	N–B1

DIAGRAM 165

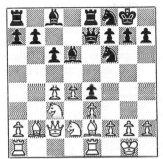

14 P–B3!

A frequently occurring way of eliminating the opponent's central pawn; White thereby gains a pawn superiority in the centre. Such a manoeuvre, however, requires careful consideration, as it can lead to a perceptible weakening of the King-pawn: for example, in the French Defence Black is often left with hanging pawns on e6 and d5 after the freeing move P–KB3; these frequently are a serious weakness if White can succeed in blockading the pawn on e6. In the present position, however, White can easily force the advance P–K4 and thus build a strong pawn centre.

171

14 ...	P×P
15 B×P	N–N5
16 N–B1	

Now the meaning of White's eleventh move becomes clear: White cannot be prevented from playing P–K4 (16 ..., P–KB4?; 17 P–K4, P×P; 18 R×P), and he can still hold on to his Bishop-pair for the time being.

16 ...	Q–N4
17 P–K4	

It is important to note that Black cannot afford 17 ..., P–QB4 with the intention of inducing White to play P–Q5, giving Black the chance to occupy e5; for White can reply 18 P–K5, B–N1 (18 ..., P×P?; 19 N–K4, Q×P; 20 N×B); 19 N–K4, Q–N3; 20 P–KR3, N–R3; 21 P×P!, B×KP; 22 B×B, R×B; 23 Q–B3!, P–B3 (23 ..., R–K2?, 24 N–B6 ch); 24 N–Q6 with a won position.

17 ...	B–B5
18 B×N!	

Meeting the threat 18 ..., N–K6. Exchanging his Bishop in these circumstances is good for White, as the Black Bishop on f4 is on an unfavourable diagonal.

18 ...	B×B?

Recapturing and developing at the same time seems the natural thing; yet it is a mistake. It was necessary to take with the Queen in order to open up the retreat square h6 for the Bishop on f4.

19 P–K5	B–B4

20 Q–KB2	B–Q6

Meeting White's threat of 21 P–KN3, which can now be answered by 21 ..., B×N; 22 K×B, B–Q7.

21 N–K4	Q–R3
22 P–KN3	B×N(f1)
23 K×B	Q–R6 ch
24 K–N1	B–R3
25 N–Q6	R–K2
26 P–Q5!	

White has already attained his strategical goal and by the advance of the central pawns severely cramps the enemy position. The text-move is much better than 26 Q–B5, Q×Q; 27 N×Q, R–Q2.

26 ...	P×P
27 P×P	R–B2
28 QR–Q1	B–N4
29 R–K2	P–KR4
30 R–KB1	

The attack on the square f7 brings quicker results than the preparation of the advance of the central pawns.

30 ...	Q–Q2
31 P–KR4	B–R3
32 Q–B3	P–KN3
33 Q–N3!	

The pawn on f7 can no longer be protected. If 33 ..., Q–Q1, White wins by either 34 N×NP or 34 N×BP, R×N; 35 P–Q6, Q–Q2; 36 R(2)–KB2.

33 ...	N–R2
34 N×BP	B–N2
35 P–Q6	Resigns

In this game White used the mobility of his central pawns to obtain a break-through in the centre. Sometimes, however, it is not so straightforward, and the centre only makes itself felt indirectly: in this case the enemy pieces are restricted in their movements because of the need to block the break-through that is always in the air; then the side with the pawn centre is favourably placed to begin various sorts of operations.

KOTOV–ELISKASES
(Interzonal 1952)

DIAGRAM 166

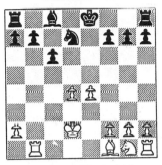

Position after White's 14th move

Without Queens it is more difficult to use a pawn centre as a basis for a flank attack; yet White again has the advantage, for he can post his King actively behind his pawns and after an eventual break-through quickly penetrate the enemy position.

14 ...	N–N3
15 B–Q3	B–K3
16 P–QR4	O–O–O
17 N–K2	

Not 17 P–R5?, N–B5 ch; 18 B×N, R×P ch!; 19 B–Q3, B–B5; 20 K–B3, B×B, etc.

| 17 ... | N×P |
| 18 R–R1 | N–N7 |

| 19 R×P | K–N1 |
| 20 R(1)–QR1 | B–B5! |

A strategical blunder would be 20 ..., N×B, for White's Knight, which can effectively support the advance of his pawns, would be considerably stronger than the Black Bishop.

21 B×B	N×B ch
22 K–Q3	N–N3
23 P–N4!	

White thus forestalls a possible P–KB4 by Black and at the same time begins the advance of his King-side pawns.

| 23 ... | K–B2 |
| 24 P–B4 | R–Q2 |

Black could indeed have exchanged both Rooks but that would have left his Knight and King unfavourably placed and thus cost him a pawn, e.g. 24 ..., R–R1?; 25 R×R, R×R; 26 R×R, N×R; 27 N–N3 (threatening N–R5), P–KN3; 28 P–K5, K–Q2; 29 N–K4, K–K2; 30 N B6, etc.

| 25 R(7)–R5 | KR–Q1 |
| 26 R–KN5! | |

This move, in connection with the next, is a very good manoeuvre; the intention is to advance with the pawns on the King-side and then

173

break through in the centre at a suitable moment. The immediate advance of the King-side pawns (e.g. 36 P–B5 followed by P–N5) would be pointless, as the Black pawns have not yet been weakened; for this reason White forces the advance of one of the Black pawns.

26 ...   P–B3

After 26 ..., P–KN3; 27 R(5)–QR5, White can continue with 28 P–N5, cramping Black's King-side; he can then follow this with P–R4–R5 and P–B5.

27 R(5)–QR5

Now he threatens 28 P–B5 followed by K–K3 and N–B4–K6.

27 ...   N–B1!
28 P–B5(?)

More precise was 28 P–R4!, N–Q3; 29 N–B3, after which White can choose P–B5, P–K5, or P–N5 as the position demands. The text-move complicates the situation considerably.

28 ...   P–KN4!
29 P–R4   P–R3
30 P×P   RP×P
31 R–KR1

Now White must arrange his pieces as favourably as possible and then prepare the break-through P–K5; that is the only winning plan.

31 ...   N–Q3
32 R–KR6   R–K2!
33 N–B3   R(1)–K1!

Passive defence of the pawn lets

White make the winning advance P–K5; Black therefore counters by an attack on the King-pawn, whose advance is now seemingly prevented.

DIAGRAM 167

Position after 33 ..., R–K1

34 P–K5!   P×P
35 N–Q5 ch!

The break-through is achieved by a combination that leaves White with the better end-game.

35 ...   P×N
36 R–B5 ch   K–N1

Weaker is 36 ..., K–Q2; 37 R×P, etc.

37 R×N   P×P

Stronger is 37 ..., P–K5 ch!; 38 K–K3, R–R1; 39 R(5)×P, R–R6 ch; 40 K–K2, R–R7 ch; 41 K–B1, P–K6; 42 R–K6!, R–QB2; 43 R–B5, and although White has good prospects, it is doubtful whether he can win against the best defence. After missing his chance, Black sees his opponent convert his passed-pawn on f5 in a most instructive manner.

38	R(5)×P!	R–K6 ch
39	K–B4!	R–QB1 ch
40	K×P	R–KN6
41	P–B6	R×P ch
42	K–K5	R–KB5

After 42 ..., R–K1 ch; 43 K–B5, R–B5 ch; 44 K×P, R(1)–K5; 45 R–KB5 White has a won position.

43	R–Q8!	R×R
44	R×R ch	K–B2
45	R–KN8	K–Q2
46	R–N7 ch	K–K1

White also wins after 46 ..., K–B3; 47 R×KNP, R–B8; 48 K–K6, R–K8 ch; 49 K–B7, P–N4; 50 K–N7.

47 R×QNP!

It is interesting to note that Black only loses because of the existence of his King-Knight-pawn, which shields the White King from perpetual check.

47	...	R–B7
48	K–K6	R–K7 ch
49	K–B5	P–N5
50	K–N6	R–KB7
51	P–B7 ch	K–B1
52	R–N8 ch	K–K2
53	R–K8 ch	Resigns

Our examples have shown cases in which the attainment of the classical centre brought with it an obvious positional advantage; this occurred because the central pawns were supported by pieces and, being mobile, constantly threatened various break-through operations. It should be remembered that the pawns on Q4 and K4 ventured from these squares only at a favourable moment, when their advance was accompanied by strong tactical threats; this is similar to the case of united passed-pawns. The advance of one of these central pawns must be well prepared, and great care should be taken to ensure that, after an advance, the neighbouring pawn is not left behind in a position from where it can be blockaded. The centre pawns are strongest on Q4 and K4; a premature advance can change the picture completely and make the centre a serious weakness.

In our next example we show a successful attack against the classical centre.

SLIVA–PACHMAN

(Moscow 1956)

1	P–Q4	N–KB3
2	P–QB4	P–KN3
3	N–QB3	P–Q4
4	P×P	N×P
5	P–K4	N×N
6	P×N	B–N2
7	B–QB4	O–O
8	N–K2	N–B3!?

The Grünfeld Defence is an opening that puts pressure on White's centre from the wings. This necessitates the advance P–QB4 by Black; consequently the text-move seems illogical; yet it contains a profound idea worked out by the Soviet master Simagin: Black does not give up the move P–QB4 altogether, but merely postpones it until after the development of his pieces (e.g. P–QN3, B–QN2, Q–Q2, KR–Q1, N–QR4), when he hopes that its execution will occur with added force.

9 O–O(?)

White should counter Black's plan to attack his centre by preparing an action on the King-side. Well suited for this is the move 9 B–KN5!; then if Black replies 9 ..., P–KR3, White gains an important tempo by 10 B–K3 followed by Q–Q2; Black's best reply is 9 ..., Q–Q2!; 10 Q–Q2, R–Q1; 11 B–R6, with a very complicated position, in which White has the better prospects.

9 ...   **P–N3**
10 R–N1

With this move White impedes the advance P–QB4 by Black. After 10 ..., N–R4; 11 B–Q3, the move 11 ..., P–QB4 is answered by 12 P–Q5. P–K3; 13 P–QB4—a manoeuvre made possible by the movement of the Rook to b1.

10 ...   **B–N2**

DIAGRAM 168

11 B–R3?

With this White hopes to stem the anticipated attack on his centre; but he merely furthers his opponent's plans. Correct was 11 B–K3, Q–Q2; 12 Q–Q2, KR–Q1, with approximate equality.

11 ...   **N–R4**
12 B–Q3   **Q–Q2**
13 P–KB4(?)

Such an aggressive procedure is effective only when the central formation is sufficiently firm; under the present circumstances it is a strategical mistake, after which White's centre, despite the imposing appearance of the pawns on d4, e4, and f4, soon falls apart. However, Black's P–QB4 could not have been prevented even by an attempt at repetition of moves; e.g. 13 B–N4, N–B3; 14 B–R3, KR–Q1!; 15 P–KB4, P–K3!; 16 P–B5, KP×P; 17 P×P, N–R4!; 18 B–N4, P–QB4!; 19 B×N, P×B; 20 P×NP, RP×P; 21 B–B4, B–Q4; 22 B×B, Q×B, and Black, in view of his pressure against the remnants of White's centre, has the advantage.

13 ...   **P–QB4!**
14 P×P

If 14 P–Q5, Black delivers a blow from the other wing (14 ..., P–KB4) to liquidate the centre.

14 ...   **KR–Q1**
15 B–B2   **Q–B2**
16 Q–K1

After 16 Q–B1, N–B5, Black has also a decided positional advantage.

16 ...	N–B5
17 P×P	P×P
18 B–B1	N–R6!

The pawn on a2 cannot escape; Black has therefore time to secure the lasting advantage of the *two Bishops*.

19 B×N	R×B
20 P–K5	

The attempt to protect the pawn on a2 by R–N2 fails for tactical reasons: 20 R–N2, R×BP!; 21 N×R, B×N; 22 Q–B1, B×R; 23 Q×B, R–Q7; 24 R–QB1, Q–B4 ch! followed by B×P, and Black has a won game. White therefore decides to give back the pawn and close the diagonal to the Bishop on g7.

20 ...	R×RP
21 B–N3	R(7)–Q7
22 R–B2	P–K3
23 R–Q1	R×R
24 B×R	

Of the proud central formation there remains only shadow; there is indeed still the pawn on e5 blocking the Black Bishop, but soon this last bastion will be undermined too.

DIAGRAM 169

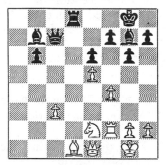

Position after 24 B×R

24 ...	P–KN4!
25 P×P	

Or 25 P–N3, Q–B3; 26 K–B1, Q–R8 ch; 27 N–N1, B–KB1; 28 R–Q2, B–Q4, and Black wins.

25 ...	Q×KP
26 P–R4	Q–K6
27 Q–B1	R–Q7
28 K–R1	R×B
29 Resigns	

In this game Black broke up his opponent's centre by the advance of a Bishop-pawn. Another means of fighting a strong centre is pressure by the pieces on Q4 and K4; then it is often possible to force the pawns into an early advance so that they can be liquidated by exchange against one's own pawns. A simple example is the Alekhine Defence: 1 P–K4, N–KB3; 2 P–K5, N–Q4; 3 P–QB4, N–N3; 4 P–Q4: if White's King-pawn were still on e4, he would have a decided advantage; but, as it is, Black can proceed with success against the centre by 4 ..., P–Q3; 5 P–B4, P×P; 6 BP×P, N–B3; 7 B–K3, B–B4; 8 N–KB3, P–K3; 9 B–K2, and now can force the exchange of either White's Queen-pawn (9 ..., N–N5 followed by P–QB4) or his King-pawn (9 ..., B–K2 followed by P–KB3).

We are now in a position to sum up the aims and principles that should be borne in mind when the classical centre makes its appearance—

For the player who possesses the pawn-centre

1. The pieces should be so posted that they protect the central pawns and at the same time are ready to support a possible advance.

2. He should manoeuvre in such a way that the opposing pieces are forced into a less favourable position.

3. He should advance the central pawns at a suitable moment and, by a break-through in the centre, create tactical threats on one or both wings.

For the player fighting the pawn-centre

1. Advantageous posting of the pieces to immobilize the enemy central pawns.

2. Piece pressure against the centre to force the opposing pieces into a passive position.

3. Weakening the opponent's centre so that he is forced to advance one pawn allowing the other to be blockaded.

4. Liquidation of one or both central pawns by an attack with the c-pawn or f-pawn.

Basically the classical pawn centre is strong only when it is sufficiently protected by pieces and possesses mobility; when immobilized or blockaded it becomes a weakness.

B. THE LITTLE CENTRE

By this concept we mean the possession by one side of a pawn on K4 or Q4 while the opponent has one on the third rank on an adjacent central file; Diagram 170 shows a position in which White has the *little centre*. In this position White must endeavour to use the open d-file by occupying the square d5, while Black will seek in a similar way to draw advantage from the e-file by occupation of e5. As, however, a White piece on d5 is in the opponent's half of the board, it will exert greater pressure on the opponent's position than a Black piece on e5; therefore the possession of the *little centre* gives

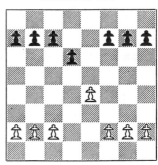

DIAGRAM 170

a certain space advantage and so allows greater freedom in the movement of one's pieces. The following game shows how this space advantage can be used to mount an attack on the enemy position.

TARRASCH–SCHLECHTER

(Leipzig 1894)

1 P–K4	P–K4
2 N–KB3	N–QB3
3 B–N5	P–Q3
4 P–Q4	B–Q2
5 N–B3	N–B3
6 O–O	B–K2
7 R–K1	N × QP
8 N × N	P × N
9 B × B ch	Q × B
10 Q × P	O–O

DIAGRAM 171

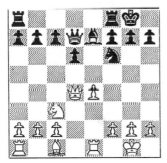

11 P–QN3!

The Bishop will work most effectively on the diagonal a1–h8. Besides, White impedes the possible counter-manoeuvre by Black of KR–K1, B–B1, R–K3, P–KN3, and B–N2, which would improve the co-ordination of Black's pieces and turn the bad Bishop on e7 into an active piece.

11 ...	KR–K1
12 B–N2	B–B1
13 QR–Q1	

Now White threatens P–K5. Thus the *little centre*, although less mobile than the classical centre, can nevertheless generate a certain dynamic strength.

13 ...	Q–B3
14 R–Q3	R–K3
15 R(3)–K3	QR–K1
16 P–KR3	Q–N3

It is doubtful whether Black could have improved the co-ordination of his pieces by P–KN3, for White would then have been able to occupy the outpost d5 with great effect; e.g., 16 ..., P KN3; 17 N–Q5!, B–N2; 18 P–QB4, N–R4; 19 Q–Q2, and White, in view of the weakness of f6, has a clear advantage.

17 Q–Q3   P–B3

Bars d5 to the White Knight, which could have gone there after P–KN4–5. That Black has been induced to play P–QB3, however, is a strategical success for White.

18 N–R4!   Q–B2
19 P–QB4

A very important manoeuvre, which prevents P–Q4 by Black and allows the White Knight to go over to the King-side; rather strangely, it was the move N–QR4 which laid the basis for the Knight's impending King-side excursion.

19 ...   N–Q2?

Here Black had his first and last opportunity to play P–KN3; the position of the Bishop on g2 would then, it is true, leave the pawn on d3 weak, but this weakness would be offset by the activity of the Bishop. Instead, Black opts for passive defence, allowing White to use his space advantage to storm the King-side.

20 K–R1

Preparing an attack on the g-file. The square g1 is made available to the Rook, which takes up the offer nine moves later.

20 ...	P–B3
21 Q–B2	N–K4
22 N–B3	

Threatening 23 N–K2 followed by N–N3.

22 ...	N–B2
23 P–KN4!	

Not 23 N–K2?, P–KB4!, after which the *little centre* is eliminated and White's advantage gone.

23 ...	Q–R4
24 R–Q1	Q–N3
25 P–KR4!	

Again N–K2 is premature, as Black replies N–N4, forcing the Knight back to c3.

25 ...	N–K4
26 R–N3	N–B2
27 P–B3	N–R1

Black has no longer any counter-play and can only await White's attack.

DIAGRAM 172

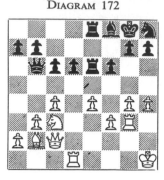

28 N–K2	Q–B2
29 R(1)–KN1!	

Threatening storm clouds are gathering over the square g7. White's plan is simple; he will open the g-file by P–KN5 and then bring his Knight to f5, after which the square g7 is attacked four times. Black is powerless to thwart this manoeuvre.

29 ...	Q–KB2
30 N–Q4	R(3)–K2
31 P–N5	P × P
32 R × P	P–N3
33 N–B5	R–K4

Or 33 ..., R–Q2; 34 Q–B3, etc.

34 P–B4!	R × N
35 P × R	B–N2
36 P × P	Resigns

In this game White's space advantage enabled him to build up an attack against the enemy King. It is worth noting that the central pawn created an important support point for the Knight on f5.

In positions where the pawn on the fourth rank is supported by a pawn (e.g. pawns on Q4 and QB3, or K4 and KB3), the centre is not very mobile; on the other hand, it does not bind pieces to its defence. If the protecting pawn should subsequently advance, the centre gains in mobility, but with the loss of protection that results it can often become an object of attack.

There are two principal means of playing against the *little centre*. The first, which usually occurs when the neighbouring pawn has advanced leaving the central pawn without its natural protection, is to subject this central pawn to pressure. The second, and more frequent, is to liquidate the central pawn by the advance of a pawn on an adjacent file. We find numerous examples of this in opening theory: for example, in the Rubenstein variation of the French Defence (1 P–K4, P–K3; 2 P–Q4, P–Q4; 3 N–QB3, P×P; 4 N×P) an eventual P–QB4 is the corner-stone of Black's set up; we also meet the advance of a central pawn in several variations (1 P–K4, P–K4; 2 P–Q4, P×P; 3 Q×P, N–QB3; 4 Q–K3, N–B3; 5 N–QB3, B–K2!; 6 B–Q2, P–Q4!). The *little centre* is therefore an impermanent creation and can only be maintained for a short period; with its liquidation, the resulting opening of the central files can sometimes give the opponent an advantage, if he can manage to occupy them.

C. OTHER TYPES OF PAWN CENTRE

Pawn centres can, of course, be of many different types. One possibility is the symmetrical pawn formation, which, from the strategical point of view, does not require a detailed examination; an example is the formation that occurs after 1 P–K4, P–K3; 2 P–Q4, P–Q4; 3 P×P, P×P. In such positions the struggle for the centre is merely a matter of active piece development, which makes the control of the central squares possible.

DIAGRAM 173   DIAGRAM 174

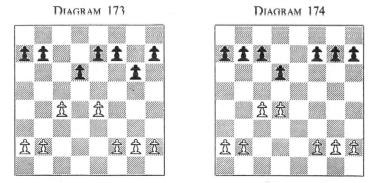

A common type of pawn formation is that shown schematically in Diagram 173. Here Black still possesses both his central pawns, whereas White has already exchanged his Queen-pawn for a Bishop-pawn; yet it is White who has the superiority in the centre. The reason for that is the lack of mobility of the Black centre: the d-pawn is completely immobilized by White's c-pawn, and an advance of the e-pawn would weaken the d-pawn considerably. Such a pawn centre generally gives White a greater space advantage than the *little centre*, and it is a strategical necessity for Black to liquidate at least one of White's fourth-rank pawns; so, for example, after the opening moves 1 P–K4, P–QB4; 2 N–KB3, N–QB3; 3 P–Q4, P×P; 4 N×P, P–KN3; 5 P–QB4, B–N2; 6 N–B2, P–Q3; 7 B–K2, Black generally continues 7 ... N–R3!; 8 O–O, P–B4! and gets a satisfactory game.

In Diagram 174 we again have a formation that gives White superiority in the centre, for his Queen-pawn is mobile, while Black's is hampered in its advance by the pawn on c4. A pawn centre of this type is, as a rule, of temporary duration: either White soon makes the advance P–Q5, which gives him a certain space advantage and leaves the square d4 open for a minor piece, or Black achieves the advance P–Q4; in the latter case, the central pawn position becomes symmetrical and White, if he is to keep the upper hand, must endeavour to obtain a space advantage on the Queen-side by P–QB5. If, however, Black does not manage to play P–Q4, he allows White to maintain his central superiority and thereby facilitates his piece development.

We now follow with two examples in which the schematic pawn formations of diagrams 173 and 174 are incorporated in actual games.

LISSIZYN–BOTVINNIK
(Leningrad 1932)

1 N–KB3	P–QB4
2 P–B4	N–KB3
3 P–KN3	P–Q4
4 P×P	N×P
5 B–N2	N–QB3
6 O–O?	

Better is 6 P–Q4.

6 ...	P–K4
7 P–Q3	

After his mistake on the sixth move, White has no effective means of fighting the opponent's centre.

7 ...	B–K2
8 QN–Q2	

More active is 8 N–B3 followed by B–Q2, N–K1, and P–B4; but even then White's pieces are so badly placed to support this advance that he cannot obtain complete equality.

8 ...	O–O
9 N–B4	P–B3
10 B–K3	B–K3
11 P–QR4	

White's strategical conduct of the game is faulty. The text-move, it is true, secures the square b5 for the Knight, but simultaneously weakens the Queen-side; in addition it amounts to a renunciation of P–QN4 and thereby the struggle to eliminate Black's pawn on c5.

| 11 ... | Q–Q2 |
| 12 Q–Q2 | P–QN3! |

DIAGRAM 175

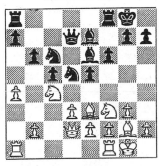

The pawns on c5 and e5 have become strong bulwarks for Black, whose space advantage is now so great that he can calmly prepare his attack on the enemy position.

13 KR–QB1	QR–B1
14 Q–Q1	K–R1
15 B–Q2	KR–Q1
16 Q–N3	N–B2
17 B–B3	QR–N1
18 Q–B2	N–Q4
19 KN–Q2	QR–QB1
20 N–B1	N–Q5!

A move that is typical in such positions. It should, however, be made only at a moment when retaking by one of the pawns is favourable. In this position, Black

will open the e-file and exert pressure on the pawn on e2.

| 21 Q–Q1 | B–N5! |

This forces White to make an exchange that he would sooner avoid.

22 B(3)×N	KP×B
23 Q–Q2	B–B1
24 R–K1	R–K1
25 P–R4	

With the intention of developing the Knight via h2. Hopeless is 25 P–K4, P×P *e.p.*; 26 P×P, N–N5, etc.

| 25 ... | B–R6 |

Part of Black's plan is an attack on White's King-side, which is already cramped by the pawn on d4; but he first seeks to deprive White of his most important piece, the Bishop on g2.

26 B–B3	R–K2
27 N–R2	QR–K1
28 K–R1	B–K3
29 P–N3	N–N5!

Black now intends to exchange the important Bishop by means of B–Q4. A mistake would be 29 ..., N–B6 on account of the strong reply 30 P–K4.

| 30 B–N2 | B–Q4 |
| 31 N–B3 | R–B2 |

In order to bring the Bishop on f8 into play.

32 K–R2	B–Q3
33 B–R3	Q–Q1
34 QR–N1	R(2)–K2
35 N–N1	B–QB2

36 N–R3	B–N2!

At last Black induces the exchange of the White Bishop; the threat is 37 ..., Q–Q4.

37 B–N2	B × B
38 K × B	N–Q4
39 N–B2	Q–Q3!

DIAGRAM 176

The stage is set for the final stroke; there is no defence against Black's threat of N–K6 ch.

40 N–QR3	N–K6 ch!
41 K–R1	N–N5
42 Q–B4	

No better is 42 K–N2, N × P; 43 K × N, Q × P ch; 44 K–B1, R–K6; 45 N–B3, Q–R6 ch; 46 K–N1, B–R7 ch.

42 ...	Q × Q
43 P × Q	N × P ch
44 K–N2	N × P
45 Resigns	

BOLESLAVSKI–
BONDAREVSKI

(Leningrad 1948)

1 P–K4	N–KB3
2 P–K5	N–Q4
3 P–Q4	P–Q3

4 P–QB4	N–N3
5 P × P	KP × P
6 B–Q3	P–N3

This move, instead of the normal 6 ..., B–K2, is recommended by Mikenas. The intention is to develop the Bishop on g2 and so weaken any possible advance P–Q5 by White, for in such an eventuality the Bishop would have good prospects on the long diagonal. If White does not make the advance, the Bishop will put pressure on the Queen-pawn, which can be immobilized by P–Q4 on Black's part.

7 N–K2	B–N2
8 O–O	O–O
9 QN–B3	N–B3
10 B–K3	

DIAGRAM 177

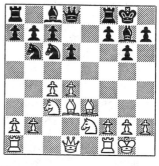

10 ...	N–N5

Black sets a higher value on the *two Bishops* than on the superior centre he leaves White. Correct was 10 ..., P–Q4!; 11 P–B5, N–Q2!, and Black can equalize with N–B3, N–K2, and B–B4.

11 P–QN3	N × B

184

Already P–Q4 has lost some force, since, after 11 ..., P–Q4; 12 P–B5, N–Q2; 13 B–N1 followed by 14 P–QR3 and 15 P–QN4, White begins his Queen-side action with the gain of a tempo.

12 Q×N   R–K1

At this stage P–Q4 is poor, as Black's King-side position is weakened after 12 ..., P–Q4; 13 P–B5, N–Q2; 14 N×P, P–QB3; 15 N(5)–B4, P–KN4 (the only way to recover the pawn); 16 N–R5, N×P; 17 Q–B2.

13 QR–Q1   N–Q2
14 Q–Q2   P–QB3

Black cannot bring himself to try 14 ..., N–B1; 15 B–N5, as that would leave him the choice between two unattractive alternatives: restricting the mobility of the Bishop after 15 ..., P–KB3, or allowing its exchange after 15 ..., B–B3. However, both these continuations would have offered better prospects than the text-move, which does, it is true, open a path for the Queen to the Queen-side, but which has the disadvantage of seriously weakening the square d6.

15 KR–K1   Q–R4

Still preferable was 15 ..., N–B1. The alternative, 15 ..., N–B3, is answered by 16 B–N5, Q–B2; 17 N–N3, B–Q2; 18 N(N3)–K4.

16 B–B4   B–B1
17 N–N3   R×R ch
18 R×R

DIAGRAM 178

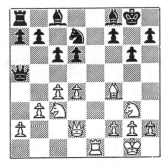

Now White is threatening 19 R–K8, which cannot be countered by either 18 ..., N–B3?; 19 N–Q5!, Q–Q1; 20 N×N ch, Q×N; 21 B–N5, Q–N2; 22 R–K8, etc., or 18 ..., Q–Q1; 19 N(N3)–K4, N–N3; 20 B–N5, B–K2; 21 B×B, Q×B; 22 Q–B4.

18 ...   P–QN4

In order to answer 19 R–K8 by B–QN2.

19 N(N3)–K4   P×P

Just as hopeless is 19 ..., P–N5; 20 N–N1, P–Q4; 21 N–Q6, B–QR3; 22 P–B5, with a decisive positional advantage for White.

20 B×P   B–QR3

Or 20 ..., P×P; 21 B×B, N×B; 22 N–B6 ch, K–R1 (22 ..., K–N2; 23 N–K8 ch and 24 Q–R6); 23 R–K8, K–N2; 24 R–K5! followed by 25 N–K8 ch, and White wins.

21 P–QN4   Q–KB4
22 B×B   R×B
23 P–Q5!   N–K4

If 23 ..., P×P, there follows 24

N×P, K–N2; 25 N–K7, Q–K3;
26 N–QB5 winning.

| 24 P×P | P–B3 |

After 24 ..., N×P; 25 P–N5,
B×P; 26 N–Q6, Black loses a
piece.

25 P–N5	B–B1
26 Q–Q4	P–QR3
27 N–Q5	K–N2
28 N(4)×P	Resigns

After 28 ..., R×N, there
follows 29 N×R, K×N; 30 P–B4.

D. TENSION IN THE CENTRE

The central pawn formations that we have discussed in the first three
sections of this chapter all arose after an exchange of pawns; now
we shall examine the positions that occur before the exchange of
pawns. Let us look first at the French defence after the moves
1 P–K4, P–K3; 2 P–Q4, P–Q4. The centre contains a certain tension,
derived from the position of White's King-pawn in relation to
Black's Queen-pawn; but it will only be a tension of temporary
character, for sooner or later a change must occur. This change can
even take place on the next move: White can continue with 3 P×P,
P×P, producing a symmetrical centre in which the tension has disappeared; or he can play 3 P–K5 and build a blocked pawn chain
that is also without tension. White can, however, maintain the
central tension by covering the King-pawn with a Knight (e.g.
3 N–QB3); in that case the decision rests with Black, who can play
3 ..., B–N5, 3 ..., N–KB3 or 3 ..., P×P. If Black opts for
the immediate exchange, he gives up his only pawn that is already
posted in the centre. Tarrasch called this exchange "giving up the
centre" and considered it wrong in all cases; Nimzowitsch, on the
other hand, pointed out that the exchange did not necessarily mean
the entire loss of the centre, the fight for which could be continued
by exerting pressure on the squares e4 and d4. (We have already
seen that the *little centre* can often be effectively fought by piece
pressure and by the advance of the c-pawn and f-pawn.) In their
comprehension of the centre, Tarrasch and Nimzowitsch fell into
opposite extremes: Tarrasch over-estimated the importance of
central occupation, while Nimzowitsch did not accord the *little
centre* its true worth. Today we know that the exchange 3 ...,
P×P gives White a decided space advantage, and for that reason it
remains out of favour.

A central formation that sometimes occurs is the one in Diagram
179; in such a case the tension is usually of short duration. It
should be noted that the opening of the position brings a definite
advantage to the player with a lead in development. Another

interesting fact is that it is often better to force the opponent to liquidate the centre rather than to do so oneself; in Diagram 179, for example, White's strongest move is **1 B–N5**, which forces Black to open the game; then if **1 ...**, **P×QP**, White replies **2 O–O**, and after **2 ..., B–Q2; 3 P×P, N–N5; 4 Q–K2 ch, B–K2; 5 P–Q6, P×P; 6 N×P**, Black has a difficult game.

DIAGRAM 179

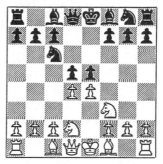

The evaluation of the advantages and disadvantages of an exchange in the centre depends always on the whole character of the position; the tension presents complicated strategical and tactical problems, and the possibilities that could occur with any change in the pawn structure require very careful assessment.

In our next example Black attempts to maintain his central pawn formation, though only by restricting the mobility of his pieces; the result is that White obtains a strong attack by opening the game at a suitable moment.

SMYSLOV LUBLINSKI

(17th U.S.S.R. Championship)

1 P–K4	P–K4
2 N–KB3	N–QB3
3 B–N5	P–QR3
4 B–R4	P–Q3
5 P–B3	B–Q2
6 P–Q4	N–B3
7 QN–Q2	B–K2
8 O–O	O–O
9 R–K1	

(*See* Diagram 180).

DIAGRAM 180

Position after 9 R–K1

In this position it is customary to continue 9 ..., P×P; 10 P×P, N–QN5; 11 B×B, Q×B; 12 N–B1, P–QB4! and take up the fight against White's classical centre.

9 ...   B–K1

Black intends to maintain his pawn centre by means of N–Q2 and P–KB3.

10 B–N3

This move has a double purpose: on the one hand it thwarts the counter-action in the centre that could arise after an immediate N–B1 (e.g. 10 N–B1, P×P; 11 P×P, P–Q4; 12 P–K5, N–K5); on the other it hampers any attempt to strengthen the square e5 by means of P–B3 (e.g. 10 P–KR3, N–Q2; 11 N–B1, P–B3).

| 10 ... | N–Q2 |
| 11 N–B1 | B–B3? |

More in line with Black's set-up is 11 ..., K–R1 followed by P–B3; then at least he has a firm centre as compensation for his passive position.

| 12 N–K3 | N–K2 |

He does well to avoid 12 ..., P–KN3; 13 N–Q5, B–N2; 14 B–N5.

13 N–N4	N–KN3
14 P–N3	B–K2
15 P–KR4!	

The prelude to an attack on the King-side; White creates a base on g5 for his Knight.

15 ...	N–B3
16 N–N5	P–R3
17 N×N ch	B×N
18 Q–R5!	N–R1

DIAGRAM 181

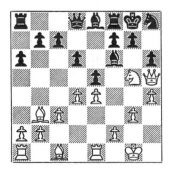

19 P×P!

Opening up at the right moment. Black can hardly avoid the complete opening of the d-file, as after 19 ..., B×P; 20 P–KB4, B–KB3; 21 N–B3 White's central and King-side pawns are extremely mobile; then, faced with threats like P–KN4–5 or P–K5, Black would be in an uncomfortable position.

| 19 ... | P×P |
| 20 B–K3! | Q–K2 |

Accepting the Knight offer is not good, for White's attack on the h-file would be decisive: 20 ..., P×N; 21 P×P, P–KN3; 22 Q–R4, B–N2; 23 K–N2, B–QB3; 24 R–R1, R–K1; 25 Q–R7 ch, K–B1; 26 B–B5 ch, R–K2; 27 Q×N ch!, and White wins

| 21 B–Q5! | P–B3 |

It seems that 21 ..., B–B3; 22 B×B, P×B would have been the lesser evil, although Black then has weakened pawns and a bad Bishop. After the text-move Black succumbs to the onslaught of White's pieces.

| 22 B–N3 | B–Q2 |

By his manoeuvre on the previous move White prevented the active posting of Black's Bishop on c6; now he has time to begin operations on the d-file.

23 QR–Q1	QR–Q1
24 R–Q2	B–B1
25 KR–Q1	R×R
26 R×R	Q–B2

The Knight is still taboo: 26 ..., P×N; 27 P×P, P–KN3; 28

P×B, Q×P; 29 Q–R6, Q–N2;
30 Q–R4, with clear advantage to
White. By the text-move Black
hopes to force his opponent's
unpleasant Knight to a decision,
but instead he opens the way for a
pretty combination.

| 27 B–B5! | R–Q1 |

Useless is 27 ..., P×N; 28
B×R, and the alternative 27 ...,
B–K2; 28 B×B, Q×B; 29 N–B3,
R–K1; 30 Q×KP!, Q×Q; 31

N×Q, R×N; 32 R–Q8 ch gives
White a pawn.

28 R×R ch	B×R
29 N×P!	N×N
30 B–N6!	Q–Q2

After 30 ..., Q×B; 31 Q×N ch,
K–R2; 32 P–R5, the mate on g8
cannot be averted.

31 B×B	K–R2
32 B×N	Q×B
33 B–N6 ch	Resigns

In this game White's active central position gave him a marked
space advantage. We may say that in general the maintenance of
tension in the centre for a long time is seldom good for the defending
side. There are, however, two important ways of proceeding when
one is on the defensive—

1. Exchange at a suitable moment in order to liquidate the
centre completely.

2. Pressure against the opponent's central pawns, thereby
forcing him to end the tension.

In the following game we show the first method at work.

TARRASCH–ALEKHINE
(Baden-Baden 1925)

1 P–K4	P–K4
2 N–KB3	N–QB3
3 B–B4	B–B4
4 P–B3	B–N3
5 P–Q4	Q–K2
6 O–O	N–B3
7 R–K1	P–Q3
8 P–QR4	P–QR3
9 P–R3	

There are difficulties involved in
maintaining the centre: White
must prevent B–KN5 in order to
preserve sufficient control over d4.

| 9 ... | O–O |
| 10 B–KN5 | |

Stronger is either 10 P–QN4, in
order to develop the Bishop to a3,
or 10 N–QR3, followed by N–B2,
with consolidation of the central
position.

| 10 ... | P–R3 |
| 11 B–K3 | |

After 11 B–R4 the direct advance
11 ..., P–N4? gives White a
decisive attack by 12 N×NP!,
P×N; 13 B×NP; but Black can
simply prepare the advance by
K–R1 and R–KN1.

189

DIAGRAM 182

Position after 11 B–K3

The position of the Bishop on e3 is unfavourable, as it hampers the defence of the King-pawn. It is not easy for Black to make use of this; for example, 11 ..., N×KP?; 12 P–Q5, N–QR4; 13 B×B, P×B; 14 B–R2, P–B4; 15 P–QN4 loses a piece: Alekhine, however, succeeds in finding a very clever way to eliminate his opponent's central superiority.

| 11 ... | Q–Q1! |

A fine positional move, which threatens to liquidate the opposing pawn centre by 12 ..., P×P; 13 P×P, P–Q4. White can forestall this by simplifying (12 P×P, P×P), but, if he is not content with this, he must, in order to maintain the tension in the centre, withdraw his Bishop from its active position on c4.

| 12 B–Q3 |

Not so good is 12 B–R2, R–K1!; 13 QN–Q2, P×P, which forces White to take on d4 with his Bishop.

| 12 ... | R–K1 |
| 13 QN–Q2 | B–R2! |

A very good waiting move, which also removes the Bishop from attack by a possible Knight move to c4.

| 14 Q–B2(?) |

White wants to facilitate the transfer of his Knight to g3; but the tactically unfavourable position of the Queen on c2 allows Black to eliminate the tension in the centre. Better is 14 Q–N1!, so that after 14 ..., P×P; 15 P×P!, N–N5 White can safely retreat with his Bishop to f1 (16 B–B1, N×P?; 17 N×N, B–KB4; 18 B–Q2!).

DIAGRAM 183

| 14 ... | P×P! |
| 15 N×P |

Not good is 15 P×P, N–QN5; 16 Q–B3, N×B; 17 Q×N, N×P!; 18 N×N, B–KB4; 19 B–B4!, Q–K2! (not 19 ..., P–Q4; 20 B×BP!); 20 N–B5, Q–B3; 21 N–K4, Q–N3, with advantage to Black. But after the text-move White's centre will soon be completely broken up.

| 15 ... | N–K4 |
| 16 B–B1 | P–Q4! |

17 QR–Q1

Black wins a pawn after 17 P–KB4, N–N3; 18 P–K5, N–R4.

17 ...	**P–B4!**
18 N(4)–N3	**Q–B2?**
19 B–KB4	

White should have been content with the modest 19 P×P, N×P, which leaves Black with only a slight advantage.

19 ...	**N–B6 ch!**
20 N×N	**Q×B**
21 P×P?	

Now Black's advantage takes on a concrete form. Alekhine recommends 21 P–K5, B–B4; 22 Q–Q2, Q×Q; 23 R×Q, N–K5; 24 R(2)–Q1 (24 R×P?, B–K3), QR–Q1 as White's best line; but

the *two Bishops* give Black a lasting advantage.

21 ...	**B–B4**
22 B–Q3	

White hopes for 22 ..., B×B?; 23 Q×B, P–B5; 24 Q–Q2!, but he is out of luck. In answer to 22 Q–Q2, the continuation 22 ..., Q×P; 23 N–B1, B–B7; 24 R×R ch, R×R; 25 R–K1, N–K5; 26 Q–B4, P–B5; 27 N–Q4, B×N; 28 P×B, Q–N5! is given by Alekhine.

22 ...	**B×P!**
23 P×B	**Q×N**
24 R×R ch	**R×R**
25 B–B1	**R–K4**
26 P–B4	**R–N4 ch**
27 K–R2	**N–N5 ch**
28 P×N	**R×NP**
29 Resigns	

The other method of eliminating central tension—forcing the opponent to initiate the change—often occurs in the opening. Let us consider the well-known closed variation of the Ruy Lopez (**1 P–K4, P–K4; 2 N–KB3, N–QB3; 3 B–N5, P–QR3; 4 B–R4, N–B3; 5 O–O, B–K2; 6 R–K1, P–QN4; 7 B–N3, O–O; 8 P–B3, P–Q3**). At this stage 9 P–Q4 is no longer considered the best continuation, as it allows Black to reply 9 ..., B–N5, forcing the advance 10 P–Q5 (10 B–K3 enables Black advantageously to break up the centre by 10 ..., P×P; 11 P×P, N–QR4; 12 B–B2, N–B5; 13 B–B1, P–B4); instead **9 P–KR3** is generally preferred, in reply to which Black must fight sharply to eliminate the tension: one possibility is the Tschigorin variation, **9 ..., N–QR4; 10 B–B2, P–B4; 11 P–Q4, Q–B2; 12 QN–Q2, N–B3**, after which White is practically forced to the exchange 13 P×P or the advance 13 P–Q5.

To sum up positions in which two central pawns on the fourth rank (d4, e4) are opposed by one on the fourth defended by one on the third (e.g. d6, e5), we can say that the side with both pawns on the fourth will endeavour to maintain the central tension, except in cases where the change brings him a clear advantage. His opponent, on the other hand, will attempt to eliminate the tension, provided that he thereby removes the enemy superiority in the centre.

To finish this section on central tension we shall examine the position in Diagram 184.

DIAGRAM 184

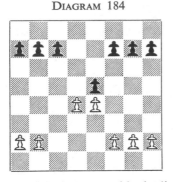

It might be supposed that basically there is no difference whether the exchange is made by White or Black; tactically, however, there is often a very important difference, for the exchange usually allows the opponent to obtain an advantageous centralization of the retaking piece. It should be noted that the advance P–Q5 rarely takes place in such positions; it merely strengthens Black's King-pawn and gives him a favourable post on d3, which can possibly become a blockading square, should White's Queen-pawn eventually become isolated.

E. PIECE CENTRALIZATION

We have already mentioned that a strong pawn-centre is not the only means of controlling the centre. We shall now examine one of the other ways—piece centralization. In books on the opening we come across the variation 1 P–Q4, P–K3; 2 N–KB3, P–QB4; 3 N–QB3, P–Q4; 4 P–K4, P×KP; 5 N×P, P×P; 6 Q×P, Q×Q; 7 N×Q (Diagram 185). Now, although Black possesses the only pawn in the centre, it is White, with his two Knights, who dominates the centre: an immediate attempt to drive off the Knights fails (e.g. 7 ..., P–K4; 8 N–QN5, or 7 ..., P–B4; 8 N–KN5), and the preparatory move 7 ..., P–QR3 gives White the chance to obtain the two Bishops (8 B–KB4 followed by N–Q6 ch).

DIAGRAM 185

The piece centre as shown in Diagram 185 is admittedly an exceptional case; more usually only one piece is centralized: even so, that one piece, with its enhanced power, is often enough to dictate the entire situation in the centre. The piece most frequently centralized is the Knight, which benefits enormously in view of its limited reach; but other pieces, too, gain in strength when operating from the centre of the board. In the next game it is the Bishop which takes up a central position and thereby determines the character of the game.

BOTVINNIK–KAN
(Leningrad 1939)

1 P–Q4	N–KB3
2 P–QB4	P–K3
3 N–QB3	B–N5
4 N–B3	P–B4
5 P–QR3	B × N ch
6 P × B	Q–R4?

Better is 6 ..., P–Q3 or 6 ..., P–QN3.

7 B–Q2	N–K5
8 Q–B2	N × B
9 N × N	P–Q3
10 P–K3	

A mistake would be 10 P–K4?, P × P; 11 P × P, N–B3; 12 Q–Q3, P–K4!, after which Black can keep White's central pawns blocked on the same coloured squares as White's Bishop.

10 ...	P–K4?

Now this advance is a strategical error, as it allows White's Bishop to reach the weakened square d5 by way of e4.

11 P × KP!

At first sight it looks as if White is weakening his central position and saddling himself with doubled isolated pawns; in reality, this move is merely the first stage in his plan to establish superiority in the centre.

11 ...	P × P
12 B–Q3	P–KR3

13 O–O	O–O

DIAGRAM 186

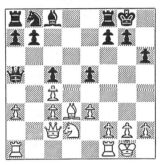

It is clear that White must now endeavour to occupy the square d5. The most natural piece with which to effect this plan is the Knight, but unfortunately a Knight excursion to d5 in the present position is not good, e.g. 14 P–K4?, N–QB3; 15 KR–Q1, B–K3; 16 N–B1, QR–Q1; 17 N–K3, N–K2; 18 N–Q5, B × N!; 19 BP × B, N–B1 followed by N–Q3, and Black's blockade gives him the better game.

14 P–B4!

A very important move. White intends the further advance P–B5 in order to deprive Black of the natural developing square for his Bishop on e6, thereby assuring control of d5. If Black now attempts to forestall this plan by 14 ..., P × P, he will find that the opening of the game favours White, who already has a lead in development.

14 ...	N–Q2

193

15 P–B5	N–B3(?)

After this the position in the centre soon becomes clear-cut. Black ought to have held his Knight in reserve for a possible exchange on d5; his best plan was to try 15 ..., P–B3 in order to counter any tactical threats generated by the advance P–B6 on White's part; however, even then White would have had the advantage after 16 B–K4 and B–Q5 ch.

16 N–K4!	Q–Q1
17 N×N ch	Q×N
18 B–K4	R–N1
19 QR–Q1	P–QN3

Black apparently thinks that he can exchange the opposing Bishop simply by developing his own to b7; this plan, however, is not practicable, as he must always watch out for the danger of White's Rooks making inroads into his position along the d-file. Black is also suffering from the handicap that his Queen must remain for a long time on f6 to prevent White from breaking up his King's position by P–B6.

20 P–R3

While waiting for 20 ..., B–N2, White opens a useful haven for his King. If now Black goes ahead with his plan, there follows 20 ..., B–N2; 21 B×B, R×B; 22 Q–K4!, R–K2 (22 ..., R(2)–N1; 23 R–Q7); 23 R–Q5 followed by 24 KR–Q1. In view of this, Black decides to complicate the game by preparing P–QN4.

20 ...	B–R3
21 B–Q5	P–QN4
22 P×P	R×P(?)

Better is the line given by Botvinnik: 22 ..., B×P!; 23 P–B4, B–B3; 24 Q–K4, B×B; 25 R×B, and although Black loses a pawn he obtains certain drawing chances in an end-game with heavy pieces.

23 P–B4	R–N3

DIAGRAM 187

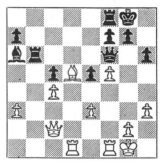

The strong position of the Bishop ensures White a clear superiority. If White's Bishop were on d3 instead, and his King-pawn on e4, then it would be Black, with his good Bishop against a bad one, who would have the advantage. As it is, although most of White's pawns are on white squares, his Bishop is nevertheless much more powerful than Black's, which can only move about aimlessly; there is, of course, the threat 24 ..., B–N2 in the offing, but that can be suitably dealt with.

24 R–N1!	R–Q1

194

The continuation 24 ...,
KR–N1; 25 R × R, R × R (not
25 ..., Q × R?; 26 P–B6! with the
threat of Q–N6!); 26 Q–R4 (also
good is the simple 26 R–N1),
Q–K2; 27 P–B6!, P × P; 28 Q–B2,
K–N2; 29 R–B3 gives White a
strong attack.

25	R × R	P × R
26	P–K4	B–B1
27	Q–R4	B–Q2
28	Q–R7	B–K1
29	R–N1	R–Q3
30	P–QR4	

There is no way to prevent the
further advance P–QR5, which
leads by force to the win of a pawn.

30	...	K–R2
31	P–R5	P × P
32	Q × RP	R–R3
33	Q × P	R–R7
34	Q–K3	Q–R3
35	R–N8	Q–R5
36	K–R2	R–R6
37	Q–B5	R–R7
38	R–R8	Q × R
39	B × Q	R × B
40	Q × P	B–B3
41	Q–B7	Resigns

It is less frequent that the centralizing of heavy pieces is the
dominant feature of the game; yet under certain circumstances this
is the case; generally it is most effective when an attack is made on
an enemy central pawn (e.g. e5). The following is a typical example.

BOTVINNIK–TSCHECHOVER
(Leningrad 1938)

DIAGRAM 188

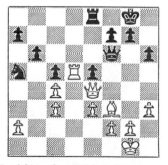

Position after White's 21st move

Here we have the characteristic
position in which the centralized
heavy pieces are a threat to the
pawn on e5; Black cannot therefore force any exchanges for the
moment (e.g. 21 ..., R–Q1; 22

R × KP, N × P?; 23 R–K8 ch,
R × R; 24 Q × R ch, K–R2; 25
Q–K4 ch, etc.). It is interesting to
note that, despite Black's superior
pawn formation, which would
make itself felt in the end-game, he
nevertheless has the inferior position on account of the lack of
co-ordination of his pieces.

21	...	Q–K2
22	B–N4	Q–N2

Countering the threatened 22
R–Q7.

23 B–B5!

The Bishop contributes its share
to controlling the centre by keeping
the Queen covered; it thereby
makes the advance of the Rook to
d7 possible. Black cannot reply 23
..., P–N3 on account of 24 B × P,

P×B; 25 Q×NP ch, K–B1; 26 R–Q6.

23 ...	Q–N1
24 R–Q7	R–Q1
25 Q×P	N×P
26 Q×Q	R×Q
27 B–K4!	

First the Bishop heads for d5; then White will initiate a Kingside pawn advance, which Black is powerless to stop.

27 ...	N–R6
28 B–Q5	R–KB1
29 P–K4	P–QR4
30 P–QB4	P–QN4

31 P×P	N×P
32 P–K5	P–R5
33 P–B4	N–Q5
34 K–B2	P–N4
35 P–N3	P×P
36 P×P	N–K3
37 K–K3	

Towards the end of the game, King centralization makes its appearance—a typical end-game phenomenon.

37 ...	P–B5
38 P–B5	N–B4
39 R–B7	N–Q6
40 P–K6	Resigns

Our final example is one in which both sides manage to centralize a piece; but in one case the centralized piece works in harmony with its fellow pieces, while in the other this co-ordination is lacking.

TEICHMANN–TSCHIGORIN

(Cambridge Springs 1904)

1 P–Q4	P–Q4
2 P–QB4	N–QB3
3 N–KB3	B–N5
4 P×P	B×N
5 P×N	B×BP
6 N–B3	P–K3
7 B–B4	N–B3
8 P–K3	B–N5
9 Q–N3	N–Q4
10 B–N3	O–O
11 B–Q3	Q–N4!
12 Q–B2	

Avoiding 12 O–O?, B×N; 13 P×B, N×P!, which is bad for White.

12 ...	P–B4!

Black secures the square d5 for his Knight, but at the same time leaves e5 to the opposing Bishop. The further course of the game, however, shows that it is not a simple matter of one centralized piece cancelling the other out.

13 B–K5	R–B2
14 O–O–O	B×N
15 P×B	

DIAGRAM 189

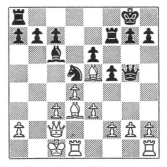

At first sight White's position

196

does not look too bad: he has the Bishop pair and a central pawn majority; his Bishop on e5 appears to have possibilities of eventually promoting an attack on the enemy King. Nevertheless, within a few moves Black succeeds in completely breaking up the position around White's King. What is the cause of this rapid catastrophe? First of all, Black's pieces are in harmony: the centralized Knight is supported by the Bishop, and the Queen can transfer quickly to the Queen-side. Compared with this, the strength of White's Bishop on e5 is an illusion; it is trained on g7, but is ineffective until supported by the opening of the g-file; however, as Black is not likely to oblige by capturing the pawn on g2, there is no time for this. Finally the Bishop is cut off by its own pawn on d4 from the defence of the Queen-side.

15 ...	P–QN4!
16 KR–N1	Q–K2
17 QR–B1	

Transferring the King to a1 would lose quickly: 17 K–N2, R–N1; 18 P–N4, P–N5; 19 P–QB4, N–B6; 20 QR–KB1, N–R5 ch; 21 K–R1, P–N6, etc.

17 ...	Q–R6 ch
18 K–Q2	P–N5
19 P–QB4	B–R5!
20 Q–N1	N–B6

With White's forces in disarray, Black has several ways of strengthening the attack.

21 Q–R1	R–Q1
22 P–N3	N–K5 ch
23 K–K2	N–B4
24 Q–N1	N × B
25 Q × N	Q × P ch
26 K–B3	B–B7!
27 Resigns	

F. CONTROL OF THE CENTRAL SQUARES

In the previous section it may have been observed that the fight for the centre was conducted not only by the pieces actually placed there; those that controlled the centre from the side-lines also played their part. We shall now see how control and occupation differ, how occupation of a central square by a piece actually diminishes control over that square. After the moves 1 P–Q4, N–KB3; 2 N–KB3, for example, it is clear that if Black continues with 2 ..., N–K5 (which in any case is an important loss of tempo) he alters his control over the square c4: before the move Black had the square under observation; by occupying it he relinquishes his control over it. Likewise it would be quite pointless for White after 1 N–KB3, P–Q4 to continue with 2 N–K5, for Black could simply drive off the Knight by P–KB3. Centralizing of pieces, therefore, is only practicable when adequate control over the centre has already been obtained.

Looking at the moves 1 P–Q4, N–KB3; 2 N–KB3 we might ask

how Black can increase his control over the square e4 and thereby strengthen his central position. Basically there are two ways: he can continue by 2 ..., P–Q4, setting up a pawn centre; or he can choose 2 ..., P–QN3 followed by B–N2, putting piece pressure on e4. The creators of the *Neo-Romantic School*, Nimzowitsch and Réti, have shown that, though a pawn posted in the centre is indeed in most cases a guarantee for its stable occupation, there is the disadvantage that the pawn is a barrier to the effective working of one's own pieces. So, for example, after 1 P–Q4, N–KB3; 2 N–KB3, P–Q4 the pawn on d5 restricts the power of a Bishop that may be developed to b7 (e.g. in the Tartakower system). For this reason Nimzowitsch advocated in the French Defence (after 1 P–K4, P–K3; 2 P–Q4, P–Q4; 3 N–QB3) the exchange 3 ..., P×P; he claimed that Black would thereby increase the force exerted on the centre by his pieces (the Bishop along the diagonal a8–h1 and the heavy pieces on the d-file).

The opening systems discovered by the *Neo-Romantics* have as their strategical basis not the occupation of the centre with pawns but pressure against the centre by pieces and pawns. We have already dealt with the use of the Bishop-pawns to exert central pressure; control of the centre by pieces is generally characterized by the fianchetto of a Bishop to QN2 or KN2. Examples of this are the Queen's Indian Defence (1 P–Q4, N–KB3; 2 P–QB4, P–K3; 3 N–KB3, P–QN3), the Nimzowitsch System (1 N–KB3, P–Q4; 2 P–QN3), and the Réti System (1 N–KB3, P–Q4; 2 P–B4, P–K3; 3 P–KN3, or 2 ..., P–QB3; 3 P–QN3). Another important strategical factor in these openings is the exchange of opposing pieces controlling the centre; so, in the Nimzo-Indian Defence after 1 P–Q4, N–KB3; 2 P–QB4, P–K3; 3 N–QB3, the move 3 ..., B–N5 serves to pin, and later exchange off, the Knight on c3, which controls d5 and e4.

The use of pawn and piece pressure against the centre has been known since the beginning of the modern form of chess. Piece pressure against the squares d4 and e5 is the basic idea behind the Ruy Lopez (1 P–K4, P–K4; 2 N–KB3, N–QB3; 3 B–N5); and in the Scotch game (1 P–K4, P–K4; 2 N–KB3, N–QB3; 3 P–Q4, P×P; 4 N×P) Black defends himself by piece pressure on either d4 (4 ..., B–B4; 5 B–K3, Q–B3) or e4 (4 ..., N–B3; 5 N–B3, B–N5). Pawn pressure against the centre is the idea behind not only the Queen's gambit (1 P–Q4, P–Q4; 2 P–QB4) but also one of the oldest of all chess openings, the King's Gambit (1 P–K4, P–K4; 2 P–KB4). Formerly, however, the use of pieces and pawns in the fight to control the centre was seen as a means to its occupation:

the *Neo-Romantics* showed that command of the centre was possible without direct occupation.

Our first example shows an interesting transition from one centre form to another: Black begins his struggle against White's pawn centre by piece pressure; then he occupies the centre with his pieces; finally he establishes a pawn centre himself.

FEIGEN–FLOHR
(Kemeri 1937)

1 P–Q4	N–KB3
2 P–QB4	P–KN3
3 N–QB3	P–Q4
4 Q–N3	P×P
5 Q×BP	B–K3
6 Q–N5 ch?	

Although considered good at the time, this move is not good; correct is 6 Q–Q3.

6 ...	N–B3
7 N–B3	N–Q4
8 N×N	

If 8 P–K4, then 8 ..., KN–N5; 9 Q–R4, B–Q2; 10 Q–Q1, P–K4!.

8 ...	B×N
9 P–K3	P–K3
10 B–Q2	P–QR3
11 Q–R4	B–Q3!

As a result of White's mistaken sixth move, Black obtained a lead in development, which he has used to secure control over the central squares. The Bishop is better placed on d6 than on g7, for, besides bearing on e5, it is positioned for a possible King-side attack.

12 B–K2	O–O
13 Q–B2	N–N5

This move cannot be considered

good, as it temporarily diminishes control over the centre; better was the immediate P–KB4.

14 Q–N1	P–KB4
15 O–O	N–B3!

White was threatening simplification by 16 B×N, B×B; 17 N–K5; Black recognizes in time the mistake on his fourteenth move and prepares the transfer of his Knight to the favourable post f6.

16 B–B3	Q–K2
17 R–Q1	N–N1!
18 N–Q2	

After 18 N–K5, B×N; 19 P×B, Q–N4; 20 B–B1, N–Q2, Black also has the advantage, in view of the active position of his pieces and his Queen-side pawn majority.

18 ...	N–Q2
19 B–B3	N–B3

DIAGRAM 190

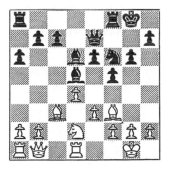

Black's domination of the square e4 has been made possible by the re-development of the Knight; White cannot now play 20 P–K4?, P×P; 21 N×P, N×N; 22 B×N, Q–R5; this variation shows the importance of Black's 11 ..., B–Q3.

| 20 Q–Q3 | N–K5! |

At last Black can occupy the square e4; White dare not play 21 N×N, P×N; 22 B×P, B×P ch.

| 21 Q–K2 | N–N4! |

The Knight leaves its central post for a moment; the intention is to play Q–N2–R3 in order to force White to exchange Bishops. White does not wait to be forced and lightens Black's task by exchanging at once, perhaps fearing 22 ..., N×B ch? and loss of his Bishop-pair.

| 22 B×B(?) | P×B |

Black has now a firm bastion in the centre—his Queen-pawn. His good Bishop and the open e-file with the outpost on e4 give him a decisive advantage.

23 N–B3	N–K5
24 QR–B1	P–B3
25 B–K1	QR–K1
26 P–KN3	Q–Q2
27 Q–B1	P–KN4

White has not the slightest counter-chance and is powerless against the King-side attack.

28 R–Q3	P–B5
29 KP×P	P×P
30 N–R4	K–R1
31 Q–N2	P×P
32 RP×P	N–N4
33 P–B3	N–R6 ch
34 K–R1	

If 34 K–R2, Black has the strong reply 34 ..., N–B5.

34 ...	B–K2
35 B–Q2	B×N
36 P×B	Q–B4
37 R–N3	R–KN1
38 Q–R2	R–K3
39 R–KB1?	N–B7 ch
40 Resigns	

In the next game White attacks the enemy centre by piece pressure combined with pawn pressure from the sides; he finally destroys it by advancing his Queen-pawn, which had been held back in reserve.

PACHMAN–DONNER
(Rotterdam 1955)

1 P–QB4	P–KN3
2 N–QB3	B–N2
3 P–KN3	N–KB3
4 B–N2	O–O
5 P–K4	P–K4

Better is 5 ..., P–B4.

6 KN–K2	P–Q3
7 O–O	KN–Q2
8 P–Q3	P–KB4
9 P×P	P×P

Although Black has a pawn majority in the centre, the position is not favourable for him. White's plan is straightforward: he will increase his pressure on the centre by P–KB4 and finally break it up by the advance P–Q4 at a suitable moment. All the while, the pressure exerted by his pieces on the centre plays an important part.

10 B–K3

The immediate P–KB4 is also good: but it is usually better not to unfold one's strategical plan too early; so the completion of his development is quite logical.

| 10 ... | N–KB3 |
| 11 Q–Q2 | P–B3 |

If 11 ..., N–N5, White replies 12 B–N5.

| 12 P–KR3 | N–R4? |

After 12 ..., P–Q4; 13 P×P, P×P; 14 P–Q4, P–K5; 15 N–B4 followed by 16 KR–QB1, White does indeed stand better: but the text-move leads to even greater difficulties; instead of preventing 13 P–KB4, Black makes this move more effective by withdrawing a piece from the centre for an unjustified flank action.

DIAGRAM 191

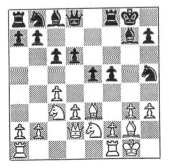

13 P–KB4!

The strategical importance of this move has already been explained; tactically it is possible because the continuation 13 ..., P×P; 14 N×P!, N×P?; 15 R–B3, Q–R5 (15 ..., Q–N4; 16 N–K6); 16 B–B2 is bad for Black.

13 ...	Q–K1
14 K–R2	Q–N3
15 Q–K1!	

Protecting the g-pawn in this way enables White to recapture with the Knight should Black play P×P.

| 15 ... | N–Q2 |

Somewhat better is 15 ..., N–R3, which leaves the Bishop's line of fire unblocked.

| 16 R–Q1 | K–R1 |
| 17 P–Q4! | |

The struggle for the centre has reached its climax. After 17 ..., P–K5; 18 P–KN4!, P×P; 19 N×P, P×P; 20 B–B3, White's fine central position combined with the open g-file gives him a decisive King-side attack. In this variation the typical break-through move P–KN4 shows how a pawn two files away can nevertheless participate in the struggle for the centre.

17 ...	R–KN1
18 Q–B2	B–B3
19 QP×P	P×P
20 R–Q6!	

White now breaks into the enemy position.

| 20 ... | P×P |

Black chooses this as the moment to open the game on the

King-side; but his attempt is foiled by a little combination.

21 N×P!

A very unpleasant surprise; the pawn on g3 is again taboo, as after 21 ..., Q×P ch; 22 Q×Q, N×Q; 23 KR–Q1! White's pressure is irresistible, e.g. 23 ..., R–N2; 24 R×B!, N×R; 25 R–Q8 ch, R–KN1; 26 B–Q4!, R×R; 27 B×N ch, winning.

21 ...	N×N
22 B×N	Q–B2
23 R–K1!	

An important strengthening of the control over the central squares; above all, it prevents the centralizing of the Black Knight by N–K4, which would free Black's position considerably. If now 23 ..., Q×P, White wins by 24 R×B!, N×R; 25 B–K5, R–B1 (25 ..., Q–B2; 26 N–K4!); 26 N–K4!, P×N; 27 R×P!, Q–B2; 28 R–KB4. White's present plan foresees an exchange sacrifice some moves later.

23 ...	B–N2
24 R(6)–K6!	N–B1

After 24 ..., N–B3 the game would be decided in a similar manner.

25 R–K7	Q×P?

After 25 ..., Q–B3; 26 R×B!, R×R; 27 B–K5, Q–B2; 28 N–K4! Black has likewise a very bad position, though one that affords rather longer resistance.

DIAGRAM 192

26 R×B!

This exchange required no precise calculation; the Bishop on g7, which is directed towards the centre, is Black's only active piece; after its elimination White's pieces completely dominate the scene.

26 ...	R×R

Or 26 ..., K×R; 27 B–K5 ch, K–B2; 28 N–K4!, and White's pieces are all poised for the decisive action.

27 R–K8

The point of the sacrifice was to paralyse all Black's pieces; the recovery of material by 27 B–K5? is unimportant.

27 ...	K–N1

After 27 ..., R–KB2 or 27 ..., Q–B2, White replies 28 Q–K3! leaving Black defenceless against numerous threats.

28 B–Q6	R–KB2
29 Q–K3	P–B5

Other moves allow 30 Q–N5 ch.

30 Q–K5	R–B4
31 R×N ch!	R×R
32 Q–N5 ch	Resigns

There is no hope after 32 ... K–B2; 33 Q–K7 ch, K–N3; 34 Q×R followed by B–K4 ch.

G. THE PARTLY BLOCKED CENTRE

In this section we shall examine positions in which the opponent has a central pawn on the fourth rank (e.g. the pawn formation d4, e3 opposed by d5, e6). Sometimes it is possible to eliminate this central pawn by exchanging it against a Bishop-pawn; sometimes it is necessary to advance one's own rear central pawn. It is with the second case that we are concerned in this section.

OPOCENSKÝ–IVKOV

(Rogasskaslatina 1948)

DIAGRAM 193

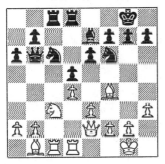

Position after Black's 17th move

White's advantage lies in his two Bishops; but they can only be exploited fully in an open position. White must therefore endeavour to open the game by an advance in the centre.

| 18 P–KN4! | N–QR4? |

White's eighteenth move was played in order to drive off the Knight on f6, thereby giving White more control of the centre. Black has misinterpreted the move as the beginning of a King-side attack and decides to start a counter-action on

the c-file; but the decentralization of the Knight enables White to break through strongly in the centre.

| 19 P–N5 | N–K1 |

After 19 ..., N–Q2; 20 P–K4, P×P; 21 P–Q5!, Black cannot reply 21 ..., P–K4 on account of 22 Q×KP.

| 20 P–K4! | P×P |
| 21 P–Q5! | |

White now has achieved the liquidation of the centre and with it the break-up of Black's position. After 21 ..., P×P; 22 N×QP, Q–K3; 23 R×R, R×R; 24 Q×KP, Q×Q; 25 B×Q, White's Bishop pair and centralized pieces give him a clear advantage.

21 ...	P–B4
22 P×P e.p.	N×P
23 B–K3!	Q–Q3
24 N×P	N×N
25 R×R	R×R
26 B×N	P–K4

Obviously not 26 ..., P×P; 27 B×QP ch, K–R1; 28 B×P, Q–N3 ch; 29 B–N2, and Black has lost a pawn.

27 P–N3	P–QN4
28 Q–N4	R–Q1
29 R–QB1	

By means of his successful break-through White has already obtained a decisive positional advantage; his centralized Bishops are in control, and he threatens 30 B–QB5, Q–KB3 (30 ..., Q–B2; 31 Q–K6 ch, K–B1; 32 Q–B5 ch);

31 P–Q6!, B×P; 32 B–QN6. There is no adequate defence to this: e.g. 29 ..., N–N2; 30 R–B6, or 29 ..., Q–KB3; 30 Q–K6 ch, Q×Q; 31 P×Q.

29 ...	Q–Q2?
30 B–QN6	Q×Q ch
31 P×Q	N–N2
32 R–B7	Resigns

In the next game White succeeds in playing P–K4 after preparation by P–KB3; he thereby achieves a strong classical centre.

BOTVINNIK–KERES
(20th U.S.S.R. Championship)

1 P–Q4	N–KB3
2 P–QB4	P–K3
3 N–QB3	P–Q4
4 P×P	P×P
5 B–N5	B–K2
6 P–K3	O–O
7 B–Q3	QN–Q2
8 Q–B2	R–K1

In this position White has the choice of several different strategical plans; he decides to prepare the advance P–K4

9 KN–K2	N–B1
10 O–O	P–B3
11 QR–N1	

To prepare the advance P–K4 by P–B3 would not be good at this stage, as, after 11 P–B3, P–KR3; 12 B–R4, N–K3; 13 B–B2, P–QB4!, the isolated pawn that Black gets on d5 is no weaker than White's pawn on e3. White therefore first prepares another advance, the minority attack (this will be treated

in a subsequent chapter); his plan of advance in the centre will be held back until the circumstances are more propitious.

11 ...	B–Q3(?)

This is the cause of Black's later difficulties. The correct way to meet the threatened minority attack will be shown in another chapter. Black's threat of B×P ch is easily countered by White.

12 K–R1!	N–N3
13 P–B3!	

After 13 P–QN4 Black had intended 13 ..., P–KR3; 14 B×N, Q×B, with counter-play on the King-side; now, however, things are different and White gains a clear advantage if Black attempts the same plan, e.g. 13 ..., P–KR3; 14 B×N, Q×B; 15 P–K4.

13 ...	B–K2

Preventing P–K4 for the moment, e.g. 14 P–K4, P×P; 15 P×P, N–N5!; 16 B×B, Q×B with the threats N–K6 and Q–R5.

DIAGRAM 194

Position after 13 ..., B–K2

14 QR–K1!   **N–Q2**

White's eventual P–K4 cannot easily be stopped by 14 ..., N–R4 either; e.g. 15 B×B, Q×B; 16 P–KN4!, N–B3; 17 N–N3, etc. Black's best continuation was 14 ..., B–K3; 15 N–N3 (15 P–K4, P×P; 16 P×P, N–N5; 17 B–B1, B KN4!), Q–N3; 16 N–B5, B×N; 17 B×B, QR–Q1, after which he is indeed without his Bishop pair, but is in a position to hamper White's P–K4.

15 B×B	R×B
16 N–N3	N–B3
17 Q–KB2	B–K3
18 N–B5	

Again P–K4 is premature, e.g. 18 P–K4, P×P; 19 P×P, N–N5. The text-move, by inducing Black to exchange his Bishop, deprives the square f7 of valuable protection; this could prove important when the f-file is eventually opened.

18 ...	B×N
19 B×B	Q–N3
20 P–K4	P×P

21 P×P	R–Q1
22 P–K5!	N–Q4

No better is 22 ..., N–K1; 23 B×N, RP×B, for White then has a strong attack along the h-file. White's last move has given Black the opportunity to blockade the backward pawn on d4, but in return White will obtain the very fine square d6 for his Knight.

23 N–K4	N–B1
24 N–Q6	Q–B2

Meeting the threat 25 N–B8. If, instead, 24 ..., N–K3?, then 25 N×BP! followed by 26 B×N is decisive; likewise hopeless for Black is 24 ..., R–B2; 25 N×BP!, K×N (25 ..., R×N; 26 B–K6); 26 B–K6 ch, K×B; 27 Q–B5 ch, K–K2; 28 Q–B7 mate.

25 B–K4   **N–K3**

Or 25 ..., N–QN3; 26 Q–N3!, N–K3 (26 ..., P–KN3; 27 N–B5, R(2)–Q2; 28 Q–N5); 27 R–K3, and Black is faced with the threat 28 B×P ch followed by Q–R4 ch and R–KR3.

26 Q–R4!	P–KN3
27 B×N	P×B
28 R–B1	Q–Q2
29 R–QB3	R–KB1

Otherwise White would decide the issue by 30 R–KR3, which can now be answered by 30 ..., P–B4. However, the poor position of Black's King allows a combination that soon finishes the game.

30 N–B5!   **R(1)–K1**

After 30 ..., P×N; 31 R–KN3 ch followed by Q–B6, mate cannot be avoided. White can now pick up the exchange, but he declines to do so, preferring to press on with his attack.

31 N–R6 ch	K–B1

Or 31 ..., K–R1; 32 Q–B6 ch, N–N2; 33 N×P ch, etc.

32 Q–B6	N–N2
33 QR–KB3	

Threatening mate in three beginning with 33 Q×BP ch.

33 ...	R–B1
34 N×P	R–K3
35 Q–N5	N–B4
36 N–R6	Q–N2
37 P–KN4	Resigns

CHAPTER X

Superiority on the Wings

IN the previous chapter we examined the important question of the struggle for the centre; but it is not only in the centre that an effective action can be launched: most games are characterized at some stage by an action on the wings. In an earlier part of the book we stated that a successful attack can be carried out only when the equilibrium has been disturbed, that is, when one side has acquired a superiority somewhere; this can arise from a weakness in the opponent's position, from a numerical superiority, or from the general superiority of one's own pieces. When applying this principle to an attack on the wings we can say that at least one of the following conditions should be fulfilled before such an attack is undertaken—

1. The opponent's wing position should be seriously weakened.

2. The attacking side should possess a pawn majority on the wing or a superiority in piece strength there.

In this chapter we shall deal with cases in which the second condition has been fulfilled, weaknesses in the opposing pawn chain will be treated in a later chapter. Our material will be spread over the following sections—

A. Pawn majority on the wing
B. Piece concentration on the wing
C. Space superiority on the wing
D. The blocked pawn chain
E. Flank attack and the centre.

A. PAWN MAJORITY ON THE WING

Often in the earliest stage of the game, an exchange of central pawns takes place, leaving an unsymmetrical pawn formation; for example, after the moves 1 P–K4, P–QB4; 2 N–K2, N–KB3; 3 QN–B3, P–Q4; 4 P×P, N×P; 5 N×N, Q×N; 6 P–Q4, P×P; 7 Q×P, Q×Q; 8 N×Q White has three pawns on the Queen-side compared with Black's two, while on the King-side Black has a majority of four to three. The reader will remember that in the chapter on pawns such positions occurred, and the result was usually that the pawn majority made the creation of a passed-pawn possible. It is this creation of a passed-pawn which is the most important strategical goal in utilizing a pawn majority. We shall now examine the different cases in which the pawn majority can be used to produce a passed-pawn and the effect of the pawn so created.

Let us imagine a position in which both sides have castled short and the material strength is equal. Is it, in such a case, better to have a pawn majority on the King-side or Queen-side? Anyone who has played over a game from a magazine or chess book is sure to have come across the annotation, "White has the advantage on account of his Queen-side majority." Most players know that a Queen-side majority is an advantage; but not all know the reason for it. In order to explain this advantage we shall consider first the end-game and then the middle-game.

We shall assume first an end-game position in which the pieces have been exchanged off and the Kings are in their castled positions on g1 and g8; Black has a majority on the Queen-side, White on the King-side. If both sides advance their pawns on the wing on which they are in a majority, Black will obtain a passed-pawn on the Queen-side, White on the King-side. Now, the way to the queening square is much more difficult for White, as his pawn is barred by the opposing King; Black's pawn, on the other hand, is farther away and therefore more dangerous, for it is not impeded by any King. However, one thing should be mentioned: in the end-game an important strategical principle is the centralization of the Kings, and both Kings generally hurry at the first suitable opportunity towards the centre, from where they can watch over both wings. Once the centralization of the Kings has taken place the Queen-side majority ceases to be an advantage.

In the middle-game the King is rarely employed as an active piece, and the role of stopping an opposing pawn is not, as in the end-game, one which it often has to play. The importance of the Queen-side majority in the middle-game lies in the fact that it can be advanced, whereas the attempt to set a King-side majority in motion denudes one's own King rather dangerously; without its natural pawn protection, the King would invite all sorts of unpleasant attacks.

Summing up, we can say that the conversion of a Queen-side majority, that is, the creation of a passed-pawn, is easier in both the middle-game and end-game than a King-side majority. In the middle-game the Queen-side pawns can advance without endangering the King's position: in the end-game, providing the Kings have not been centralized, they can create a passed-pawn out of reach of the enemy King.

Up to now we have assumed that both players have castled on the King-side. Of course, if they castle instead on the Queen-side, the position is reversed, and the Queen-side must be considered as the King's wing. If they castle on different sides, there is no King's wing and all the above remarks lose their validity.

We must now add a word of warning. In coming to the conclusion that a Queen-side majority is advantageous we assumed that the force exerted by the pieces of both players was equal; where this is not so the position is obviously different. Often a piece attack may be launched against the King of the player with the Queen-side majority, and the resistance to the attack may be lessened by the absence of the King-side pawn that gives the defending player his Queen-side majority. Thus with the pawn formation f2, g2, and h2 against g7 and h7, Black's ability to repel an attack is reduced by his lack of a pawn on f7; should he be under fire from a Bishop on d3 and a Queen on h5, he must think twice about defending himself by P–KN3, for he has always to reckon with the sacrifice B×NP, which would hardly be possible if Black still had his pawn on f7. To take another case: where Black's Queen-side majority means giving his opponent a four to three majority on the King-side, White can sometimes work up considerable pressure against the pawn on f7; he may even use his own e- and f-pawns in the attack and by advancing them break up Black's King-side position.

Having shown some of its limitations, we may now say that the Queen-side majority is of greatest and most lasting value in positions where the Kings have not been centralized and where the material is sufficiently reduced to exclude the danger of a piece attack on the King. Such positions generally occur in the transitional stage between the middle-game and the end-game; they include positions in which the Queens, but not the Rooks or all of the minor pieces, have been exchanged, and those in which the Queens remain, supported by some minor pieces but no Rooks.

And now some examples.

BRONSTEIN–KOTOV

(16th U.S.S.R. Championship)

(*See* Diagram 195)

The diagram shows a characteristic pawn position that allows White to use his Queen-side majority. It must be admitted that White's majority is in itself a relatively small advantage, and were it not for the unfavourable positions of the Black Knight on a6 and the Queen on f6, he would have a difficult task to convert it.

17 ...   N–B2
18 B–R5!

With this fine manoeuvre White

DIAGRAM 195

Position after White's 17th move

weakens the opposing King's position considerably: Black must reply P–KN3, and as he will probably have also to play P–KB3 at a later stage, in order to drive off the menacing Knight on e5, he will have difficulties in defending his King; in addition his seventh rank will be weakened, which could be an important factor in a possible Queen end-game.

18 ...	P–KN3
19 B–K2	N–K1
20 P–B3	

This reduces the scope of Black's Bishop and at the same time prepares for the centralization of the King in the event of most of the pieces being exchanged off.

20 ...	Q–K2
21 R×R	R×R
22 R–Q1	R×R ch
23 B×R	

The present material is favourable for the conversion of White's

pawn majority; White must now endeavour to post his pieces as advantageously as possible and then begin the march of his pawns. Although the exchange of Queens is not good for him, there is nothing to be feared from the exchange of both his minor pieces, so long as that does not prevent him from securing an advanced passed-pawn.

23 ...	P–B3
24 N–Q3	N–B2
25 B–N3	K–N2
26 P–QR4	Q–Q3
27 P–B5	P×P
28 N×P	B–B1 ?

Black realizes that the game would not be tenable after the exchange of both minor pieces; but he ought to allow the exchange of one by B–Q4 rather than disrupt the co-ordination of his pieces by this retreat.

| 29 P–N5 | P–K4 |

DIAGRAM 196

The position is clearly won for White. He should now play K–B2 followed by K–K2, in order to prevent the enemy Queen from penetrating his second rank; with the square d2 under cover the White Queen is free for duty elsewhere and should be brought to c4, from where it can create threats along the diagonal a2–g8; at the same time the further advance of the Queen-side pawns should be undertaken. If White had followed this plan, Black would have had no possibilities of active counter-play, for any advance of his King-side pawns exposes his King to great danger. White, however, opts for another plan and decides to settle the issue by tactical means: he brings about an exchange of Queens and calculates that he can win a piece by force; but he does not realize until too late that this leads to a drawn position.

30 N–K4?	Q–N3!

Not 30 . . ., Q–N5?, after which White can continue with 31 Q–B1.

31 Q × Q	

Now K–B2 is no longer of any use, as Black has the reply 31 . . ., B–K3, which gives him the chance to transfer his King to the Queen-side.

31 . . .	P × Q
32 N–Q6	B–Q2

33 B–B4	N–R1!

Not 33 . . ., K–B1?; 34 P–R5, K–K2; 35 P × P, K × N; 36 P–N7!, and White wins.

34 B–Q5	N–B2

Now White realizes that the hoped-for win of a piece leads to a clearly drawn position: 35 B–N7, B–K3!; 36 P–R5, P × P; 37 P–N6, N–Q4!; 38 B × N, B × B; 39 P–N7, B × NP; 40 N × B, P–R5; 41 K–B2, P–R6; 42 N–B5, P–R7; 43 N–N3. With this possibility ruled out, White can do nothing, as the exchange of Queens has made it possible for Black's King to cross the board to take care of any passed-pawn that may arise on the Queen-side.

35 B–B6	B–K3
36 N–N7	K–B2
37 P–R5	P × P
38 N × P	K–K2
39 K–B2	B–Q2

Even safer is 39 . . ., K–Q3.

40 P–N6	N–R3
41 B–N7	

The game is also drawn after 41 B × B, K × B; 42 K–K3, N–B4; 43 P–B4, P × P ch; 44 K × P, K–Q3. After the text-move the game was agreed drawn, as White cannot convert his passed pawn.

If a pawn majority is to be put to use, it is important that it should be mobile. Often a mobile King-side majority is much more valuable than an immobilized one on the Queen-side. The next example shows how Black is prepared to give up a pawn simply to immobilize his opponent's majority.

SPIELMANN–COLLE

(Dortmund 1928)

DIAGRAM 197

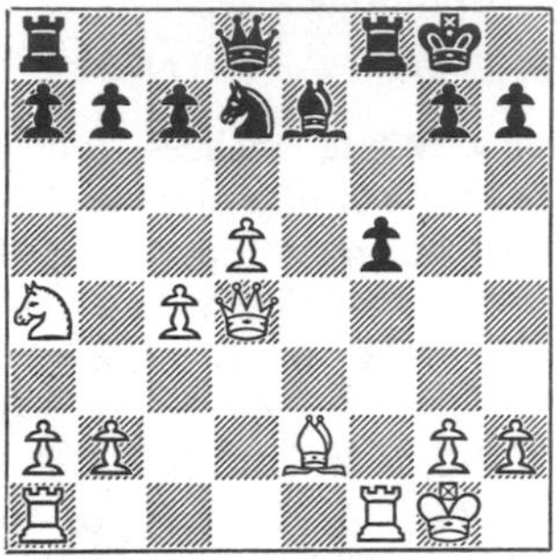

Position after White's 17th move

White has just taken his Knight from c3 in order to prevent B–B4 and at the same time to prepare the advance P–B5; however, he allows Black the chance to make a fine reply.

17 ...   P–QN4!

White will now have two extra pawns on the Queen-side, but as they are broken up their value is not so great; any attempt to create a passed-pawn will be accompanied by considerable difficulties. Black, on the other hand, will obtain a fine square on d6 for his Bishop

and will quickly be able to work up a strong King-side attack.

18 P × P	B–Q3
19 QR–K1	Q–K2
20 B–Q3	N–K4!

A good example of centralization. The continuation 21 B × P, R × B!; 22 R × R, N–B6 ch; 23 R × N, Q × R ch; 24 R–B1, B × P ch is not good for White.

| 21 K–R1 | P–B5! |
| 22 R–K2(?) | |

Hastens defeat. The only possibility of counter-play lies on 22 N–B5! followed by N–K6 or N–K4. Obviously 22 R × P??, R × R; 23 Q × R, N × B is out of the question for White.

22 ...	QR–K1
23 N–B3	Q–R5
24 N–K4	N–N5
25 P–KR3	

There is also no salvation in 25 P–KN3, Q–R6!, or 25 Q–N1, N × P; 26 Q × N, Q × Q ch; 27 K × Q, P–B6 dis ch.

25 ...	P–B6!
26 R × P	R × R
27 N–B6 ch	K–B2!
28 Resigns	

We shall now take a look at an opening that is based on the creation and conversion of a pawn majority; this is the Exchange Variation of the Ruy Lopez, with which Lasker achieved many successes.

LASKER–JANOWSKI

(Match 1909)

1 P–K4	P–K4
2 N–KB3	N–QB3
3 B–N5	P–QR3
4 B × N	QP × B
5 P–Q4	P × P
6 Q × P	

The character of the position is

now clear: by the exchange of central pawns White has acquired a King-side pawn majority and left Black with a Queen-side one that is badly disrupted by the doubled pawns; Black, however, has the Bishop pair, which could be put to good use in this open position. White's plan is now to simplify the position and use his pawn majority to create a passed-pawn that can be converted in the end-game; Black must seek his chances in play with his pieces. Already in 1894 Steinitz had found the right method for Black: in his match with Lasker he continued 6 ..., Q×Q; 7 N×Q, P–QB4; 8 N–K2, B–Q2; 9 QN B3, O–O–O; 10 B–B4, B–B3; 11 P–B3, N B3; 12 O O, B–K2, with a good game. Later Alekhine also used a good system: 6 ..., Q×Q; 7 N×Q, B–Q2; 8 B–K3, O–O–O; 9 N–Q2, N–K2; 10 O–O–O, R–K1!; 11 KR–K1, N–N3; 12 N–K2, B–Q3; 13 P–KR3, P–KB4, and Black stands better.

6 ... B–KN5(?)

Diagram 198

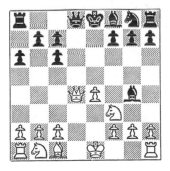

Black's last move was played with the idea of exchanging off the Knight on f3 and breaking up White's King-side pawns. That, however, is not a logical plan, for White's doubled pawns would be more mobile than those of his opponent. To convince ourselves that this is so, let us imagine that the exchange has been made and White is left with doubled pawns on f2 and f3. In this case he has the possibility of playing his fore-most King-Bishop-pawn to f5, assisted of course by suitable piece support; then he can advance his rear King-Bishop-pawn to f4 and his King-pawn to e5, and afterwards force the creation of a passed-pawn; he must of course take care that Black does not nip the whole plan in the bud by blockading the doubled pawns before they begin their advance; so he must fore-stall the manoeuvre P–KN4, N–K2–N3. When we look at Black's doubled pawns on the Queen's wing, the picture is entirely different; there is no clear way of creating a passed-pawn, and Black will have great difficulty in doing so. We can now see that White's majority would be the more mobile; the reason is that his pawn on e4 stands on a file not barred by an enemy pawn.

7 N–B3 Q×Q

With this move Black renounces his plan to disrupt White's pawns; his sixth move therefore proved a waste of time, for the Bishop can always be driven back by P–KB3.

8 N×Q	O–O–O
9 B–K3	B–N5
10 N(4)–K2!	

After 10 P–B3, B×N ch; 11 P×B, B–Q2; 12 K–B2, White would also have the better game, but, as unlike Bishops would be left after a possible exchange of Knights, Black would have drawing chances.

10 ...	B×N(7)?

A complete misapprehension of the strategical character of the position. Black gives up his only trump—the two Bishops—in order to saddle White with double pawns; but his prospects on the Queenside are in no way improved as a result. Correct was 10 ..., N–K2; 11 P–B3, B–Q2 followed by P–KB4, and Black can attempt to obtain play with his pieces.

11 K×B	B×N
12 P×B	

DIAGRAM 199

How are we to assess this position, in which both sides have doubled pawns? White's doubled pawns, on the same wing as his opponent's majority, are even isolated; but although doubled pawns are weak when mobility is desired, they can be very effective in defence; and in this position the pawns on c2 and c3 are just as able to stop the creation of an enemy passed-pawn as pawns on b2 and c2. On the King's wing it is only a matter of time before White can produce a passed-pawn; in addition his Bishop is very active. It can therefore be said that White has a clear positional advantage, and even without the minor tactical errors made by his opponent later in the game, Lasker could have won.

12 ...	N–B3

At last the Knight heads for c6, from where it can energetically fight the advance of White's pawns. Although the direct route to c6 with 12 ..., N–K2 is frustrated by 13 B–B5, there was a quicker way than that chosen by Black: 12 ..., P–QN3; 13 QR–Q1, N–K2 followed by P–QB4 and N–QB3.

13 P–B3	N–Q2
14 QR–Q1	N–K4

This costs two further tempi; better was 14 ..., P–QN3 followed by P–QB4 and N–N1–B3.

15 R–Q4	P–QN3
16 P–KB4	N–Q2
17 KR–Q1	P–QB4
18 R(4)–Q3	N–N1
19 K–B3	QR–K1

Black thinks that by holding on to his Rooks he will be better able to meet the opposing pawn advance; the drawback is that his King is cut off for a long time from where it is most needed—the King-side. The exchange of Rooks would have offered him better prospects: 19 ..., R×R; 20 R×R, R–Q1, or 20 P×R, K–Q2.

20 P–B5!

This move stands in contradiction to the rule that the pawn not directly opposed by an enemy pawn should advance first; but the move consistent with the rule, 20 P–K5, would have been faulty in this case, for the later advance of the f-pawn would present difficulties, as the pawn on e5 would be left *en prise*. The text-move is strong because it allows the Bishop access to f4, from where it can play a more active role.

20 ...   P–KB3

No better is 20 ..., N–B3; 21 B–B4, R–K2; 22 R–K1, KR–K1; 23 R–Q5, N–K4 ch; 24 B×N, R×B; 25 R×R, R×R; 26 K–B4, P–KB3; 27 R–Q1, and White can proceed with the pawn march P–N4, P–KR4, P–N5.

21 P–N4	R–K2
22 B–B4	KR–K1
23 R–K3	N–B3
24 P–N5	N–R4

The Knight will be no better placed on c4 than on c6; but Black has no means of improving his position. The move P×P,

recommended by Alekhine, is bad: 24 ..., P×P; 25 B×NP, N–K4 ch; 26 K–B4, R–Q2; 27 R–Q5!, and White can force the advance of his King-pawn as the continuation 27 ..., R×R?; 28 P×R loses Black a piece.

25 P–KR4	N–B5
26 R–K2	R–B2
27 R–KN1	K–Q2

Somewhat better is 27 ..., P–N3; White would then continue with 28 BP×P, RP×P; 29 P×P, R×BP; 30 R–N5! followed by P–R5.

28 P–R5   N–Q3(?)

Facilitates the decisive breakthrough.

29 P–R6!   BP×P

Obviously not 29 ..., P–N3; 30 BP×P, RP×P; 31 P×P, R×BP; 32 P–K5, R(3)–K3; 33 R–Q2.

30 R×P   P–N3

This loses a pawn; but after 30 ..., P×P; 31 R–R5 the position is hopeless for Black in view of the two united passed-pawns.

31 P×P	P×P
32 R×NP	R(1)–KB1
33 R–N7	R×R

Or 33 ..., K–K3; 34 R(2)–N2.

34 P×R	R–KN1
35 R–N2	N–K1
36 B–K5	K–K3
37 K–B4	K–B2
38 K–B5	Resigns

215

B. PIECE CONCENTRATION ON THE WING

It is not only a pawn majority which makes a flank attack possible; piece concentration can do so too. By this we do not mean simply the concentration of all pieces on a small section of the board, but rather the concentrated power of pieces directed towards a particular area; it must therefore be borne in mind that a piece can work effectively from a distance, as, for example, a Bishop on b2 trained towards the square g7. An important requirement for the proper use of piece superiority in a particular area is the opening of lines; we have already seen in the chapters on the individual pieces that a single open file for a Rook was the means to a decisive superiority; the same can apply to an open diagonal controlled by a Bishop.

Piece pressure on the wing can take several forms, but always the goal will be the attainment of such superiority in piece strength that the opponent is left powerless to defend adequately all points attacked. We shall make do with one example.

AVERBACH–FUCHS

(Dresden 1956)

1	P–QB4	P–KN3
2	N–QB3	B–N2
3	P–Q4	N–KB3
4	P–K4	P–Q3
5	B–K2	O–O
6	B–N5	P–B4
7	P–Q5	P–QR3
8	P–QR4	P–K3
9	Q–Q2	Q–R4
10	R–R3!	

This move looks merely like a defence to the threat 10 ..., P–QN4, which can now be answered by 11 RP×P; but it also serves another purpose: White, who cannot launch a successful action in the centre or on the Queen-side, will eventually play his Rook to the King-side and obtain a superiority there.

10	...	P×P
11	KP×P	QN–Q2(?)

With this move Black interferes with his development; better is 11 ..., R–K1 followed by B–N5.

12	N–B3	N–N3
13	O–O	B–N5

Black's previous manoeuvre was probably intended as the prelude to 13 ..., Q–N5, but now Black realizes that this can be answered by 14 Q–B1. As 14 ..., N×BP?; 15 N–R2 is then out of the question, Black would have to look for a way to extricate his Queen from the dangerous situation that White could create by 15 P–R5 followed by R–R4.

14	Q–B4!	B×N
15	Q×B	KN–Q2?

Black persists with his version of a Queen-side attack and consequently weakens his King-side further. Correct is 15 ..., QN–Q2.

16 N–K4!

216

All of a sudden White has two threats: 17 B–Q2, trapping the Queen, and 17 N×QP. Black's reply is forced.

16 ...   N–B1
17 Q–R3!   Q–B2
18 Q–R4   R–K1
19 R–KR3

DIAGRAM 200

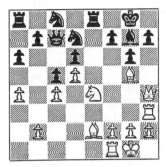

All White's pieces, apart from the Rook on f1, are poised for the decisive attack on Black's insufficiently defended castled position; even the Bishop on e2 is ready to join in by sacrificing itself on h5. All that remains is the tactical execution of the attack.

19 ...   P–KR4

Clearly 19 ..., N–B1; 20 N–B6 ch, B×N; 21 B×B is hopeless.

20 N–N3!

The final preparation for the deciding stroke. The Bishop sacrifice is at this stage premature: 20 B×P, R×N!; 21 Q×R, P×B; 22 R×P, N–B1.

20 ...   N–B1
21 B×P!   B×P

Or 21 ..., P×B; 22 N×P, N–KN3; 23 N–B6 ch!, B×N; 24 B×B, N×Q; 25 R×N, etc.

22 N–B5!   P×B

After 22 ..., P×N; 23 B–B6!, B×B; 24 Q×B, Q–K2; 25 B×P ch!, Black cannot avoid mate.

23 B–B6   N–KN3
24 Q–N5   N(1)–K2
25 N–R6 ch   K–B1
26 B×B   Resigns

C. SPACE SUPERIORITY ON THE WING

It often happens that a particular pawn structure confers a space advantage on one of the players; even with a balance in material this advantage can become the prerequisite for an attack. The characteristic feature of a space advantage on the wing is the greater mobility of one's pawns there. In Diagram 201 Black's King-side pawns are held in check by the pawn on e5, while White's on the Queen-side suffer the same fate at the hands of the pawn on c4. If Black plays P–KB3 or P–KB4 he gets a weak e-pawn after White's reply P×P; if instead he attempts P–KN3 or P–KN4, he is left with a dangerous weakness on f6. On the other wing it is White who has problems with mobility.

In general there are two ways of using the space advantage on the wings—a piece attack against the enemy wing or the advance of one's pawns. In the second case the motive is either to open the lines for attack or to constrain the enemy position; in Diagram 201 White would proceed with P–KB4, P–KN4, and P–KB5, and then, according to circumstances, either P × KP or P–B6; Black's plan of campaign on the other wing would be characterized by P–QN4, P–QR4, and P–QN5. It is hardly necessary to add that such advances as these should be well prepared by a suitable posting of the pieces. The pieces may also be so placed as to thwart the enemy advance; for example, a Black Bishop controlling the diagonal a8–h1 will probably stop White from playing P–KN4 if his King is on g1. And now some examples.

DIAGRAM 201

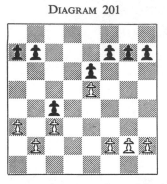

BOTVINNIK–RESHEVSKY

(AVRO Tournament 1938)

1	P–QB4	P–K4
2	N–QB3	N–QB3
3	P–KN3	P–KN3
4	B–N2	B–N2
5	P–K3	P–Q3
6	KN–K2	KN–K2

Better is 6 ..., B–Q2.

7	P–Q4	P × P
8	P × P	O–O
9	O–O	N–B4
10	P–Q5	N–K4

Better is 10 ..., N(3)–Q5

11	P–N3	P–QR4
12	B–N2	N–Q2

(*See* Diagram 202)

The force of the pawn on d5 is increased by the Bishop in g2, so that Black's Queen's wing is paralysed. The correct plan for White is the advance of the Queen-side pawns and the break-through P–QB5 at a suitable moment.

DIAGRAM 202

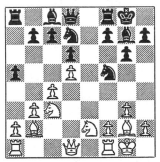

Position after 12 ..., N–Q2

13 P–QR3!	N–B4(?)

As White is planning P–QN4, this move is a waste of time; more logical is 13 ..., R–K1.

14 P–QN4   **N–Q2**

After 14 ..., P×P; 15 P×P, R×R; 16 B×R, N–QR3; 17 Q–N3, the Knight on a6 is not particularly well placed; this shows that Black's previous move was quite pointless.

15 Q–N3	N–Q5
16 N×N	B×N
17 QR–Q1	B–N2
18 KR–K1	P×P
19 P×P	N–B3

Black must develop his Bishop somehow; but this move reduces control over c5 and facilitates White's break-through.

20 P–R3!   **P–R4**

The intention of this move is to secure the square f5 for the Bishop by preventing White from driving it off with P–KN4. However, as the further course of the play shows, the Bishop is well placed neither on f5 nor on d7.

21 P–B5!	B–B4
22 N–N5	B–Q2

Or 22 ..., R–K1; 23 N–Q4, B–Q2; 24 P–B6, P×P; 25 P×P, B–QB1; 26 P–N5, with clear advantage to White, who can always obtain a dangerous passed-pawn by P–N6.

23 P–B6!	P×P
24 P×P	

By the advance P–B6, White has destroyed the symmetrical pawn formation; but he need not rest content with having eased the path of his pawn to the queening square:

with Black's pieces so badly placed there is generally a quicker decision to be obtained by combinative means.

24 ...   **B–B1**

Other moves by the Bishop are likewise inadequate: 24 ..., B–B4; 25 N–Q4, Q–B1; 26 R–K7, or 24 ..., B–K3; 25 R×B!, P×R; 26 N–Q4, Q–K2; 27 N×P, Q–B2; 28 B×N, B×B; 29 B–Q5, K–R1; 30 N–B4, Q–N2; 31 Q–Q3, and White wins.

DIAGRAM 203

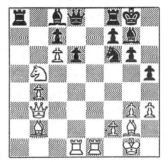

25 N×QP!

An elegant combination. It is quite clear that 25 ..., P×N; 26 P–B7 is out of the question; but Black hopes to save himself with his next move.

25 ...	B–K3
26 R×B!	P×R
27 N–B5!	Q–K1

There is also little hope of a sustained defence from 27 ..., Q×R ch, e.g. 28 Q×Q, KP×N; 29 P–N5, QR–N1; 30 Q–N3 ch, K–R2; 31 B–R3 followed by Q–B7.

219

28	N×B	K×N	30 ...	K–N1
29	R–Q7 ch	R–B2	31 R×P	R×R
30	B–K5		32 B×R	R–R8 ch

Winning the pawn on c7, as 30 ..., R–QB1 is answered by 31 Q–KB3. White's two united passed-pawns supported by the Bishop pair will quickly decide the game.

33	K–R2	R–R2
34	B–K5	R–KB2
35	P–B7	N–Q2
36	Q–B2	R–B1
37	P–B8=Q!	Resigns

The following game contains a very interesting motif: White obtains a superiority on the King-side, forcing the opponent on to the passive defence of the points attacked; then White suddenly switches to the other wing, where the Black King had meanwhile sought refuge. Such a change of fronts is frequently the conclusion of a wing attack, for the defending player's pieces are often so unfavourably placed, as a result of having to ward off continual tactical threats, that they cannot easily regroup in time to protect the other wing.

KERES–EUWE

(Match 1939)

1	P–Q4	N–KB3
2	P–QB4	P–K3
3	N–QB3	B–N5
4	Q–B2	N–B3
5	N–B3	O–O
6	B–N5	P–KR3
7	B–R4	P–Q3
8	P–K3	

Better is 8 P–QR3.

8	...	Q–K2
9	B–K2	P–K4
10	P–Q5	N–N1
11	N–Q2!	

This move has a tactical as well as a strategical purpose. From the tactical point of view White prevents the opponent from building up a strong King-side attacking position as would happen after 11 O–O, B×N; 12 Q×B, P–KN4;

13 B–N3, N–K5; 14 Q–B2, P–KB4. Strategically seen, White prepares the advance P–KB4 after castling short; he will then be ready to obtain a superiority on the King-side.

11 ...	QN–Q2

But not 11 ..., R–K1?; 12 B×N, Q×B?; 13 Q–R4, and Black loses a piece.

12 O–O	P–QR4!

White's pawn on d5 would normally give him a space advantage on the Queen's wing; Black therefore sets up an obstacle to the exploitation of this advantage. White can now hardly continue with 13 P–QR3?, B×N; 14 Q×B, P–R5!, because his pawns would then be blocked.

13 QR–K1!

The continuation of the plan to

make the advance P–KB4. Black can indeed frustrate White's intentions by 13 ..., B×N; 14 Q×N, P–K5, but then White brings his Knight to d4 and has two possibilities to obtain active play: on the Queen's wing, after the preparatory moves P–QN3, P–QR3, and P–QN4, he can carry out the advance P–QB5; on the opposite wing he can, at a suitable moment, open the f-file by P–KB3 and launch a King-side attack.

| 13 ... | R–K1 |
| 14 P–B4 | B×N |

It would not be good to continue 14 ..., P×P?; 15 P×P because he would soon lose control of the e-file as a result of backward development. The text-move, by which Black seeks to lessen White's King-side attacking chances through exchange, is therefore quite correct.

15 Q×B	N–K5!
16 N×N	Q×B
17 P–KN3	Q–K2
18 B–N4!	

Strategically well played. White will eventually advance his King-Bishop-pawn to f5 in order to secure a King-side space advantage; in that case the Bishop will be hampered by the pawns on d5 and f5; so White now prepares to exchange it.

18 ...	N–B3
19 N×N ch	Q×N
20 B×B	QR×B
21 R–B2	

Black cannot now, or even on the next move, exchange on f4 without jeopardizing his King-side pawns, e.g. 21 ..., P×P; 22 Q×Q, P×Q, 23 R×P, K–N2; 24 P–K4, R–K2; 25 R(1)–KB1. White therefore delays P–KB5 until it can be played with a gain in tempo. It should be noted that 21 Q×RP is not good for White on account of the reply 21 ..., P×P followed by Q×NP.

21 ...	P–QN3
22 R(1)–KB1	Q–N3
23 P–KB5!	Q–B3
24 P–K4	

DIAGRAM 204

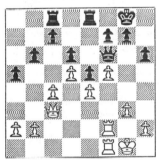

Thanks to his pawn on f5 White has a space advantage on the King's wing; his plan will be the preparation of the break-through P–KN4–5 (e.g. by P–KN4, Q–KN3, P–KR4, and P–KN5). Black is suffering from the handicap of having his Queen tied to the square f6, from where it dare not move for the time being, as White would then continue with P–KB6, adding force to the attack. Black now intends to transfer his King to the opposite side, in accordance with the principle examined in the chapter on the King; but first he must guard against a possible Queen-side break-through by White (P–QN3, P–QR3, P–QN4, P–QB5) so that the King's place of refuge is not quickly subjected to danger.

24 ...	P–B3!
25 P×P	R×P
26 P–QR4	

Meeting the threat 26 ..., P–QN4.

26 ...	K–B1
27 R–Q1	KR–B1
28 P–N3	K–K2
29 Q–KB3	K–Q2
30 P–R4	K–B2
31 K–B1	

White's King too leaves the King-side; the reason is to avoid hindering further action there by the White pieces.

31 ...	K–N2
32 K–K2	R(1)–B2
33 R–KR2	Q–Q1

Black's King is in safety and his Queen has been relieved of its duty on f6, which will soon be occupied by a Black pawn; then White's break-through P–KN5 will be more difficult to carry out. If White tries to forestall 34 ..., P–B3 by 34 P–B6, Black replies with 34 ..., P–N3! (stronger than either 34 ..., Q×P; 35 Q×Q, P×Q; 36 R–B2 or 34 ..., P×P; 35 R–B2), and the ensuing position is one in which White cannot open

any lines on the King-side (e.g. 35 P–R5, P–KN4).

34 P–KN4	P–B3
35 R–N2	R–B1
36 R–N3	

White intends to prepare the break-through with thoroughness; he wants to be able to occupy the eventual open h-file without difficulty. After 36 P–N5, RP×P; 37 P×P, Q–R1, Black can defend himself.

36 ...	Q–Q2

In order to answer 37 P–N5 by 37 ..., RP×P; 38 P×P, R–KR1.

37 Q–Q3	Q–KB2
38 R–KR1	R–KR1
39 R(1)–R3!	R(3)–B1
40 P–N5!	

After 40 Q×P?, R(B1)–Q1; 41 Q–R3, R–Q5 followed by R(1)–Q1, Black obtains strong counter-play on the open d-file.

40 ...	RP×P
41 P×P	Q–QB2
42 Q–Q5 ch	K–R2
43 R–Q3	R×R(?)

With this move Black surrenders the open file and hastens his defeat. In the Rook end-game after 43 ..., P×P; 44 R×R, R×R; 45 Q×QP, Q×Q; 46 R×Q, R–R5, Black still has certain drawing chances (e.g. 47 K–B3, R–R6 ch; 48 K–N4, R×P; 49 R–Q7 ch, K–R3!).

44 R×R	P×P
45 R–R7	Q–K2
46 K–B3	R–KB1

47 K–N4   R–B2

Meeting the threat 48 Q–K6, which can now be answered by 48 ..., Q×Q; 49 P×P, R–K2.

DIAGRAM 205

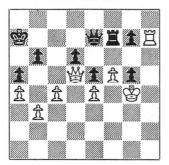

48 P–N4!

The decisive break-up of the Black King's position. It is worth noting the power exerted by the centralized White Queen.

48 ...   P×P
49 P–R5!   Q–N2

Now two pawns are lost, but after 49 ..., P×P; 50 Q×RP ch, K–N2; 51 Q×NP ch, K–B2; 52 Q–R5 ch, Black cannot escape: e.g. 52 ..., K–Q2; 53 Q–R7 ch, K–K1; 54 Q–N8 ch, K–Q2; 55 Q–N7 ch, K–K1; 56 Q–B8 ch, Q–Q1; 57 R–R8 ch; or 52 ..., K–B3; 53 Q–R6 ch, K–B2; 54 R–R8, R–B1; 55 Q–R7 ch.

50 P×P ch   K×P
51 Q×QP ch   K–R2
52 Q×KP   P–N6
53 R–R3!   R–B3

Not 53 ..., P–N7; 54 R–QR3 ch.

54 Q–Q4 ch   R–QN3

The alternatives 54 ..., Q–N3; 55 Q–Q7 ch, K–R3 (55 ..., K–R1; 56 R–R8 ch); 56 Q–R4 ch and 54 ..., K–N1; 55 R–R8 ch, K–B2; 56 R–Q8 are also insufficient.

55 R×P   Resigns

In positions in which one side creates a space advantage by P–KB5, as in the preceding game, it usually pays to continue with the advance of the other pawns in order to open lines of attack for the heavy pieces. If this is not done, the attack with mere pieces (e.g. Queen and minor pieces) is less effective and can often be withstood. The advance of the pawns is the preparation for a break-through, which, besides opening lines of attack, can produce weaknesses in the enemy position, deprive the King of its pawn armour, and possibly create a passed-pawn. It can be seen then that the break-through is a very important way of converting a space advantage on the wings; it played an important role in the previous two games. Often the break-through is carried out by positional means—thorough preparation by favourable piece and pawn placing. Sometimes, however, there is no time for such preparations, and combinational methods are called for, as in the following example.

White–Black

DIAGRAM 206

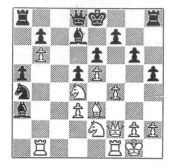

The pawn structure indicates a break-through on the King-side by P–KB5. However, if White proceeds in the normal manner with the preparatory moves P–KN3, P–KR3, and P–KN4, he wastes too much time and also give Black the chance of counter-play on the open h-file. He therefore rejects this plan in favour of the combinative break-through, which is made possible by the unfavourable position of the Black pieces on h3 and h4.

1 P–B5!   NP×P

After 1 ..., KP×P; 2 N–B4, Black's Queen-pawn falls, for he cannot continue with either 2 ..., B–B3; 3 R–R1, Q–K2; 4 N×B, P×N; 5 Q–R2, or 2 ..., N×P; 3 N–B2, on account of the loss of a piece.

2 N–B4

White is now threatening 3 Q–N3 followed by Q–N7 and N×RP. After Black's natural defensive move, another, more subtle, threat appears.

2 ...	P–R5
3 R–R1	B–K2
4 R×N!	B×R
5 N(Q4)×KP!	P×N
6 N×KP	

Now Black's position is in shreds. In the actual game he gave up his Queen by 6 ..., B–Q2; 7 N×Q, after which the win for White was only a matter of time. However, if Black retains his Queen, he is exposed to an irresistible attack, as the following moves show.

6 ...	Q–B1
7 Q×BP	Q–B3

Or 7 ..., B–QB3; 8 B–N5!, B–B4 ch ; 9 K–R1, etc.

8 B–N5!	Q×P ch
9 P–Q4	Q–N5
10 Q–B7 ch	K–Q2
11 B×B	Q×B
12 N–B5 ch	K–Q1
13 N×P ch	K–Q2
14 N–B5 ch	K–Q1
15 Q×P ch	

And Black is left completely helpless.

D. THE BLOCKED PAWN CHAIN

In the chapter on the centre we saw that sometimes the elimination of central tension led to a blocked pawn chain; an example is shown in Diagram 207. Many textbooks call this simply a pawn chain, but in my opinion this is not correct: the term pawn chain can be applied to any pawn formation strung together; in the diagrammed position, the chief characteristics are the blocked positions of two White and two Black pawns.

DIAGRAM 207

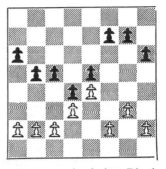

What possibilities are open to both players in this position? As will be clear from the preceding section, Black's pawn on d4 restricts White on the Queen-side, giving Black a space advantage there; White's pawn on e4 performs a similar function on the other wing, though more modestly, as it has not crossed the middle of the board. Black's pawns are more mobile on the Queen-side, while the position is reversed on the opposite wing. It should be noticed that Black will not often try to expand on the King-side in such positions, because his advance P–KB4 would leave the King-pawn weak after White's reply KP × P. The blocked pawn chain often determines the character of the position by giving each player a qualitative, not quantitative, pawn superiority on a particular part of the board, the qualitative element being mobility. Black's field of operations will therefore be on the Queen-side, White's on the King-side. Black's plan will be the execution of the advance P–QB5 followed by BP × KP or possibly the break-through P–QB6; it is generally advisable after P–QB5 to maintain the tension until the moment when its elimination brings some concrete advantage. For White, his action on the King-side will usually commence with P–KB4; then if Black defends his King-pawn with P–KB3, there are two possible continuations: White can open the f-file by P × P, or he can increase his space advantage by P–B5; in the latter case, which adds a third limb to the blocked pawn chain, the character of the position remains the same; White will merely continue his King-side advance with P–KN4, P–KR4, and P–KN5.

The addition of an extra limb to the blocked pawn chain occurs with relative frequency. Often one of the players in the course of his flank action eliminates the tension for a while and shifts his attack one rank to a less advanced member of the opposing pawn chain; in the case above, White, after P–KB5, can transfer his pressure from e5 to f6, and in the French Defence, after 1 P–K4, P–K3; 2 P–Q4, P–Q4; 3 P–K5, P–QB4; 4 P–B3, Black sometimes, at a later stage in the game, plays P–QB5 followed by the advance

P–QN4–5. Any plan to increase the number of limbs in the blocked pawn chain must always be carefully considered, for there are both advantages and disadvantages in such an undertaking. The advantage is that the space superiority on that wing will be enhanced; the disadvantage that the tension is released for a few moves, during which time the opponent may press his action home on the other wing. It is especially on the Queen-side that the greatest care must be taken in making this tension-relieving advance, for the opponent's attack against the King may have proved decisive before it is possible to renew the Queen-side tension and create further threats. The temporary release of the tension on the King-side is generally more effective, as it soon produces dangerous threats to the enemy King.

We shall now add some remarks on examples taken from opening theory. After the moves **1 P–K4, P–K3; 2 P–Q4, P–Q4; 3 P–K5, P–QB4,** White has two basically different continuations to choose from: 4 P–QB3 and 4 P × P. If he chooses the latter, he must, after **4 P × P, N–QB3!; 5 N–KB3, B × P,** endeavour to maintain his pawn on e5 and benefit from his King-side space advantage; he has, however, relinquished a certain amount of control over e5 by his exchange P × P, and, after **6 B–Q3, P–B4!,** will hardly be able to continue **7 P × P** *e.p.,* **N × P;** for, if he did, he could not keep sufficient control of e5 to prevent Black from forming a strong pawn centre with P–K4. White's alternative on move four is to defend the base of the pawn chain with P–QB3; this gives Black the opportunity to exert pressure on d4. A typical variation is **4 P–QB3, N–QB3; 5 N–B3** (White is behind in his development and has not time for the advance 5 P–KB4, Q–N3; 6 N–B3, N–R3!, for Black can then continue with N–B4 putting intolerable pressure on d4), **Q–N3; 6 B–Q3, P × P!; 7 P × P, B–Q2; 8 B–K2, KN–K2; 9 P–QN3, N–N4; 10 B–N2, B–N5 ch; 11 K–B1, O–O; 12 P–N4, N–R3; 13 R–N1, P–B3!; 14 P × P, R × P; 15 P–N5, R × N!; 16 B × R, N–B4,** with advantage to Black, who, by his exchange sacrifice, has broken up White's pawn chain and will soon capture its base, the pawn on d4 (e.g. 17 R–N4, B–K1, threatening B–KR4). All Black's moves in this variation were characterized by the constant pressure they exerted on d4. The move 3 ..., P–QB4 was important on two accounts, which also apply to all similar advances against a blocked pawn chain. First of all, it was the basis of the action on the Queen-side (where the particular pawn formation gave Black a space advantage) and enabled him at any time to open the game by P × P or increase his space advantage by P–B5. Secondly, the move put pressure on the base of the enemy pawn chain (d4);

such pressure can generally be strengthened by suitable piece development (Q–N3 and N–QB3) and often forces the opponent to give up this most important limb by QP×P.

In our remarks on the French Defence, we have considered the attack on the base of a blocked pawn chain: sometimes, however, the most advanced limb can be advantageously liquidated, as Black's thirteenth move (P–KB3) in the second variation showed. Any such freeing advance must be well prepared by suitable piece support, and care must be taken to ensure that the resulting backward pawn (in the French Defence the pawn on e6) does not become a serious weakness or, if it does, that the weakness is balanced by an advantage elsewhere (e.g. active piece play). In general, however, the advance against the foremost limb of the blocked pawn chain can be considered as the exceptional case, and usually takes place only with the support of pieces tactically well placed. The normal procedure, as we have seen, is advance on the other wing with pressure against the base of the blocked pawn chain; this we shall witness in our first example.

FORGACS–TARTAKOWER
(Petersburg 1909)

1 P–K4	P–K3
2 P–Q4	P–Q4
3 N–QB3	N–KB3
4 B–KN5	B–K2
5 P–K5	N–K5(?)
6 N×N	B×B
7 N×B	Q×N
8 P–KN3!	

The tempo win by 8 N–B3 looks attractive but that would impede the execution of White's strategical plan—attack with pawns on the King-side.

8 ...	P–QB4
9 P–QB3	N–B3
10 P–KB4	Q–K2
11 Q–Q2	

After 11 N–B3, B–Q2; 12 B–Q3? (with the intention of replying to 12 ..., O–O by 13 B×RP ch!),

Black continues with 12 ..., P×P; 13 P×P, N×QP!, winning a pawn.

11 ...	B–Q2
12 N–B3	O–O
13 B–Q3	P–B5?

An example of the faulty shifting of the attack to another limb of the pawn chain: before Black can achieve counter-play, he will succumb to the attack on his King. Correct is 13 ..., P×P; 14 P×P, Q–N5, or 14 N×P, N×N; 15 P×N, QR–B1, and in both cases White would only have the slight advantage of good against bad Bishop.

14 B–B2	P–QN4
15 O–O	P–N5
16 QR–K1	P–QR4

(*See* Diagram 208)

Obviously Black underestimates his opponent's attacking chances

227

on the King-side. He continues with his action on the Queen-side, probably counting on answering the preparatory 17 P–N4 by 17 ..., P–B3! and obtaining an equal game after 18 P×P, Q×P, as his weak King-pawn is balanced by White's weak pawn on f4. But White can reverse the order of his moves and by a double pawn sacrifice obtain an irresistible attack.

DIAGRAM 208

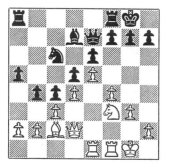

Position after 16 ..., P–QR4

17 P–B5!   **KP×P**

Necessary, for White was threatening 18 P–B6.

18 P–N4!   **BP×P**

Pushing on is also insufficient; e.g. 18 ..., P–B5; 19 Q×P, P–B3; 20 P–K6!, B×P; 21 B–B5, N–Q1; 22 B×B ch, N×B; 23 Q–B5, KR–K1; 24 Q×QP, QR–B1; 25 Q×RP, R–R1; 26 Q–N6 with the threat 27 P–Q5.

19 N–N5   **P–N3**

After 19 ..., P–R3; 20 N–R7 Black must give up the exchange, for moving the Rook loses at once; e.g. 20 ..., KR–Q1; 21 N–B6 ch!, P×N; 22 Q×P, P–B4; 23 B×P, B×B; 24 R×B, P–B3; 25 R×P, etc. The text-move, however, weakens the black squares and aids White's attack.

20 R–B6!   **K–N2**

If 20 ..., P–R3, White continues with 21 B×P!, P×B; 22 R×P ch, K–R1; 23 R×P ch, K–N1; 24 R–N6 ch, K–R1; 25 P–K6, B–K1; 26 N–B7 ch!, R×N; 27 P×R, Q×P; 28 Q–R6 ch, etc.

21 R(1)–KB1   **B–K1**

Other defences are also insufficient—

(a) 21 ..., B–K3; 22 Q–B2, N–Q1; 23 Q–R4, P–R3; 24 N×B ch, N×N; 25 R×NP ch, etc.

(b) 21 ..., N–Q1; 22 Q–K1!, P–R3; 23 N×P, N×N (23 ..., R×N; 24 B×P, B–K3; 25 Q–R4, R–KB1; 26 B–K8!); 24 R×P ch, K–R1; 25 P–K6, QR–K1; 26 P×N!, Q×Q; 27 R×P ch, K–N2; 28 R–R7 mate.

22 Q–B4	N–Q1
23 P–K6	R–R3
24 Q–K5	K–R3
25 R(1)–B5	P×KP
26 N–B7 ch!	Q×N
27 R–R5 ch	K–N2
28 R×NP mate	

So far we have only considered positions in which the blocked pawn chain is composed of both central pawns; sometimes, however, it can be completely confined to one side of the board. After the moves 1 P–Q4, N–KB3; 2 P–QB4, P–B4; 3 P–Q5, P–Q3, the blocked pawn chain is on the Queen-side; in this position White will endeavour to break through in the centre by P–K4–5 and Black on the Queen-side by P–QN4–5. A similar position arises in those variations of the Queen's Gambit where White plays P–QB5; in this case it is Black who strives for the central break-through and White the Queen-side one; if White can stop Black's action in the centre, his own attack on the Queen-side can often be decisive, as the following example shows.

MARCÓZY–SÜCHTING

(Barmen 1905)

DIAGRAM 209

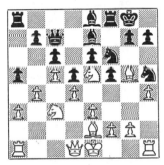

Position after Black's 14th move

The pawn structure clearly indicates that White's strategical plan is a break-through on the Queenside. The immediate advance P–N5, however, is not possible tactically, on account of the reply B×P; but, in any case, White is in no hurry: he will first secure himself against a possible break-through in the centre (P–K4) or on the King-side (P–B5) before proceeding with his own advance.

| 15 P–N3! | P×P |
| 16 P×P | R×R |

17 Q×R	N–K5
18 P–N4!	N×N
19 Q×N	N–B3

After 19 ..., P×P; 20 B×P, Black cannot save his e-pawn.

20 B–KB4!

Threatening 21 N–N6. White thereby wins the necessary tempo to make the advance P–KN5 and block the position on the King-side.

20 ...	Q–B1
21 P–KN5	N–Q2
22 N–Q3!	

In view of his great advantage in space, White will not want to exchange pieces, especially in this case, for the Knight is needed for duty on the Queen-side.

| 22 ... | B–B2 |
| 23 K–Q2 | |

The King would be quite safe after castling short; but White prepares for the possibility of an end-game, in which the penetration of the King into the Queenside could prove decisive.

229

23 ...	B–Q1
24 R–QR1	B–B2
25 R–R7	R–K1

Still hoping to carry out the freeing advance P–K4. Just to be sure, White stops this once and for all.

26 B × B	Q × B
27 P–B4	R–N1
28 P–N5	Q–B1

Or 28 ..., P × P; 29 N–N4, B–K1; 30 P–B6! (not 30 B × P?, N × P), N–N3; 31 P × P, etc.

DIAGRAM 210

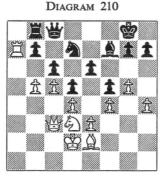

29 P–N6!

In this position a very strong continuation, by which White transfers the attack from c6 to b7. He will carry out his plan by N–B1–N3–R5; then he will capture the pawn on b7 with his Knight and, if Black recaptures

with his Rook, the pin by B–R6 should be decisive. Black, for his part, lacks the space to indulge in corresponding manoeuvres and will be left without an adequate defence.

29 ...	B–K1
30 N–B1	N–B1
31 N–N3	P–K4

This sacrifice is the only way to protect the square b7.

32 QP × P	N–K3
33 B–Q3	P–N3
34 P–R5	B–B2
35 N–R5	N–Q1
36 P–K6!	Q × P
37 P–R6	

Black will be able to parry the mating threat but not save the b-pawn.

37 ...	P–Q5
38 Q × P	Q–R7 ch
39 K–K1	N–K3
40 Q–K5	R–K1
41 N × NP	Q–N6
42 B–K2	Q–N8 ch
43 K–B2	Q–KR8
44 N–Q6	Q–R5 ch
45 K–N2	N × KBP ch
46 Q × N	B–Q4 ch
47 B–B3	B × B ch
48 K × B	Resigns

In this game the advance P–QB5 proved to be a very strong weapon; in some variations of the Queen's Gambit, however, it is wrong, because it allows the break-through P–K4. An example is the following variation: 1 P–Q4, P–Q4; 2 P–QB4, P–K3; 3 N–QB3, P–QR3; 4 P–B5?, P–K4!; 5 P × P, B–K3; 6 B–K3, N–K2 followed by N–B4 and N–QB3.

And now a few remarks about blocked pawn chains. We have seen that each player has an obvious field of action—the area in which his foremost pawn limb is situated. If he can manage to set his pawns in motion in his field of action and attack the base of the blocked pawn chain, he can often obtain a decisive advantage. It follows, therefore, that obstacles to the natural advance, such as an enemy blockading piece or doubled pawns of one's own, must not be allowed to appear or, if they do, must be eliminated as soon as possible. In the variation 1 P–K4, P–K4; 2 N–KB3, N–QB3; 3 B–B4, B–K2; 4 P–Q4, P–Q3; 5 P–Q5, N–N1; 6 B–Q3, N–KB3; 7 P–B4, O–O White would be committing a serious blunder if he continued 8 P–QN4?, for, after 8 ..., P–QR4!; 9 P–QN5 (or 9 P×P, R×P followed by QN–Q2), the natural break-through P–QB5 is permanently impossible. From this we can see that generally the advance P–QN4 in similar situations should not be undertaken until the counter P–QR4 can be met by P–QR3.

We have seen that basically the most effective procedure against the blocked pawn chain is a pawn advance directed against the enemy's most backward limb. This, however, is not always possible, because the opponent can sometimes thwart the plan tactically. In the French Defence, for example, the developing move N–KB3 is sometimes forced before P–KB4 can be played; as a result the King-side pawn advance is badly hampered and another plan must be sought. Generally, with the pawn formation d4 and e5 against d5 and e6, White can also use his space advantage to build up a King-side piece attack: he can, by Q–KN4 and B–Q3, work up certain tactical threats such as the Bishop sacrifice on h7, attack on the square g7 by means of B–KR6, and weakening of the King's position by P–KR4–5–6. In the position in Diagram 211 it might seem natural to prepare the advance P–KB4–5 by means of B–K3 and N–K1; but, if White does that, Black

DIAGRAM 211

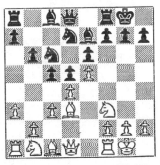

Position after 9 ..., N–Q2

will get the chance of freeing himself by P–KB3. The proper course is, therefore, to renounce the King-side pawn advance and thwart Black's freeing manoeuvre by increasing control over e5 with moves such as Q–K2 and B–KB4; then it should be possible to proceed with a King-side attack unaided by a pawn advance.

E. THE FLANK ATTACK AND THE CENTRE

In the chapter on the Centre we saw that, in general, a strong central position makes an effective flank action possible. It is sometimes believed that superiority in the centre is a necessary prerequisite for any flank attack; but this is not so: many examples from practice have shown that a successful flank attack can be carried out when the position in the centre is balanced or even when the opponent has a superiority there. However, such an attack will almost always fail if the opponent can open the game in the centre and obtain open lines and operation bases for his pieces; or if he can force the attacking pieces back by a break-through in the centre. We can therefore express the relationship between a flank action and the centre as follows: the prerequisite for a successful flank action will be either a superiority in the centre or, at least, a firm, though passive, centre. The correct assessment of the centre and the possibilities offered for a flank attack is a complicated strategical problem; even in the games of leading masters we find flank attacks initiated when the position in the centre indicates that they are doomed to failure.

Now let us examine the positions in the two diagrams and see whether White would be justified in proceeding with a King-side

DIAGRAM 212

DIAGRAM 213

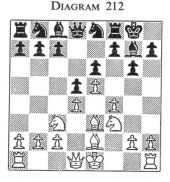

attack. In the first case (Diagram 212) Black has lost a lot of time and will have difficulty in making the natural advance P–QB4; White will therefore have a free hand to carry out a decisive King-side attack. He should begin with 1 P–KR4 and follow up with P–KN4 and P–KR5; if Black should attempt to cut across this plan by 1 ..., P–KR4, then the continuation 2 P–KN4!, P×P; 3 N–KN5 followed by B×P and P–R5 is the way to victory. In the second case (Diagram 213) the position is different. White, it is true, possesses the *little centre*, and so has a certain advantage in space; but we know that in the centre it is not only pawns which count: the pieces must be considered too, and here, we observe, all Black's minor pieces are participating in the fight for the centre—which cannot be said of White's Bishop on d2. Besides this, the possibility of Black's playing P–QB4 must not be overlooked; this move would not only eliminate White's little centre but would also open the d-file. It is therefore clear that the central position does not justify a flank attack by White; his best plan is to castle short and then centralize his heavy pieces (QR–Q1 and KR–K1). In the actual game White misjudged the position and embarked on an immediate King-side attack with P–KR4; after the reply 1 ..., P–QB4, he soon paid the penalty for his strategical blunder.

Another interesting example is shown in Diagram 214, a position characteristic of the Sicilian Defence. The correct strategical plan for White is a sharp attack on the King-side by moves such as P–KN4–5, B–KN2, R B3, R–KR3, Q–KR4; Black will seek counter chances on the Queen-side, where he can operate on the c-file. It should be noticed that White, in making his advance on the King-side, must ensure that he maintains sufficient control of the centre to

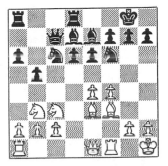

DIAGRAM 214

prevent a break-through by Black. In this respect his Knight on c3 and Bishop on f3 play an important part by their pressure on d5; therefore, before proceeding with his attack, White ought to secure the position of his Knight by P–QR3. In the game he failed to do so and proceeded at once with **1 P–N4**. Black countered vigorously with **1 ..., P–N5; 2 N K2, P–K4!; 3 P–B5** (or 3 P–N5, N–N5; 4 B × N, B × B; 5 P–B5, B × N; 6 Q × B, P–Q4), **P–Q4**. White's best course now was 4 P × P, P–K5!; 5 P × N, P × B; 6 P × B, P × N; 7 Q × KP, R × P, but even here Black, despite his pawn minus, would have had the better game in view of White's weak pawns and exposed King's position. In the game White spurned this line and continued with his attack at the cost of a pawn by **4 P–N5, N × KP;** but Black's central superiority was already too great to offer White much hope of success: after generating a few threats, White found his attack beaten off and Black was able to launch a successful counter-attack on his opponent's weakened King-side.

This example showed how an insecure centre is a serious obstacle to a pawn attack on the King's wing: Black's central break-through proved to be a very effective counter. In our next example White's central position is passive; but it is also secure. White is quite justified in undertaking a flank attack.

STEINITZ–TSCHIGORIN

(Match 1892)

1	P–K4	P–K4
2	N–KB3	N–QB3
3	B–N5	N–B3
4	P–Q3	P–Q3
5	P–B3	P–KN3
6	QN–Q2	B–N2
7	N–B1	O–O
8	B–R4	N–Q2

Better is 8 ..., N–K1 followed by P–KB4.

9	N–K3	N–B4
10	B–B2	N–K3

DIAGRAM 215

The moves P–Q3 and P–QB3 in conjunction with the transfer of the Bishop to c2 characterize the Steinitz set-up. White renounces any ideas for the present of gaining superiority in the centre by P–Q4; in fact he leaves Black the possibility of advancing there. The plan will be to open the h-file by P–KR4–5 and gradually build up an attacking position on the King-side.

11	P–KR4!	N–K2

Black attempts to answer his opponent's flank action by a push in the centre; but White's forces are sufficiently well posted to deal with this threat. The alternative for Black, 11 ..., P–KB4, would lead to an opening of the game and the dangerous exposure of his King; e.g. 12 P×P, P×P; 13 P–Q4, P–K5 (13 ..., P–B5; 14 Q–Q3!); 14 N–N5, N×N; 15 P×N, Q×P; 16 N–Q5, Q×P (16 ..., Q–Q1; 17 Q–R5); 17 Q–R5, Q–N3; 18 Q×Q, P×Q; 19 N×P, R–N1; 20 B–N3 ch, and White wins.

12	P–R5	P–Q4
13	RP×P	BP×P(?)

It will soon be seen that the opening of the diagonal a2–g8 greatly jeopardizes the King's position. Better is 13 ..., RP×P, which gives a position that Steinitz's strategical plan was prepared for; the continuation would be Q–K2 followed by B–Q2, O–O–O and, if necessary (after N–B5 by Black), Q–KB1; White would then maintain his defensive position in the centre while increasing his pressure on the King-side.

14 P×P!

Black's previous move has changed the position radically; White no longer needs to hold the point e5, for Black's isolated pawn will not be sufficiently mobile to threaten a break-through in the centre. With the text-move, White is enabled to develop pressure on the diagonal a2–g8 and, at a suitable moment, break through in the centre himself.

14 ...	N × P
15 N × N	Q × N
16 B–N3	Q–B3
17 Q–K2	

Putting a stop to any possible advance P–K5 and at the same time preparing to complete his development by O O O.

17 ...	B–Q2
18 B–K3	K–R1
19 O–O–O	QR–K1
20 Q–B1!	

Preparing for a complete opening of the game by P–Q4. White already envisages a Rook sacrifice on h7, after which his Queen will enter the h-file with decisive effect. Black's position is no longer tenable; the following attempt at a counter-attack merely hastens defeat.

| 20 ... | P–QR4 |
| 21 P–Q4! | P × P |

| 22 N × P | B × N |

Or 22 ..., N × N; 23 R × P ch.

| 23 R × B! | N × R |

DIAGRAM 216

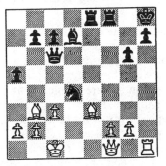

Black hopes to offer some resistance after 24 B × N ch, R–B3, but Steinitz now consummates the combination begun with his fine twentieth move.

24 R × P ch	K × R
25 Q–R1 ch	K–N2
26 Q–R6 ch	K–B3
27 Q–R4 ch	K–K4

Or 27 ..., K–N2; 28 B–R6 ch and 29 B × R mate.

| 28 Q × N ch | Resigns |

The mate after 28 ..., K–B4; 29 Q–KB4 is a tasty morsel for the problemist; it is clean and economical.

CHAPTER XI

The Minority Attack

ONE of the main principles of strategy is that an attack can be successfully made only in a place where the attacking forces possess some superiority. This is merely an expression of the fact, well known in the science of warfare, that to conquer an enemy defensive position requires sufficient attacking means to overcome the defending forces. But already Napoleon gave practical proof that such a superiority cannot be calculated mechanically in terms of a numerical superiority: it can also consist, to a large extent, of a better concentration of forces, of their greater mobility, of their better mutual contact, and of many other factors. Up to the twenties the mechanical assessment of superiority in numerical terms was generally the basis for a strategical plan; then the value of the Minority Attack was discovered.

To clarify exactly what is meant by the term Minority Attack let us look at Diagram 217. In this position White's best continuation is P–QR4 followed by P–QR5; this advance constitutes an attack by a pawn minority against a pawn majority. The reason for White's

DIAGRAM 217

DIAGRAM 218

procedure is to give Black an isolated pawn on the Queen-side whether Black himself exchanges or waits for White to do so; although Black will then have a passed-pawn, it will be very weak, and White can combine an attack on it with his own King-side pawn advance. This is a simple example of a Minority Attack. More

236

generally, however, the concept "minority attack" is applied to a strategical plan adopted in several variations of the Queen's Gambit with pawn structures similar to that in Diagram 218. Here we can see that on the Queen-side Black has four pawns against three, while on the King-side the position is reversed. A closer look at the position, however, shows that Black's majority on the Queen-side is hampered by White's Queen-pawn: the advance P–QB4 would, after P×P, weaken the pawn on d5 and also deprive Black of his pawn majority; the advance P–QN3 or P–QN4 would weaken the pawn on c6. Equally worthless is White's pawn majority on the King-side. In positions with pawn chains similar to those in Diagram 218, the correct strategical plan for White is the advance P–QN4–5. If Black then plays BP×P, or recaptures with a piece on c6 after allowing White to exchange pawns, his Queen-pawn becomes weak; if he recaptures on c6 with a pawn, his c-pawn becomes weak. Black can, of course, reply to White's initial advance P–QN4 by P–QR3; then White continues with P–QR4 and P–QN5, and if Black exchanges twice on b5 he is left with two weak pawns—on b7 and d5. On the King-side it is Black who plays the aggressive role; he can strive to obtain counter-play by P–KB4–5. The following extract shows both plans at work. From the simplified position in

Diagram 219 White begins his Minority Attack first: 1 P–N4!, P–KB4!; 2 P–N5, P–B5!; 3 KP×P. Now Black can obtain equality either by 3 ..., P×P; 4 Q–QN3, Q–Q2 or by 3 ..., Q×BP; 4 P×P, Q–QB2. In the latter case White will have a weak pawn on d4 and Black on c6, and, although Black's weakness is more likely to be felt, because it is on an open file, the reduced material makes this a negligible factor.

DIAGRAM 219

We have seen how Black's logical counter-action, P–KB4–B5, can be an adequate defence against the Minority Attack. Very often, however, Black does not get a chance to set this in motion, for its preparation, in practice, runs up against considerable difficulties. Consequently other methods of defence have to be sought. In most games before the war, Black endeavoured to work up active piece play to meet White's Queen-side advance by a tactical counter-action on the King-side; but the methods adopted did not correspond to the demands of the pawn structure. After many years it became clear that Black's counter-play was insufficient, and for that reason the Minority Attack was looked on as a dreaded weapon. One of the last occasions on which this method of counter-action was employed in a game between two leading grandmasters was at the World Championship in 1948; we give the game below.

SMYSLOV–KERES
(World Championship Moscow 1948)

1 P–Q4	P–Q4
2 P–QB4	P–K3
3 N–QB3	N–KB3
4 B–KN5	P–B3
5 P–K3	QN–Q2
6 P×P	KP×P
7 B–Q3	B–K2
8 N–B3	O–O
9 Q–B2	R–K1
10 O–O	N–B1
11 QR–N1	N–N3
12 P–QN4	B–Q3

Black does nothing to meet White's advance on the Queen-side. He intends, by P–KR3, to secure the Bishop pair and seek his chances in a King-side attack.

DIAGRAM 220

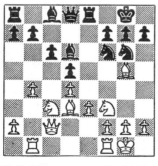

13 P–N5	B–Q2(?)

More in accord with the spirit of his plan is 13 ..., P–KR3; 14

B×N, Q×B, after which White achieves nothing if he continues with 15 P–K4, N–B5!; 16 P–K5, Q–K3; 17 P×B, Q–N5.

14 P×P	B×BP

In almost all positions of this type, it is a mistake to retake on c6 with a piece: a pawn on c6 can generally be defended more easily than the weak pawns on b7 and d5. Black would therefore have had more prospects after 14 ..., P×P; 15 B–B5, Q–B1; 16 B×B, N×B.

15 Q–N3!	

Now the weakness of d5 becomes apparent. Black has no alternative but to withdraw his active Bishop and revert to his previous piece formation; he has, however, wasted two tempi.

15 ...	B–K2
16 B×N!	

This exchange is often an important motif in the Minority Attack. If White had played, say, 16 B–QN5, then, after 16 ..., N–Q2; 17 B×B(K7), N×B, Black could have used his Knight to good effect in the defence of his Queen-side weaknesses. After the text-move the Bishop on f6 will be out of active play for a rather long time.

16 ...	B×B

17 B–N5	Q–Q3
18 KR–QB1	P–KR4
19 N–K2	P–R5
20 B × B	

The pressure on d5 has borne fruit in the passive position of the Black pieces. White now shifts the weakness to the point c6.

20 ...	P × B
21 Q–R4	N–K2

The position is strategically lost for Black, who cannot in the long run cover all the weaknesses in his position. The correct procedure is now 22 Q–R6!, after which there is no adequate defence to the threat 23 R–N7: the continuation 22 ..., P–R6; 23 P–N3, instead of giving Black attacking chances, merely weakens his King-Rook-pawn. White, however, missed his way and chose a line that gives Black good defensive possibilities.

22 R–N7?	P–R4!
23 P–KR3	

After 23 R(1) N1, KR–N1!; 24 R × R ch, R × R; 25 R × R ch, Q × R; 26 Q × RP, Q–N8 ch; 27 N–K1, N–B4; 28 K–B1, N–Q3

Black has, in return for the pawn, very active pieces.

23 ...	KR–N1
24 R(1)–N1	R × R
25 R × R	P–B4!
26 R–N5	

Avoiding 26 P × P, Q × P; 27 N × P?, P–Q5.

26 ...	P × P
27 N(3) × QP	R–QB1?

A mistake; much better is 27 Q–B2!, after which Black has good prospects of holding the game.

28 N–QN3	B–B6
29 Q × KRP	R–B5
30 P–N4!	P–R5
31 N(3)–Q4	B × N
32 N × B	Q–K4?

Better is 32 ..., N–B3.

33 N–B3	Q–Q3
34 R–R5	R–B1
35 R × RP	N–N3
36 Q–R5	Q–KB3
37 Q–B5	Q–QB3
38 R–R7	R–KB1
39 R–Q7	P–Q5
40 R × QP	R–R1
41 P–QR4	Resigns

Although this game was not completely free from mistakes, it did show the difficulties that Black is faced with if he decides to meet the Minority Attack by active piece play alone. It is clear that Black needs to seek a plan corresponding to the strategical character of the position. We have already mentioned that the logical advance P–KB4–5 is hard to carry out; what then of other plans? In tournament praxis the following three strategical plans have predominated—

A. The exploitation of the weakness of the square c4, and in certain cases e4 as well.

B. The prevention of the advance of White's Queen-Knight-pawn by means of P–QN4 on Black's part; this is followed by the neutralization of the square c6 through occupation of c4 with a Knight.

C. Changing the pawn formation by playing a Knight to e4 and forcing White to exchange, Black retaking with a pawn.

We shall now look at these strategical plans in more detail.

A. THE STRUGGLE FOR CONTROL OF C4

(without the advance P–QN4 by Black)

White's advance P–QN4, which always introduces the Minority Attack, has the disadvantage that, by ruling out P–QN3, it weakens the square c4. A good strategical plan for defending against the Minority Attack is the occupation of the square c4 by a Knight; Black thereby shields any possible weakness in his Queen-side pawn position from a frontal attack by White's heavy pieces. Diagram 221

DIAGRAM 221

shows a position in which Black has carried out his plan successfully, for after N–Q3 control over c4 will be secured. If White, who has the move, continues immediately with 1 P–N5, Black can quite calmly answer by 1 ..., RP×P; 2 P×P, N–Q3; but there is an even stronger reply: 1 ..., BP×P!; 2 P×P, P–QR4. The diagram position is in Black's favour and shows the prospects open to Black if he can succeed in his struggle to control c4.

In order to carry out the plan to control c4 it is necessary to force the exchange of white-squared Bishops. But a word of warning is needed here: often this exchange is taken to be the whole object of Black's defence without any thought being given to the subsequent fight for control of the white squares; so frequently Black plays the exchange manoeuvre B–KN5–R4–N3 automatically. The exchange of white-squared Bishops, however, is quite pointless unless Black can support it by favourable piece development leading to control of c4.

Now we shall mention some points that occur in the Minority Attack. First of all, the move P–QR3, which is often made by Black to hold up his opponent's advance. This move has both advantages and disadvantages. On the one hand it favours Black by the simplification it causes on the Queen's wing after White's advance P–QN5: on the other, it weakens b6, and also indirectly c5, for the pawn on a6 would be under fire should Black play P–QN3; in addition, White is enabled, after simplification, to combine occupation of the open a-file with his attack on the pawn on c6. So the advance P–QR3 has its bad as well as its good sides for Black. Another point for consideration is the timing of White's exchange NP×BP. When White's b-pawn has reached b5, he often makes the exchange as soon as possible; generally, however, Black is presented with greater difficulties if this exchange is delayed; White does better to precede the exchange by N–QR4 and N–QB5, and perhaps R–N7.

We saw in Diagram 221 a case in which Black had carried out his plan successfully; the contribution of his two Knights to the strategical plan is clear. In view of this White often exchanges off one of the Knights, thereby presenting Black with new problems. The opening moves of the game Kotov *v.* Pachman at Venice 1950 show this to some extent.

White	Black
1 P–Q4	P–K3
2 P–QB4	N–KB3
3 N–QB3	P–Q4
4 B–N5	B–K2
5 P–K3	O–O
6 N–B3	QN–Q2
7 R–B1	P–QR3
8 P×P	P×P
9 B–Q3	R–K1
10 O–O	P–B3
11 Q–B2	N–B1
12 P–QR3	

White prepares the advance P–QN4 without taking his Rook from the Queen-Bishop file.

12 ...	P–KN3
13 P–QN4	N–K3
14 B×N!	

A well-known exchange, which refutes the dogmatic assertion of the superiority of the Bishop pair.

14 ...	B×B
15 P–QR4	N–N2
16 P–N5	RP×P
17 P×P	B–B4
18 B×B	N×B

DIAGRAM 222

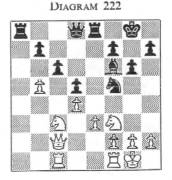

In this position Black has only one Knight to assist in the defence, although it will be strongly placed on d6. White's best continuation is now 19 N–QR4, after which he has some advantage.

241

Sometimes Black can increase his prospects by speeding up the exchange of white-squared Bishops. The following opening exemplifying this occurred in the game Pachman *v.* Ragosin, Saltsjöbaden, 1948.

White	Black
1 P–Q4	P–Q4
2 N–KB3	N–KB3
3 P–QB4	P–K3
4 N–B3	P–B3
5 P×P	KP×P
6 Q–B2	P–KN3
7 B–N5	B–N2

Not 7 ..., B–KB4?; 8 Q–N3.

8 P–K3	B–B4
9 B–Q3	B×B
10 Q×B	QN–Q2
11 O–O	O–O

DIAGRAM 223

The value of Black's timely manoeuvre P–KN3 and B–KB4 is now clear: one Knight is trained on b6 and the other, after the withdrawal of the Black Queen, will make for either e4 or d6 (via e8).

The same position occurred in a game Botvinnik-Euwe, which continued 12 N–K5, Q–K1!; 13 N×N, Q×N; 14 P–QN4, KR–K1, drawn; if White tries 15 B×N, B×B; 16 P–N5 the answer is 16 ..., P–B4!, and if 15 P–N5, Black replies 15 ..., N–K5.

12 QR–N1	Q–K2
13 KR–QB1	Q–K3

Threatening 14 ..., N–K5.

14 N–Q2	KR–K1
15 B×N!	B×B
16 P–QN4	QR–B1
17 P–QN5?	

This advance is premature; it should have been prepared by 17 Q–B2, B–N2; 18 Q–N3. Black would then have had to use the method described in the next section, 18 ..., P–QN4, in order to maintain himself (see page 247).

17 ...	P–B4!
18 P×P	N×P

Black has now the upper hand; it is clear that 19 Q×QP?, B×N; 20 Q×Q, N×Q is out of the question. In the game, White only managed to save himself after a long and unusual defensive action.

These opening moves showed how Black can find it advantageous to accelerate the exchange of white-squared Bishops. But this is not always possible, and other ways of strengthening the fight for c4 must be used. The following moves, showing slight differences in Black's approach to the problem, occurred in two games.

White	Black
1 P–QB4	P–K3
2 P–Q4	P–Q4
3 N–QB3	N–KB3
4 B–N5	B–K2
5 N–B3	O–O
6 P–K3	QN–Q2
7 R–B1	P–QR3
8 P×P	P×P
9 B–Q3	R–K1

Black wastes no time on P–QB3, but instead prepares at once the re-positioning of his Knights.

10 Q–B2	P–KN3
11 O–O	N–N3

DIAGRAM 224

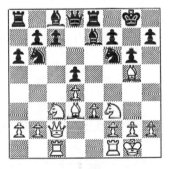

White has now the choice between several continuations. The seemingly strong 12 N–K2, P–B3; 13 N–N3 is answered by 13 ..., N–K5!, and after 14 B–KB4, B–Q3!; 15 B×N, P×B; 16 N×P, B×B; 17 P×B White's extra pawn is balanced by the weaknesses on d4 and f4. From the diagram position, one of the games,

between Filip and Fichtl, continued as follows—

12 N–Q2	N–R4
13 B×B	R×B!
14 N–N3	N–N2
15 N–B5	P–QB3

Black is now ready for B–BK4, which he will follow by the transfer of his Knight on g7 to d6; White has no prospects of carrying out his minority attack. Recognizing this, White decided to break through in the centre, but was left with a weak pawn on d4, which Black managed to exploit sufficiently to win.

Now let us return to Diagram 224 and follow the other game, between Pachman and Podgorny. In this White continued more strongly.

12 B×N!	B×B
13 N–K2	P–B3
14 N–Q2	B–N5
15 N–KN3	N–B1
16 N–N3	N–Q3
17 N–QB5	B–R5!

A correct appreciation of the situation: the so-called "good" Bishop has limited scope; so Black does best to give up his Bishop pair.

18 KR–K1	B×N
19 RP×B	Q–B3

Threatening 20 ...,.B–B4.

20 Q–N3

243

DIAGRAM 225

Position after 20 Q–N3

With his last move White has prevented B–B4, e.g. 20 . . ., B–B4?;

21 B×B, Q×B; 22 N×P, QR–N1?; 23 N×N, etc. However, he has at the same time blocked his minority attack and retains only slight pressure on the Queen-side. Black should now play 20 . . ., QR–N1, after which he should hold the game; unfortunately for him he made a strategical error and played 20 . . ., P–QN4. In this position such a measure is faulty, because White's Knight-pawn is still on b2 and can be used to secure c4 by P–QN3; Black's weakness on c6 then becomes perceptible.

Although Black was led into an error in the second game, his first nineteen moves showed that the system was adequate to obtain equality. The fight for the strategically important c4 was, as in many such positions, a very good defensive plan to the Minority Attack.

B. THE ADVANCE P–QN4 BY BLACK

The second possibility of fighting the Minority Attack is by the advance P–QN4. In the last example we saw the faulty execution of this advance, and from this we may state the rule: the advance P–QN4 by Black should be delayed until White has already played P–QN4.

A typical position is shown schematically in Diagram 226, where Black's main object will be the occupation of c4 with a Knight. The

DIAGRAM 226

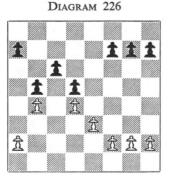

DIAGRAM 227

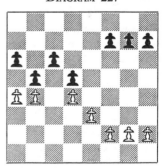

244

main weakness in Black's position is the pawn on c6, which White can attack with a Knight from e5 or with heavy pieces on the c-file; after the possible opening of the centre by P–K4, White may further increase the pressure on the pawn by placing a Bishop on f3 or e4. White can also use the weakness on c5 by occupying it with a Knight. Another possibility for White is the advance P–QR4, as in the position in Diagram 227. Here White can open the a-file and take up an active position there; he has, however, inherited a weakness on b4, which Black can subject to attack.

It will now be clear that the advance P–QN4 by Black offers his opponent many active possibilities; consequently Black must weigh up the position very carefully before deciding on such an important advance. In our first example Black makes it at an inopportune moment.

FILIP–JEZEK

(Mariánské Lázně 1951)

1	P–Q4	P–Q4
2	P–QB4	P–K3
3	N–QB3	N–KB3
4	P×P	P×P
5	B–N5	B–K2
6	P–K3	P–B3
7	Q–B2	QN–Q2
8	B–Q3	N–B1

The manoeuvring of the Knight in the direction of e6 often takes place before castling; but it has its disadvantages.

9	N–B3	N–K3
10	B×N!	

This exchange is almost always advantageous in similar positions; rather strangely, it is only in recent years that it has replaced the mechanical withdrawal B–R4.

10	...	B×B
11	O–O	P–KN3
12	P–QN4	O–O

13	N–QR4	P–QR3
14	N–B5	Q–K2
15	QR–N1	N–N2

Black has greater possibilities after 15 ..., P–N3, but it is no easy matter to decide on such a course. The text-move is played in routine fashion and leads to nothing because the whole manoeuvre is several moves too late.

16	P–QR4	P–QN4?

DIAGRAM 228

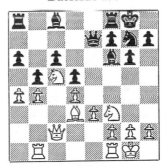

Black's plan to control c4 and take his Knight there is in itself strategically quite sound. Unfortunately it falls through tactically, for White soon gets an irresistible attack along the a-file; in this he is greatly helped by the strong position of his Knight on c5.

17	N–Q2	N–B4
18	N(2)–N3	N–Q3
19	R–R1	B–Q2
20	R–R2!	N–B5
21	KR–R1	QR–N1
22	P×P	RP×P
23	R–R7	KR–Q1
24	R(1)–R6	

The penetration of the White

Rooks completely cripples Black's position.

24	...	Q–K1
25	R–B7	B–K2
26	R(6)–R7	B×N
27	N×B	N–N3
28	N×B	R×N
29	R×R	N×R
30	Q×P	N–N3
31	Q×Q ch	R×Q
32	R–N7	N–B5
33	R×NP	

Black is now quite lost; the game, however, dragged on for another twenty moves.

In our next game Black chooses a more suitable occasion for the advance P–QN4.

PACHMAN–AVERBACH

(Saltsjöbaden 1952)

1	P–Q4	N–KB3
2	P–QB4	P–K3
3	N–KB3	P–Q4
4	B–N5	B–N5 ch
5	N–B3	P–KR3
6	B×N	Q×B
7	P×P	P×P
8	R–B1	

The strongest move is probably 8 Q–R4 ch.

8	...	O–O
9	P–QR3	B×N ch
10	R×B	P–B3
11	P–K3	R–K1
12	B–K2	P–QR4!

This important piece of tactical play often occurs in the Minority Attack. After White's P–QN4 Black will force open the a-file and

at the same time weaken White's pawn on b4; this will then be a good moment to play P–QN4 himself.

13	O–O	B–N5

After 13 ..., P–R5, the weakness of Black's pawn would sooner or later necessitate P–QN4, and it is doubtful whether Black could bring his Knight to c4 early enough.

14	P–QN4	P×P
15	P×P	N–Q2
16	Q–N3	

(*See* Diagram 229)

The immediate 16 P–N5? is answered by 16 ..., P–B4. Stronger than the text, however, is 16 Q–B2, delaying Q–N3 until Black plays B–B4; after this White retains his Knight, which can operate strongly from e5 should

DIAGRAM 229

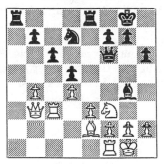

Position after 16 Q–N3

Black decide on the advance P–QN4.

16 ...   P–QN4!

The right moment for this advance; with this move Black equalizes.

17 KR–QB1   R–K3
18 Q–N2

After 18 N–K5, B×B; 19 N×N, Q–K2; 20 N–K5, B–B5!, we have one of those rare positions in which the Bishop, not the Knight, occupies c4. The text-move paves the way for an exchange of heavy pieces, a course that is essential for White if he is to avoid slipping into an inferior position.

18 ...   B×N!
19 B×B   N–N3
20 R–R3   R(3)–K1
21 R×R   R×R
22 R–R1   Q–Q1
23 P–R3
        Drawn

Having seen the advance P–QN4 played to good effect by Black, we can now state the requirements for using it as an answer to the Minority Attack—

1. Black must have the possibility of actively defending the weak pawn on c6.

2. He must be in a position to occupy the open a-file—or at least neutralize White's pressure there.

3. He must have prospects of a speedy occupation of c4 with his Knight or, in exceptional cases, his Bishop.

Now let us have another look at the game Pachman-Ragosin (page 242). In the note to White's 17th move we stated that a stronger continuation for White was 17 Q–B2, B–N2; 18 Q–N3, to which Black could answer 18 ..., P–QN4!; the resulting position is shown in

DIAGRAM 230

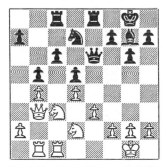

Position after 18 ..., P–N4

Diagram 230. We see that Black still has quite a good game, for his Knight threatens to go to c4 via b6 and his Bishop can attack the weak pawn on b4 from f8; besides, his pawn on f7 is ready to make its contribution by advancing to f5 and f4.

What conclusions can we come to about the move P–QN4 for Black in the Minority Attack? It must be said that it is an extremely risky advance, which can create weaknesses in Black's position; under certain conditions, however, it can be the best answer of all to the Minority Attack.

C. THE CHANGE IN PAWN FORMATION

One of the most frequent defences to the Minority Attack is the occupation of the square e4 with a Knight; mostly White will be

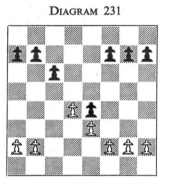

DIAGRAM 231

forced to exchange this strong, centralized piece, and after Black's recapture the pawn structure is changed to that in Diagram 231. The shifting of the pawn from d5 to e4 increases Black's tactical prospects on the King-side because White is somewhat cramped by the pawn on e4; in addition, Black secures a fine base for his pieces on d5. He does, however, lose the possibility of undertaking the struggle for control of c4.

White's basic strategical plan will be the advance P–QN4–5, which will give him a passed-pawn on d4 after Black makes the exchange BP × NP. An example of the successful execution of this advance is the following game.

SAJTAR–PEDERSEN

(Mariánské Lázně 1951)

1 P–Q4	N–KB3
2 P–QB4	P–K3
3 N–QB3	P–Q4
4 B–N5	QN–Q2
5 N–B3	B–K2
6 P × P	P × P
7 P–K3	O–O
8 Q–B2	P–B3

9 B–Q3	R–K1
10 O–O	N–B1

Not 10 ..., N–K5?; 11 B × N, after which White gains a pawn.

11 QR–N1	N–N3
12 P–QN4	

The exchange 12 B × N also deserves attention.

12 ...	P–QR3

248

Black rejects the immediate Knight sortie to e4 (12 ..., N–K5; 13 B×B, Q×B) and opts for active piece play on the King-side just as Keres did in his game against Smyslov (page 238); but the line he selects with his next move is even more innocuous than that initiated by Keres on his twelfth (12 ..., B–Q3).

13 P–QR4	N–N5
14 B×B	Q×B
15 N–K2	

Unnecessary caution, which makes White's task more difficult. Either the immediate 15 P–N5 or first 15 P–R3 and then 16 P–N5 was called for.

15 ...	N–R5
16 N×N	Q×N
17 P–R3	N–B3
18 N–N3	N–K5
19 B×N	P×B

DIAGRAM 232

20 P–N5!	RP×P
21 P×P	B–Q2
22 P×P	B×BP
23 Q–B5	Q–Q1
24 R–N6	P–N3

White clearly has the upper hand: his Knight is ready to enter the game actively by jumping to f4 via d2; Black's Bishop, on the other hand, is confined to the passive role of protecting the pawns on b7 and e4. White's task could be made more difficult if Black were to play Q–Q4, but even after the exchange of Queens White still has the better of it.

25 N–K2	R–R7
26 N–B4	R–Q7
27 Q–N4	

Threatening 28 R×B followed by 29 Q×R.

27 ...	R–R7
28 P–Q5!	B–Q2

Of course 28 ..., B×P; 29 R–Q6 is out of the question; so Black has to give up a pawn, which means that the game is decided.

29 R×QNP	B–B1
30 R–N8	Q–B2
31 P–Q6	Q–B3
32 R–Q1	K–N2

After 32 ..., Q–B7; 33 Q–K1, White threatens both 34 R–B1 and 34 P–Q7.

33 Q–Q4 ch	K–R3

The alternatives 33 ..., P–B3; 34 P–Q7 and 33 ..., K–N1; 34 N–Q5, Q–B7; 35 N–K7 ch, R×N; 36 R×B ch!, Q×R; 37 P×R are both hopeless for Black.

34 Q–B6!	R–Q7

Or 34 ..., R–R4; 35 R×B!

R×R; 36 Q–R4 ch, K–N2; 37
P–Q7, etc.

35 R×R	Q–B8 ch
36 K–R2	Q×R

37 R–N5	Resigns

There is nothing to be done
against the threat of R–KR5 mate.

In this game White's Queen-side attack was crowned with success,
though it must be admitted that Black's faulty tactical play con-
tributed to the result; for example, the line chosen by him on the
twelfth move cost two tempi as compared with the immediate
12 ..., N–K5. Black's prospects in such positions are not always so
bad, as the next game shows.

RAGOSIN–KOTOV

(Moscow 1947)

1 P–Q4	P–Q4
2 P–QB4	P–K3
3 N–QB3	N–KB3
4 B–N5	B–K2
5 P–K3	QN–Q2
6 N–B3	O–O
7 R–B1	P–QR3
8 P×P	P×P
9 B–Q3	P–B3
10 O–O(?)	

A tactical oversight, which allows
Black to free himself at once. If
instead White had continued 10
Q–B2, R–K1; 11 O–O, Black
would have had to delay N–K5
and play first N–B1, as in the
previous game.

10 ...	N–K5!
11 B–KB4	

After 11 B×B, Q×B; 12 B×N,
P×B; 13 N–Q2, N–B3 White has
no prospects of obtaining an
advantage; Black can develop his
Bishop to f5 or in some cases to b7
after P–QN3.

11 ...	QN–B3

12 N–K5	B–Q3
13 N×N	P×N
14 B–N1	B–K3!

DIAGRAM 233

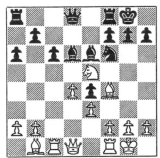

Black will now occupy d5 with
his Bishop; he will then have a
good game, for a White Queen-
side pawn advance costs too much
time.

15 B–N3	B–Q4
16 B–R4	B–K2
17 B–N3	N–K1!
18 Q–B2	N–Q3

Black now threatens to win the
Knight by P–KB3; White must
therefore leave the way open for a
pawn exchange in the centre.

19 P–B3	P–B3

20	N–N4	R–K1	24	N×N	P×N
21	N–B2	P–KB4	25	Q–K2	Q–Q2
22	P×P	N×P	26	P–KN3	Q–K3
23	B–K5	B–N4!	27	P–KR4	B–K2
			28	R–KB4	B–Q3
			29	B×B	Q×B
			30	QR–KB1	
				Draw	

Black's pieces are now so active that White can do no better than simplify the game as quickly as possible and reach a drawn end-game.

We can now make a few general comments about this method of meeting the Minority Attack. Black's best chances occur when there are still several pieces on the board; he then has prospects of a King-side attack. The position is generally difficult for Black when the minor pieces have disappeared, for White is given a free hand to proceed with his Queen-side action. With both minor and major pieces on the board the prospects vary according to the combination of pieces: for example, White has good chances with a combination of Q+2R+N against Q | 2R+B (white squared) or Q+2R+N+B against Q+2R+N+B (white squared); Black, however, is better placed when both sides have Q+2R+N, even after an exchange of one of the heavy pieces. These rules of course can only be applied very generally; they are based on the results of tournament praxis: but they can lose their validity in certain concrete cases. So it is with all the principles in chess strategy; the importance of comprehensive analysis of each individual position should never be forgotten.

CHAPTER XII

The Strategical Points

IN the earlier chapters of this book we examined the working power of the pieces and pawns; we saw then that a single piece could often determine the character of the whole position. In practice it very frequently happens that an apparently less significant factor can be decisive in determining a strategical plan—the control of one or more squares on the chessboard. In many of our examples so far the value of a single square has been clear, and we have already shown the importance of control of the central squares. Such squares of special importance for the assessment of the strategical character of the position and the consequent plan we call strategical points. The problems associated with these strategical points will be treated in three sections—

    A. The pieces in a forward position.

    B. Advanced pawns.

    C. Weak squares in the pawn formation.

A. THE PIECES IN A FORWARD POSITION

One of the most important ways of obtaining superiority is the penetration of pieces into the enemy position; the resulting superiority can be in actual material or merely the crippling of the working power of the opposing pieces. We already know that the penetration of Rooks to the seventh or eighth ranks is one of the most important strategical objects in actions along open files, and mostly the result is a decisive superiority. With minor pieces penetration need not be particularly effective if it is only of temporary character and the opponent can drive out the advanced pieces. Where, however, a piece can reach a firm base the position is different. Such a piece can often decide the game by hampering the enemy pieces, by attacking weaknesses, by increasing positional pressure, or by making a combinative solution possible.

It is difficult to lay down any concrete principles for the creation of such bases or outposts and their occupation by pieces. A few examples will be much more enlightening.

E. RICHTER–PAOLI

(Trencianske Teplice 1949)

1 P–Q4	P–Q4
2 P–QB4	P–K3
3 N–QB3	P–QB3
4 N–B3	N–B3
5 P–K3	P×P?
6 B×P	P–QN4
7 B–Q3	P–QR3
8 O–O	P–B4
9 Q–K2	

We have now reached a position from the Queen's Gambit Accepted; but Black has lost a tempo compared with normal variations.

9 ...	B–N2
10 P×P	Q–R4

Not 10 ..., B×P?, 11 B×NP ch.

11 P–K4	B×BP
12 P–K5	N–Q4
13 N–K4	B–K2
14 B–N5!	

A typical move for such positions; White eliminates the Bishop that is protecting d6. Black can now hardly complete his development by castling, for, after 14 ..., O–O; 15 B×B, N×B; 16 N(3)–N5!, he succumbs to a Kingside attack.

14 ...	Q–N3
15 B×B	K×B
16 QR–B1	N–Q2
17 B–N1	P–R3
18 KR–K1!	

This move, as will be apparent later, is an important piece of preparation for the occupation of d6.

18 ...	QR–QB1
19 R×R	R×R
20 N–Q6	R–B2
21 Q–K4!	

DIAGRAM 234

By simple moves White has been able to achieve a decisive superiority. His Knight on d6 restricts the freedom of Black's pieces, and his Queen threatens to go to h7 or h4 with great effect.

21 ...	Q–B4

Hopeless for Black is 21 ..., N×P?; 22 N–B5 ch!, P×N; 23 Q×N ch, etc; this variation is the justification of White's eighteenth move, KR–K1. Another quick losing variation is 21 ..., N–B1; 22 Q–R4 ch, P–B3; 23 P×P ch, N×P (23 ..., K×N; 24 Q–N3 ch followed by 25 P×P); 24 N–B5 ch, K–B2 (24 ..., K–Q1; 25 N×NP); 25 N–K5 ch.

22 N×B	

The simplest way to gain material. More in keeping with the character of the game, however, was 22 Q–R4 ch, P–B3; 23 P×P ch! with a decisive attack.

22 ...	R×N
23 Q–R7	Q–N5
24 Q×NP	Q–KB5
25 B–K4!	

Black has got his Queen into a difficult position and cannot meet both the threats 26 P–KN3 and 26 B×N.

25 ...	P–KR4
26 B×N	R–B2

Or 26 ..., P×B; 27 P–K6, etc.

27 P–N3	Q–KN4
28 N–N5!	Resigns

In this game the advanced Knight was on a central file. This is not always the case, but even away from the middle of the board an advanced Knight can exert great power on occasions. Witness to that is the following game by Réti.

RÉTI–RUBENSTEIN

(Karlsbad 1923)

1 N–KB3	P–Q4
2 P–KN3	N–KB3
3 B–N2	P–KN3
4 P–B4	P–Q5
5 P–Q3	B–N2
6 P–QN4!	O–O
7 QN–Q2	P–B4
8 N–N3	P×P
9 B–N2!	

If 9 N(N3)×P, Black replies strongly with 9 ..., P–K4.

9 ...	N–B3
10 N(N3)×P	N×N
11 B×N	P–N3
12 P–QR3	

Not 12 N–Q2?, Q×B; 13 B×R, N–N5.

12 ...	B–N2
13 B–N2	

Black was threatening B×N.

13 ...	P×P
14 R×P	Q–B2

15 Q–R1	N–K1
16 B×B	N×B
17 O–O	N–K3
18 R–N1	

Now R×RP becomes a threat as there is nothing to be feared from the reply R×R followed by R–R1.

18 ...	B–B3
19 P–Q4!	

The first stage of the plan to obtain an advanced post on c6.

19 ...	B–K5
20 R–Q1	P–QR4(?)

In an attempt to get rid of the weakness on a7 Black has created a new one on b5. Naturally 20 ..., Q×BP?; 21 N–Q2 is no alternative.

21 P–Q5	N–B4
22 N–Q4	B×B
23 K×B	KR–Q1
24 N–B6	R–Q3

(*See* Diagram 235)

In the previous game Black had no obvious way of exchanging off

White's advanced Knight; in this one Black could, if he had time, play N–N2–Q1 and force its exchange or withdrawal. White

DIAGRAM 235

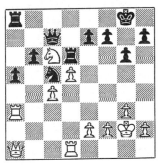

Position after 24 ..., R–Q3

must therefore lose no time in bombarding his opponent with constant threats.

25 R–K3!

Stronger than 25 P–B3, P–B3; 26 P–K4, P–K4.

25 ...   **R–K1**

The exchange sacrifice 25 ..., R × N offers little hope of saving the game, and the continuation 25 ..., P–K3? allows White to play 26 N–K5, P × P; 27 N–N4 with the threats of N–R6 ch and N–B6 ch.

26 Q–K5

White stops the freeing move P–K3 once and for all; but even after 26 Q–N2 Black can for the moment hardly risk a move such as P–K3, which would seriously weaken his King's position.

26 ...	**P–B3**
27 Q–N2	**P–K4**
28 Q–N5	**K–B2**
29 R–QN1	**N–Q2**
30 P–B3	**R–QB1**

Now Black threatens by N–N1 to force the exchange of the Knight.

31 R–Q3!

Meeting the threat to exchange Knights, for if 31 ..., N–N1, White wins by 32 P–B5. Black is now almost in *zugzwang*: if he continues with 31 ..., R–K1 (threatening P–K5); 32 P–K4, R–QB1, White can strengthen his position by 33 P–R4, P–R4; 34 P–B4 and win by a break-through on the King-side; if Black tries, instead, 31 ..., N–B4, the simple reply 32 R(3)–Q1 is the strongest, but possible is also 32 Q × NP, N × R; 33 P × N, R × N (otherwise the two passed-pawns decide the game even more quickly); 34 P × R, Q × P; 35 Q × P, and White's extra pawn is sufficient to win.

31 ...   **P–K5?!**

An attempt to free himself; but White has a pretty combination in readiness.

32 P × P	**N–K4**
33 Q × NP!	**N × N**

After 33 ..., N × R; 34 P × N the struggle against the might of the passed-pawns is hopeless.

34 P–B5!

Rubenstein had probably reckoned on 34 P × N, R × P, which

255

leads to a draw; the text-move, however, holds the pawn and secures the win.

34 ...	R–Q2
35 P×N	R×R
36 Q×Q ch	R×Q
37 P×R	R×P
38 R–N7 ch	K–K1
39 P–Q4	R–R3
40 R–N6!	R–R1

After 40 ..., R×R; 41 P×R, K–Q1; 42 P–K5, P×P; 43 P×P,

P–R5; 44 P–K6, P–R6; 45 P–N7 White wins easily.

41 R×P	P–R5
42 R–B2	P–R6
43 R–R2	K–Q2
44 P–Q5	P–N4
45 K–B3	R–R5
46 K–K3	P–R4
47 P–R4	P×P
48 P×P	K–K2
49 K–B4	K–Q2
50 K–B5	Resigns

It is not only a Knight which can yield great power in an advanced position; sometimes a Bishop too can be extremely effective. In Diagram 236 White will aim to carry out a break-through by P–K5; when he succeeds, the Bishop on e6 will prove a great menace to the opposing King. The heavy pieces are less rarely seen as the occupants of an outpost, but occasionally they can be assigned to such a

DIAGRAM 236

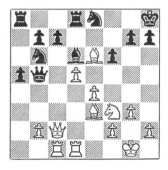

DIAGRAM 237

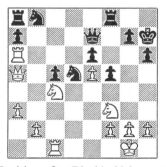

Position after Black's 30th move

role. From Diagram 237 White's best continuation is 31 R–Q6!, N–Q2; 32 Q–N5!, QR–Q1 (threatening 33 ..., N×P; 34 R×R, N×N ch); 33 K–R1; after this there is no adequate defence to White's threats of 34 N–R5 followed by N–B6, and 34 P–QN4, P×P; 35 N–Q4. Playing the Rook to d6 in the diagram position is strong because the Rook combines its occupation of that advanced post with an attack on the e-pawn. If White instead chooses to play the Knight to d6 he will restrict the opposing pieces, but will not threaten anything; this limitation makes it an inferior move.

Let us now take a look at Diagram 238, where Black has a Knight installed on d3. One difference with the previous positions is at once apparent. Normally the advanced piece is supported by a pawn: in the present case it is the pieces which maintain the Knight in its present position. Naturally a base protected by a pawn is more reliable, and a piece once there can generally be kept in its strategically advantageous position for a long time. Nevertheless the occupation of a particular strategical point controlled only by pieces can sometimes be very effective, as in Diagram 238. Here Black's Knight helps to immobilize White's pieces. The best continuation for Black is P–KB4, after which there is no adequate defence to the threat of P–KB5 followed by N × BP.

DIAGRAM 238

Black to play

B. ADVANCED PAWNS

In Diagram 239 White's advanced pawn on f6 and Black's on a3 control the space around the enemy King, creating mating threats there; with Queens on the board the threats Q–KR6–N7 mate (for White) and Q–QB6–N7 mate (for Black) are in the air. An advanced pawn can often prove so dangerous that the defending side must direct all his resources to its elimination. Chess literature abounds in examples of mating attacks made possible by an advanced pawn.

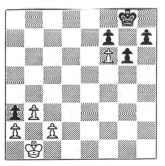

DIAGRAM 239

The advanced pawn can, however, be of use even where there is no question of direct tactical threats. For example, it can be the support for an outpost and it can also disrupt the smooth operation of the enemy pieces as in the following game.

EUWE–NAJDORF

(Candidates Tournament 1953)

1	P–Q4	N–KB3
2	P–QB4	P–KN3
3	P–KN3	B–N2
4	B–N2	O–O
5	N–QB3	P–B4
6	P–Q5	P–K4!
7	B–N5!	

This very fine move anticipates the later advance P–Q6; for if White is allowed to carry it out, his Bishop will be of less importance than Black's Knight, which on the one hand is directed towards d5 and on the other will be able to attack the advanced pawn on d6. Black's best plan is to forestall White's advance by 7 ..., P–Q3, although after that White can continue with 8 Q–Q2, securing the Bishop against P–KR3; then the unpleasant threat of P–KR4–5 is something that Black must reckon with.

7	...	P–KR3
8	B × N	Q × B
9	P–Q6!	

DIAGRAM 240

This advance is important for three reasons—

1. It hampers Black's development on the Queen-side.

2. It restricts the manoeuvrability of Black's pieces, particularly their transfer from the Queen-side to the King-side.

3. It opens the square d5 to the White pieces.

Such a move, however, is always risky, because the advanced pawn can be attacked and won by the opposing pieces (R–K1–K3 and B–KB1). In the game the important thing for White is that he obtains attacking chances on the King-side before the weakness of the pawn becomes noticeable.

9	...	N–B3
10	P–K3	P–N3
11	B–Q5	K–R1

By removing the possibility of B × P ch, Black puts the Queen-pawn *en prise*; he also prepares the advance P–KB4.

12	N–K4	Q–Q1
13	P–KR4!	P–B4
14	N–N5	B–N2!

This offers the exchange, but if White accepts (15 N–B7 ch?, R × N; 16 B × R, N–N5; 17 P–B3, P–K5), Black obtains a decided advantage.

15	P–KN4!	P–K5

Black seeks an active defence by opening the long diagonal; the disadvantage of the move is that it opens f4 to the White Knight. After 15 ..., Q–B3, however, White has two good continuations:

258

16 N–B7 ch, R×N; 17 P–N5!, and 16 P×P, Q×P (16 ..., P×P; 17 Q–R5); 17 R–R2.

| 16 N–K2 | B×P |
| 17 N–B4! | |

White must press on with his attack regardless of material loss. After 17 ..., B×R, the correct continuation is 18 P×P! (not 18 Q×B ch, Q–B3; 19 N×NP ch, K–N2), B–B6 ch; 19 K–B1, leaving White with a Rook less but a very strong attack that Black can hardly meet; in this variation Black cannot very well continue with 19 ..., P×N?; 20 P×P dis ch, K–N2; 21 N–R5 ch!, P×N; 22 Q×P.

17 ...	Q–B3
18 P×P!	B×R
19 N×NP ch	K–N2
20 N×P?	

White decides to win back at least a piece and thereby reduce his material disadvantage; but in so doing he merely increases Black's defence prospects. More precise was 20 N–B4!; e.g. 20 ..., Q–B6 ch; 21 K–B1, P×N (21 ..., R×P; 22 Q–N4!); 22 P×P, R×P; 23 R–R7 ch!!, and Black is helpless.

| 20 ... | B–B6 ch! |

Virtually forced, as after 20 ..., Q×BP?; 21 Q×B ch, K×N; 22 R–N1 ch, Black loses his Queen.

| 21 K–B1 | Q×BP |
| 22 N–B4! | K–R1! |

The best defence; withdrawing or protecting the Bishop loses the Queen—

(a) 22 ..., B–K4; 23 N–N3!, Q–R2; 24 Q–N4 ch.

(b) 22 ..., B–B3; 23 N–N3, Q–K4; 24 Q–N4 ch.

(c) 22 ..., Q–K4; 23 Q–N4 ch (Euwe).

23 N×B

DIAGRAM 241

| 23 ... | QR–K1? |

Black prevents N–K4 and prepares to return the exchange. A better method was 23 ..., N–Q1; Black can then answer 24 R–N1 by 24 ..., K–R2!, and although White has a dangerous attack after 25 B×B, N×B; 26 N(3)–Q5 the game is still undecided.

| 24 N(3)–K2 | KR–N1! |
| 25 P–R5! | |

White would remain with an extra pawn after 25 B×R, R×B, but Black's strong Bishop is adequate compensation.

| 25 ... | R–N4 |
| 26 N–N3 | R×N |

As Black cannot in any case hold his material advantage (26 ..., Q–B3; 27 N–K4, or 26 ..., Q–K4;

27 N–N6 ch), he decides to give it back at once and thereby win the pawn on e3. White's pieces, however, still remain active enough to bring about a quick decision.

27	P×R	R×P	
28	K–B2	R–K1	
29	R–K1!	R×R	
30	Q×R	K–N2	
31	Q–K8	Q–B7 ch	
32	K–N1	Q–Q8 ch	
33	K–R2	Q–B7 ch	
34	N–N2	Q–B4	
35	Q–KN8 ch	K–B3	
36	Q–KR8 ch	K–N4	
37	Q–N7 ch	Resigns	

The advanced pawn can be a very effective weapon, as this game shows. But the decision to make the advance must always be well considered, for the pawn can easily become a weakness, especially in the end-game. Care must be taken that the opponent is not permitted to force the exchange of Queens and then attack the pawn at his leisure.

C. WEAK SQUARES IN THE PAWN CHAIN

In an earlier chapter we pointed out that the pawns differ from the other pieces in that they can only move in a forward direction. Every pawn move must therefore be carefully weighed.

Steinitz once laid down the principle that the pawns are strongest on their original squares. This applies mainly to pawns on a wing that is under attack. We know that a pawn advance is often the only way to convert a space or a material advantage in the centre or on the wings; we know too that a well-prepared pawn advance can be an effective attacking weapon. But when it comes to defence, every pawn move can create a serious weakness. Beginners are frequently given the good advice never to move a pawn in an area under attack unless such a pawn move is forced by an enemy threat.

DIAGRAM 242

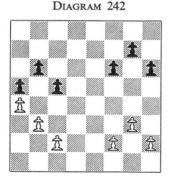

Diagram 242 shows us some weak squares; both sides have, by pawn advances, been left with squares that cannot be protected by pawns. On the King-side it is f3 and h3 which are weak for White and g6 for Black; if they are not kept under sufficient piece control, enemy pieces may be able to take up position there. It is obvious that such weaknesses are relative and vary in accordance with the position of the pieces: if, for example, White has a Bishop on g2, the weakness of f3 and h3 need not be perceptible provided that

Black does not succeed in concentrating his pieces correspondingly (e.g. Q–QB1, B–KN5, N–K4).

There are also weaknesses on the Queen-side. By advancing his a and c-pawns Black has left the square b5 weak and the pawn on b6 vulnerable; this gives his opponent the possibility of occupying b5 with a piece and attacking b6 with a Knight from c4, a Bishop from c7, or a Rook from d6. White's Queen-side pawn chain is also not free of weaknesses. There is the obvious one on c3; but b4 can also become weak if for any reason (e.g. occupation of c3 by Black) White is prevented from playing P–QB3.

As weak squares are generally caused by the advance of a neighbouring pawn, the opponent often endeavours to force such an advance. The creation and exploitation of weak squares in the enemy position is an important element in modern chess strategy; often one weak square can decide a game. It should however be stressed that the weakness of a square is not an absolute factor. Sometimes the weakness is all important; at others its influence on the play is negligible: all depends on the character of the position, the material at hand, the position of the pieces, and so on. To recognize real weaknesses—those that can be exploited—calls for a deep evaluation of the position, and that in turn requires a positional feeling that comes with practice.

In our first example we see a weak square exploited in almost brutal fashion; this is the sort of treatment a King-side weakness usually gets. Our second example shows the more difficult task of exploiting a weak point on the Queen-side.

EUWE–FLOHR

(Amsterdam 1939)

Diagram 243

Position after Black's 20th move

Black is suffering from a serious weakness on f6; he had probably played P–K3 (the cause of the weakness) in the belief that his Bishop on f8 would prevent the weakness from becoming perceptible. But White soon demonstrates the tactical attacking chances that have been thereby opened to him.

21 B–B6   Q–R4

After 21 ..., B–K2; 22 P–K5! the weakness of the squares f6 and h6 becomes more noticeable because an exchange of Bishop leaves

261

Black with a bad Bishop, which cannot be used in the fight for the black squares.

22 R–B5!

A nice piece of tactical play; Black cannot continue with 22 ..., B×R; 23 P×R, for he would then be left facing the double threat of R×B and Q–K3–R6.

22 ...	Q×P
23 R–KR5!	P–K4

There is no better way of defending against the mating attack—

(*a*) 23 ..., Q×P; 24 B–B1, and Black must reply 24 ..., P–K4, after which play continues as in the actual game.

(*b*) 23 ..., B–K2; 24 R×P!, B×B; 25 Q×B, K×R; 26 Q×BP ch, K–R1; 27 R–Q3, Q–N8 ch; 28 B–B1, P–K4; 29 Q×B winning.

(*c*) 23 ..., B–N2; 24 B×B, K×B; 25 R×P ch!, with a continuation similar to the previous variation.

24 P×P	B–K3
25 Q–B4	Q×P
26 B–B1	B–K2(!)

Obviously not 26 ..., B–N2; 27 B×B, K×B; 28 Q–R6 ch, etc. After the text-move Black can answer 27 Q–R6 by 27 ..., B×B; 28 P×B, Q×P (f6).

27 Q–R4(?)

White misses a pretty continuation leading to an immediate win: 27 R–N1!, Q–Q5 (27 ..., Q×R?;

28 Q–R6); 28 R–QN4!!, Q–R8; 29 Q–R4, etc.

28 ...	B–QB4!

By attacking the square f2, Black gains an important tempo for the defence. Naturally the continuation 29 R×P?, Q×BP ch is out of the question.

28 R–R6	P–R4!

The last counter-chance; but Black's King is too vulnerable for this to offer much hope of salvation.

29 R–Q3

In view of the threat 30 R–KB3 followed by R×RP Black is forced to give up his material advantage by sacrificing a piece.

29 ...	B×P ch
30 Q×B	Q×Q ch
31 K×Q	P–R5

DIAGRAM 244

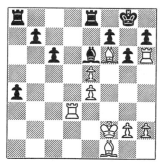

The White pieces have the squares f6 and h6 firmly in their grip. There remains only a little tactical problem: will White be able to push through his mating attack before Black gets a new Queen? The continuation 32 R–KB3, P–R6; 33 R–B4 (threatening R×RP), P–KN4! is not the right way to finish the attack.

32 B–K2!

All is now decided; there is nothing Black can do after 32 ..., P–R6; 33 P–N4!, P–R7; 34 R×RP. The following despairing sacrifice does not change the situation.

32 ...	R–R4
33 P–N4	R×P
34 B×R	B–B5
35 R(3)–KR3	B×B
36 B–B6	R–K3
37 P–K5	B×P
38 R×RP	R×B ch
39 P×R	Resigns

BOGOLJUBOW–CAPABLANCA

(New York 1924)

1 P–Q4	N–KB3
2 N–KB3	P–Q4
3 P–K3	P–K3
4 B–Q3	P–B4
5 P–QN3	N–B3
6 O–O	B–Q3
7 B–N2	O–O
8 QN–Q2(?)	Q–K2!
9 N–K5	P×P
10 P×P	B–R6!

The purpose of this move is clear; after the exchange of Bishops the weakness of White's Queen-side becomes noticeable.

11 B×B	Q×B
12 QN–B3	

Likewise after 12 N×N, P×N; 13 P–QB4 Black has the better game; e.g. 13 ..., B–R3; 14 N–B3, P×P; 15 P×P, KR–Q1; 16 Q–K2, P–B4!, etc.

12 ... B–Q2

DIAGRAM 245

Black's plan will consist of pressure on the c-file; sooner or later White will be forced to play P–QB3, after which his pawn on c3 can be attacked by the heavy pieces. White's difficulties result from his failure to prevent the exchange of his black-squared Bishop after having played P–QN3; thus he is left with a weakness on the Queen-side. The continuation 13 P–QB4, P×P; 14 P×P, KR–Q1 is not favourable to White, because the resulting isolated pawn pair is weak: without his Bishop on b2 White will have difficulty with the defence of the pawns; he will also lack the means to create attacking chances on the King-side.

13 N×N	B×N
14 Q–Q2(?)	

Somewhat better is 14 Q–B1; an exchange of Queens would then improve White's defence prospects, although not fully equalizing the game; a withdrawal of Black's Queen would also remove some of White's difficulties.

14 ...	QR–B1
15 P–B3	P–QR3!
16 N–K5	B–N4!

An important prerequisite for the attack on the Queen-side is the elimination of White's Bishop. By that, Black not only rids himself of his own bad Bishop and clears the c-file: he also deprives White of all possibilities of active play (P–KB4–5); in addition he removes one protector from the square e4, so that White must look for another way to prevent penetration of the Black Knight.

17 P–B3

No better is 17 B×B, P×B; 18 P–B3, R–B2; 19 KR–QB1, KR–QB1; 20 R–B2, N–K1 followed by N–Q3.

17 ...	B×B
18 N×B	R–B2
19 QR–B1	KR–QB1
20 R–B2	N–K1
21 KR–QB1	N–Q3
22 N–K5?	

A mistake that helps Black's attack. Correct was 22 N–B5! with the object of neutralizing the weakness on c3; Black would then have to play very precisely: 22 ..., P–QN3; 23 N–R4, R–B3 (not 23 ..., P–QN4?; 24 N–B5, N–N2;

25 P–QN4); 24 Q–Q3, R–R1! followed by N–N2; only after this preparation could Black safely drive the Knight from its defensive position by P–QN4.

DIAGRAM 246

| 22 ... | Q–R4! |
| 23 P–QR4 | |

Meeting the threat 23 ..., N–N4 but weakening the pawn on b3. After 23 N–Q3, N–N4; 24 N–B5 Black would continue with 24 ..., P–QN3; 25 N–R4, R–B3! (not 25 ..., N–Q3; 26 P–QB4!) followed by N–Q3.

| 23 ... | Q–N3! |
| 24 N–Q3 | |

The pawn cannot be held in any case; e.g. 24 P–QN4, P–QR4!; 25 P–N5, N–B5; 26 N×N, R×N; 27 R–R2, P–K4!; or 25 R–N1, P×P; 26 R×P, Q×R!, etc. But the attempt to get counter-play by its immediate sacrifice is frustrated by Capablanca's precise play, which is crowned with a fine combination.

| 24 ... | Q×NP |
| 25 N–B5 | Q–N3 |

26 R–N2	Q–R2	30 N–B5	N–N4
27 Q–K1	P–QN3	31 R–K2(?)	N×QP!
28 N–Q3	R–B5	32 P×N	R(1)×N!
29 P–R5	P×P	33 Resigns	

In the last two examples the weaknesses arose from imprecise play in the opening; the task of the attacking side was to exploit a weakness already there. Mostly, however, the opponent is not so kind as to create the weakness voluntarily; he must be forced to do so. There are two ways of doing this—

1. By piece attack. If for example White threatens his opponent's castled position by N–KB5 combined with Q–KN4, Black may be forced to play P–KN3. A similar piece manoeuvre can also be used on the Queen-side to induce a weakening advance there.

2. By the advance of one's own pawns. A frequent case is the advance of the Rook pawn (e.g. P–KR4–5–6). If it is allowed to reach the sixth rank, the opponent is generally forced to play P–KN3, after which a serious weakness may arise on f6.

In the following example White adopts the first method. Even before finishing his development he manoeuvres in such a way as to force the weakening of f6; this square eventually proves to be the deciding factor in the game.

GELLER–UNZICKER
(Interzonal 1952)

1 P–Q4	P–Q4
2 P–QB4	P–QB3
3 N–KB3	N–B3
4 N–B3	P×P
5 P–K4	P–QN4
6 P–K5	N–Q4
7 P–QR4	P–K3
8 P×P	N×N
9 P×N	P×P
10 N–N5!	B–N2
11 Q–R5	

This forces P–KN3; but that is only the beginning of the fight for f6: White must now eliminate those enemy minor pieces that protect this square; that applies especially to the Bishop on f8.

11 ...	P–N3
12 Q–N4	B–K2
13 B–K2	N–Q2
14 B–B3	Q–B2(?)

Also poor for Black is 14 ..., B×B; 15 Q×B, O–O; 16 P–R4, which gives White good attacking chances. The correct procedure for Black was employed by Petrosian against Szabó (match, Moscow-Budapest 1955). That game went on 14 ..., Q–B1!; 15 N–K4, P–B4!; 16 P×P *e.p.*, N×P; 17 N×N ch, B×N; 18 B×B, Q×B; 19 Q×KP ch, Q–K2, and Black

265

had the better prospects in the end-game.

DIAGRAM 247

Position after 14 ..., Q–B2

15 N–K4

The Knight on g5 has served its purpose there; now it is needed for the fight to control f6.

15 ...   **N–N3**

Some commentators recommended 15 ..., P–KR4. That would indeed have prevented 16 B–R6; but Black's chances would hardly have been better than in the game, because the weakness of the King's wing would likewise have precluded castling.

16 B–R6!   **R–KN1**

Meeting the threat B–N7 followed by N–B6 ch. After 16 ..., N–Q4, White could have carried out this manoeuvre after a little preparation; e.g. 17 O–O, P–R3; 18 B–N7, R–KN1; 19 B–B6, B×B; 20 P×B followed by Q–R4 and N–B5 (Ståhlberg). The continuation 16 ..., B×N; 17 B×B, O–O–O?!, recommended by some commentators, is likewise unsatis-

factory, e.g. 18 Q–B3, B–KB1; 19 B–N5, B–K2; 20 B–Q2, B–KB1; 21 O–O, N–Q4; 22 R–R6 followed by KR–R1.

17 B–N5!

With his previous move White stopped his opponent castling and thereby hindered the speedy mobilization of his heavy pieces; as a result he need not fear the exchange of all the minor pieces because he will remain for some time with an extra Rook in play.

17 ...   **B×N**
18 B(3)×B   **N–Q4**

After 18 ..., O–O–O White obtains a decisive attack: 19 R–R5, P–N5; 20 O–O, P–N6; 21 B×B, Q×B; 22 P–Q5. Euwe recommended 18 ..., R–QB1; 19 O–O, N–R5, but White can then continue strongly with 20 B×B, Q×B; 21 Q–B3, Q–B2 (21 ..., Q–Q2; 22 P–Q5); 22 B–N7, R–N1; 23 B–B6 ch, K–K2 (23 ..., K–B1; 24 KR–K1 followed by P–Q5); 24 Q–B6 ch, K–B1; 25 P–Q5.

19 B×N   **P×B**
20 B×B   **Q×B**
21 O–O   **K–B1**
22 KR–N1   **P–QR3**

It looks as if Black has overcome all his difficulties; after 23 R×NP, P×R; 24 R×R ch, K–N2 he would even have the better of it, for he then threatens to secure a passed-pawn by the breakthrough P–N5. But in reality things are not so rosy for Black;

the weakness of the square f6 has still to be reckoned with.

23 Q–B3!   Q–K3?

This leads by force to a speedy loss. After the immediate return of the pawn by 23 ..., K–N2!; 24 Q×QP, KR–QN1 he has some hope of saving the game. White can hardly continue with 25 R×NP?, P×R; 26 R×R, R×R;

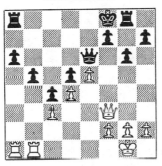

27 Q×R, P–N5!, after which Black has excellent counter-play; but 25 P–B4! still gives White good attacking chances on the King-side.

24 Q–B6!

The decisive move; Black's King is pinned to the eighth rank for the time being. After 24 ..., Q×Q; 25 P×Q, K–K1; 26 R×NP followed by R×QP, the end-game is hopeless for Black.

24 ...	Q–B1
25 P–B4	Q–N2
26 R–R5	K–K1
27 KR–R1	P–N5

Or 27 ..., K–Q2; 28 Q–Q6 ch, K–B1; 29 R×RP.

28 P×P	Q×P
29 R×QP	Q–N2
30 P–K6	Resigns

Sometimes it is not only one square which is weak; a whole complex of weak squares can arise. We have already touched on the problem in the section on good and bad Bishops; the following game is an instructive extension of the theme.

SCHLECHTER–JOHN

1 P–Q4	P–Q4
2 P–QB4	P–K3
3 N–QB3	P–KB4(?)

Black's set-up is called the Stonewall formation; the aim is to gain control of the square e4 and obtain active play on the King-side. The system can also be adopted by White (1 P–Q4, P–Q4; 2 P–K3, N–KB3; 3 P–KB4). The disadvantage of the advance P–KB4 is that it weakens the square e5, and generally the system is satisfactory only when the opponent is not in a position to exploit this weakness; for example, after the opposing Queen-Bishop has been closed in by the move P–K3, the set-up can be all right. In this game, that is not the case, and the weakness of e5 will determine the whole course of play.

4 N–B3	P–B3
5 B–B4	B–Q3
6 P–K3!	

Although 6 B×B is also quite good, the text-move is much stronger; Black will sooner or later be forced to play B×B, and after P×B, Black's backward pawn on e6 is fixed as a serious weakness in his position; in addition White will be then able to control the square e5 with a Rook on e1.

6 ...	N–B3
7 B–Q3	Q–B2
8 P–KN3!	O–O
9 O–O	N–K5

The favourable position of the Knight is the positive side of the Stonewall formation. However, the square e4 is not unduly weak for White because the Knight can be driven off by P–KB3.

10 Q–N3

Threatening to win a pawn by 11 P×P, KP×P; 12 N×N, BP×N; 13 B×P.

| 10 ... | K–R1 |
| 11 QR–B1 | B×B |

After 11 ..., Q–K2 the Queen is tied to the defence of the Bishop; the natural developing continuation 11 ..., N–Q2; 12 P×P, KP×P (12 ..., N×N; 13 P×KP); 13 N–QN5 is hopeless: it is no wonder that Black opts for the strategically unfavourable exchange of Bishops.

12 KP×B!	Q–KB2(?)
13 N–K5	Q–K2
14 B×N!	

The best way of removing the Knight from its strong post; of

course, White's next move is an important follow-up.

14 ...	BP×P
15 P–B3	KP×P
16 QR–K1	Q–QB2
17 Q–R3!	

DIAGRAM 249

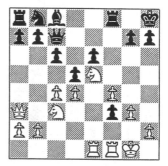

Gradually the weakness of the whole black square complex becomes perceptible. If Black now plays N–Q2, White can answer at once by Q–K7.

17 ...	K–N1
18 R×P	N–R3
19 P–N3	Q–Q1
20 P–B5!	

The blocked pawn chain has been formed under circumstances very favourable to White: he has control of e5 and also has a clear space advantage on the King-side; he can therefore operate simultaneously on both wings without giving his opponent any chances of active play.

20 ...	N–B2
21 Q–N2	B–Q2
22 Q–QB2	

As the advance P–QN4–5 still presents some difficulty, it is best to postpone the action on the Queen-side until Black is fully occupied with parrying threats on the opposite wing.

22 ...	Q–K2
23 QR–KB1	QR–K1
24 P–KN4!	B–B1
25 R–R3!	

Forcing P–KN3, which weakens f6 and h6.

25 ...	P–KN3
26 P–N4	

Although White has no intention of breaking-through on the Queen-side at the moment, he positions his pawns in such a way that a break-through is always in the air.

26 ...	Q–B3
27 R(3)–B3	R–K2
28 P–QR4	P–QR3
29 N–Q1!	

White needs a Knight on e3 in order to carry out the manoeuvre P–KN5, N–KN4, N–KB6 ch (or N–R6 ch).

29 ...	R–N2
30 N–K3	Q–K2
31 P–KN5	B–Q2
32 N(3)–N4	B–K1
33 N–R6 ch	K–R1
34 Q–K2	Q–Q1
35 N(5)–N4!	B–Q2
36 Q–K5	N–K1
37 R–KR3	Q–B2

Black cannot play 37 ..., Q–K2?; 38 Q–N8. This demonstrates that the White pieces can move virtually unhindered on the opponent's black squares.

38 N–B6!

The climax of White's black square strategy; the exchange on e5 is forced and fairly soon Black will also have to exchange on f6; then White will have not only an easy path for his King into the enemy position (via f4 and e5) but will also have a strong passed-pawn on f6.

DIAGRAM 250

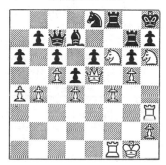

38 ...	Q × Q
39 BP × Q	R–K2
40 R(3)–KB3!	

Threatening 41 N × B (or even 41 N × QP), R × R; 42 R × R, R × N; 43 R–B8 ch, K–N2; 44 R–N8 mate.

40 ...	N × N
41 R × N	R × R
42 KP × R	R–K1
43 N–B7 ch	K–N1
44 N–K5	R–Q1
45 K–N2	K–B1
46 P–R4	B–K1
47 K–B3	B–B2
48 K–B4	K–K1
49 R–QN1	K–B1
50 P–N5!	Resigns

CHAPTER XIII

Dynamic Elements

THE character of the position is determined by elements of different types. Some of these—the type of material, the pawn formation, lasting weaknesses there—continue to affect play for rather a long time; these are termed static elements. Rather different are the lead in development, the more active position of one's pieces, the concentration of pieces for attack on a certain section of the board; it is clear that these elements mostly exert an important influence only for a short period: every tempo decides whether the active side will succeed in changing his momentary superiority into a material advantage or finishing the game by a mating attack; whether the defender will manage to parry the immediate threats, improve his position, and eventually restore the balance. Time is the most important factor here. Neither side can, under these conditions, afford to undertake lengthy manoeuvres; a single lost tempo or a superfluous move can decide the game. Elements of this sort, in which time plays a dominant role, are called dynamic elements; in this chapter they will be treated in four thematic groups—

A. Lead in development.

B. Gain in time at the cost of material.

C. Co-operation of pieces and pawns.

D. The positional sacrifice.

A. LEAD IN DEVELOPMENT

The right of each player to make a move can be carried out with several different aims. Some moves serve to develop pieces or increase their power; others help to form a suitable pawn chain. There are moves that are necessary for repelling enemy threats and securing one's own position; there are also superfluous moves and even moves that accelerate the opponent's advance. In the opening, especially, when both sides are undeveloped, economy of time is extremely important; superfluous moves here (e.g. moves of the Rook pawns) are typical beginner mistakes. In the end-game and middle-game we sometimes come across positions where waiting moves are called for: but in the opening it is necessary to use every move to build up one's forces.

In the introductory chapter of my book *Moderne Schachtheorie* I gave the most important principles for handling the opening. Summarized they are: To complete the development of the pieces as quickly as possible and secure the position in the centre. With regard to this, the following points should be remembered—

1. Place the pieces without loss of time where they can develop their greatest power.

2. Do not move a piece that is already developed unless there is a strong reason for doing so.

3. Avoid putting pieces on squares where they can be driven off by moves contributing to the development of enemy pieces and pawns.

4. Pawn moves in the opening are only an aid to development and a means of fighting for the centre; they should therefore be kept to a minimum.

These principles should, of course, not be applied dogmatically without consideration of the particular conditions obtaining. Sometimes it is possible to move a piece three or four times in the opening and still emerge with an advantage; this is the case where each move of the piece is part of a plan to restrict the power of the opposing pieces and create weaknesses in the enemy camp. Mechanical calculation of development tempi is, in itself, not a suitable measure for deciding who has the advantage; the real meaning of piece development lies in the achievement of the maximum power for the pieces.

Generally, however, a violation of one of the preceding principles helps the opponent to a lead in development or a superiority in the power of his pieces. The side having a lead in development not balanced by other factors (e.g. material disadvantage) gains the initiative, which can be either of temporary or of permanent duration. The lead in development can be a means to a direct mating attack, material advantage or even a lasting positional advantage. In the last case, which can result from forcing the opponent to weaken his pawns or give up his Bishop pair, etc., a dynamic weakness is transformed into a static one.

Often loss of time in the opening stems from an endeavour to launch an attack before one's development is complete. An example of this is the following game.

BOTVINNIK–DENKER

(U.S.S.R. *v.* U.S.A., Match 1945)

1	P–Q4	P–Q4
2	N–KB3	N–KB3
3	P–B4	P–QB3
4	P×P	P×P
5	N–B3	N–B3
6	B–B4	Q–R4(?)

Black intends to attack the point c3 by means of N–K5, P–K3, B–N5, etc. In this position such a plan is bad, for White can easily defend c3 by natural developing moves. Black's attack will merely lose time.

7	P–K3	N–K5
8	Q–N3	P–K3
9	B–Q3	B–N5
10	QR–B1	N×N
11	P×N	B–R6(?)

The start of a doubtful plan. Better is 11 ..., B–K2; 12 O–O, Q–Q1, although after 13 P–K4 White has a dangerous initiative in the centre and on the King's wing.

| 12 | QR–N1 | P–QN3 |

DIAGRAM 251

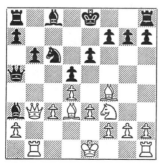

Black wants to exchange off his opponent's good Bishop; but

Black, with all his manoeuvres, is two tempi behind, and when we consider that the Queen, rather than being developed, is actually a tactical weakness in its present place, then that is another debit tempo. It is not surprising that White is able to open the game by a simple break-through in the centre; after that Black runs into great difficulties.

| 13 | P–K4! | P×P |

This move was given a question-mark by many commentators; but in view of the bad position of Black's Queen and his King Bishop (the result of the faulty action begun on move six), the game cannot be held in any case. Some possibilities are—

(*a*) 13 ..., B–R3; 14 B×B, Q×B; 15 P×P winning a pawn.

(*b*) 13 ..., B–N2; 14 P×P, P×P; 15 O–O, O–O; 16 Q–B2, and White threatens both B×P ch and R–N5.

(*c*) 13 ..., B–K2; 14 B–QN5, B–Q2; 15 P×P, and Black again loses a pawn.

| 14 | B–QN5! | B–Q2 |
| 15 | N–Q2 | P–QR3 |

The only way to meet White's threat of 16 N–B4.

16	B×N	B×B
17	N–B4	Q–KB4
18	B–Q6	P–K6!

Black's only possibility of pro-longing the game is to sacrifice his Queen; but even that is not enough. The alternative, 18 ...,

B–Q4; 19 B×B, P–QN4; 20
N–Q6 ch, however, loses at once.

19	N×KP	Q×R ch
20	Q×Q	B×B
21	Q×NP	K–Q2
22	Q–N3	QR–N1
23	Q–B2	R–N4
24	O–O	R–KR4

25	P–KR3	R–QN1
26	P–QB4	P–N3
27	N–N4	R–KB4
28	N–K5 ch	B×N
29	P×B	R×KP
30	Q–Q2 ch	Resigns

After 30 ..., K–K2 (or B2) there
follows 31 R–Q1.

A lead in development makes itself felt mainly in open positions
or in those in which the active side has the possibility of opening the
game by a break-through in the centre. In closed positions it has
less significance; there the placing of the pawns and pieces on
strategically advantageous squares is of more importance than the
number of pieces developed. From this we can postulate the
following rule: If you have a lead in development, endeavour to
keep the position open by a break-through in the centre or by
opening files and diagonals; if it is your opponent who has the lead,
keep the position closed. This is such a logical and obvious rule
that it is valid in all cases; its violation is always a bad strategical
mistake.

B. GAIN IN TIME AT THE COST OF MATERIAL

In view of the present-day state of opening theory, it is rare that in
games between experienced players one side is allowed to get a free
lead in development; generally any lead in development must be
paid for—in material, etc. In such cases the game is a sharp struggle
of static (material advantage) against dynamic elements (lead in
development). The materially weaker side will endeavour to use the
temporary superiority of his forces to launch an attack; his opponent
will strive to ward off all threats, complete his development, simplify
the position, and use his material advantage in the end-game.

The majority of the classical gambits were based on the idea of
sacrificing material to accelerate the development of one's pieces;
typical is the Danish Gambit (1 P–K4, P–K4; 2 P–Q4, P×P;
3 P–QB3, P×P; 4 B–QB4, P×P; 5 B×NP), in which White gains
a lead in development for the two pawns sacrificed. Similar gambits
proved to be fairly dangerous at a time when the technique of
defence was at a low level; the defending side generally clung
blindly to his material and was never prepared to exchange it for a
different sort of advantage. With the development of defence

strategy, most of these gambits were refuted. The two principal methods of refutation are—

1. Returning the material at a moment when the opponent's lead in development can thereby be neutralized; if possible some sort of positional advantage should be seized at the same time.
2. Declining the material offered altogether and exploiting the defective positional set-up of the opponent.

Amongst the openings of the Classical Era, the Danish Gambit gives Black the chance of using both defensive methods; this the following game will show.

MIESES–MARÓCZY

(Monte Carlo 1902)

1	P–K4	P–K4
2	P–Q4	P×P
3	P–QB3	P×P

Maróczy chooses the first method. Today many players would simply decline the gambit by 3 ..., P–Q4; 4 P×P, N–KB3!; 5 P×P, N×P (5 ..., Q×P is also good); 6 B–QB4, B–K3 followed by N–QB3.

4	B–QB4	P×P
5	B×NP	P–Q3

Black can obtain comfortable equality by giving back both pawns immediately: 5 ..., P–Q4; 6 B×QP, N–KB3; 7 B×BP ch, K×B; 8 Q×Q, B–QN5 ch, etc. Does the text-move therefore imply that Black intends to hold on to his material advantage at all costs? No; as the game shows, Maróczy is merely postponing the return of the two pawns until a moment when it brings him more than he would get from doing so immediately.

6 N–K2

The majority of opening text-books, my own included, give 6 P–B4 as more dangerous for Black. However, a careful study will show that this line does not vindicate the Danish Gambit; e.g. 6 P–B4, N–QB3 (better than the theoretical 6 ..., B–K3; 7 B×B, P×B; 8 Q–N3, Q–B1; 9 N–KB3); 7 N–KB3, B–K3; 8 B×B P×B; 9 Q–N3, Q–Q2 (9 ..., P–Q4 is also good); 10 N–N5, O–O–O; 11 N×KP (11 Q×KP, N–B3!), R–K1, etc.

6	...	N–QB3
7	O–O	B–K3
8	B–Q5	N–B3
9	Q–N3	Q–B1
10	N–B4	B×B
11	P×B	N–K4
12	R–K1	

(*See* Diagram 252)

For the pawns sacrificed White has a considerable lead in development. If Black now defends himself with 12 ..., N(3)–Q2 he runs into serious difficulties after 13 Q–KN3. Maróczy obtains a clear advantage, however, by returning both pawns.

DIAGRAM 252

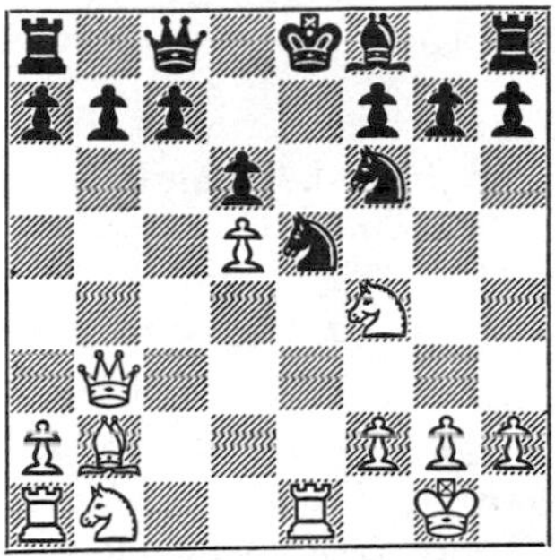

Position after 12 R–K1

12 ...	B–K2!
13 B×N	P×B
14 R×P	Q–Q2
15 Q–KN3	

Bad for White is 15 Q×P, O–O; e.g. 16 Q–B6, Q–N5; 17 N–K2, B–Q3, or 16 R–K1, B–Q3; 17 N–Q3, N×P. But even the text-move does not bring salvation; Black can simply ignore the threat to his pawn.

15 ...	O–O–O!

Black has a lead in development and his pieces are working in co-operation. White now attempts to regain material equality, but in doing so loses the exchange.

16 Q×P	Q–Q3!
17 Q–N5	KR–K1!
18 N–Q2	N–Q2
19 R×B	Q×R
20 Q–N3	Q–N5
21 N–B3	R–N1
22 Q–R4	Q–B6
23 R–N1	Q×N
24 Resigns	

A difficult strategical problem is the decision to play for the win of a pawn in the opening at the expense of development; such a manoeuvre must always be carefully weighed, for an undeveloped position cannot generally resist a sudden piece attack; chess literature abounds in games (often twenty-move miniatures) where a pawn hunt in the opening has been the cause of defeat. It is difficult to lay down any rules for deciding when it is justifiable to play for the win of a pawn; the strength of one's defensive position and the opponent's attacking chances must be carefully examined. In a number of variations theoreticians have been unable for years to assess positions where development tempi are matched by material disadvantage.

Generally it is more dangerous to take a Rook or a Knight pawn than a central pawn; the capturing of a central pawn means not only material gain but also occupation of central squares. In his book *My System* Nimzowitsch spoke of the principle: Always take a central pawn if you can do so without any great danger. But the word *if* keynotes the whole difficult problem.

In our first example we show Black taking a pawn under most unfavourable conditions: he not only loses time but also opens up lines for his opponent's attack.

FUDERER–MILIĆ

(Agram 1955)

1 P–QB4	P–K3
2 N–QB3	P–Q4
3 P–Q4	N–KB3
4 B–N5	B–K2
5 P–K3	O–O
6 R–B1	P–KR3
7 B–R4	N–K5
8 B × B	Q × B
9 Q–B2(?)	P–B3
10 B–Q3	N × N
11 Q × N	Q–N4?

White has not handled the opening accurately and Black can obtain easy equality by 11 ..., N–Q2; 12 N–KB3, P × P; 13 B × P, P–QN3. Instead he embarks on a pawn hunt that is completely unjustified.

12 N–B3!	Q × NP
13 K–K2	

DIAGRAM 253

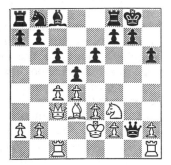

Suddenly Black is faced with defeat; he has only his Queen in play, and its exposed position is likely to cost further tempi. White has a clear plan of attack on the King-side, thanks to his opponent's foolhardiness in opening the g-file.

13 ...	Q–R6
14 QR–KN1	P–KB4

Forced, because the pawn on g7 has got to be defended by a Rook from f7. After 14 ..., N–Q2; 15 R–N3, Q–R4; 16 KR–KN1, P–KN3; 17 K–K1! White threatens 18 R × P ch, P × R; 19 B × P; if Black tries to defend himself by 17 ..., K–R1, there follows 18 Q–R3 with the threats of 19 Q–K7 and 19 N–K5.

15 R–N3	Q–R4
16 KR–KN1	R–B2
17 Q–R3!	N–Q2
18 K–K1	

Now White threatens 19 Q–Q6 followed by 20 N–K5; Black has no longer any defensive possibilities because his pieces are all tied down; e.g. 18 ..., N–N3; 19 N–K5.

18 ...	P × P
19 B × QBP	P–B5

Black wants more space for his Queen, but this move is answered elegantly by White. After 19 ..., N–N3 there is also a pretty conclusion: 20 Q–Q6!, N × B; 21 Q–Q8 ch, K–R2; 22 Q–K8 (threatening 23 R × P ch!), P–KN4; 23 R × P!, P × R; 24 R × P, etc.

20 R × P ch!	R × R
21 B × P ch	K–R1
22 R × R	K × R
23 Q–K7 ch	K–R1

24 N–K5! P×P

Naturally 24 ..., N×N; 25 Q–B8 ch is out of the question.

Black is a Rook up, but he cannot get his pieces into play.

25 P–B4

A fine finish. Of course 25 N–B7 ch, K–N2; 26 N–N5 dis ch, K–N3; 27 B–B7 winning the Queen is also sufficient; but the text-move contains the stronger threat of 27 N–B7 ch, K–N2; 28 N–N5 dis ch, K–N3; 29 Q–B7 mate, and against this there is no defence. So Black resigned.

A pawn offer to win time is not confined entirely to the opening; the middle game too presents opportunities on occasions; but here the sacrifice is generally of a tactical nature and bound up with particular variations whose outcome can be exactly calculated. In the middle-game, with both sides fully developed, such a pawn-sacrifice demands a careful follow-up.

C. CO-OPERATION OF PIECES AND PAWNS

The full working power of the forces can only be properly utilized when there is co-operation between the different units. Without this co-operation the pieces may lose a considerable amount of their power and be worth much less than their normal value; on the other hand, by working together they may well be a match for a numerically superior force. Diagram 254 (the end phase of a study by B. N. Sachodjakin) shows a position in which Black cannot win despite

DIAGRAM 254

DIAGRAM 255

his tremendous material superiority of Queen against minor piece. The reason for that is the superb co-operation of White's forces. Black cannot win the Bishop or the pawn by checking with his Queen, on account of N–B7 ch; he cannot move his Knight because of the reply B–K5 ch; and an attempt to control e5 with his Queen

277

(Q–K7 ch) would be of no avail, because that square is indirectly protected by the Knight fork (N–B7 ch). White's pieces have developed a maximum of co-operation and together are able to exert tactical threats on the opposing King. Black's pieces, on the other hand, are operating well below their potential: the King is pinned to the edge of the board and the Knight must continually guard against B–K5 ch; the result is that the only remaining force, the Queen, is severely hampered in its pursuit of the enemy King by its inability to call on the other pieces for support.

Now let us look at Diagram 255, a well-known position from end-game theory; this is the only case of a draw with Queen against Bishop and Knight. The White pieces protect each other and form a barrier to the opposing King; Black cannot therefore use his King to assist in a mating or material winning manoeuvre.

Co-operation amongst the pieces and pawns can be of two types. In some cases the different units help each other when tactical threats are involved; e.g. in attack they can concentrate on a point in the enemy camp and in defence they can cover a point in their own position; this is called *tactical co-operation*. In other cases, good co-operation can aid the execution of a strategical plan; it can, for example, involve the piece support given to the advance of a passed-pawn or the conversion of a quantitative or qualitative pawn superiority; it can also take the form of a blockade and subsequent attack of an isolated pawn. Cases of this nature are characterized by *strategical co-operation*.

DIAGRAM 256

Position after White's 45th move

The achievement of the maximum tactical co-operation of one's forces is the foundation of many combinations of different types. From the position in Diagram 256 (Fuderer–Pachman, Interzonal 1955) I managed to obtain the maximum co-operation of my forces in the attack against the White King; the way to this lay in a Rook sacrifice: **45 ..., R–N5 ch!; 46 P × R, Q–K5 ch; 47 K–N3, Q × NP ch; 48 K–B2, Q–B5 ch; 49 K–N2** (49 K–K2, B–N5 ch; 50 K–Q3, Q–Q5 mate), **B–K5 ch; 50 K–R3, Q–B6 ch; 51 K–R4, Q–B7 ch; 52 K–N4, B–B6 ch; 53 K–B4, B–K7 dis ch; 54 K–N5, Q–N6 ch; 55 Resigns.** In this attack, the pawns on c5 and b3 had a vital role to play; without just one of them, the forced mate would have been impossible. The Black King, too, played his part towards the end. The pawn on d2 was admittedly superfluous, but the co-operation of all the other units was absolutely necessary to the success of the combination.

Our next example is of strategical co-operation; in this game White's pieces operate in a way that increases the value of a passed-pawn.

GELLER–SOKOLSKI

(18th U.S.S.R. Championship)

1	P–K4	P–K3
2	P–Q4	P–Q4
3	N–QB3	B–N5
4	P–K5	P–B4
5	P–QR3	B × N ch
6	P × B	N–K2
7	Q–N4	P × P
8	B–Q3	Q–B2
9	N–K2	P × P
10	Q × P	R–N1
11	Q × RP	Q × P?

Capturing the pawn on e5 appears quite logical because Black thereby obtains a great central superiority; and it does not look as if he is in any great danger. But two moves later it will be quite clear that White's pieces are working together in wonderful harmony; the advance of the h-pawn will then be sufficient to decide the game. Correct is 11 ..., QN–B3; 12 P–B4, B–Q2 followed by O–O–O; even 12 ..., R × P!? is possible.

12 B–KB4	Q–B3

Not even forcing the exchange of Queens would ease Black's defence: 12 ..., Q–R1; 13 Q × Q, R × Q; 14 B–K5, R–B1; 15 B × P, QN–B3; 16 P–B4 followed by P–KR4, and White's passed-pawn, supported by

the Rook and both Bishops, will decide the game.

13 P–KR4!

DIAGRAM 257

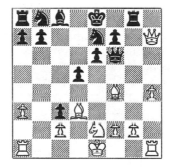

Black has an extra pawn and a seemingly sound position; nevertheless he loses quickly because he has no adequate defence to the advance of White's Rook pawn, which is well supported by the White pieces. White's only problem is the position of his Queen, which stands in the way of the passed-pawn; but the manoeuvre B–KN5, Q–R6–B6 soon changes that.

13 ...	QN–B3

After 13 ..., R–R1; 14 B–KN5, Q–K4; 15 P–B4, R × Q; 16 P × Q, R–R1; 17 P–R5, QN–B3; 18 B–B6 White's pawn cannot be stopped. Also bad for Black is

279

13 ..., P–K4; 14 B–KN5, Q–N2;
15 Q×Q, R×Q; 16 B–B6, etc.

14 B–N5	Q–K4
15 Q–R6!	B–Q2
16 Q–B6	R–QB1(?)

Hastens defeat; the exchange sacrifice 16 ..., Q×Q; 17 B×Q, P–K4; 18 B–R7, P–Q5! offered more chance of salvation.

17 P–B4!	Q–K6

18 P–R5	P–K4
19 P–R6	P–K5
20 B–N5	R×B
21 P–R7!	B–N5

Or 21 ..., R×P; 22 Q–R8 ch, etc.

22 Q×R	Q–Q7 ch
23 K–B1	B×N ch
24 B×B	N–Q5
25 P–R8=Q ch	Resigns

An important strategical plan that is possible under various conditions is to strengthen the co-operation of one's own forces and destroy that of the opponents. In our next example, Black, who gets behind in development, finds himself pressed into a position in which his pieces fail to work in unison.

RESHEVSKY–EVANS
(New York 1955)

1 N–KB3	N–KB3
2 P–KN3	P–Q4
3 B–N2	B–B4
4 O–O	P–B3
5 P–Q3	P–K3
6 QN–Q2	N–R3

For a certain time this was considered the best continuation; its aim is to forestall 7 Q–K1 (the usual answer to 6 ..., QN–Q2) by the threatened reply N–QN5. Nevertheless, the development of the Knight to a6 has its disadvantages: the Knight cannot join in the fight for the centre and lacks contact with the other minor pieces.

7 P–QR3!	B–K2

Weak is 7 ..., N–B4; 8 P–QN4, N–R5; 9 P–B4, etc. (9 ..., N–B6; 10 Q–K1).

8 P–QN4	O–O
9 B–N2	P–R3
10 R–K1	N–Q2?

Black leaves his opponent a free hand in the centre. Better is 10 ..., N–B2, after which the Knight makes some contribution, albeit a passive one, to the centre (control of d5); then Black would be in a position to strive for counter-play on the Queen-side by P–QR4.

11 P–K4	B–R2
12 P–B4	P×BP(?)

Now White obtains a numerical pawn superiority in the centre. Better is either P×KP or N–B2.

13 N×P!	P–QB4

Otherwise White plays 14 P–Q4 obtaining a classical centre. The text-move, however, means a further weakening of the Queen-side.

280

14 P–N5	N–B2
15 P–QR4	

DIAGRAM 258

Black clearly stands badly; all his pieces have been pressed back to the first and second ranks and they lack co-ordination.

15 . . .	B–B3
16 P–Q4	P × P
17 B × P	B × B
18 Q × B	P–N3

On b7 the pawn would soon come under attack by N–Q6 and P–K5; Black therefore moves it forward and at the same time secures c5 for his Knight. The move, however, opens c6 to White's Knight.

19 KR–Q1	N–B4
20 Q–K3	Q–K2
21 KN–K5	KR–Q1
22 N–B6	R × R ch
23 R × R	Q–B1
24 Q–KB4!	N–K1

(*See* Diagram 259)

The co-ordination of Black's pieces has been finally destroyed. White now forces the decision by a fine tactical break-through on the

DIAGRAM 259

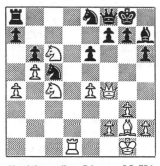

Position after 24 . . ., N–K1

Queen-side; the mutual contact of his own pieces helps him in his hunt against those of the enemy, especially the Rook on a8.

25 P–R5!	P × P
26 P–N6!	P × P
27 N × NP	P–N4
28 Q–K5	R–R3

After 28 . . ., P–B3?; 29 Q–N2, R–R3; 30 B–B1, Black loses the exchange.

29 Q–N8!

Threatens 30 B–B1 as well as 30 R–Q8. If Black now continues 29 . . ., B × P; 30 B × B, N × B; 31 N–Q7, he either is mated quickly or else loses his Queen.

29 . . .	B–N3
30 R–Q8	P–B3
31 B–B1	R × N
32 Q × R	N × P
33 Q × P	

Although all the pawns are on the same wing, the bad position of Black's King and White's exchange advantage make the win easy.

281

33 ...	N(5)–Q3	39 N–B5 ch	N×N
34 Q–R7	B–B2	40 B×N	K–B1
35 R–N8	P–K4	41 R–N7	Q–N2
36 Q–Q7	K–N2	42 Q–K7 ch	K–N1
37 N–K7	Q–R1	43 B–K6	Resigns
38 B–Q3	P–R4		

D. THE POSITIONAL SACRIFICE

A material sacrifice is aesthetically the most potent factor in a game of chess; beautiful combinations survive centuries and remain for ever in the history of chess. Wherein lies the aesthetic value of a sacrifice? The answer is that at a certain moment the value of the pieces and the meaning of material superiority apparently undergo a change; the normal values no longer apply.

Sacrifices can arise for several reasons. Often they are intended to lead to a quick mate, or a forced variation at the end of which the active side recovers his material—sometimes with interest. This is a tactical sacrifice, and the whole manoeuvre is called a combination. In other cases there is no question of exact calculation; the sacrifice is made for strategical reasons, the sacrificer hoping to gain compensation in some form—securing the two Bishops, weakening opposing squares, gaining time, promoting the co-ordination of his own pieces, etc. Sacrifices of this type are positional (or strategical) sacrifices. Sometimes a sacrifice lies between the tactical and the strategical: this arises where a player makes a sacrifice without being able to calculate its consequences exactly, yet where later analysis produces forced variations leading to some definite conclusion vindicating or refuting the intuitional sacrifice.

Our first example is a positional sacrifice intended to assist the attack on the opponent's King-side position.

RÉTI–SNOSKO-BOROWSKI

(London 1922)

(*See* Diagram 260)

White has his pieces poised for action; he now gives up a pawn to weaken Black's defence and sharpen his attack.

| 16 N–K5! | B×N |
| 17 P×B | P–N4 |

This weakening move has been provoked by the threat of N–N4.

| 18 B–N3 | R×P |
| 19 P–KR4! | |

Faced with 20 P×P, P×P; 21 Q–Q2, which would leave both his Knight pawn and Rook under attack, Black has a problem to solve. If he tries 19 ..., N(N3)–Q4?; 20 P×P, P×P; 21

DIAGRAM 260

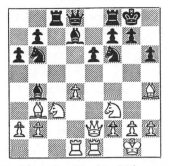

Position after Black's 15th move

Q–Q2, he still cannot hold the pawn. Also insufficient is 19 ..., R–B1; 20 P–B4!, for his King's position is too weak.

19 ...   N(B3)–Q4

This solution allows White's Queen to penetrate the King-side.

20 Q–R5   K–N2
21 B×N!   P×B

Black cannot recapture with the Knight, for after 21 ..., N×B; 22 N×B, Q×N, the Black Queen is no longer available for the defence of g5.

DIAGRAM 261

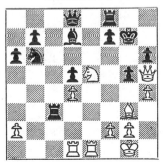

White can now use the weakened position of Black's King to bring off a very pretty combination; the point will become clear on move twenty-seven.

22 N×P!   R×N
23 B–K5 ch   R–KB3

This, the only defence, is seemingly adequate.

24 P×P   P×P
25 Q×P ch   K–B2
26 Q–R5 ch   K–N1
27 R–N1!

A very fine move, by which White transfers his Rook to the King-side. The immediate threat is 28 Q–N5 ch followed by Q×R; if Black tries 27 ..., B–N4, he falls to a nice combination: 28 R×B!, P×R; 29 B×R, Q×R; 30 R–K8 ch, etc.

27 ...   R(B6)–B3
28 R–N3   B–K1
29 R–KN3 ch   B–N3
30 R×B ch!   R×R
31 Q–R8 ch   K–B2
32 Q×Q   R–B1
33 Q–R4   Resigns

In the last few years the exchange sacrifice has occurred with surprising frequency, especially in the games of Soviet masters. We know that a Rook needs open lines if it is to function properly; in the absence of these a minor piece may well be worth more than a Rook and a sacrifice justified. In our next example White sacrifices the exchange to open up the enemy King to attack.

SMYSLOV–TRIFUNOVIĆ

(Agram 1955)

DIAGRAM 262

Position after Black's 23rd move

24 R×B!

A well-based exchanged sacrifice. It is true that White does not get a direct mating attack, despite his menacing Bishop on f6. But Black will be kept so busy trying to ward off all threats that the manoeuvring of his pieces will become a matter of great difficulty.

24 ...	P×R
25 QB×P	Q–KR4

Black is being forced to use his strongest pieces for defensive purposes. If instead of the text-move Black tries 25 ..., Q–B3, threatening R–K1, White can employ the variation given by Smyslov: 26 Q–N2!, KR–K1; 27 R–QB1, P–N4; 28 B–R8, K–B1; 29 B–N7 ch, K–N1; 30 B–R6, etc.

26 Q–K3	P–KR3
27 P–KR3	Q–KB4
28 B–B3	K–R2

29 P–KN4!	Q–KN4

Any other move by the Queen allows the decisive 30 B–Q2.

30 P–B4	Q–KR5
31 K–N2!	

The immediate advance P–B5 only draws: 31 P–B5, QR–K1; 32 Q–B2 (32 P×B ch, P×P; 33 B–K5, R×B; 34 Q×R, Q–B7 ch, and Black has a perpetual check), Q×RP; 33 R×R (33 P×B ch, P×P; 34 R×R, Q×P ch), Q×P ch; 34 K–B1, Q–R6 ch, and White cannot win.

31 ...	R–KN1
32 Q–K7!	

The simplest way to win; after the exchange of Queens Black cannot avoid losing material, for besides the threat to his pawns he has to watch his Bishop.

32 ...	Q×Q
33 R×Q	QR–K1
34 R×R	R×R
35 P–B5	P–R3
36 K–B3	R–QB1
37 B–Q4	P–N4
38 B–Q3	R–B8
39 P×B ch	P×P
40 P–KR4	R–Q8
41 K–K2	R–KR8
42 P–R5	R–R7 ch
43 B–KB2	K–N2
44 P×P	P–KR4
45 P×P	R×P
46 B–Q4 ch	K–N1
47 B–K4	P–R4
48 K–B3	Resigns

CHAPTER XIV

Methods of Conducting the Fight

A. ATTACK AND DEFENCE

THE climax of an active strategical plan is direct action against an enemy position and the endangering of its weak points—in short, an attack. A positional advantage can, as a rule, only be converted by an attack; therefore the principles for correctly handling an attack make up an important part of chess strategy. The majority of the games in this book contain examples of attacks, some successful, some not. We shall confine ourselves here to a re-statement of the principles that have emerged in the previous chapters—

1. For the successful execution of an attack it is necessary to possess some sort of superiority; this can be of several types: better co-ordination of one's pieces, greater pawn mobility, the occupation of open files and diagonals, local superiority on a particular section of the board (wing pawn majority, piece concentration on the wing).

2. The target cannot be chosen at will; the attack must be directed at the weak points in the enemy position.

3. A necessary prerequisite for an attack on the wing is either superiority in the centre or a firm, though passive, centre.

4. The attacking side should endeavour to open the game and use the power of the pieces to their fullest.

5. The attack rests on a given strategical plan, which, however, consists of many different elements, e.g. double attack, deflexion and enticing of enemy pieces, the pin, sacrificial combination, etc.·

Now let us turn to defence. It is logical that the aims of the defending side should be opposed to those of the attacker. If, for example, the opening of the game is an important element in conducting the attack, then keeping it closed where possible is the task of the defender. This basic rule hardly admits of an exception; the opening of the game in defence, except as part of a counter-attack, is always a mistake. Yet it is surprising how often this very mistake is repeated; Réti, in his book *Masters of the Chessboard*, gives us a good example from a game by Morphy (Diagram 263). Here Black has two extra pawns and his position is quite solid; White has only slight compensation in his two Bishops and space advantage (little centre). A player familiar with the principles of modern positional play would find the right plan: prevention of White's advance P–K5 and holding the position closed. After the correct 1 ...., P–KB3; 2 P–B4, N–B3 (or N3) Black would have had the advantage. In Morphy's day, however, the Steinitz theories of defence were

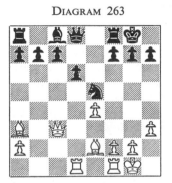

unknown; most masters of that time would have undoubtedly made the same mistake as Morphy's opponent, who wanted to free himself at once by P–KB4; this error quickly got Black into severe difficulties, and Morphy was able to finish the game elegantly in twelve more moves.

This does not mean, however, that every attempt to free oneself from a constricted position is, in principle, wrong. But the freeing manoeuvre is generally only playable after the gradual liquidation of enemy pressure, the improvement in the coordination of one's pieces, and the extension of one's defensive space. The freeing manoeuvre should not introduce the defensive measures but should be, rather, the result of a correctly conducted defensive operation.

The technique of defence and the preparation of a freeing push have had their effect on opening theory; an interesting and important case is the Ruy Lopez.

EVANS–ROSSOLIMO

(U.S.A. Open, 1955)

1	P–K4		P–K4
2	N–KB3		N–QB3
3	B–N5		P–QR3
4	B–R4		N–B3
5	O–O		B–K2
6	R–K1		P–QN4
7	B–N3		P–Q3
8	P–B3		O–O
9	P–KR3		N–QR4
10	B–B2		P–B4
11	P–Q4		Q–B2
12	QN–Q2		N–B3
13	P–Q5 (?)		

DIAGRAM 264

By blocking the centre, White prepares the famous Spanish Attack on the King-side; this is characterized by the moves N–B1, K–R1, P–KN4, N–N3, and R–N1. In many games Black was unable to find a satisfactory defensive system, and at the beginning of this century the Spanish Attack was a much feared weapon. Tartakower, however, was of the opinion that Black had nothing to fear if he defended correctly; the Spanish Attack was, he believed, routine and ineffective.

13 ...   N–Q1

Black has two possibilities here, both of which involve quite different strategical plans—

(*a*) Withdrawal of Knight to a5 (13 ..., N–QR4). With this Black intends to employ only a small part of his forces in defending the King; he will concentrate mainly on a Queen-side counter-attack.

(*b*) The continuation in the game (13 ..., N–Q1). Black reckons that the Queen-side will remain passive and that the fight will be confined to the King's wing. As this game shows, Black has not only good defence prospects but also the possibility of making the freeing advance P–KB4.

14 P–QR4

If White intends to achieve a superiority on the King-side, then this move in conjunction with the next is his most logical continuation, for he will thereby close up the Queen-side.

14 ...   R–N1

Premature is 14 ..., P–N5 on account of 15 N–B4! with the threat of KN×KP.

15 P–B4

After 15 P×P, P×P; 16 P–B4, P–N5 White's King-side attack has even less chance of success, for Black can in this case operate later on the open a-file.

15 ...   P–N5

At the time 15 ..., B–Q2 was considered best by theory; but this game shows that even after the complete blocking of the Queen-side Black is not condemned to lasting passivity.

16 K–R2   N–K1
17 P–N4   P–N3

Players not sufficiently well acquainted with the subtleties of the Ruy Lopez will find such a move surprising. The intention is to stop White's Knight from occupying f5 (N–B1–N3–B5) and also to fortify the King's wing by preparing for a later N–KN2 and N–KB2.

18 R–KN1   P–B3
19 N–B1   N–B2
20 N–N3   N–N2

(*See* Diagram 265)

Black has his pieces well placed and his opponent is denied the

DIAGRAM 265

Position after 20 ..., N–N2

possibility of launching an effective attack on the King-side. In similar positions White often gets the chance of sacrificing his Knight on f5 to good effect; but here such a manoeuvre is impossible because of the Knight on g7; e.g. 21 N–B5?, P×N; 22 P×P, K–R1 followed by R–N1. From the diagram position Black can possibly play for a win by getting ready to make the advance P–KB4; this requires very thorough preparations of course.

21 P–N3   B–Q2

22	B–K3	K–R1
23	Q–Q2	QR–K1
24	R–N2	Q–B1!
25	R–KR1?	

White still dreams of an attack; he intends to prepare P–KR4 after withdrawing his King to g1. Better is 25 QR–KN1, although after that Black can prepare the advance P–KB4 by 25 ..., R–N1.

25 ...   P–B4!

Black now frees himself from his cramped position; after the ensuing exchanges he will obtain the better pawn position.

26	NP×P	P×P
27	P×P	N×P
28	N×N	B×N
29	R(1)–KN1	R–N1

Obviously not 29 ..., B×P?; 30 Q–Q3.

30	N–N5	N×N
31	B×N	B(2)×B
32	R×B	B×B
33	Q×B	R×R
34	R×R	

Black has now a slight advantage because of White's weak pawn on f2. In the game Black was able to win after thirty-three more moves, but only as a result of weak play on White's part.

A correctly conducted defence should put the greatest obstacles in the way of the opponent's attack and at the same time be combined with a good strategical plan (e.g. the preparation of a counter-attack or forced transposition into an end-game). It is clear that positions of different characters demand different defensive methods; we shall therefore consider the most important methods separately in the following three sections.

1. REPULSION OF TACTICAL THREATS

In many cases it is sufficient to limit the defence to a repulsion of the enemy tactical threat. This is the case where one side has gained the foundation for his attack—space advantage, better piece co-ordination, lead in development—at the cost of a positional disadvantage; the defender has only to parry the immediate attack and the balance then automatically shifts in his favour.

SPASSKI–GELLER

(Candidates Tournament 1956)

1 P–Q4	P–Q4
2 P–QB4	P–K3
3 N–QB3	P–QB3
4 P–K3	N–KB3
5 N–B3	N–B3
6 P–QR3	BP×P
7 KP×P	B–K2
8 B–Q3	P×P
9 B×BP	O–O
10 O–O	P–QR3
11 B–KN5	

The continuation 11 B–R2, P–QN4; 12 P–Q5, P×P; 13 N×P, N×N; 14 B×N, B–N2 leads to equality.

11 ...	P–QN4
12 B–R2	B–N2
13 R–B1	P–N5!
14 P×P	N×NP
15 B–N1	

By his clever manoeuvring on the Queen-side (11 ..., P–QN4, 13 ..., P–N5) Black has succeeded in gaining control of d5, so crippling White's isolated pawn. White, on the other hand, has obtained a space advantage on the King-side, where his actively placed pieces and the base e5, which may well prove useful for his Knight, give him good attacking chances.

15 ...	Q–R4

After 15 ..., B×N; 16 Q×B,

Q×P White, with the two Bishops and good co-ordination of his pieces, has several tactical possibilities (17 KR–Q1 or 17 N–K4). The position would then be dynamically balanced, just as in the game.

DIAGRAM 266

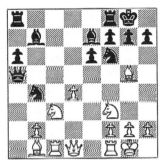

16 N–K5	QR–B1
17 R–K1	N(5)–Q4

Both sides set up their forces in a way that corresponds to the requirements of the isolated pawn. With his next move White unleashes a dangerous attack against the opponent's King.

18 Q–Q3

Threatening the strong move 19 N–N4.

18 ...	P–N3
19 Q–R3!	

Threatening 19 B–R6 followed by N×P.

19 ...   **Q–N5!**

In view of the above threat Black must give extra protection to his Bishop on e2; he combines this with a measure giving him active counter-play in the form of an attack on the pawn on d4.

20 B–R6   **KR–Q1**
21 B–R2

In order to pass a proper judgement on Black's defensive play we must consider whether the move 21 N×BP would have been dangerous for him. An exhaustive analysis after the game showed that Black could weather the storm; e.g. 21 N×BP, K×N; 22 Q×KP ch, K–K1; 23 B–N5!, Q–Q3; 24 Q–R3, N×N; 25 P×N, B–Q4; 26 B×N, Q×B; 27 Q×P, B–B2, and the game, though still very sharp, is about equal.

21 ...   **R–Q3**

An important defensive move; it answers the threat of N×BP for the moment.

22 B–N5   **Q×QP**

DIAGRAM 267

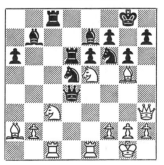

The critical moment in the attack; White ought now to continue 23 N×N, N×N; 24 N×BP!, R×R!; 25 N–R6 ch!, K–N2; 26 B×R, N–B5; 27 B×N, Q×B with equality. In the game he tries to strengthen his attack but fails against the very precise defensive play of his opponent.

23 QR–Q1?   **N–B5!**
24 B×N   **Q×B**
25 R×R   **B×R**
26 N×BP

Spasski had probably relied on this move, but failed to see Geller's very fine tactical counter. Of course, 26 ..., K×N?; 27 B×P ch is out of the question.

26 ...   **R×N!**

The exchange sacrifice has a double purpose: first it removes the Rook without loss of time from a threatened square; secondly it gives Black control over e4.

27 N–R6 ch

After 27 P×R, N–K5!; 28 N–R6 ch, K–N2; 29 N–N4, P–KR4 White is also lost.

27 ...   **K–N2**
28 P×R   **B–B4**

Obviously 28 ..., N–K5 is also possible.

29 Q–N3   **Q×Q**
30 RP×Q   **K×N**
31 B×P   **N–K5**
32 R–K2   **N×QBP**
33 R–N2   **B–B3**
34 K–R2   **B–N4**
35 P–B3   **K–N2**

36 R–N3	B–Q5	40 P–N3	K–B3
37 B–B8	P–QR4	41 P–B4	B–B3
38 R–R3	P–R5	42 B–B5	P–R3
39 P–N4	P–N4	43 Resigns	

A characteristic feature of this game was the combination of mere defence and active counter-play; Black was able to protect his endangered points and parry all threats, at the same time putting pressure on d4 and, towards the end, on f2. Such an active defence is not always possible: but even where a player is forced by enemy threats to confine himself to the passive protection of endangered points, he must at least see to it that his pieces obtain the maximum co-ordination and that those forces tied to purely passive defence are kept to a minimum. It is a typical beginner's mistake to go on the defensive at the first sign of an enemy attack: guarding against non-existent dangers can involve giving up all possibilities of active counter-play. A correctly conducted defence parries enemy tactical threats as economically as possible; one's own forces must be left with the maximum working power.

2. THE COUNTER-ATTACK

The well-known saying "attack is the best defence" is a very important tenet in chess strategy. Conducting an attack is always bound up with a certain risk: to endanger the enemy position necessitates a complete build up of one's reserves; the defending side has therefore plenty of scope to obtain superiority on another part of the board; besides, the attack often demands radical measures, such as a pawn advance, which leave important weaknesses in the position of the attacker. An actively conducted defence should therefore always have in mind the possibility of a counter-attack at a suitable moment.

BISGUIER–FUDERER

(Interzonal 1955)

1 P–K4	P–QB4
2 N–KB3	P–Q3
3 P–KN3	N–KB3
4 P–Q3	P–QN3
5 B–N2	B–N2
6 O–O	P–N3
7 N–R4	

White prepares the advance P–KB4 in order to attack on the King-side. Although this plan is frequently adopted in such positions it is not really effective; White ought to pay more attention to the centre and by moves like P–QB3, QN–Q2, R–K1, and P–Q4 attempt to gain a superiority there.

7 ...   N–B3

8 P–KB4	B–N2
9 N–Q2	O–O
10 P–B3	

DIAGRAM 268

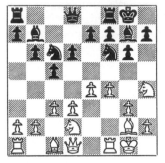

White's position looks good and elastic. The game shows, however, that his pawns possess little dynamic power; their advance can hardly cause Black much trouble.

10 ...	N–Q2

A very good move: not only does Black increase the power of his Bishop on g2 and prepare the advance P–QN4–5; he also strengthens his control of the central squares and hinders the advance P–Q4; e.g. 11 N(2)–B3, P–QN4; 12 P–Q4?, P×P; 13 P×P, Q–N3; 14 B–K3, P–K4, and Black wins a pawn, or 12 B–K3, Q–N3; 13 Q–Q2, P–N5; 14 P–Q4, P×BP; 15 NP×P, N–R4, and Black has good counter-play on the Queen-side.

11 P–QR4?

This only delays Black's advance P–QN4 by one move; on the other hand it opens the Rook file, which is advantageous for Black. Better is either 11 N(2)–B3 or 11 P–B5.

11 ...	P–QR3
12 P–B5	

This is the logical follow-up of the plan initiated by White's seventh move. White intends to open the f-file and then increase his pressure on the King-side by the manoeuvre N(2)–B3–N5; the disadvantage is that it gives Black the important strategical point e5.

12 ...	P–QN4
13 RP×P	RP×P
14 R×R	Q×R
15 P×P	RP×P
16 N(2)–B3	Q–R7!

DIAGRAM 269

It is now clear how White's seemingly innocent eleventh move (P–QR4) has harmed his position: the entry of the Black Queen not only cripples him on the Queen-side, but also increases the force of the coming P–QN5. The continuation 17 P–Q4, P×P; 18 P×P, Q–R2; 19 B–K3, P–K4 loses a pawn for White.

17 R–B2	Q–N8

Again preventing P–Q4; e.g. 18 P–Q4, P×QP; 19 P×QP, N×P!; 20 N×N, B×N; 21 Q×B, Q×B ch.

18 N–Q2

With this White virtually gives up his King-side attack, leaving Black to continue his Queen-side action undisturbed.

18 ...	Q–R8

Obviously not 18 ..., Q×QP??; 19 R–B3.

19 Q–B2	N(2)–K4

Threatening 20 ..., N×P. White is now forced completely on to the defensive.

20 B–B1	N–KN5
21 R–K2	P–N5
22 N–N3	Q–R2!
23 P–B4	

This move, which gives Black control of d4, was criticized by some commentators; but White can hardly allow his opponent to play P–B5 in view of the tactical threats that would follow.

23 ...	Q–R5!
24 N–B3	

Hoping to free himself from the unpleasant pin by 25 N(N3)–Q4. Black, however, soon stops this.

24 ...	R–R1
25 B–N5	B–QB1

A very useful move, which prepares the transfer of the Bishop to g4. It also plays a part in the final combination by preventing White from taking the Black Rook on a8 with check.

26 R–K1	N(5)–K4!
27 N×N	

After 27 N(B3)–Q2, B–N5!; 28 R–R1, Q×R; 29 N×Q, R×N, Black has a decisive advantage.

27 ...	B×N

White is now threatened with the loss of a piece. The best defence is 28 K–N2, after which Black can obtain an advantageous end-game (28 ..., N–Q5; 29 N×N, B×N; 30 Q×Q, R×Q; 31 B×P, B×P; 32 B×P, B–Q5, leaving him with a menacing pawn on b4) or indulge in a Queen sacrifice (28 ..., B–N5!?; 29 R–R1, Q×R; 30 N×Q, R×N).

28 R–R1?

Falling into a trap.

28 ...	Q×N!
29 Resigns	

If 29 Q×Q, then 29 ..., R×R; 30 Q–B2 (30 K–N2, N–Q5), B–R6.

The counter-attack is not only the best method of defence; it is one of the most effective ways of conducting the entire chess struggle. When parrying dangerous enemy threats, one must never forget that hidden possibilities may lurk in even the most difficult positions; they need only to be uncovered. The counter-attack has also a strong psychological effect. The moment when the attacker becomes the defender often decides the fate of the game.

3. PREVENTIVE DEFENCE

Just as in modern medical science more and more emphasis is being laid on the prevention of illness, so too in modern chess strategy preventive measures are frequently employed to meet an enemy attack before it has fully developed. By preventive defence we mean the strengthening of weak points in advance of an enemy attack; the possibility of tactical threats is eliminated before they can develop.

It might be thought that this method of defence is in contradiction to the rule demanding economy in defence; for we have noted that only real threats should be dealt with, and these with the minimum of one's forces. This contradiction is only an apparent one: preventive defence is in order, and effective, when it demands less time and force than the repulsion of a direct attack. It therefore underlines the call to economy in defence. In many cases it is indispensable; its neglect can lead to a sharpening of the enemy attack, as in the following example.

SÄMISCH–GRÜNFELD

(Karlsbad 1929)

DIAGRAM 270

Position after White's 29th move

Black has a fairly solid position and in view of his better Bishop has prospects of obtaining an advantage. White, however, has his forces concentrated menacingly on the King-side; so Black ought first to give some thought to defence. The main threat is the opening of the h-file by R(R3)–N3, which Black ought to meet by the preventive 29 ..., N–K1!; then if White does play 30 R(R3)–N3 (instead of the superior 30 R–R5, N–N2, with repetition), Black gets a very good game after 30 ..., K–N2!; 31 N–B5 ch, B×N; 32 NP×B, P–KR4. Black, however, fails to take the necessary precautions and thereby allows White to mount a decisive attack.

29 ...	B–Q2?
30 R(R3)–N3	B–K1
31 P–KR4!	P×P
32 R–N2	P–R6
33 R×RP	B–N3
34 R–B3!	QR–N1
35 Q–R4!	

The game is virtually over; Black can do nothing about White's threats of R(2)–KB2 and P–N5, after which the pawn on f6 falls.

35 ...	R–N6
36 R(2)–KB2	R×BP
37 P–N5	N–K1

Or 37 ..., R×B; 38 P×P!, R×R; 39 P×Q, R×R; 40 P×R=Q ch, R×Q; 41 Q–K7, etc.

| 38 P×P | Q–Q1 |

There is a pretty finish after 38 ..., N×P; viz. 39 R×N, R×R; 40 R×R, R×B; 41 R×B!, Q×Q; 42 R–N8 mate.

| 39 N–N4 | R×B |

A final attempt; but the position is hopeless.

40 R×R	B×P
41 R–K3	N–Q3
42 N×P	B–B4
43 R×B!	N×R
44 N–N6 ch	K–N1
45 R–K7!	

The point of White's forty-third move; three White pieces are under attack, yet none can be taken.

45 ...	R–B2
46 R×R	K×R
47 N–K5 ch	K–B1
48 Q×P	Resigns

Preventive defence is very important as a means of countering an enemy pawn advance; it can be used against a numerical majority or, as in the next game, against purely qualitative superiority.

NIMZOWITSCH–BERNSTEIN

(Karlsbad 1923)

1 N–KB3	N–KB3
2 P–Q4	P–Q4
3 P–QB4	P–K3
4 N–B3	B–K2
5 P–K3	O–O
6 P–QR3	P–QR3 (?)
7 P–B5!	

Such an advance in the Queen's Gambit is generally two-edged. In this case, however, White is in a position to make it, because Black, with his last move, has wasted a tempo in the fight for the centre.

| 7 ... | P–B3 |

We now have a familiar blocked pawn chain.

8 P–QN4	QN–Q2
9 B–N2	Q–B2
10 Q–B2	P–K4
11 O–O–O	

We have already noted a similar manoeuvre in the chapter on the King. White's King moves to the wing on which his pawns will advance; but despite the early loss of the pawns' protection, the King will be safer here than on the opposite wing; the reason is that White's space superiority is very great on the Queen-side, whereas on the King-side Black has the advantage in space.

11 ...	P–K5

DIAGRAM 271

Black has lengthened the blocked pawn chain and intends to attack White's support point e3 by means of the advance P–KB4–5. If White now carelessly plays 12 N–Q2, the game continues 12 ..., N–N5; 13 N–N3, P–B4; 14 P–R3, N–R3, and there is no way of preventing Black from carrying out the important break-through P–B5. Nimzowitsch, however, finds an excellent four-move manoeuvre to hold up Black's King-side advance.

12 N–KR4!	N–N1
13 P–N3	N–K1
14 N–N2	P–B4
15 P–KR4	

Now that the break-through P–B5 has been virtually stopped for ever, White will be able to devote his whole attention to his Queen-side action. Although Black can try the freeing advance P–QN3, he will still remain with a clear positional disadvantage.

15 ...	B–Q1

16 P–R4	P–QN3
17 P–N5!	

After Black's previous move this advance is very strong because it puts the d-pawn under pressure. The threat is now 18 P × BP, Q × BP; 19 N × QP!, Q × N?; 20 B–B4.

17 ...	N–B3
18 N–B4	RP × P
19 RP × P	Q–KB2
20 B–K2	

Premature is 20 P × BP, N × P; 21 N(3) × QP (21 P × P, N–QR4!; 22 N–R4, B–Q2), N × N; 22 N × N, B–K3! followed by B–N6 and Black wins the exchange. By the text-move White maintains the tension on the Queen-side; he will now benefit if Black exchanges either of the pawns.

20 ...	B–B2

Black temporarily gives up a pawn in order to eliminate the pressure on d5 by exchanging off White's Knight on f4. His counter-action is well conceived; it fails only against a very fine combination.

21 P × NP	B × N
22 NP × B	B–Q2
23 K–Q2!	

The c-file is no longer healthy for the King; and 23 P–N7, R–R2 eases Black's problems.

23 ...	P × P
24 R–R1	N–B3
25 B × P	N–QR4
26 B–K2	KR–N1

DIAGRAM 272

Position after 26 ..., KR–N1

It seems that Black, after winning back his pawns, will have reached equality; but White succeeds in maintaining the initiative by a surprising manoeuvre.

27 N–R4!   B×N?

Stronger is 27 ..., N–B5 ch; 28 B×N, P×B, although after 29 B–B3!, B×N; 30 R×B, R×R; 31 Q×R, R×P; 32 Q–R5, N–Q2 (32 ..., N–Q4?; 33 Q–R8 ch); 33 R–KN1 White still has a positional advantage.

28 R×B   R×P
29 B–QB3!

Not 29 KR–QR1, N–N6 ch; 30 Q×N, R×Q; 31 R×R ch, N–K1; 32 K–B2, R–N2, and Black can ride the attack.

29 ...   N–N6 ch

Or 29 ..., N–B5 ch; 30 B×N, R×R; 31 B×P!, N×B (31 ..., R×P ch?; 32 B×R, Q×B; 33

Q–B8 ch); 32 Q×R, N×B; 33 Q–R8 ch, and White has a won end-game.

30 Q×N!   R×Q
31 R×R ch   N–K1
32 B–Q1!

The point of the Queen sacrifice; after 32 ..., R–N3; 33 B–R4, R–K3; 34 R–QN1, there is no adequate defence against the threatened 35 R(1)–N8. Black therefore tries to maintain himself by sacrificing the exchange; but after that his Queen is powerless against the two Rooks.

32 ...   R×B
33 K×R   Q–B2 ch
34 K–Q2   K–B2
35 B–R5 ch!   P–N3
36 KR–QR1   Q–N3
37 B–K2   K–N2
38 K–K1   N–B2
39 R(8)–R5   K–R3
40 K–B1   Q–N6
41 P–R5!   N–K1

Or 41 ..., P×P; 42 R–B1, Q–N2; 43 R(5)–B5, and the attack against the naked King is decisive.

42 R–R6   Q–N7
43 P×P   P×P
44 R(6)–R2   Q–N2
45 R–R7   Q–N7
46 K–N2!   N–B3
47 R–R1 ch   N–R4
48 B×N   P×B
49 R(1)–QR1   Resigns

Similar in its conception to preventive defence is the theory of over-protection, which stems from Nimzowitsch. We shall now explain what this really means.

297

As we have already seen, the character of a whole position can be determined, or at least greatly influenced, by an important strategical point; but the opponent will naturally strive to destroy or weaken one's control over this: therefore it is in order to strengthen the strategical point in advance by over-protection. An example will make this clear. In Diagram 273 White has an important strategical point on e5, which gives him a space advantage on the King-side. Sooner or later Black must endeavour to eliminate this pawn by putting piece pressure on it (e.g. KN–K2–N3, Q–QB2, or possibly B–QB4–N3–B2 combined with Q–QN1). White therefore should take preventive action and cover e5 with all the pieces that can be used for the purpose; the game can continue 1 R–K1,

DIAGRAM 273

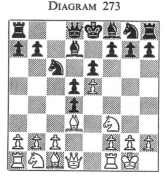

DIAGRAM 274

KN–K2; 2 B–KB4, N–N3; 3 B–N3 followed by Q–K2. White's manoeuvres are directed towards over-protection of his strong strategical point.

Another example is the position in Diagram 274, which occurred in a game between Nimzowitsch and Alekhine at Baden-Baden, 1925. An important strategical point is d4, the pawn on which limits the freedom of Black's Bishop. White must maintain control over this point and avoid being forced to make the advance P–Q5. So far White has succeeded in doing this, but now Black has set up his forces to direct pressure on d4; another dose of over-protection is therefore needed: 1 QR–Q1, QR–K1; 2 R–Q2!, Q–KN4; 3 KR–Q1. After this Black's Bishop is shut out of play for rather a long time; White, as a result, was able to gain a positional advantage: 3 ..., B–R2; 4 N–B4, N–B4; 5 N–N5, B–N1; 6 R–K2 followed by 7 R(1)–K1.

B. TACKING

This concept as applied to chess strategy is comprehended in various ways. Some authors take it to mean every lengthy manoeuvre designed to improve one's own position or lure the opponent into a tactical or strategical mistake; some go even so far as to apply it to the planless movement of the pieces back and forward. In his book *My System*, Nimzowitsch attempted to give it a more precise definition; he defined it as the manner of play in which an enemy weakness (e.g. a weak pawn) is attacked alternately in at least two ways (e.g. horizontally and vertically) until the defending pieces are driven into an unfavourable position; then the weakness can be captured or the opponent forced into accepting some other form of disadvantage. In my opinion the meaning of *tacking* should be expanded; I think it should include every positional manoeuvre in which the enemy position is alternately subjected to tactical threats of various kinds.

In the following example White employs *tacking* strategy. First he attacks on the King-side to force Black's pieces, especially the Queen, into an unfavourable position; then he decides the game by a simple break-through in the centre.

STEINITZ–SHOWALTER

DIAGRAM 275

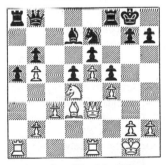

Position after Black's 18th move

White's main advantage is the strong position of his Knight on d4; the problem is to achieve an opening of the game so that he can use the superior power of his pieces. The best possibility of opening the position lies in the advance P–QB4; but if White plays this immediately Black can cover all the important central points with his pieces (Q–N2, QR–B1, KR–Q1, and, at a suitable moment, P×BP followed by N–Q4). Steinitz therefore chooses to *tack* by preceding his central break-through by threats on the King's wing.

19	Q–B2	Q–Q1
20	R–K3!	P–N3
21	R–R3	R–B2
22	K–R1	K–N2 (?)

This eases White's task; better is 22 ..., R–N2 followed by R–B1.

23	N–B3	P–R3
24	R–KN1!	

Threatening 25 P–KN4; Black is thereby forced to weaken his King-side further

24	...	P–R4

25 Q–N3!	Q–R1
26 N–N5	KR–B1
27 Q–R4!	

Threatening 28 N×P ch!; after Black's best defence, 28 ..., QR–K1, White can prepare the break-through P–QB4 with 28 R–Q1!; but Black's reply removes the need for such preparation.

27 ...	N–N1

(*See* Diagram 276)

28 P–B4!

White's manoeuvres have so destroyed the co-ordination of the opposing pieces that the opening of the game by P–QB4 suddenly unleashes unparriable threats.

28 ...	P×P
29 B×QBP	KR–K1
30 R–Q3	R–R2

DIAGRAM 276

Position after 27 ..., N–N1

31 R–Q6	R–N2
32 R(1)–Q1	B–B1
33 N×P ch	B×N
34 B×B	Q–R2
35 R–Q7 ch	R–K2
36 R×R ch	N×R
37 Q–B6 ch	K–R3
38 R–Q8	R–B2
39 P–R3	Resigns

C. TECHNICAL CONVERSION OF SUPERIORITY

In playing over games we often come across the remark that the rest is a matter of technique. It would be a mistake, however, to think that accurate and determined play was no longer needed in such cases; it repeatedly happens that a great advantage is left unconverted because the stronger side plays inattentively and without a plan, or else underestimates the opponent's counter chances. Throughout this book we have sought to impress upon the reader that every position on the chess-board requires a clearly thought-out plan. This applies even to those positions where the win is merely a technical matter.

Let us consider the two types of advantage—material and positional. The conversion of material advantage gives rise to several problems, especially when the opponent has some form of positional compensation like actively placed pieces. Obviously the strategical plan to be adopted will depend on the individual position, but in the majority of cases the superior side should endeavour to simplify and transpose into an end-game. How this should be done we have already examined in the section dealing with the exchange of material (Chapter VII).

Where the advantage is purely positional we must consider whether it is of a lasting or passing character. If the opponent has broken pawns, a bad Bishop, or pieces almost permanently locked out of play, it does not matter much whether the active side loses a tempo or so; it is sufficient to strengthen one's own position and deprive the opponent of effective counter-play. Things are quite different, however, when the advantage consists of a superior striking power and co-ordination of pieces or their concentration on a particular section of the board. Very accurate procedure is necessary here; every tempo must be properly used, and preparations for a decisive combinative solution must not be overlooked.

Diagrams 277 and 278 show the two different types of positional advantage. In the first case Black has a seriously weakened pawn

DIAGRAM 277   DIAGRAM 278

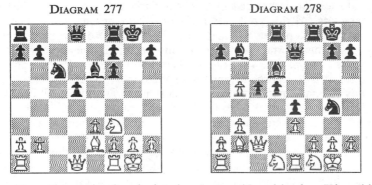

position, the result of an isolated pawn on d5 and broken King-side pawns. This gives his opponent a decisive advantage, which can be converted in several ways: for example, White can combine a King-side attack in the middle-game with threats to the isolated Queen-pawn, or he can wait and exploit the enemy weaknesses in the end-game. White's superiority is of such lasting character that no exact order of moves is necessary; he must only prevent Black from eliminating the weak pawns (e.g. by the advances P–Q5 or P–KB4–5) and adopt a plan to harass Black's weaknesses (e.g. Q–Q2, KR–Q1, N–Q4, B–B3, etc.). The position is quite different in the second diagram. Here Black has a decisive positional advantage owing to his strong centre, his Bishop pair, his open lines, and the excellent co-ordination of his pieces. But his opponent has an extra pawn. The conversion of Black's advantage will require very precise tactical play: Black cannot allow simplification, for White would have good prospects in an end-game; the way to victory lies in an accurate and energetic attack on the King-side and the centre.

CHAPTER XV

Individual Style: Psychological Play

IN our analysis of individual strategical elements, we have, up to now, considered a game of chess as an impersonal process involving thirty-two pieces and sixty-four squares. This is, of course, a very simplified presentation. A game of chess is a struggle between two adversaries taking place under certain concrete conditions: but people are never free from fault; they are unavoidably, to a lesser or greater extent, influenced by particular moods; they have differing characters. All this is reflected in their performance in a game of chess.

Every chess player, whether an eminent master or a rabbit, brings to his games certain elements of his personal style of play. His style is not only the sum of his chess knowledge and views on the game; it is to a large extent the expression of his character. If we study the games of a player personally unknown to us, we can discover much about his character from his play; on the other hand when we know someone well, we can with a fair amount of certainty guess what style of play he will choose in a game of chess. A man cautious and anxious in life will not be quick to indulge in daring play; a gambler, or someone of frivolous nature, will conduct his game in a risky manner, often without a proper evaluation of the possibilities open to him and his opponent. The optimist tends to overestimate his position, whereas the pessimist sees dangers and difficulties in every position. The individual style of play is a reflection of the character of the player.

A very important problem is the influence of external factors on the course of a game. An example is the state of the tournament at the moment when the game is played: if a player in the last round needs only half a point to win the first prize, he will set out his game in a manner different from what he would if he had to win at all costs. Time-trouble is also an important external factor; so too are one's present mood and the background conditions under which the game is played. Nor must we forget the players' health. Everyone knows from his own experience how even a common cold can affect one's play and influence the result; we could draw some important conclusions here about the importance of physical preparations and the preservation of good nerves; but to elaborate upon this is not the task of a book on chess strategy.

Individual Style: Psychological Play

We may now ask an important question: Wherein lies the connection between the choice of strategical plan on the one hand and the individual style of the players and the various external factors on the other? The former world champion Dr. E. Lasker laid down the profound principle that in many positions it is impossible to speak of the *best move*; there are, rather, several possibilities, and from these, one move may be the best against a particular opponent under particular conditions. In other words the strategical plan should in many cases be determined by the style of the opponent and the prevailing external conditions. Diagram 279 shows a position (World Championship match between Tarrasch and Lasker in 1908) in which Black, with a cramped position, must reckon on an attack against his King. A passive defensive plan would be 1 ..., Q-K3; 2 N-B5, P-B4 followed by B-B1. In the game, however, Lasker chose a different, and objectively much weaker, way. What were his reasons? It was well known that Tarrasch could convert a space advantage with great sureness and mastery without giving his opponent any counter-chances. Lasker, therefore, did not want to be confined to passive defence against Tarrasch in a cramped position, so he chose a very risky continuation, which gave him counter-play at the cost of a pawn. As the course of the game showed, Lasker had judged his opponent well. The game continued 1 ..., N-N5?!; 2 B×P!, N×BP!; at this stage White has two possibilities: to win a pawn by 3 K×N, K×B; 4 Q-Q4 ch followed by Q×RP, or to play for attack with 3 Q-Q4. Analysis after the game showed that White's pressure after 3 Q-Q4, N-N5; 4 N-B5 is irresistible. Does this mean that Lasker's 1 ..., N-N5 was a mistake? Not at all; Lasker had simply assessed the position on a psychological basis; he knew that Tarrasch preferred to select clear continuations rather than indulge in complications that could not be exactly calculated. Tarrasch remained true to style and continued 3 K×N, K×B; 4 N-B5 ch, K-R1; 5 Q-Q4 ch, P-B3; 6 Q×RP, B-B1; 7 Q-Q4, R-K4!, which allowed Black some counter-play in the form of pressure on the isolated pawn; Lasker then played very energetically and was even able to win the game by taking advantage of some small errors on the part of his opponent.

In many positions one is faced with the choice between two or more plans of practically equal value but leading to completely different types of game. From the position in Diagram 280, which arises from the Queen's Gambit after 1 P-Q4, P-Q4; 2 P-QB4, P-K3; 3 N-QB3, N-KB3; 4 B-N5, B-K2; 5 P-K3, O-O; 6 N-B3, QN-Q2; 7 Q-B2, P-B4, White has two possibilities. First he can by 8 P×QP, N×P; 9 B×B, Q×B; 10 N×N, P×N;

303

11 B–Q3, P–KN3; 12 P×P isolate his opponent's Queen-pawn and, after simplification, exploit this weakness. Alternatively, he can play 8 O–O–O, P–KR3 (8 ..., Q–R4; 9 K–N1); 9 P–KR4!, Q–R4; 10 P–KN4, securing a sharp position in which both sides will undertake an attack against the opposing King. The theoreticians cannot

DIAGRAM 279

DIAGRAM 280

Position after 7 ..., P–B4

agree on which of these continuations is objectively stronger: the choice must rest on purely psychological factors.

Of great importance psychologically is the choice of opening. One should select that which, as far as possible, accords with one's own style and is far from the opponent's. Often it is worthwhile selecting an objectively weaker system in order to confront the opponent with unpleasant problems. A classical example is Lasker's choice in his game against Capablanca at the St. Petersburg Tournament in 1914. Three rounds before the end both players had the same number of points; Lasker, however, had played one game more and so he had to win this encounter if he were to entertain hopes of securing the first prize. Playing the White pieces he chose the Exchange Variation of the Ruy Lopez (1 P–K4, P–K4; 2 N–KB3, N–QB3; 3 B–N5, P–QR3; 4 B×N), which even then was considered completely innocuous. No one at the time recognized the profundity of Lasker's conception, as the remarks of Dr. Tarrasch in the tournament book verify—

"Why did you choose the Exchange Variation?" I asked Lasker in the lunch break. "You had to play sharply for a win, didn't you?"

"I had no other choice," replied Lasker, "for against the defence employed by you against Bernstein and me there is nothing to be found." So radically has the opinion about attack and defence in the once feared Ruy Lopez changed!

Tarrasch, however, did not catch the irony in Lasker's reply. It was not the fear of the Tarrasch defence (4 B–R4, N–B3; 5 O–O, N×P) but a much deeper reason which caused Lasker to choose the colourless drawing variation in this decisive game. In order to understand this let us look at the position that arises after the moves actually played: 4 B×N, QP×B; 5 P–Q4, P×P; 6 Q×P, Q×Q; 7 N×Q, B–Q3 (Diagram 281).

The diagram shows that White has a clear pawn majority on the King-side, while Black's Queen-side majority is crippled by doubled pawns; White will naturally seek an end-game where he can convert this advantage. As compensation Black has the two Bishops, and objectively seen has rather the better game: but in order to use his Bishop pair he must play actively and be ready to go on the attack. Lasker, however, knew that his opponent had sat down at the board with the intention of getting a draw in order to make sure of winning first prize in the tournament. But this is in direct conflict with the character of the position arising from the Exchange Variation of the Ruy Lopez. Lasker's psychological calculation in this game was fully justified: Capablanca played passively and in the end lost the game and first prize in the tournament.

DIAGRAM 281

Position after 7 ..., B–Q3

In studying the games of routine players we can discern a preference for particular types of position. One will endeavour to obtain a quiet positional game, another will opt for complicated positions, a third will attempt to attack at the first opportunity, and a fourth may be inclined towards defence. One's style of play reflects one's preference for a particular strategical set-up. Styles of play can show considerable variation, and there is not an eminent master whose style is not influenced to some extent by his personal predilections.

Generally, chess literature puts styles of play into two basically different groups; these are the combinative and positional styles. The combinative player likes to solve difficult tactical problems; he is happy when the play is razor sharp and welcomes positions that allow surprise combinations. The positional player is content to

305

win small advantages, which he will systematically try to enlarge; he will avoid unclear combinations and complicated play whose outcome cannot be reckoned exactly. The truly great master, however, is never one-sided; he is able to conduct a sharp attack in a combinative way even when he prefers a quiet positional game, and vice-versa. His predilection comes to the fore in those positions whose character admits of a choice of strategical plans; for example, in Diagram 280 Smyslov and Petrosian would almost certainly prefer the continuation 8 P×QP whereas Bronstein and Geller would most probably decide on 8 O–O–O.

A thorough knowledge of the style of one's opponent is a very important part of the general preparations for a tournament or match. A typical example of the importance of such psychological preparation is the famous match between Alekhine and Capablanca in 1927. Alekhine subjected his opponent's play to a thorough examination and arrived at certain conclusions, which he described in the book of the 1927 New York tournament; in the match he adapted his play to suit the discoveries he had made. Capablanca, on the other hand, intoxicated by his victory in the New York tournament, considered it unnecessary to study in detail the style of his opponent; this neglect proved to be one of the main causes of his defeat in the contest between the two chess giants.

There are some psychological elements that are not directly connected with the opponent's style or an evaluation of the position on the board. To this category belong those traps set with the intention of inveigling an unsuspecting opponent into a certain course by offering him prospects of a material or positional advantage. In a game between Nimzowitsch and Leonardt at San Sebastian in 1911, the position in Diagram 282 was reached after 26 moves. With his last few moves Black had repeatedly tried to force his opponent to play P–QB4 so that he could then move his Queen to d4. Nimzowitsch, seeing Black's intention, managed to set a nice trap. The game continued 27 R(1)–N2!, Q–Q3; 28 Q–B1!; at this stage Leonardt was still unaware of the trap being set and went on with his original plan: 28 ..., Q–Q5?, but after 29 N–Q5!, his Queen was closed in and powerless against the threat of 30 P–QB3. Black tried 29 ..., R×N; 30 P–QB3!, Q×QP; 31 KP×R, Q×P (B5); 32 P×B, Q×P (K3); 33 Q–B2, but White won in a few more moves.

This last example was a tactical trap; but a strategical trap is also possible. Here it is a case of disguising one's real strategical plan so that the opponent undertakes measures that actually assist that plan. Let us look at the position in Diagram 283, which arose in a game between Thelen and Treybal in Prague, 1927. White's real plan was to occupy the c-file without allowing his opponent the opportunity of wholesale exchanges. Knowing that his opponent feared attacks on the King, he set up his forces as if he intended to launch a King-side attack. His calculations were correct; Black removed the Rook from the c-file with R(2)–KB2 as a preventive measure against the imaginary attack; White was then able to play

DIAGRAM 282

Position after Black's 26th move

DIAGRAM 283

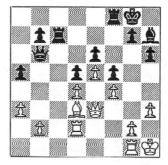

R–QB1 and carry out his real plan, which brought him victory within twenty moves.

We now come to the psychological problems associated with time-trouble. What is the proper course to adopt when you have sufficient time for reflection and your opponent is in time-trouble? A frequent mistake of the unpractised player is to move quickly and in so doing throw away his advantage completely; the correct course is to seek difficult tactical and strategical problems. On no account should one move planlessly; every move should go towards strengthening one's position: a definite and thought-out plan of campaign exerts tremendous psychological pressure on a player in time-trouble. In positions where one already has a clear advantage—material or positional—one should pay no attention to the opponent's time-trouble and proceed calmly with the conversion of the advantage. How wrong it is to play on the opponent's time-trouble

DIAGRAM 284

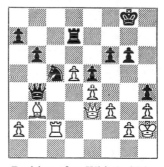

Position after White's 37th move

307

in such cases I know from my experience in a game that cost me my place in the 1956 Candidates' Tournament. In this game, which was played towards the end of the Göteborg Interzonal, the position in Diagram 284 occurred. I saw clearly that the superiority of my Knight over the bad Bishop gave me a definite advantage; the correct way to make use of this was as follows—

1. Block the King-side by P–KN4.
2. Withdraw the Queen to d6 and transfer the King to b8.
3. Occupy the open c-file with the Rook and force the exchange of one or both heavy pieces.

By following this plan I should have reached a won end-game; unfortunately I happened to glance at my opponent's clock and observed that he had only seconds left for his next three moves. As a result I decided to give him a few surprises in order to disrupt his line of thought. The game continued 37 ..., P–R4?; 38 B–B4, P–R5?; 39 P–R3, Q–N8??; 40 Q–B3!; and now my opponent was out of time-trouble and my Queen virtually trapped. As 40 ..., N–N6; 41 B×N followed by R–N2 is hopeless, I tried 40 ..., Q–Q8; 41 R–B1, Q–Q5; 42 Q×Q, P×Q; 43 R–Q1, but then resigned.

What conclusion can we draw from this terrible example? Simply that we should not overestimate the importance of time-trouble. It is always best to stick to a sound and strategically based plan: particularly in favourable positions it's illogical to fish in troubled waters on the basis of the opponent's time-trouble.

CHAPTER XVI

Conformity and Contradiction in Chess

THE application of laws to chess is a very interesting, but extremely difficult, philosophical problem. Although it deserves detailed treatment, we cannot possibly exhaust it in this book; we shall confine ourselves to the question of the character of the principles used in chess strategy.

The relationship between the pieces on the chessboard can undoubtedly be expressed mathematically. After all, the question is, basically, the particular movement of individual pieces and their mutual co-ordination, though it does extend to threats, protection, capturing, checking, and mating. We could, without undue difficulty, express the principles for correct play mathematically in a simple end-game (e.g. K+R against K, or K+B against K). But with an increasing number of pieces the task becomes more and more complicated and would in most cases be impossible despite all the possibilities opened up by modern mathematics.

In this connection there has been talk in recent years of building a chess automaton or, more precisely, using a modern cybernetic machine (i.e. an electronic apparatus capable of solving extremely difficult mathematical and logical problems) to play a game of chess or solve chess problems. The question whether such a machine would be capable of playing chess is important, because in its answer lies the key to the true character of chess laws.

It is a simple matter to teach the cybernetic machine the basic rules about the movement and capturing of pieces; check, mate, and stalemate; pawn conversion; etc. But that is not enough; the machine must actually play. For this, two methods can be used. With the first, the automaton examines all possible variations and selects the best move by rejection. This method can be employed for solving problems in which the number of possible moves is relatively small; for example, an electronic automaton in the Soviet Union (see *Chess in the U.S.S.R., 1956*, page 177) was able to solve the problem in Diagram 285 (1 P–K8=B!, K×QP; 2 P–B8=R, or 1 ..., K×BP; 2 P–N8=R). But the machine took twelve minutes, whereas I was able to do it in one minute. What then is the difference between the thinking power of a chess player and the working of a machine? The chess player does not examine anything approaching all the possibilities in the position; automatically, and to a certain extent subconsciously, he rejects all clearly bad moves, thus enabling himself to solve his problem in a relatively short time. The machine, on the other hand, must examine an enormous number of variations, and despite the extraordinary rapidity with which electrons work, the process takes a lot of time.

It is quite clear that this method cannot be used for playing a game. If the machine had to calculate for only seven moves in advance in a position with thirty alternatives, it would need 10,000 years to select the right move!

DIAGRAM 285

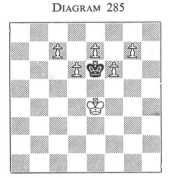

Mate in three moves

The second method is to teach the machine the most important principles of strategy and tactics. A cybernetic machine can solve not only mathematical, but also logical operations—even extremely complicated ones. And, after all, the principles of strategy and tactics have a logical form. This attempt was also made in the Soviet Union and the machine was indeed able to play a game of chess: but it played very weakly and was beaten by an average player.

We may well ask how this result could be possible, for we know that the electronic brain has performed brilliantly in many scientific fields. The reason is that play at the chessboard crosses the limit of logic and enters the field of dialectics. This is a field that is outside the scope of even the most perfect machine; it is a field of activity reserved for the human brain, and will always remain so. An example will make this clear. We can teach the machine the principle that a Bishop is stronger than a Knight or vice versa: but we cannot teach it that a Bishop is stronger or weaker than a Knight depending on a number of other factors. We chess players have therefore no need to fear that the use of an electronic apparatus will end the development of chess and make its practice impossible. The reason why chess is so fine a game is that it has a personal character and is able to bring out the many-sidedness of human thought.

The contention that chess belongs to the field of dialectics must of course be given some basis. To do this, let us consider material advantage. When we say that material superiority is an advantage we are merely expressing something obvious (though we must remember that the materially weaker side may have some form of compensation). We know that material superiority is one of the elements that enable a win to be forced. But now look at Diagram 286, which contains a position shortly before the adjournment in a game Pachman-Hromadka, Championship of Prague, 1944. If it

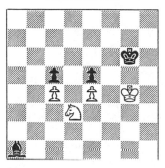

had been Black's turn to move, I should, after 1 ..., B–Q5, have employed the correct winning method: 2 N–K1, B–B7; 3 N–B3, K–B3 (3 ..., B–Q5; 4 N–R4 ch, K–B3; 5 K–R5); 4 K–R5, B–N6; 5 N–R4!, B–B7; 6 N–B5, B–N8; 7 N–R6, B–Q5; 8 N–N4 ch, K–K3; 9 K–N6 followed by N–B6–R7–N5 ch and K–B5. Unfortunately it was my turn to move, and I seized the opportunity to gain an immediate material advantage by the faulty 1 N×BP, after which the game can no longer be won: the Bishop-pawn cannot be converted without the help of the King, which, however, can only render the necessary assistance by letting the King-pawn fall; if, on the other hand, White should revert to the plan he mistakenly rejected, we should probably arrive at a position like that in Diagram 287; but from there after 1 N–B7 ch, K–B4; 2 N×P, B–B6 White still cannot win, despite his two pawn advantage.

There are also other cases of apparent contradiction in chess. One example is the disadvantage of having to make a move (*zugzwang*). We know that time is an important factor in a game; the right to make a move is something that we would, under normal circumstances, never renounce. But sometimes positions arise in which the obligation to make a move is a serious, sometimes decisive, disadvantage. And this is not only confined to simple positions, as Diagrams 288 and 289 show. In the first it is White who is in *zugzwang*, in the second, Black; in this latter position Black still has two pawn moves available (P–N4 and P–R4), but they will not alter the position.

Another example of the dialectical nature of chess is the question of the character of the position. In many positions the character is

DIAGRAM 288

DIAGRAM 289

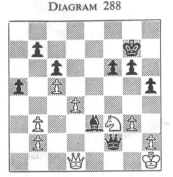

White in zugzwang

Black in zugzwang

determined by elements that in isolation are completely opposed but that together produce unity; they produce the equilibrium of the

DIAGRAM 290

Position after Black's 12th move

position. An example is material advantage opposed by superior development and piece co-ordination. In Diagram 290 the position is equal, judged in the present-day state of theory. White has the superior pawn structure: not only has he an extra pawn, but Black's pawn on c7 is isolated on an open file. Black, on the other hand, has more effective pieces: he has two Bishops, a lead in development, excellent co-ordination of all his pieces, and open files for his Rooks. Here we see contrasting elements—static (White) against dynamic (Black). The equilibrium of this position is an example of the dialectical unity of contrasts.

The dialectical character of chess obtrudes even more when we consider psychological factors. The fact that in a particular position the same move can be bad or good according to the nature of the opponent is an obvious contradiction, but one that can only be grasped after a deep study of the application of laws to chess.

312

In this book we have dealt with many principles of chess strategy; we may now ask what character these principles have. The majority of valid relationships on the chess-board have been built up empirically from *praxis*. But they have a limited validity because chess is full of contradictions. Just as in nature, in human society, in human thought, so too in chess complications occur that are beyond the scope of simple logical laws. In chess we often have situations that cannot be explained by the usual tenets of chess theory; and the higher the level of the chess, and the more advanced and developed chess theory is, the more often do these cases occur: but their very uniqueness and peculiarity makes them characteristic of chess. For the principles of chess are only a sign-post; they cannot be considered under all conditions to be reliable pointers to correct procedure. Sometimes we have players who, besides their basic command of chess principles, use something more—the intuition of an artist. This helps them discover hidden possibilities, unearth surprising combinations, and create games of lasting aesthetic worth. In this union of scientific and artistic elements lies the true greatness of chess—that wonderful product of the human brain.

Index of Openings

(numbers refer to pages)

Index of Games